JOHN PAUL II AND MORAL THEOLOGY

Readings in Moral Theology No. 10

Edited by
Charles E. Curran and
Richard A. McCormick, S.J.

PAULIST PRESS
New York / Mahwah, N.J.

Cover design by Tim McKeen.

Library of Congress Cataloging-in-Publication Data

John Paul II and moral theology / edited by Charles E. Curran and Richard A. McCormick.
      p.   cm. — (Readings in moral theology ; no. 10)
      Includes bibliographical references.
      ISBN 0–8091–3797–6 (alk. paper)
      1. John Paul II, Pope, 1920—Ethics.   2. Christian ethics—Catholic authors.
3. Catholic Church—Doctrines—History—20th century.   I. Curran, Charles E.
II. McCormick, Richard A., 1922–   . III. Series
BJ1249.J586   1998
241'.042'092—dc21   98–16737
                                                                                                    CIP

Published by Paulist Press
997 Macarthur Boulevard
Mahwah, New Jersey 07430

www.paulistpress.com

Printed and bound in the
United States of America

Contents

PART TWO:
SEXUALITY, GENDER, MARRIAGE AND FAMILY

PART THREE:
SOCIAL TEACHING

To the editors and staff of Paulist Press,
especially
Kevin A. Lynch, C.S.P.
and
Donald F. Brophy
for their encouragement and support of this series

Acknowledgments

Leslie C. Griffin's *"Evangelium Vitae:* The Law of Abortion" is reprinted from *Choosing Life: A Dialogue on Evangelium Vitae,"* edited by Kevin Wm. Wildes, S.J. and Alan C. Mitchell, by permission of Georgetown University Press. *"Familiaris Consortio*: A Review of Its Theology" by Michael D. Place is reprinted from *The Changing Family: Views from Theology and the Social Sciences in the Light of the Apostolic Exhortation Familiaris Consortio,* edited by Stanley L. Saxton, Patricia Voydanoff and Angela Ann Zukowski, by permission of Loyola University Press. Richard Grecco's "Recent Ecclesiastical Teaching" appeared in *The Sexual Revolution*, edited by Gregory Baum and John A. Coleman (Concilium, 1984, vol. 3), published by T&T Clark, and is reprinted by permission of Concilium. "Tested by Our Own Ideals" by Michael Novak is taken from *National Review*, June 14, 1991, © 1991 by National Review, Inc., 215 Lexington Avenue, New York, N.Y. 10016, and is reprinted by permission. Richard A. McCormick's "Some Early Reactions to *Veritatis Splendor"* and David Hollenbach's "Christian Studies after the Cold War" are reprinted by permission of *Theological Studies*. J. Bryan Hehir's "Reordering the World" is reprinted by permission of *Commonweal*. "An Argument about Human Nature" by Richard John Neuhaus is reprinted by permission of the *Wall Street Journal*, © 1991 by Dow Jones & Company. All rights reserved. "Concern and Consideration" by Donal Dorr is reprinted with the permission of Orbis Books from his book *Option for the Poor: A Hundred Years of Vatican Social Teaching*. "Neoconservative Economics and the Church's 'Authentic Theology of Integral Human Liberation'" by David L. Schindler is reprinted by permission of Wm. B. Eerdmans Publishing Company and T&T Clark Ltd. from *Heart of the World, Center of the Church,* © 1996 by David L. Schindler. *Communio* has granted permission to reprint "The Mystery of Easter and the Culture of Death" by Marc Ouellet, *Communio* 23 (Spring 1996), pp. 5–15, and "Sincere Gift: The Pope's 'New Feminism,'" by Léonie Caldicott, *Communio* 23 (Spring 1996), pp. 64–81. Charles Curran's *"Evangelium Vitae* and Its Broader Context" is reprinted from his book *History and Contemporary*

Issues: Studies in Moral Theology with permission of Continuum. "Pope John Paul II's Theology of the Body" by Ronald Modras appeared in *The Vatican and Homosexuality,* edited by Jeannine Gramick and Robert Nugent (Crossroad, 1988), is reprinted by permission of the editors. Grateful acknowledgement is made to *The Tablet* and its individual authors for permission to reprint "Revelation and Dissent" by Germain Grisez, "A Distrust That Wounds" by Bernard Häring, "Good Acts and Good Persons" by Joseph Fuchs, and "Accent on the Masculine" by Lisa Sowle Cahill. "The New 'New Things'" by George Weigel is reprinted with the permission of the author from his book, *A New World Order,* published by the Ethics and Public Policy Center, Washington, D.C. "Economic Justice for Whom?" by Pamela K. Brubaker and "An Ethical Critique of Capitalism" by Gregory Baum are reprinted from *Religion and Economic Justice,* edited by Michael Zweig, © 1991 by Temple University. Reprinted by permission of Temple University Press. "The Family and Sexuality" by Richard M. Hogan and John M. Levoir is reprinted with permission of Ignatius Press from their book *Covenant of Love* (pp. 71–102), published in 1992 by Ignatius Press, San Francisco. All rights reserved.

Foreword

John Paul II has been one of the most active and energetic popes of this or any century. His many pastoral trips all over the globe together with his almost countless speeches on these journeys testify to this. These visits almost define the public *persona* of this pope. Hence it is easy to overlook his huge written output.

This is certainly the case in moral theology. Since John Paul II's encyclicals and addresses tend to be long, meditative, and at times repetitious, there is the real danger that they will remain largely the province of experts and special interest groups. Many, including those who would ordinarily be expected to explain them, will not have read them.

We are convinced that this pope's moral writings will exercise an impact for years to come. This does not mean that we believe that they all are of equal value, or that we agree with all the papal emphases and analyses. Far from it. It simply means that these encyclicals and pastoral statements are part of the Church's heritage, and that we receive them, to cite the late Bishop Christopher Butler, with "a welcoming gratitude that goes along with the keen alertness of a critical mind and of a good will concerned to play its part both in the purification and the development of the Church's understanding of its inheritance."

Our previous nine volumes of *Readings in Moral Theology* had as their overarching purpose a contribution to this "purification and development." For this reason we have included contrasting, even opposing views. We do the same in this volume of reactions to the moral teaching of John Paul II, convinced that the truth is deeper and richer than any partial presentation of it.

To facilitate the discussion of John Paul II's voluminous teachings in the area of moral theology, we have divided our book into three parts: 1) Ethical Theory; 2) Sexuality, Gender, Marriage, and Family; 3) Social Teaching. The pertinent papal encyclicals and documents are mentioned at the beginning of each part.

Charles E. Curran
Richard A. McCormick, S.J.

Part One

ETHICAL THEORY

Pertinent Encyclicals of Pope John Paul II

Veritatis Splendor, 1993
Evangelium Vitae, 1995

1. Some Early Reactions to *Veritatis Splendor*

Richard A. McCormick, S.J.

This chapter first appeared in *Theological Studies* in 1994.

Veritatis Splendor has elicited a broad range of reactions, both favorable and unfavorable. In this article, I shall first review comments on, responses to, and studies of the papal letter, and then outline what appear to be critical issues in the encyclical or associated with it.

COMMENTS, RESPONSES, AND STUDIES

The encyclical letter *Veritatis Splendor*[1] was signed by John Paul II on August 6, 1993 and released the following October 5. Addressed to "all the bishops of the Catholic Church regarding certain fundamental questions of the Church's moral teaching," it understandably got a reading far beyond episcopal ranks. At the outset I want to glance at some reactions from around the world, both in the media at large and within the Church. I realize that sound bites are hardly adequate to a long and complicated papal letter. They can, however, convey a tone.

The Press

The journal *30 Days* gathered a sampling of journalistic reaction. For example, the widest circulating Polish daily, *Gazeta Wyborcza*, referred to the letter as "an encyclical of the counter-reformation for a Church in crisis." Rome's *La Repubblica* asserted that "Wojtyla wants a silent Church." Its summary stated that "the Pope's final effort introduces only one great innovation: the abolition of theological dissent." Milan's

Corriere della sera found nothing new in the encyclical. "Nor is the call to obedience directed at theologians new: it merely reproduces an 'Instruction' of 1990." The *Frankfurter Allgemeine* had a different tone. It saw in the encyclical "a point of reference for believers and moral theologians alike." *The Times* (London) spoke of the risk of schism. *The Guardian* judged the document fundamentalist and inspired by nostalgia for pre-Vatican II days. The French Catholic daily *La Croix* viewed the letter as "the most important of the pontificate of John Paul II." The Spanish daily *El Pais* wrote that "even the most inveterate detractors will have problems presenting this intellectual effort in sensational tones, however polemical the static nature of the document may prove to be."[2]

Episcopal Statements

With few exceptions episcopal statements followed a fairly predictable pattern. Cardinal Roger Mahoney praised the encyclical for its "magnificent vision of the Christian life" and its "stunning" insight that "the moral life is a response to the gift of faith and a path to perfection."[3] Cardinal Bernard Law said that it "presents a teaching which has to be pondered and appropriated at a deeper level of consciousness."[4] Bishop Donald W. Wuerl called the letter "a beacon that shines in the midst of the gloom of confusion."[5]

At the press conference for the release of the encyclical, Archbishop J. Francis Stafford pointed up its emphasis on natural law and called it "an outstanding contemporary presentation of the Catholic natural law approach to moral reason."[6] Archbishop Adam Maida stated that he was most impressed by the pope's reflections on Jesus' dialogue with the rich young man.[7] Somewhat mysteriously, Archbishop Elden Curtiss referred to the encyclical as "a discernment made by the Church's magisterium (the body of bishops in the world under the leadership of the Pope) with regard to certain modern positions and controversial problems in moral theology."[8] Most of us would judge that a letter to the world's bishops is hardly a product of their own magisterium, as indeed it was not.

Archbishop John Quinn noted that "a supremely important emphasis in the encyclical is its insistence that the foundation of Christian morality lies in the paschal mystery of Christ."[9] Cardinal James A. Hickey stated that it warns about the "grave pastoral dangers of flawed theologies...and of public dissent."[10] Bishop Daniel P. Reilly asserted that "the basic concern of the Holy Father is that in much of today's thinking the exercise of human freedom has been separated from its essential relationship with truth."[11] Bishop Alfred C. Hughes acknowledged that the encyclical contains nothing new. John Paul II "is basically reasserting that there is an objective moral order."[12]

Cahal Daly, the Catholic Primate of All Ireland, states that "the overriding message is that the human being is created for truth."[13] Interestingly, Daly's summary includes no mention of fundamental option or proportionalism. Cardinal Basil Hume, after admitting that the letter is "highly technical," says that "the heart of the Pope's message is that there are acts which in themselves are always seriously wrong."[14] Hume calls it "a prophetic document that would be seen to be right in 500 years' time." One cannot resist calling this a far-sighted comment. Bishop Karl Lehmann, speaking as chairman of the German Bishops' Conference, asserted that moral theologians will have to determine whether they maintain the positions rejected by the encyclical, or whether it is a question of the working out of their teaching for which they themselves bear no responsibility.[15] Cardinal Godfried Daneels confessed that the letter is "not the best of encyclicals" but judged it to be "an important text."[16] Cardinal Jean-Marie Lustiger concluded that the pope and bishops are simply fulfilling their mission "to stay awake while the conscience of men sleeps."[17] Finally, Chicago's Cardinal Joseph Bernardin sensibly noted that some theologians and pastoral leaders, "while agreeing with the substance of the encyclical, perhaps will disagree with its evaluation of the ethical theories it discusses."[18]

This sampling will have to suffice, with appropriate apologies to those who have been omitted from the overview. Most of the episcopal statements on the encyclical that I have read have an air of court formality about them. They express gratitude to the pope (often enough for his courage), pick out and display general and noncontroversial truths, note that the teaching is an authentic act of the magisterium, and urge theologians and others to study it carefully. In a sense, these episcopal statements are noteworthy for what they do not say. I suppose it is understandable that the bishops' statements do not say that the letter is prolix and repetitious, its analyses too frequently obscure and convoluted, and its presentation of revisionist tendencies tendentious, extreme, and ultimately inaccurate.

The Encyclical's Contents

At this point a brief summary of the encyclical's content is in order since it would be unreal to assume, given its length and technical density, that even most theologians have managed to read it.

In the Introduction the pope laments the fact that dissent against the Catholic Church's authentic teachings on moral issues is no longer "limited and occasional" but questions them in an "overall and systematic" way. Exactly what this means I do not know, but the encyclical takes dead aim at this "overall and systematic" dissent and its underlying philosophical and theological underpinnings. If "overall and systematic dissent" is meant as a description of moral theologians, I would disagree. We must not forget the late John Tracy Ellis's statement over ten years ago: "I have the impression that certain curia officials are listening too much to one side—and that side is usually the far right."[19]

The first of three chapters is a protracted and beautiful meditation on Christ's dialogue with the rich young man of Matthew 19:16 who asks, "What good must I do to inherit eternal life?" Jesus responds, "Keep the Commandments." When pressed further he adds, "Come, follow me" (Matt 19:21). Thus, Chapter 1 basically presents the moral life as a response to Christ's invitation. Its biblical base is a breath of fresh air. As theologian Ronald Modras notes, Chapter 1 "shows all the signs of not only being written by the pope but of arising out of his own deeply personal, introspective reflections on the gospel story."[20]

Chapter 2 is a different matter. It begins with an attack on relativism in contemporary culture. Such relativism rests on "certain anthropological and ethical presuppositions." The pope then states that "at the root of these presuppositions is the more or less obvious influence of currents of thought which end by detaching human freedom from its essential and constitutive relationship to truth." The pope rightly deplores this separation of freedom from truth, a separation that implies that conscience *creates* truth rather than *discovers* it.

The relativism that leads to the dead end of individualism is rooted in cultural biases and drifts. But the encyclical sees Catholic moral theology adrift on this relativistic sea. It singles out so-called proportionalism and consequentialism as recent developments that are incompatible with revelation. Why are they incompatible? Because, so it asserts, they justify morally wrongful acts by a good intention, and thus deny the existence of intrinsically evil acts.

The final chapter discusses the personal and institutional practices that the teachings of Chapters 1 and 2 require, practices that can require great sacrifice, even martyrdom. In this connection the pope reminds the bishops that they are "to have recourse to appropriate measures to ensure that the faithful are guarded from every doctrine and theory contrary to" the Church's moral teaching. They are urged to be "personally vigilant."

Authorship

One of the very first questions to arise concerns the authorship of the encyclical. John Wilkins, editor of *The Tablet* (London), notes that the style of Chapter 2 is different, a fact that "suggests that other hands have been at work."[21] Joseph Selling of the Katholieke Universiteit, Leuven, agrees. Chapter 2 "uses a vocabulary that John Paul II has never used before, includes very few references to the pope's earlier writings and speeches, a common trait in papal encyclicals, and is written in an acrimonious tone that is not typical of previous documents."[22]

Whose hands have been at work here? Ronald Modras, cited above, suggests those of Andrzej Szostek. After stating that Chapter 2 will be a difficult read for bishops and priests, Modras notes that "that is because it is largely drawn from a doctoral dissertation written by Father Andrzej Szostek," the Pro-Rector of the Catholic University of Lublin. Szostek was in Rome on Tuesday, October 5, 1993, as part of the panel charged with clarifying the encyclical to the press. Szostek wrote his doctoral dissertation on *Norms and Exceptions (Normy i Wyjatki)* for the University of Lublin.[23] The then Cardinal Wojtyla was on his board. In this dissertation Szostek examined the writings of what he called the "new wave" of Catholic moralists. Among them: the late Franz Böckle, Charles Curran, Joseph Fuchs, Bernard Häring, Louis Janssens, Peter Knauer, Giles Milhaven, Bruno Schüller, and myself. These and many more theologians share the general teleological directions rejected by the encyclical. Szostek criticizes them for their impoverished anthropology. Chapter 2 refers to "some theologians" and "certain theologians." Szostek's book tells us who they are—with one exception. He does not mention Karl Rahner, the greatest theologian of this century; but the encyclical surely has him in its cross hairs. It is Rahner's anthropology that the cited theologians share.

If another pair of hands was at work, it could well belong to John Finnis, lecturer in jurisprudence at Oxford University and a member of the International Theological Commission. I (along with others) see his hands at work in Chapter 2 because that chapter contains some of the same caricatures that I find present in Finnis's work.

Symposium-Like Presentations

COMMONWEAL

After the encyclical's appearance, several publications offered symposium-like presentations on it. *Commonweal* led off with Lawrence S. Cunningham who regarded *Veritatis Splendor* as "this generation's *Humani Generis.*" The papal letter, "while paying lip service to various theological schools, quite clearly opts for one."[24] Joseph Komonchak also saw parallels with *Humani Generis.* Dennis M. Doyle, while admitting its many positive aspects, judged that the letter "may do more to divide the Church than to unite it." Charles Curran scores the defensive nature of the document and its unfair demolition of straw persons: "The Encyclical does not accurately portray the true picture of Catholic moral theology today."

As if footnoting Curran's assertion, Janet Smith states that the letter "carefully discusses the claim that such acts as 'having sexual intercourse with someone against that person's will' is considered a premoral or ontic evil in the view of dissenters." Of course, no one says that.[25] As soon as one adds "against that person's will," a qualifier has been added that makes the described action morally wrong, much as does "against the reasonable will of the owner" in the definition of theft.

Lisa Sowle Cahill believes the encyclical gives impetus to theologians who are renewing the natural-law tradition in service of humane and consensus-seeking public discourse. Unfortunately its fideist and authoritarian tone undercuts this impetus and Cahill fears that the result will be further divisions within the Church. Stanley Hauerwas praises the encyclical as "a great testimony to the Catholic ability to withstand the ethos of freedom." At one point Hauerwas states: "I must admit as one who has always found the concept of 'fundamental option' and particularly the corresponding idea of 'pre-moral' evil, mystifications, I particularly enjoyed the encyclical's criticisms of those peculiar notions." These notions will, of course, remain "peculiar" to Hauerwas if his grasp of them is as confused as it appears to be here. In what sense, for example, is the notion of pre-moral evil a "corresponding idea" to the fundamental option?

Anne E. Patrick concludes this symposium by noting that, while sexuality is not the stated theme of the letter, it is "the subtext that occasioned and governed this text," a claim made by a number of commentators. She praises the emphasis on human dignity and moral objectivity but fails to recognize the positions of theologians like Häring, Curran, and this author in the encyclical's portrayals.

FIRST THINGS

A symposium of quite a different type and quality is presented in Richard John Neuhaus's *First Things*. After general introductory remarks Neuhaus states: "Here John Paul takes on those moralists, including Catholic theologians, who say that an evil act may be justified by the end to which it is directed ('consequentialism') or by weighing the other goods at stake ('proportionalism'). It is never licit to do evil in order to achieve good. To those of a contrary view the question might be put: When is rape morally justified? Or torture of children? Or Auschwitz? John Paul's answer is *never*."[26] So is mine and so is that of anyone identified as a proportionalist, as anyone with a rudimentary knowledge of the literature will realize.

Given Neuhaus's confusion, it is perhaps understandable that he would publish the essay of Princeton's Robert P. George. Repeatedly George misrepresents proportionalists as maintaining that rape, murder, and adultery could be justified by a proportionate reason. In his words (which he takes from Germain Grisez without attribution), "For centuries, no Jew or Christian imagined that precepts such as 'Do not murder' and 'Do not commit adultery' meant not to kill or commit adultery unless one had a proportionate reason for doing so."[27] I suppose it would be asking too much to suggest to George that he read Louis Janssens' seven-page article in which he discusses a fourfold variety of human actions. The very first class consists of actions which involve an insepa-rable deformity such as fornication and adultery. The very terms "sig-nify both sexual acts *and* their immorality." Of these Janssens concludes: "So the names of some actions denote that they are simply and intrinsically evil and that they can never be done in a good way."[28]

Hadley Arkes of Amherst College delivers an analytic howler. He excoriates proportionalism with grave vigor. But he never defines it. That enables him to reject the name but unwittingly to adopt its content. Thus he notes that the papal teaching "lends itself to layers of shading and calibration." One example: "The injunction to avoid killing is an injunction to avoid the killing of the innocent." Another is that of the Dutch householders who refused to reveal to the prying Gestapo the Jews they were hiding. Of them, Arkes states: "The Dutch householders were not seeking to injure the Nazis when they spoke falsely. Nor were they endorsing deceit as a general rule of life. They were willing, rather, the protection of the innocent, and they were thoroughly justified in misleading the wicked." At this point Arkes notes that this is "not spelled out in the encyclical," but, he adds, "we can assume that it is folded into the teaching." If this is the case, then (remarkably) there is folded into the teaching the very thought structure the pope wants to reject. Arkes states that he has "crossed swords" with proportionalists on many occasions. What he fails to realize is that he sees one in the mirror every day. But on one point I believe he is correct: "'Proportionalists' are not likely to find here [in *Veritatis Splendor*] any new arguments that might encourage them to think anew about their position."[29]

The symposium also contains a supportive essay by Russell Hittinger and a laudatory one coauthored by David Burrell and Stanley Hauerwas.[30]

THE TABLET

The most ambitious symposium was that put together by John Wilkins of *The Tablet*.[31] It includes eleven essays from various points of view. I can pick out only threads in this overview. The very first article is by Germain Grisez. Basically Grisez passes in review "four ways various dissenters have tried to soften received moral teaching about intrinsically evil acts." Confronted with the encyclical's criticisms, "dissenting theologians undoubtedly will respond that the Pope has misinterpreted them, missed them altogether, and/or found no new or convincing arguments against their views." Grisez sees this as inadequate because the papal argument is from revelation. He concludes that dissenting theologians are left with three choices: "to admit that they have been mistaken, to admit that they do not believe God's word, or to claim that the Pope is grossly misinterpreting the Bible."[32]

Grisez's essay did not go unchallenged. Moral theologian Seán Fagan saw it as an exercise in fundamentalism, "a bitter and simplistic attack on theologians who are 'looking for ways around the precepts.'"[33] He would especially reject the notion of revelation-as-dictation implied in Grisez's account and states that there is a fourth choice open to theologians if history is our guide: respectful dissent.

The revered Bernard Häring authored the second piece. It is quite remarkable. It begins as follows:

> After reading the new papal encyclical carefully, I felt greatly discouraged. Several hours later I suffered long-lasting seizures of the brain, and looked forward hopefully to leaving the Church on earth for the Church in heaven. After regaining my normal brain function, however, I have a new feeling of confidence, without blinding my eyes and heart to the pain and brain-convulsions that are likely to ensue in the immediate future.
>
> *Veritatis Splendor* contains many beautiful things. But almost all real splendor is lost when it becomes evident that the whole document is directed above all towards one goal: to endorse total assent and submission to all utterances of the Pope, and above all on one crucial point: that the use of any artificial means for regulating birth is intrinsically evil and sinful, without exception, even in circumstances where contraception would be a lesser evil.

After pointing out that the encyclical is part of a structural pattern of suspicion and distrust, Häring fairly cries out;

> Away with all distrust in our Church! Away with all attitudes, mentalities and structures which promote it! We should let the Pope know that we are wounded by the many signs of his rooted distrust, and discouraged by the manifold structures of distrust which he has allowed to be established. We need him to soften towards us, the whole Church needs it. Our witness to the world needs it. The urgent call to effective ecumenism needs it.[34]

When Häring writes like this, we know that something is quite wrong, and, I suggest, not with Häring. What so exercises Häring is the caricature of contemporary theologians encased in the encyclical: "Clearly the Pope and his special adviser do not have a proper picture of what moral theology today is like. Very grave insinuations are made. What moral theologian of good reputation in the Church would recognize himself in the picture which *Veritatis Splendor* draws?"[35]

At this point it would be appropriate to mention an open letter of sixty theologians of Quebec to the bishops of Quebec. It was printed October 17, 1993 in *La Presse,* Quebec's principal newspaper, and also in the monthly *L'Eglise canadienne.* At one key point it states:

> In its care to invite prudence in the teaching of ethics or morals, the encyclical tries to describe certain currents of thought that have appeared in the last several decades. This is a very delicate enterprise, because most often it is difficult in several sentences to present an accurate and really fair description of ideas requiring rather lengthy elaboration. Theological movements well situated in Catholic moral thought can thus be more or less targeted. It seems to us that the Magisterium of the Church should avoid getting involved in quarrels among theological schools: as history, even recent history, teaches us, when this happens, the danger always exists that it is one school of theology getting even with another. It seems to us that this wise rule, which the last council adopted, has not been followed in the recent encyclical, especially where there is question of teleological morality and proportionalism.[36]

My own article follows Häring's. It dwells especially on the encyclical's presentation of proportionalism. We read there: "Such theories however are not faithful to the Church's teaching, when they believe they can justify, as morally good, deliberate choices of kinds of behavior contrary to the commandments of the divine and natural law" (no. 76). Later we read: "If acts are intrinsically evil, a good intention or particular circumstances can diminish their evil, but they cannot remove it" (no. 81). In brief, the encyclical repeatedly and inaccurately states of proportionalism that it attempts to justify *morally wrong actions* by a good intention. This, I regret to say, is a misrepresentation, what I earlier called a caricature. If an act is morally wrong, nothing can justify it.[37] I shall return to this below.

Joseph Fuchs discusses the encyclical's treatment of fundamental option and finds it wanting. Basically the papal advisers see the fundamental option "as though it were a precise, definite and determinable *act,*" and indeed as belonging "to the objective realm of the ethical consciousness of the person." Fuchs concludes: "In this way the fundamental option as defined by its protagonists is misunderstood in the encyclical."[38]

Nicholas Lash notes that Chapter 2 is written in quite different language. It resembles 19th-century textbooks. In spite of John Paul's insistence that "the Church's magisterium does not intend to impose upon the faithful any particular theological system, still less a philosophical one," the letter does precisely that. In Lash's words, "the encyclical appears to argue that the richness and integrity of traditional Catholic ethics is adequately represented by only one school of moral philosophy." Lash sees the portrayal of other schools of thought as "not without distortion" and urges bishops to exercise their magisterium by disagreeing with the pope when appropriate and by "correcting, in the name of justice and in the measure that circumstances warrant it, the account given in the letter of the teaching and intentions of moral theologians in their churches."[39]

Maciej Zieba, a Polish Dominican, in an interesting article, sees the document's stress on truth, loyalty to the truth, and paying the price for this loyalty as a kind of theological assessment of the experience of the churches of Central and Eastern Europe. He compares *Veritatis Splendor* with *Centesimus Annus.* This latter expressed the experience of the churches of the Western democracies and was explicitly directed mainly at countries which had recently liberated themselves from Communism. The theological trends criticized by *Veritatis Splendor* have few supporters in the theology departments of Prague, Krakow, or Vilnius.[40]

Oliver O'Donovan, Regius Professor of Moral and Pastoral Theology at the University of Oxford, lauds the pope's insistence on truth as the condition of freedom. "On this chosen ground the encyclical is at home. Its maladroit moments come when it leaves it to pursue more traditional scholastic exercises." If it misrepresents contemporary moral theologians, says O'Donovan, "no harm has been done and some good. We can all learn from misunderstandings that careful readers form of our positions."[41] True enough, but perhaps not enough of the truth.

O'Donovan's Olympian detachment reflects little knowledge of Catholic Church life and of the way misunderstandings can be turned against individuals.

Herbert McCabe argues that the encyclical makes a bad case for a good thesis: "that we need absolute prohibitions as well as instruction in the path of virtue." These absolutes concern actions that cut at the root of human community and thereby cut at the roots of our community in *caritas* (e.g., killing of the innocent). Where the encyclical fails is in the central role it gives these prohibitions and in its attempt to *base* Christian morality on the ten commandments. This has the effect of reducing the virtues to dispositions to follow rules, whereas Christian morality is not primarily a written code but the presence in us of the Holy Spirit.[42]

Lisa Sowle Cahill approaches the subject from a feminist perspective. The encyclical resists the idea that the body is simply freedom's raw material. But it does not advance the discussion of how the body sets parameters for freedom. Church teaching "tends to revert to a sacralization of physical processes whenever sex is the moral issue." The encyclical obfuscates the notion of intrinsically evil acts by giving examples on disparate levels. For instance, murder, adultery, stealing, genocide, torture, prostitution, slavery, etc., would have no defenders among Catholic theologians. These phrases, Cahill correctly notes, do not define acts in the abstract, "but acts (like intercourse or homicide) *together with the conditions or circumstances* in which they become immoral." The same is true of intentionally killing an innocent person. Cahill asserts that "about this there is little disagreement." She ends by faulting the letter's neglect of changing gender roles.[43]

John Finnis, professor of law at University College, Oxford, concludes the symposium. He lashes out at moral theologians who use proportionate reason as the basis for establishing exceptions. He lists several objections. First, exceptions (e.g., against killing the innocent) cannot be contained, because "none of these theologians has ever explained how one can rationally tell when a reason is not, in their sense, proportionate." Therefore, proportionalists are leading people to decisions grounded in what they *feel* appropriate. Second, while professing only adjustments, moral theologians "should not be surprised by what their adjustment of traditional moral teaching has wrought." His example: widespread approval by Catholics of abortion.

But more basic in Finnis's view are certain reconceptions of revelation and faith. Finnis wants the pope and bishops to define these reconceptions out of existence. Only by solemn definitions can the crisis of faith be adequately met.[44]

Peter Hebblethwaite correctly senses that in calling for such definitions Finnis seems to be volunteering for the role of inquisitor. Hebblethwaite impishly recalls that in 1503 the Holy See asked the Spanish lawyer, Francisco Peña, to produce a new *Manual for Inquisitors.* The "exceptionless moral norm" about never killing the innocent did not apply. Peña taught: "Let everything be done so that the penitent cannot proclaim his innocence, so as not to give the people the slightest reason to believe that the condemnation is unjust." Hebblethwaite sees this as "exactly the import of Finnis's article."[45]

Individual Studies[46]

Notre Dame's Todd Whitmore, in an insightful study, sees the letter's very positive features as the source of its shortcomings. Thus this encyclical is more biblical and theological than others. But Whitmore senses a gradual shift in emphasis away from invited response, which is rooted in the Bible, toward commanded obedience, away from response to God's invitation toward obedience to the magisterium's command.

Another example adduced by Whitmore is relativism. He lauds the encyclical's unflinching condemnation of relativism in contemporary culture, but suggests that seeing Catholic moral theologians as contributing causes risks trivializing the problem in the wider culture. Finally, Whitmore lauds the stress on the need of lived Christian witness. However, he fears that the accent on negative prohibitions "directs attention away from the task of creating the positive social conditions that are necessary for those prohibitions to be met with any regularity."[47]

Several philosophers have taken issue with me. After summarizing some of the letter's more general themes, Russell Hittinger cites this paragraph of mine from the *National Catholic Reporter*:

Take an example sometimes cited by opponents of proportionalism: the solitary sex act. This, it is urged, is intrinsically evil from its object. This is the view of the Pope. Proportionalists would argue that this ("solitary sex act") is an inadequate description of the action. For self-stimulation for sperm testing is a different human act from self-pleasuring, much as self-defense is different from homicide during a robbery. They are different because of different reasons for the act, i.e., different goods sought and aimed at different intentions. Intention tells us what is going on.[48]

Hittinger says this is an example of "how intending a good end defines the morality of an act" and states that it is "an example of what the Pope criticizes." Hittinger continues:

By analogy to masturbating for the sake of scientific research, one could just as easily insert aborting fetuses for population control, killing for world peace, pre-marital sex for psychological maturation, or whatever. This is not to say that a proportionalist like Father McCormick holds that these acts are morally good; rather, it is only to say that the example he gives of his own method does not indicate why he shouldn't conclude that such acts are good in some cases. It seems that by shifting intention to and fro, the agent constitutes out of whole cloth the moral properties of his act.[49]

Hittinger refers to the agent's "shifting intention to and fro" and to "ends which might be brought into view by the agent." In contrast to this, the pope holds that there are acts that are intrinsically wicked and "no intention can ever legitimate such an act." I am surprised to see a philosopher fall into such a trap. For Hittinger, intention means one thing and one thing only: something *in addition to an action already constituted.* Thus, he can refer to "shifting intention to and fro." Thus, he, too, argues that no good intention can justify a morally wrong act — as if somebody actually held that it could.

What Hittinger fails to do is distinguish intention from motive. The intention makes the act what it is, as several articles reviewed below point out. Thus, we refer to an *act of self-defense,* not to an act of killing for the added purpose of defending my life.[50] We refer to an act of transplantation of organs, not to an act of mutilation done for the good purpose of saving another's life. It is precisely this structure I had in mind when I wrote that "self-stimulation for sperm testing is a different human act from self-pleasuring." Similarly "intention [not motive] tells us what is going on." That is why theologians like Bernard Häring, Marciano Vidal, L. Rossi, Ambrogio Valsecchi, Franz Scholz, and Louis Janssens distinguish "moral" from merely "biological" self-stimulation, or masturbation from "ipsation." They see them as different human acts, not the same act with different motives.

Another example. Taking another's property (food) for survival and for self-enrichment are two different actions, not the same action with different motives. That is why the manualist tradition defined theft as "taking another's property *against his reasonable will."* This was regarded as the very object of the act.[51] It is, of course, the task of human reason to determine what elements must be present before we can speak meaningfully of the object, or a fully constituted action. This exercise of reason, as is obvious from Catholic tradition, is teleological in character.

The examples given by Hittinger (e.g., killing for world peace) are by and large of actions fully constituted (therefore, with the intention) plus supervening motive. This seems to be the encyclical's idea, too. It states that certain acts are intrinsically evil, "in other words on account of their very object and quite apart from the *ulterior* intentions of the one acting" (no. 80; my emphasis). Intentions that are ulterior to the object of the act or apart from "kinds of behavior" (no. 76) are motives. It is this understanding of intention as referring only to the motive that allows *Veritatis Splendor,* and by implication Hittinger, to accuse proportionalists of saying that a good intention justifies a morally wrong action. I have said it before and I say it here again: the encyclical misunderstands and misrepresents the teleological tendencies it describes.

Perhaps it would be helpful here to refer to some interesting remarks of Sebastian Moore, O.S.B., on intention. Moore insists that intention is of the essence of action. Action cannot be understood without it. There are many actions whose intention may be presumed. Citing Herbert McCabe, Moore calls these presumed intentions "privileged descriptions." Thus, most taking of another's property is not for survival; it is theft. Most killing is not for self-defense; it is murder. We must hold on to these privileged descriptions, but to do so "we have to sacrifice the much neater notion that we can have actions definable as bad *apart* from intention."[52] Clearly for Moore intention is not reducible to a motive added to an action, but determines its very meaning or object in the broadest sense.

The second philosopher to discuss this matter is Ralph McInerny. I think McInerny would clearly admit the difference between intent and motive, for he distinguishes the aim of the action (object) from some further aimed-at good. He then states: "What the Pope is concerned with in [the encyclical] is actions which may never be done regardless of their circumstances or the *further purpose for which one might do them.*"[53] I believe all Catholic theologians would admit this. "Further purpose" refers to what I have called motive. Once the action is said to be wrong, no "further purpose" will purge that wrongfulness. As the Québecois theologians word it: "To our knowledge, Catholic moralists as a group recognize that there are such [intrinsically evil] acts, even if they do not all say so in the same way. This conviction can be found among the proponents of a teleological approach to morality as well as among others called 'proportionalists.'"[54] Exactly.

McInerny then expresses surprise that revisionist theologians do not recognize themselves in *Veritatis Splendor.* He believes the encyclical has described them accurately. I do not. Not a single theologian would hold that a good intention could sanctify what has already been described as a morally wrong act. And that is what the encyclical says proportionalists do. Revisionist writers should both reject and resent that.

Since this matter is central, let me pursue it briefly here. The pope is saying that certain actions can be morally wrong from the object *(ex objecto)* independently of circumstances. As the German theologian Bruno Schüller, S.J., one of the most influential of proportionalists, has shown, that is analytically obvious *if the object is characterized in advance as morally wrong.*[55] No theologian would or could contest the papal statement understood in that sense. But that is not the issue. The key problem is: What objects should be characterized as morally wrong and on what criteria? Of course, hidden in this question is the further one: What is to count as pertaining to the object? That is often decided by an independent ethical judgment about what one thinks is morally right or wrong in certain areas.

Let the term "lie" serve as an example here. The Augustinian-Kantian approach holds that every falsehood is a lie. Others would hold that falsehood is morally wrong (a lie) only when it is denial of the truth to one who has a right to know. In the first case, the object of the act is said to be falsehood (a lie), and it is seen as *ex objecto* morally wrong. In the second case, the object is "falsehood to protect an important secret" and is seen as *ex objecto* morally right (*ex objecto,* because the very end must be viewed as pertaining to the object).

These differing judgments do not trace to disagreements about the fonts of morality (for example, about the sentence "an act morally wrong *ex objecto* can never under any circumstances be made morally right"), but to different criteria and judgments about the use of human speech, and therefore about what ought to count as pertaining to the object. In this sense one could fully agree with the pope that there are "intrinsically illicit acts independent of the circumstances" and yet deny that this applied to the very matters apparently of most concern to him (sterilization, contraception, masturbation).

Some of these very points are reprised by Peter Knauer, S.J., who began this discussion in the first place. Knauer[56] concentrates his attention on Chapter 2, and especially on its understanding of human acts. The encyclical states of teleological theories such as proportionalism that they maintain that it is "never possible to formulate an absolute prohibition of particular kinds of behavior" (75). Knauer asserts that "hardly a moral theologian will recognize his own actual statement in such descriptions." Why? Because the key issue concerns not the ends or purposes of the agent *(Ziel des Handelnden)* but the determination of the end of the action itself, its object *(Handlungsziel).*

Knauer next turns to the notion of the object of an act and points out that the object is that to which the will consciously directs itself. It is necessarily intended. Photographing a happening will not tell us the object of the act. For instance, handing money to another can be a variety of different things: payment of a debt, a loan, a gift, an alms, a bribe, etc. It is not possible to determine the morality of an action prior to determining what is objectively willed in it.

If, in addition to the object, we speak of intention as a second criterion for moral rightness or wrongness, this really refers to the object of a second act to which the first act has been related. Thus, one takes a vacation trip in order to commit adultery. There are two distinguishable actions here, each with its own object *(Handlungsziel),* taking a vacation trip, adultery. If the first action (vacation trip) is not pointed at the second (adultery) but stands by itself, there is no additional intention *(Ziel des Handelnden).* Scholastic tradition gave the erroneous impression that every action had an intention in addition to the object.

Knauer also argues that both the new Catechism (no. 1754) and

Veritatis splendor (no. 74) err when they consign the consequences of an act solely to its circumstances. Sometimes these consequences constitute the very object of the act, at least in a larger sense.

When? Here Knauer turns to the teaching on double effect and repeats his conviction that it has been badly misunderstood as applying only to marginal dilemmas, when actually it applies to nearly all human actions. In nearly all actions a gain is tied to a loss. The central concept of double effect is that of commensurate reason. A reason is truly commensurate when "the action does justice to the universally formulated premoral value or value-complex sought in the action, in the long run and overall." By "universally formulated" Knauer means, e.g., "wealth overall," not "*my* wealth," or "life in general," not just "*this* life."

When there is no commensurate reason in the sense just described, then the evil effect or harm is direct in the moral sense and constitutes the very object of the act. When there is a commensurate reason, that constitutes the object, and the evil effect is morally indirect.

Here Knauer makes several points. First, we have language describing actions independently of the presence of commensurate reason and language describing actions with such reason. Thus: taking another's property and theft; killing and murder; false statements and lying; termination of pregnancy and abortion; amputation and mutilation. Knauer feels that lack of such distinctions in other areas causes confusion.

Next, he faults the erroneous formulation of the new Catechism. It states: "Except when there are strictly therapeutic grounds, directly willed amputations, mutilations and sterilizations of innocent persons violate the moral law" (2297). When therapeutic reasons exist, the disvalues in these procedures are indirect.

Finally, Knauer argues, correctly I believe, that we must be careful to analyze an act accurately. Organ donation from a living donor is not two acts, one a means to the other. It is a single act whose very object is saving the life of the recipient. Presumably he would say that self-stimulation is but a single element of the action of sperm testing.

Joseph Fuchs, S.J., uses the notion of mortal sin as the centerpiece around which he gathers some reflections on *Veritatis splendor*. For instance, he reminds us that the *intrinsece mala* in Catholic tradition are human interpretations and judgments, and therefore, neither share in the absoluteness of divine wisdom nor exclude the possibility of error.

There are three areas (prescinding from blasphemy) where this tradition has located such evils: life, sexuality, speech. The identification of "naturalness" with moral rightness is mistaken. Furthermore, Fuchs regards Grisez's attempt to find *intrinsece mala* in 1 Corinthians 6:9–10 and Romans 3:8 as an incompetent use of scripture.

Next, Fuchs discusses pluralism and argues that we should not expect all peoples of all times and cultures to arrive at the very same conclusions on ethical matters. For instance, Israel was at various times nomadic, agrarian, and urban. This influenced its value judgments. Similarly African societies evaluate procreation somewhat differently than do European-American peoples.

Fuchs then argues that it is a mistake to expect the Bible to lay out rights and wrongs in detail. Rather the Bible, especially the New Testament, aids our discernment in a different way. It provides a new and deeper understanding of the human person, of our vocation in Christ, of our being led by the Spirit, of our personal worth, etc. It is in such matters that the Church finds its original teaching function in moral matters.

When he presents proportionalism, Fuchs insists that it is the act in its fullness (with concrete circumstances and foreseeable results) that is the one object of decision. "The object of the ethical decision for an action is, therefore, not the basic (e.g., physical) act as such (in its ethical relevance, such as killing, speaking falsehood, taking property, sexual stimulation), but the entirety of the basic act, special circumstances, and the chosen or (more or less) foreseeable consequences." Thus, killing in self-defense and during a robbery are two different ethical acts. Fuchs underlines the fact that no proportionalist says or can be forced (logically) to say that a good end justifies a morally wrong means. Once an action is said to be morally wrong, nothing can justify it.

The notion of fundamental option traces to Karl Rahner, who developed the ideas of Jacques Maritain and Joseph Maréchal. However, Fuchs once again argues that the authors of Vatican documents *(Persona Humana, Reconciliatio et Paenitentia, Veritatis Splendor)* are not familiar with the thought-world of Rahner and therefore misrepresent the notion, especially by conceiving it as an act like any other choice.

Fuchs mentions the encyclical only a few times, but his entire study is a series of qualifications and counter-statements to the encyclical's absolutisms.[57]

An entirely different point of view is taken by Martin Rhonheimer.[58] In a long article he argues that a key assertion of the encyclical is the following: "In order to be able to grasp the object of an act which specifies that act morally, it is therefore necessary to place oneself in the perspective of the acting person." But teleological approaches do not do this. They view actions from the outside as "events which cause determinate effects." Therefore, they "fail to see that, independently from *further* intentions required to optimize consequences or good on the level of caused states of affairs, an action may already be qualifiable as *morally evil.*" This means that a particular type of action can be "qualified as causing an *evil will* simply because it is *evil* to want…certain actions as practical objects." Why? Because in doing so "the acting subject, that is, its *will,* takes a position with regard to good and evil already by *choosing* concrete actions." His example: "the choice of killing a person." This is wrong because it is "to set one's will against another man's life." It is never permissible. Of course, the action must be properly described, that is, with its basic intentional content, before this can be said.

Rhonheimer concedes that everything depends on what one considers to be the object. Some (e.g., Knauer and Fuchs, though Rhonheimer does not mention them) want to include foreseen and intended consequences as part of an expanded notion of object. Rhonheimer rejects this as contravening experience. We must distinguish two intentionalities. Thus if I break a promise of repaying money to someone, causing thereby his economic ruin, because I, simultaneously, intend thereby to prevent the ruin of many others, "I have *chosen* to break the promise given to my creditor *for the sake of* realizing an intention which is very laudable in itself." This Rhonheimer sees as morally wrong. "The same applies to killing or lying with good further intentions." Presumably a falsehood spoken to deceive a homicidal maniac intent on murdering a third party is unacceptable.

It would not stretch the imagination too much to see the work of Grisez and Finnis in Rhonheimer's essay. Indeed, he acknowledges the debt. I cannot touch on all aspects of this study here. One question, however, appears to be central: the question of intentionality. Rhonheimer asserts that for teleologists the acting subject disappears together with an intentional concept of action. The subject is replaced by events and states of affairs, the optimum of goods and minimum of bads. This, I believe, is simply wrong, as the articles of Fuchs and Knauer show. Both have intentional concepts of action but they include more than Rhon-heimer does. What is responsible for Rhonheimer's error? Is it that he has taken one general description of consequentialism and applied it indiscriminately to all recent revisionist analyses? Possibly.

Whatever the case, this opens up on a key question to be put to Rhonheimer: Why, in choosing to kill a person or deceive a person, does one necessarily "take a position with his will with regard to 'good' and 'evil'"? One could understand why if the description of the action already includes the wrong-making characteristics. For Rhonheimer, in at least one case, it does. He defines theft as misappropriation of another's goods. Finnis and Grisez have encountered this same question in the past. Why, it has been asked, does every concrete choice to speak a falsehood or take a life necessarily involve one in directly rejecting the basic good of truth itself or the good of life?

CRITICAL ISSUES

Our sampling of early responses to *Veritatis Splendor* has already revealed many issues. There are, of course, any number of critical issues raised by a papal letter as long and sprawling as this one. Others will undoubtedly pick up on these as time passes. Here I would like to mention three: the positive value of the letter; its central issue: the meaning of object; and the issue behind other issues: ecclesiology.

The Positive Value of the Encyclical

It would be a huge mistake to dwell only on the controversial aspects of the encyclical. For that would be to miss its positive value. The papal letter is a strong indictment of contemporary relativism and individualism. It rightly rejects the false dichotomies that lead to these twin errors. There are the dichotomies between freedom and law; the ethical order and the order of salvation; conscience and truth; faith and morality.

That the world needs a strong statement of this type is beyond question. There is a school of thought in the contemporary world that makes a double move. First, it moves from the factual plurality of beliefs and practices to the conclusion that there is no truth regarding right (and wrong) belief and practice. Second, from this relativistic premise it concludes that individuals should enjoy all but unlimited freedom in determining what is right and wrong belief and practice. Against this, John Paul II argues that freedom is in the service of truth and that truth is the precondition of freedom (nos. 34, 84, 86–88, 96). In a word, the pope scores radical relativism in moral thinking and radical subjectivism in moral judgment.

I have seen those noxious tendencies over and over again in mores as well as in moral arguments. Medicine offers an example. In contrast to an earlier paternalism, against which we appropriately react, we now live in an era of patient self-determination. What can easily be missed is that reactions can easily become overreactions. In the religious sphere, a reaction against authoritarianism can usher in anarchy. This has happened in contemporary medicine. In overreacting against paternalism, autonomy has been absolutized. Doctors John Collins Harvey and Edmund Pellegrino have underlined this in a recent paper.[59]

When autonomy is absolutized, very little thought is then given to the values that ought to inform and guide the use of autonomy. Given such a vacuum, the sheer fact that the choice is the patient's tends to be viewed as the sole right-making characteristic of the choice. That trivializes human choice. It is no coincidence that the notorious Jack Kevorkian is drum major for absolutized autonomy. "In my view the highest principle in medical ethics—in any kind of ethics—is personal autonomy, self-determination. What counts is what the patient wants and judges to be a benefit or a value in his or her own life. That's primary."[60] Stop. Period. No qualifications. As Leon Kass notes, "The autonomy argument kicks out all criteria for evaluating the choice, save that it be uncoerced."[61] And it is no coincidence that Kevorkian regards medicine as a "strictly secular endeavor." It should be entirely separate from religious ethics. His example: a Catholic doctor should be prepared to provide an atheistic woman with an abortion.[62] Behold the indissoluble union of a secularized medicine with absolutized autonomy that trumps every other consideration. In this system Kevorkian has become what he provides: a machine.

Relativism and individualism can be seen in many other areas of life, both domestic and public. The encyclical directs its fire against the assumptions of the liberal society: absence of any sense of an objective moral order; the assertion of freedom over truth; conscience seen as the creator of moral law. This is right on target.

However, the most vulnerable aspect of the encyclical is that it travels simultaneously along two tracks as it lays bare contemporary errors: that of the general culture and the other of Catholic moral theology. Indeed the pope attempts to relate these two by insisting that Catholic moral theologians share the blame for the cultural relativism and individualism he deplores. As Richard McBrien has observed, this lumping of moral theology with modern culture can only be achieved by misrepresentation.[63]

The Central Issue: The Meaning of Object

Veritatis Splendor insists that the morality of an act depends primarily upon the object rationally chosen. I think there is very little controversy on that general statement. What is this object? The letter responds: "a freely chosen kind of behavior." When one looks at the past literature and that reviewed above, it becomes clear that disagreements begin to occur when authors discuss what goes into the object, what counts as a "kind of behavior." Rhonheimer (and presumably Finnis, Grisez, etc.) would say that "the choice to kill a person" or "the choice to speak a falsehood" is a sufficient description of the object. In contrast to this, Knauer insists that the reason for the act must be included. Thus the very object *(Handlungsziel)* of a transplant from a living donor is the saving of another person. Equivalently he is saying that this *ratio* is what makes it a certain kind of action. Fuchs is saying much the same thing when he insists that all elements in the act constitute the object of choice.

I know of no way to solve this except by appeal to experience. Most people would not view the removal of a kidney from a living donor as an act separate from its transfer to the ill recipient. They would view the whole process as an *act of organ transplantation.* Contrarily—and here is where I disagree with Hittinger as noted above—they would judge aborting fetuses for population control, killing for world peace, etc., as fully constituted acts (therefore, with their own intentional objects) aimed by ulterior intent to a further end. I await further comment from others on this matter.

The fact that people disagree about what the notion of object should include, plus the fact that in the textbook tradition the notion of object included or excluded elements depending on what one wanted to condemn as wrong *ex objecto,* lead to a further reflection. It is the question of just how determinative of rightness or wrongness the object is. Could it be that this determination is made on other grounds, and then the conclusion is presented by use of the term "object"? If this is indeed the case, then the encyclical's repeated appeals to actions wrong *ex objecto* does not aid analysis; rather it hides it.

A possibly analogous situation is the use of the terms "ordinary" and "extraordinary" with regard to the means to preserve life. Judgments about the obligatory or nonobligatory character of measures to preserve life are to be made in terms of burden and benefit to the patient. The terms "ordinary-extraordinary" do not forge such judgments. They simply display the conclusion. As the President's Commission noted: "The claim, then, that the treatment is extraordinary is more of an expression of the conclusion than a justification for it."[64]

The Issue behind Other Issues: Ecclesiology

At some point it is necessary to stand back from this encyclical and see it in its historical context. The Irish Augustinian Gabriel Daly notes that the papal letter "forms part of the program of 'restoration' which has been launched in the Catholic Church during the present pontificate."[65]

Daly sees a double context for the papal letter: the world and the Church. As for the world, it is widely admitted that we are suffering a moral malaise. People yearn for moral leadership. They "seem glad that somebody claims to know what is right and wrong and is prepared to speak out against a climate of moral lassitude." Thus there is a widespread secular admiration for John Paul II. People may not agree with what he says, but they like the idea that somebody is ready to take a stand and crack a whip against a widespread moral decomposition, especially when their own personal lives are a comfortable distance from the pope's concrete conclusions.

The primary context of *Veritatis Splendor* is the Church. Here the encyclical is linked, as both Häring and Daly note, with a pyramidal, noncollegial ecclesiology. Some of its elements are: centralization of the teaching function; centralized control of the appointment of theologians and of the appointment of bishops; the imposition of loyalty oaths on office-holders; the blocking of scholars seeking posts in church-controlled institutions, the sacking of theology teachers, etc. The symbol of all this is the attempt to suppress any dissent.[66] Moral theologians are told to "set forth the Church's teaching and to give, in the exercise of their ministry, the example of a loyal assent, both internal and external, to the magisterium's teaching" (no. 110). The persuasiveness of the arguments seems to mean little. Later the encyclical adds that "opposition to the teaching of the Church's pastors cannot be seen as a legitimate expression either of Christian freedom or of the diversity of the Spirit's gifts" (no. 113). When it occurs, bishops are "to have recourse to appropriate measures" (no. 116) to protect the faithful.

For me, *Veritatis Splendor* is a symbol of a notion of the Church—of the Church as a pyramid where truth and authority flow uniquely from the pinnacle. Vatican II adopted the concentric model wherein the reflections of all must flow from the periphery to the center if the wisdom resident in the Church is to be reflected persuasively and prophetically to the world. That this was not the case with *Veritatis Splendor* seems clear. Cardinal Ratzinger states that "theologians of various continents and most varied orientations have had a part in its coming to be."[67] It would not be difficult to give a fairly large list of the theologians who were *not* consulted. Some were mentioned earlier and are the very ones whose work is criticized in the encyclical.

The most concrete reflection of the notion of Church operative in the document is its statement about dissent. On that matter this roundup will conclude by citing the theologians of Quebec:

> The recommendations made to bishops about repressing all dissent in regard to any teaching of the magisterium, without distinction, seem to come from another age. Put in operation, the suggested measures would be extremely dangerous for the intellectual life and the progress of thinking within the Church, especially in the area of morals and ethics. Such limits on freedom of thought and expression lead to a danger we should be very aware of today, at a time when reflective thought should be very active in order to respond to the needs and ever new problems of our time. These limits on freedom of thought and expression cannot

respect what we call academic freedom here. Moreover, they come out of a notion of the Church which really takes very little into account that the pursuit of truth, moral questions included, necessitates the participation of everyone. Frankly stated, as human persons and believers, we cannot proudly embrace the description proposed by the Encyclical of our role in the Church and the world.[68]

Notes

1. *Origins* 23 (1993) 297–334.
2. Rossana Ansuini, "Original Sin and *Veritatis Splendor*," *30 Days* 10 (1993) 34–37.
3. *The Tidings*, 10 October 1993, 9.
4. *The Pilot*, 8 October 1993, 2.
5. *Pittsburgh Catholic*, 8 October 1993.
6. J. Francis Stafford, "Moral Reason Is Basis of Virtue," *L'Osservatore Romano*, Weekly Edition, no. 41, 13 October 1993, 10.
7. *The Michigan Catholic*, 15 October 1993, 3.
8. *The Catholic Voice*, 29 October 1993, 5.
9. *The Catholic Voice*, 15 October 1993, 15.
10. Ibid.
11. *The Catholic Transcript*, 15 October 1993, 3.
12. *The Buffalo News*, 6 October 1993, 4.
13. *The Irish Times*, 6 October 1993, 11.
14. *The Daily Telegraph*, 6 October 1993, 4.
15. I take this from a xerox copy of a statement whose letterhead reads *Pressmitteilungen der deutschen Bischofskonferenz.*
16. *30 Days* 10 (1993) 34.
17. Ibid.
18. I take this from a statement issued 5 October 1993 by Bernardin and copyrighted by Reuters.
19. *Catholic Review*, 18 November 1983, cited in my *The Critical Calling* (Washington: Georgetown University, 1994) 93.
20. Ronald Modras, "Some Notes on the Margin of *Veritatis Splendor*," *ARCC Light* 159 (January 1994) 1–2.
21. John Wilkins (ed.), *Understanding Veritatis Splendor* (London: SPCK, 1994) xi. This volume brings together the series of articles published in *The Tablet*. Since some may not have access to this volume, I provide below the indi-

vidual references to *The Tablet.* Another volume, *Fundamentalmoral als Quaestio Disputata: Moraltheologische Antworten auf "Veritatis Splendor,"* edited by Dietmar Mieth, appeared in the fall of 1994. Some of the authors included are: Alfons Auer, Marciano Vidal, Johannes Gründel, Günter Virt, Bernard Häring, Hans Rotter, Joseph Fuchs, Klaus Demmer, Peter Hünerman, Bernhard Fraling, Mieth, and this author.

22. Joseph Selling, "Ideological Differences: Some Background Considerations for Understanding *Veritatis Splendor.*" *The Month,* 27 January 1994, 12.

23. Andrzej Szostek, *Normy i Wyjatki* (Lublin: Katolicki Universytet Lubelski, 1980).

24. The responses cited here are all found in *Commonweal* 120 (22 October 1993) 11–18.

25. For instance, see Joseph Fuchs, S.J., "'Intrinsece malum': Überlegungen zu einem umstrittenen Begriff," in *Sittliche Normen,* ed. Walter Kerber (Düsseldorf: Patmos, 1982) 88; also Bruno Schüller, S.J., "Neuere Beiträge zum Thema 'Begründung sittlicher Normen,'" in *Theologische Berichte* 4 (1974) 115–17.

26. Richard John Neuhaus, "The Splendor of Truth: A Symposium." *First Things* 39 (January 1994) 14–29, at 15.

27. Ibid. 24–25.

28. Louis Janssens, "A Moral Understanding of Some Arguments of St. Thomas," *Ephemerides Theologicae Lovanienses* 63 (1987) 354–60.

29. Neuhaus, "The Splendor of Truth" 25–29.

30. Ibid. 16–19, 21–23. The Burrell-Hauerwas piece refers to Catholic authors "who have long been attempting an elaborate accommodation with the spirit of the age." It is difficult to find language strong enough to condemn such motivational attribution. This is especially regrettable from authors who have played no significant role in these developments and manifest no realistic grasp of the problems, concepts, and language that surround them.

31. See n. 21 above.

32. Germain Grisez, "Revelation vs. Dissent," *The Tablet* 247 (16 October 1993) 1329–31. For discussion of Grisez's notion of basic goods, see Bernard Hoose, "Proportionalists, Deontologists and the Human Good," *Heythrop Journal* 33 (1992) 175–91; Robert P. George, "Liberty Under the Moral Law: On B. Hoose's Critique of the Grisez-Finnis Theory of the Human Good," *Heythrop Journal* 34 (1993) 175–82; B. Hoose, "Basic Goods: Continuing the Debate," *Heythrop Journal* 35 (1994) 58–63.

33. Seán Fagan, "The Encyclical in Focus," *The Tablet* 247 (20 November 1993) 1519.

34. Bernard Häring, "A Distrust that Wounds," *The Tablet* 247 (23 October 1993) 1378–79.

35. Ibid.

36 . "Lettre ouverte aux évêques du Québec," *L'Eglise canadienne* 27 (January 1994) 14–15. Joseph Selling (see n. 22 above) refers to the fact that the encyclical "represents the victory of one school of thought over another." That such "victories" can be short-lived and extremely costly to the Church is clear from Thomas O'Meara's fine article "Raid on the Dominicans: The Repression of 1954," *America* 170 (5 February 1994) 8–16. O'Meara explicitly compares 1954 and 1994.

37. Richard A. McCormick, S.J., "Killing the Patient," *The Tablet* 247 (30 October 1993) 1410–12; this same piece also appeared as "*Veritatis Splendor* and Moral Theology" in *America* 169 (30 October 1993) 8–11.

38. Joseph Fuchs, S.J., "Good Acts and Good Persons," *The Tablet* 247 (6 November 1993) 1444–45. For a summary of some fundamental questions raised by Fuchs since Vatican II, see James F. Keenan, S.J., "Joseph Fuchs at Eighty: Defending the Conscience while Writing from Rome." *Irish Theological Quarterly* 59 (1993) 204–10.

39. Nicholas Lash, "Teaching in Crisis," *The Tablet* 247 (13 November 1993) 1480–82.

40. Maciej Zieba, "Truth and Freedom in the Thought of Pope John Paul," *The Tablet* 247 (20 November 1993) 1510–12.

41. Oliver O'Donovan, "A Summons to Reality," *The Tablet* 247 (27 November 1993) 1550–52.

42. Herbert McCabe, "Manuals and Rule Books," *The Tablet* 247 (18 December 1993) 1649–50.

43. Lisa Sowle Cahill, "Accent on the Masculine," *The Table* 247 (11 December 1993) 1618–19.

44. John Finnis, "Beyond the Encyclical," *The Tablet* 248 (8 January 1994) 9–10.

45. Peter Hebblethwaite, "*Veritatis Splendor* in Focus," *The Tablet* 248 (15 January 1994) 46.

46. I shall not review those articles that are mostly summaries of the contents of the encyclical. These would include the following: Sergio Bastianel, S.J.,"L'Enciclica sulla morale: 'Veritatis Splendor,'" *La Civiltà Cattolica* 144 (6 November 1993) 209–19; Yves Daoudal, "Veritatis Splendor," *La Pensée Catholique* 49 (November-December 1993) 15–17; Georges Cottier, O.P., "L'encyclique 'Veritatis Splendor,'" *Nova et Vetera* 69 (1994) 1–13; Dario Composta, "L'Enciclica 'Veritatis Splendor' del Sommo Pontefice Giovanni Paolo II: Riflessioni sulla sua attualità," *Divinitas* 38 (1994) 9–22; A. Chapella, S.J., "Les enjeux de Veritatis Splendor," *Nouvelle revue théologique* 115 (1993) 801–17.

47. Todd Whitmore, "Three Cheers and a Number of Hard Questions: Veritatis Splendor," *Bostonian Magazine* (Spring 1994) 28–34.

48. Russell Hittinger, "The Pope and the Theorists," *Crisis* 11 (December 1993) 31–36. The quote from the *National Catholic Reporter* is from 15 October 1993, 17.

49. Ibid.

50. There was a school of thought within Catholicism that held that the death of the aggressor could be intended as a means. On this point, see M. Zalba, S.J., *Theologiae Moralis Summa II,* 2d ed. (Madrid: B.A.C., 1957) 79. Zalba holds this himself and refers to appeal to double effect as "obscurior." He cites Lugo, *De iustitia et iure* d. 10, n. 149, who cites Navarro, Valentia, Molina, Vitoria, Vasquesz, and others as holding the same view.

51. On this point H. Noldin writes: "All those things pertain to the object of the act that constitute its *substance*, viewed not physically but *morally*; furthermore, all those things constitute the substance of an act which are so essential and necessary to it that if something is lacking or added, the act is different. Thus, the object of theft is someone's property taken against his reasonable will; for if the thing is not someone else's, or is taken with the owner's consent, or not against his reasonable opposition, it is not theft" (H. Noldin, A. Schmitt, G. Heinzel, *Summa theologiae moralis,* 34th ed. [Innsbruck: F. Rauch, 1962] 75 n. 70).

52. Sebastian Moore, "The Encyclical in Focus," *The Tablet* 247 (6 November 1993) 1449.

53. Ralph McInerny, "Locating Right and Wrong," *Crisis* 2 (December 1993) 37–40, at 38 (my emphasis).

54. See n. 36 above.

55. Bruno Schüller, S.J., "Die Quellen der Moralität," *Theologie und Philosophie* 59 (1984) 535–59, at 547.

56. Peter Knauer, S.J., "Zu Grundbegriffen der Enzyklika 'Veritatis Splendor,'" *Stimmen der Zeit* 212 (January 1994) 14–26.

57. Joseph Fuchs, S.J., "Das Problem Todsünde," *Stimmen der Zeit* 212 (February 1994) 75–86.

58. Martin Rhonheimer, "'Intrinsically Evil Acts' and the Moral Viewpoint: Clarifying a Central Teaching of *Veritatis Splendor,*" *The Thomist* 58 (1994) 1–39.

59. John Collins Harvey and Edmund D. Pellegrino, "A Response to Euthanasia Initiatives," *Health Progress* 75 (March 1994) 36–39, 53.

60. *Free Inquiry* Interview, "Medicide: The Goodness of Planned Death," *Free Inquiry* 11 (Fall 1991) 14–18, at 14.

61. Leon R. Kass, "Suicide Made Easy," *Commentary*, December 1991, 22.

62. *American Medical News*, 10 February 1992, 3.

63. Richard P. McBrien, "Teaching the Truth," *Christian Century* 110 (1993) 1004.

64. President's Commission for the Study of Ethical Problems in Medicine

and Biomedical and Behavioral Research, *Deciding to Forego Life-Sustaining Treatment* (Washington: U.S. Government Printing Office, 1983) 88.

65. Gabriel Daly, O.S.A., "Ecclesial Implications," *Doctrine and Life* 43 (1993) 532–37, at 532.

66. Here it must be noted that the encyclical defines dissent as "carefully orchestrated protests and polemics carried on in the media" (no. 113). This is also the view of Cardinal Joseph Ratzinger. He refers to "attitudes of general opposition to Church teaching which even come to expression in organized groups" ("Instruction on the Ecclesial Vocation of the Theologian," *Origins* 20 [1990] 123). In a certain sense, then, expressed disagreement by an individual is not really dissent.

67. *L'Osservatore Romano*, Weekly Edition, no. 40, 6 October 1993.

68. See n. 36 above.

2. Revelation vs. Dissent

Germain Grisez

This chapter first appeared in *The Tablet* in 1993.

The descriptive title of Pope John Paul II's new encyclical, *Veritatis Splendor,* indicates its subject matter: "De fundamentis doctrinae moralis Ecclesiae (On the foundations of the Church's moral teaching)." And speaking directly to the bishops, to whom the document as a whole is addressed, the Pope is more specific: "Each of us knows how important is the teaching which represents the central theme of this encyclical and which is today being restated with the authority of the Successor of Peter." That central theme, he continues, is: "the reaffirmation of the universality and immutability of the moral commandments, particularly those which prohibit always and without exception intrinsically evil acts" (115).

The Pope addresses his brother bishops, he says, "in obedience to the word of the Lord who entrusted to Peter the task of strengthening his brethren" (115). The Pope and the bishops are "facing what is certainly a genuine crisis" (5). For "a new situation has come about within the Christian community itself....It is no longer a matter of limited and occasional dissent, but of an overall and systematic calling into question of traditional moral doctrine" (4).

The encyclical does not deal with specific kinds of acts, such as contraception or abortion, homosexual behavior or adultery. Rather, it examines and finds wanting dissenting views that attempt to find a way around some or all of the precepts which exclude those or other acts as always wrong.

As the foundation for his criticism of such dissent, the Pope recalls that faith includes specific moral requirements. The encyclical's whole first chapter unfolds the significance of Jesus' dialogue with the rich young man described in chapter 19 of Matthew's gospel. Here the

Pope finds Jesus reaffirming as God's word some specific requirements which everyone must meet if he or she is to be saved.

These requirements are not arbitrary: "The commandments of which Jesus reminds the young man are meant to safeguard the good of the person, the image of God, by protecting his goods. 'You shall not murder; You shall not commit adultery'" and so on, formulated as prohibitions, "express with particular force the ever urgent need to protect human life, the communion of persons in marriage" (13), and so on. Moreover, "Jesus shows that the commandments are not to be understood as a minimum limit not to be gone beyond, but rather as a path involving a moral and spiritual journey toward perfection, at the heart of which is love" (15). While perfection is far more, "one can 'abide' in love only by keeping the commandments" (24).

The encyclical points out that God has communicated the same moral requirements both as natural law, by giving human persons understanding of what is right and wrong, and as revealed truth. Since grace perfects human nature, Christian morality, while going beyond natural law, always includes it. "From the very lips of Jesus, the new Moses, man is once again given the commandments of the Decalogue" (12). Indeed, Jesus' "way of acting and his words, his deeds and his precepts constitute the moral rule of Christian life" (20). That is why the requirements of natural law are included in the Gospel, so that "the Gospel is 'the source of all saving truth and moral teaching'" (28).

While the encyclical's first chapter provides an inspiring articulation of the Gospel's teaching about following Jesus, its second chapter takes up and criticizes four ways in which various dissenters have tried to soften received moral teaching about intrinsically evil acts.

One way is to affirm that Christians must love their neighbor and respect everyone's dignity but to deny that love and respect always forbid "intrinsically evil acts"—such as killing the innocent and adultery. Of course, proponents of this view can say that murder and adultery are wrong provided "murder" means unjust killing and "adultery" means unchaste or irresponsible intercourse involving someone married to a third party. But until some moralists began looking for ways around the precepts forbidding intrinsically evil acts, no Jew or Christian ever gave the fifth and sixth commandments so vacuous an interpretation. A more substantive defense of this view asserts that specific prohibitions result from "biologism" or "naturalism" (47), i.e., from confusing what is naturally given with what morally ought to be.

In replying, the Pope recalls the Church's definitive teaching on the human person's unity and argues: since the human person "entails a particular spiritual and bodily structure, the primordial moral requirement of loving and respecting the person as an end and never as a mere means also implies, by its very nature, respect for certain fundamental goods" (48), such as bodily life and marital communion.

Ultimately, however, attempts to limit Christian morality's requirements to generalities such as love and respect are rejected by the Pope on the ground that they are "contrary to the teaching of Scripture and Tradition" (4). He quotes St. Paul's condemnation (in 1 Cor. 6:9–10) of "certain specific kinds of behavior the willful acceptance of which prevents believers from sharing in the inheritance promised to them" (49), and recalls Trent's use of the same passage against a view somewhat like the one rejected here.

A second way around the precepts forbidding intrinsically evil acts is to treat them as sound guidelines, but mere guidelines, for conscience. On this view, only conscience can decide whether an act bad in general might be appropriate in a concrete situation. The Pope's reply is that this view mistakenly treats conscience as a creative decision rather than as a judgment following from moral truths, including negative precepts which oblige in every case (see 56). Once more, the Pope appeals to St. Paul, this time to Romans 2:15, which "clarifies the precise nature of conscience: it is a moral judgment about man and his actions, a judgment either of acquittal or of condemnation, according as human acts are in conformity or not with the law of God written on the heart" (59).

Certain theories of fundamental option provide a third way of softening the impact of precepts excluding intrinsically evil acts. Though such acts may be intrinsically wrong, doing them in particular cases, even with full awareness and deliberate consent, need not reverse one's opinion for the good and for God, and so need not be mortal sin.

The Pope rejects such theories as inconsistent with the makeup of the acting person. But even before doing so, he rejects them as "contrary to the teaching of Scripture itself, which sees the fundamental option as a genuine choice of freedom and links that choice profoundly to particular acts" (67). The "choice of freedom" which "Christian moral teaching, even in its biblical roots, acknowledges" as fundamental is "the decision of faith...the obedience of faith (cf. Rom. 16:26)" by which (again quoting Vatican II's constitution on divine revelation) "man makes a total and free self-commitment to God, offering 'the full submission of intellect and will to God as he reveals'" (66). Since faith is a commitment to covenantal communion with God, which is to bear fruit in works, it entails the specific requirements of the Decalogue, reaffirmed by Jesus as conditions for entering the Kingdom.

The fourth and final way by which many dissenting moralists circumvent traditional teaching is by flatly denying that the precepts forbidding certain kinds of acts as intrinsically evil really are exceptionless. Proportionalists or consequentialists maintain that one cannot always tell that an act excluded by such a precept would be morally evil without taking into account, in the actual circumstances, the greater good or lesser evil which it might bring about. They maintain that the foreseen proportions of "pre-moral" or "ontic" goods to bads in the available alternatives can require an exception even to such precepts as the fifth and sixth commandments, as traditionally understood.

Against these theories, the Pope points out "the difficulty, or rather the impossibility, of evaluating all the good and evil consequences and effects—defined as pre-moral—of one's own acts" (77). He goes on to argue that the morality of human acts depends on their "object," which, being "a freely chosen kind of behavior"...is "the proximate end of a deliberate decision which determines the act of willing on the part of the acting person" (78). But the objects of certain kinds of acts are at odds with "the goods safeguarded by the commandments" (79). Thus: "Reason attests that there are objects of the human act which are by their nature 'incapable of being ordered' to God, because they radically contradict the good of the person made in his image. These are the acts which, in the Church's moral tradition, have been termed 'intrinsically evil' *(intrinsece malum):* they are such always and *per se,* in other words, on account of their very object, and quite apart from the ulterior intentions of the one acting and the circumstances" (80).

But, once again, the Pope's critique finally invokes revelation: "In teaching the existence of intrinsically evil acts, the Church accepts the teaching of Sacred Scripture" (81). Two texts are cited, Romans 3:8 and (once more) 1 Corinthians 6:9–10. The former first appears in a quotation from St. Thomas (78), then in the heading to sections 79–83, and finally in a quotation from *Humanae Vitae* 14, where Paul VI taught that "it is never lawful, even for the gravest reasons, to do evil that good may come of it (cf. Rom. 3:8)" (80). Finally, John Paul also teaches: "The doctrine of the object as a source of morality represents an authentic explicitation of the biblical morality of the Covenant and of the commandments" (82).

In chapter three, the Pope develops a further consideration: "The unacceptability of 'teleological,' 'consequentialist' and 'proportionalist' ethical theories, which deny the existence of negative moral norms regarding specific kinds of behavior, norms which are valid without exception, is confirmed in a particularly eloquent way by Christian martyrdom" (90). If there were ways around exceptionless moral norms, many martyrs could have survived. The encyclical affirms that in raising such martyrs "to the honor of the altars, the Church has canonized their witness and declared the truth of their judgment, according to which the love of God entails the obligation to respect his commandments, even in the most dire of circumstances, and the refusal to betray those commandments, even for the sake of saving one's life" (91).

Confronted with the encyclical's criticisms of the various ways around received teaching regarding intrinsically evil acts, dissenting theologians undoubtedly will respond that the Pope has misinterpreted them, missed them altogether, and/or found no new or convincing arguments against their views. Such responses, however, will not suffice. For, even if one granted that the encyclical's analyses and arguments from reason are inadequate, its main point and its arguments from revelation would remain intact. Its main point, in effect, is that passages such as 1 Corinthians 6:9–10 mean exactly what they say: those who do certain kinds of acts, such as adultery and sexual perversion, will not inherit the Kingdom—assuming, of course, that the sin, committed with full awareness and deliberate consent, remains unrepented. The Pope makes it clear that, though the "magisterium does not intend to impose upon the faithful any particular theological system, still less a philosophical one," he "has the duty to state that some trends of theological thinking and certain philosophical affirmations are incompatible with revealed truth" (29).

Dissenting moralists, of course, will reply that the prohibitions found in scripture are less absolute than they seem. But that reply will contradict the encyclical which, referring to "the moral commandments expressed in negative form in the Old and New Testaments," teaches: "Jesus himself reaffirms that these prohibitions allow no exceptions" (52).

No doubt that will be denied by some scripture scholars. However, until recent times, when some Jewish and Christian theologians began denying that there are intrinsically evil acts, no Jew or Christian ever imagined that "You shall not murder, You shall not commit adultery" mean no more than that one may not kill the innocent without a proportionate reason or engage in extramarital intercourse unchastely or irresponsibly. Any attempt to interpret God's words as allowing such exceptions would imply that for millennia the moral truth which God meant to communicate was radically misunderstood—that God failed to communicate effectively. God, however, cannot have failed to communicate effectively.

Moreover, if the view that the commandments admit exceptions were correct, the whole body of believers would have been mistaken until almost today. But ever since Pentecost it has been true that the Holy Spirit is permanently present in the Church, so that "the universal body of the faithful...cannot be mistaken in belief...in matters of faith and morals" (109, quoting *Lumen Gentium* 12). Consequently, the rejection of the Pope's interpretation of scripture is implicitly inconsistent with any Catholic conception of divine revelation and its transmission.

Those who nevertheless continue to dissent no doubt will take comfort from the fact that the encyclical never so much as mentions the magisterium's infallibility. I think, however, it would be a mistake to interpret this silence as a concession to the view that the received teaching about intrinsically evil acts falls outside the scope of infallibility. For one thing, *Donum Veritatis,* the Congregation for the Doctrine of the Faith's 1990 instruction concerning theologians' role in the Church, recalled the magisterium's infallibility not only in general but also specifically in moral matters. The present encyclical, in the passage quoted just above from *Lumen Gentium* 12, refers, though without using the word, to the infallibility of the whole Church in matters of morals.

More important, however, is that John Paul II by no means weakens past claims for the authority of the moral teaching he reaffirms in this encyclical. While nowhere treating the magisterium's infallibility, he everywhere teaches that the exceptionlessness of the relevant norms is a revealed truth—that is, a truth demanding from every Catholic the assent of faith. Thus, the appeal is to God's authority in revealing, which is the source of the Church's infallibility in believing and the magisterium's authority in teaching.

Theologians who have been dissenting from the doctrine reaffirmed in this encyclical now have only three choices: to admit that they have been mistaken, to admit that they do not believe God's word, or to claim that the Pope is grossly misinterpreting the Bible. No doubt, many will make the third choice. In doing so, they will greatly escalate the conflict which has divided the Catholic Church during the past thirty years.

In claiming that the received teaching concerning intrinsically evil acts is a revealed truth, the Pope also implicitly asserts that it is definable. That implicit assertion will be denied by those rejecting the teaching. This argument is undeniably over essentials, and cannot long go unresolved. It cannot be settled by theologians. Only the magisterium's definitive judgment will settle it.

3. A Distrust that Wounds

Bernard Häring

This chapter first appeared in *The Tablet* in 1993.

After reading the new papal encyclical, I felt greatly discouraged. Several hours later I suffered long-lasting seizures of the brain, and looked forward hopefully to leaving the Church on earth for the Church in heaven. After regaining my normal brain function, however, I have a new feeling of confidence, without blinding my eyes and heart to the pain and brain-convulsions that are likely to ensue in the immediate future.

Veritatis Splendor contains many beautiful things. But almost all real splendor is lost when it becomes evident that the whole document is directed above all towards one goal: to endorse total assent and submission to all utterances of the Pope, and above all on one crucial point: that the use of any artificial means for regulating birth is intrinsically evil and sinful, without exception, even in circumstances where contraception would be a lesser evil.

The Pope is confident that he has a binding duty to proclaim his teachings with no calculation whatsoever about the foreseeable practical consequences for the people concerned and for the whole Church. He would consider such considerations unlawful and dangerous, because they take into account a weighing of values. Whatever the risk, whatever the danger, he believes that his insights brook no dissent, but can be met only with obedience.

The recent *Catechism of the Catholic Church* issued with the Pope's authority shows that he does acknowledge that negative precepts allow of exceptions. For example, the prohibition against killing can be set aside in cases of self-defense, exaction of the death penalty, and even just wars. For him, the wrongness of contraception is much more absolute than the commandment, "Thou shalt not kill."

What about the negative precept proclaimed by the Lord himself to all his disciples, "You are not to swear at all" (Mt. 5:34)? In this case not only does the Pope allow exceptions, but imposes them as a rule on whole groups of members of the Church.

There is here a striking difference between our Pope today and John Paul I, who before his election had for many years been an outstanding teacher of moral theology. As Albino Luciani, he had suggested a change of doctrine; then when Paul VI in his encyclical *Humanae Vitae* reiterated the ban on contraception, he decided to keep silent. Soon after his election as pope, however, he left no doubt that he would propose a review of the teaching, with emphasis on a consultative approach (cf. Camillo Bassoto, *Il mio cuore è a Venezia,* Albino Luciani, Venice, 1990). Although he had given much attention to the issue, he never felt such a confidence in his own competence as to remove the need to listen patiently to all concerned and to engage in dialogue with theologians and bishops. As a moral theologian John Paul I shared fully the conviction of the vast majority of moral theologians of the past and of the present that it is unlawful and possibly a great injustice to impose on people heavy burdens in the name of God unless it is fully clear that this really is God's will.

John Paul II's mentality is different. His starting point is a high sense of duty, combined with absolute trust in his own competence, with the special assistance of the Holy Spirit. And this absolute trust in his own powers is coupled with a profound distrust towards all theologians (particularly moral theologians) who might not be in total sympathy with him.

In *Veritatis Splendor* John Paul II makes no secret that he has for a number of years felt driven to write an encyclical to bring theologians into line with his teaching on sexual morals, particularly on contraception. Yet he trusts moral theologians like Carlo Caffarra who organized a congress of other "trustworthy" moralists and produced the incredible assertion that the Church until 1917 considered contraception, whether within marriage or outside it, as "murder." Caffarra was referring to the *Corpus Juris Canonici* which only said that "those who afflict men or women with magical means or poison so that they become unable to procreate, to conceive or to give birth to a child, and do so inspired by hate or enmity, should be considered as murderers." Caffarra is still head of the John Paul II Institute in Rome, despite such incredible use of church documents.

The Pope's approach has been expressed in many talks and disciplinary measures. It has been expressed also in structures:

1. The new code of canon law criminalizes dissent (canon 1371, number 1). Anyone who is admonished for an utterance and does not declare full assent, commits a punishable crime. Not the slightest possibility is admitted of doing so with a good, sincere conscience. This text was introduced at the last moment by the Pope without any consultation of the international commission which prepared the new code.

2. There is a complete central control of nominations of all theologians, including moral theologians, teaching in church-related institutions at the higher level. For the controllers, no doubt, the heart of the matter is that any theologian, to be approved, must give the fullest assent to all papal pronouncements about contraception and similar questions.

3. To a large extent, a similar control operates over the nominations of bishops and other office-holders in the Church.

4. When the previous three measures did not work perfectly, the next step was to require a new form of confession of faith, including now wholehearted assent to non-infallible (that is, fallible) papal teaching, and a particular oath of fidelity towards the supreme pontiff. The *Acta Apostolicae Sedis* say that this measure was approved by the *Sanctissimus* (Most Holy). The text speaks of the Pope as *Beatissimus* (Most Blessed). Should one see some special significance in that? Do not these titles given to the Pope sacralize his authority unduly?

5. It is by now well known that papal agencies take enormous trouble to find out who is "trustworthy" and who is not. And who has the say in this process? What role does assent to papal sexual ethics play?

6. Now comes the encyclical *Veritatis Splendor*. Its words will press hard on the consciences of all who might be concerned, though clearly the Pope and his special adviser do not have a proper picture of what moral theology today is like. Very grave insinuations are made. What moral theologian of good reputation in the Church would recognize himself in the picture which *Veritatis Splendor* draws?

The Pope's objective is to fulfill in this way the mission entrusted by Christ to Peter and his successors: "You must lend strength to your brothers" (Lk. 22:32). But these words must be set in their immediate context. Peter assures his master and fellow disciples: "Everyone else may fall away, but I will not" (Mk. 14:29). The Lord warns him against this self-confidence and says: "I have prayed that your faith may not fail. When you have been converted, you must lend strength to your brothers." It is clear from this what conversion means for Peter. It is also clear how he should strengthen his brothers.

Peter's downfall came from his inability to believe in a humble, suffering and non-violent Servant-Messiah. Having been converted, the main task of Peter, and of all who join him, is to confess and to profess through the witness of their whole lives that the Father has raised to life and exalted to glory his suffering Servant, Jesus Christ. There is surely nothing whatsoever in this text that could be taken as relating to a task laid on Peter to teach his brothers about an absolute norm forbidding in every case any kind of contraception. Nor did Jesus tell Peter to teach a complete set of norms and laws to be fulfilled by everyone, including negative laws constraining everyone. Was not Peter wavering about whether the new Christian converts should observe Jewish law? Did not Paul have to confront him and set him right about this?

The Pope is aware that the vast majority of married people are unable to fall into full agreement with the absolute ban on contraception, that they resist the emphasis with which it is inculcated, and cannot follow the arguments by which it is justified. Most moral theologians, probably, are of the same mind. The papal response to this public opinion in the Church is not new but is now delivered with a new emphasis: the Church is not democratic, but hierarchical. Let us ask our Pope: are you sure your confidence in your supreme human, professional and religious competence in matters of moral theology and particularly sexual ethics is truly justified?

As to contraception, there is no word on the subject anywhere in divine revelation. This is a matter of what we call the natural law written deep in the hearts of men and women, and therefore we must and can find a fruitful approach which is appropriate. Since natural law is "open to the eyes of reason," we should reason together gently and patiently as we consider the case "on either side" (Rom. 2:12, 16). The hierarchical constitution of the Church cannot in the least contradict or disallow this approach in any matter which concerns the law written in our hearts and calling for a response from our consciences

Away with all distrust in our Church! Away with all attitudes, mentalities and structures which promote it! We should let the Pope know that we are wounded by the many signs of his rooted distrust, and discouraged by the manifold structures of distrust which he has allowed to be established. We need him to soften towards us; the whole Church needs it. Our witness to the world needs it. The urgent call to effective ecumenism needs it.

Let me suggest, for a start, one healing and encouraging event. Let the Vatican destroy all its lists—I have seen one of them—of those who are considered "trustworthy" ("*affidabili*") and of those who are not, simply as regards this one issue of the absolute wrongness of artificial contraception. The Church has greater concerns than this, more urgent needs: to proclaim the good news and to encourage all to set out on the road to holiness.

And let us honor God's gracious forgiveness by forgiving each other for the harm we have inflicted on each other and the anger we may have harbored in our hearts.

4. Good Acts and Good Persons

Joseph Fuchs

This chapter first appeared in *The Tablet* in 1993.

St. Augustine tied himself in knots attempting to explain why, though even venial sins conflict with God's will, not all sins are equally mortal. Many moral theologians today say the problem is not so much theological as anthropological, because it touches the depths of the human person. To deal with it, they have developed the theory of the "fundamental option," as it is called. But this approach is not universal in the Church. Some theologians do not take seriously this complex of problems, if indeed they consider them at all. They betray themselves by the paucity of their writings on the topic.

The encyclical *Veritatis Splendor* (nos. 65–70) addresses the question in very critical fashion. For the most part it hews close to the line laid down by the 1984 apostolic exhortation, *Reconciliatio et Paenitentia,* and the 1975 declaration of the Congregation for the Doctrine of the Faith, *Persona Humana.* But the encyclical does not mention this declaration.

The theory of a "fundamental option" goes back mainly to the development by the late Karl Rahner, S.J., of ideas borrowed from Jacques Maritain and Joseph Maréchal, S.J. Rahner's preferred term was not in fact "fundamental option" but "the human person's disposition of his self as a whole." Without some such theory, Rahner maintained, many church statements on dogmatic or fundamental theology and above all on moral theology were unintelligible.

The theory does not aim to deal with practical questions. Rather, it focuses on a more thorough understanding of the theological and anthropological depths of the human person as the subject of moral action. So the preoccupation with the distinction between mortal and venial sins found in the Vatican documents of 1975 and 1984 and to some extent in *Veritatis Splendor* misses the point, as we shall see later.

As understood by its proponents, among whom I include myself, the theory goes something like this. Human freedom is one single reality—but its effects occur in two different but related spheres. On the one hand, we experience freedom in everyday moral choices: here the person, more or less free, chooses the most morally significant actions. On the other hand, in such decisions about particular actions, already the person commits himself as a whole, as a person: hence one can talk of *fundamental* freedom. Thus, not only are the person's particular actions good or bad, but also the person himself as a whole.

Whereas freedom of choice is encountered within our reflective conscious experience, this is not true of the fundamental freedom. In order to be aware of it consciously and as an object, a person would have to be able to stand outside himself in order to inspect himself, but the self as a whole cannot do that. So awareness of *fundamental* freedom is not directly accessible to observation and verification. Necessarily a-thematic (that is, not conceptual and not reflectively conscious), it is also termed "transcendental," echoing what St. Thomas says in speaking of the person as *present* to himself (*Summa Theologiae* I.67.1; *Summa contra Gentiles* 4.11).

So one may say that a person, in terms of fundamental freedom, has his own ethical quality—that is, a person may be good or evil; it is not just his *actions* that come under moral judgment as right or wrong. The ethical *fundamental option* made by the person, based on his fundamental freedom, is not itself a single *act* of self-disposition, though it is always felt *in* (though not *through*) particular acts of deciding. Rather than act, it is best seen as a process towards an ethical disposition which can grow or decline.

The fundamental option is expressed in decisions about individual actions, exercised with free choice. It influences them, while also being influenced by them. This reciprocal relation between the fundamental option and freedom of choice has certain consequences, according to those who defend this view.

First, it is just not possible for us to examine the core of our person from the outside so as to establish whether we are fundamentally good or evil—or rather, since we can only be good through grace, whether we are living in God's grace and love. What we can know about good and evil is limited to our actions, decisions and desires. But—as St. Thomas puts it—we can also to some extent conclude by a conjecture based on our actions (*per coniecturam, Summa Theologiae* I–I.112.5c) whether we really are as persons good or evil: that is, whether we are bound firmly in God's grace and love or not.

A second consequence follows. Since the fundamental ethical option goes so much deeper than particular ethical choices about concrete actions, it is not as easy for a good person to change his or her fundamental option as it would be to swap morally good particular actions for morally bad ones, as St. Thomas explicitly says (*De Veritate* 27.1. ad. 9).

Finally, individual decisions and actions that may be called "peripheral" (that is, not substantially penetrated by the central fundamental option) can nevertheless gradually bring a person to a point at which he is now committed to the contrary of his previous direction and disposition. When this happens, his fundamental option is reversed.

The critical assessment of the theory of the "fundamental option" found in *Veritatis Splendor* suggests that the Pope's theological advisers have not understood deeply enough the thought-world of Karl Rahner and its widespread development of the theory among moral theologians and others. Manifestly, they do not grasp that the fundamental option and everyday moral choices happen on different levels of the same person, and so cannot be categorized on the same level of objective awareness.

The papal consultors do indeed know about the way a host of personal basic inclinations can provide, as it were, a riverbed for everyday particular decisions to run along (65). They even find such fundamental tendencies in the Bible (66). But for them all this belongs to the objective realm of the ethical consciousness of the person. They do not see it as the necessarily a-thematic (that is, not conceptually conscious) reality present at the core of the person.

In this way the fundamental option as defined by its protagonists is misunderstood in the encyclical. In its negative and therefore sinful form, this option is seen by the encyclical as the "explicit and formal rejection of God and one's neighbor"; and it is presented as though it were a precise, definite and determinable *act* (69). I know no proponent of the fundamental option who has said this. The encyclical's theologians *assume* that ethical judgment on a person can be delivered solely on the basis of his conscious and free decisions about individual acts (67).

When they criticize the theory of the "fundamental option," these consultors see a split or dissociation between the fundamental option, on the one hand, and the individual acts, on the other (III and 66), which in their view drags those acts down and would make them insignificant as far as the person is concerned (65). In truth, precisely because the fundamental option and moral choices are on different levels, the theory stresses rather their mutual relationship and interpenetration, and thus is the very contrary of division and separation.

The encyclical attacks the idea that the moral quality of individual acts may be determined only by the intention and the fundamental option of the person concerned (67). Then it states that every particular act involves some reference to good or evil. But who would wish to deny this? The problem is how this relates to the ethical status of the person as a whole, which is on another level.

A similar comment applies when the encyclical asserts that the fundamental option can sometimes be determined by a particular action or even overthrown by it (67 and 70). Yet how can decisions on the objective and conceptual level determine the personal inaccessible "fundamental option" unless they attain to the same non-conceptual level? Likewise, the possibility is calmly envisaged of people going to their eternal damnation on the basis of grave sins (88) without having a personal fundamental option. To repeat: the fundamental option is not an individual act, and particular serious sins do not lead as such to eternal damnation unless embodied in a fundamental option to reject God. For at the end of the road of genuinely free acts, there remains only the sinner as he or she is. At this point, in the furthest depths of the person, the fundamental option becomes a final option.

The International Theological Commission (ITC) got it right in its 1982 declaration on reconciliation and conversion: "According to the teaching of the Church, the *fundamental decision* ultimately determines the ethical constitution of the human person. But the concept of fundamental decision cannot provide an everyday *criterion* for distinguishing between serious and non-serious sins. Its purpose is rather to make clear what serious sin is.

"True, the human person may be able to express or alter his or her (fundamental) decision *in* (my italics) an individual act, provided the act is undertaken consciously and freely; but this does not mean that every particular act involves the entire fundamental decision, or that each individual sin must *ipso facto* be a revocation of the fundamental decision" (published in, for example, *Internationale Zeitschrift Communio* 13, 1984, pp. 44–63).

Veritatis Splendor is in fact very restrained when it comes to clear condemnation of any of the schools of moral theology. For instance, in the formulation of no. 70 the encyclical says, using the conditional, that the fundamental option should be rejected "if it is understood in such a way that at the objective level it alters or puts in doubt the traditional concept of mortal sin." The theory certainly does not do that. On the contrary, it deepens the sense of mortal sin.

At the end of the encyclical the Pope turns his gaze towards moral theologians. He makes a modest request for help which seems clearly to point in a precise direction. He says: "While recognizing the possible limitations of the human arguments employed by the magisterium, moral theologians are called to develop a deeper understanding of the reasons underlying its teachings." But there can be no guarantee in advance—as moral theologians and presumably the Pope all know very well—that moral theologians will be successful in doing so.

5. The Pope on Proportionalism

James Gaffney

This chapter first appeared in *Veritatis Splendor: American Responses,* eds. Michael E. Alsopp and John J. O'Keefe, in 1995.

In the Vatican's official summary of *Veritatis Splendor* the matter with which this essay is concerned is identified as the encyclical's "opposition to the moral theories called *teleologism, consequentialism,* and *proportionalism.*"[1] What is held in opposition to these undefined "moral theories" is that "the moral evaluation of human acts is not drawn solely from the weighing of their foreseeable consequences or from the proportion of 'premoral' goods or evils resulting from them."[2] Immediately afterwards comes the very strange statement that "even a good intention is not enough to justify the goodness *(sic)* of a choice."[3] Sense can best be made of this statement by simply omitting "the goodness of"—since goodness hardly needs justifying.

These negative assertions are then followed by an affirmative one that apparently states an ethical theory. "The morality of an act, while certainly taking into account both its subjective intention and consequences, depends primarily on the object of the choice which reason grasps and proposes to the will."[4] This statement requires us to distinguish three factors in moral behavior, namely the action of a particular moral kind that one has rationally chosen to perform (the "object" in a peculiar scholastic sense of that word), the purpose for which one has chosen to perform it (the "subjective intention"), and the effects expected to result from its having been performed.[5] What is meant by saying that the "object" is what the morality of an act depends on "primarily" becomes clear in two assertions which immediately follow, that "it is possible to hold as 'intrinsically evil' certain kinds of behavior opposed to the truth and the good of the person" and that "the choice by which they are made can never be good, even if that choice is made with a subjectively good intention and with a view to positive consequences."[6]

Simply stated, the pope's teaching thus far seems to be that a deliberately chosen course of action may fall within a category of moral classification every instance of which is *ipso facto* immoral, quite regardless of intentions however high-minded, or results however desirable in themselves. Since this is proposed in opposition to "teleologism, consequentialism, and proportionalism," those "moral theories" are understood to reject this doctrine.

The doctrine as I have stated it can hardly be dismissed as patently absurd. Indeed it is in no way extraordinary, and seems to have had defenders, including some very illustrious ones, in every age of serious ethical analysis. It can even lay claim to a firm place in popular moral wisdom, as reflected in such familiar proverbial admonitions as "the end does not always justify the means" and "the streets of hell are paved with good intentions." Probably most educated citizens of modern democracies think of at least some "human rights violations" precisely as kinds of behavior whose moral condemnation is simply not negotiable on a plea of lofty intentions or useful results.[7] And in the history of the Roman Catholic and of other Christian churches, the pope's position, as stated above, can certainly claim to be solidly traditional.

That is not, of course, to claim that there is not or has not been any serious opposition to that doctrine. Within the history of Christian theology, the name of Peter Abelard is associated with a doctrine asserting the primacy of intention in determining the morality of an act. But since the intention he had in mind was the intention of pleasing God, if he were persuaded that God had revealed that certain kinds of behavior were never pleasing to him, his position could, in practice, be equivalent to the pope's.[8] Much more serious is the opposition offered by a school of thought that for the past two centuries has been called utilitarianism, and in particular what has been sub-distinguished as "act utilitarianism."[9] In its unqualified form, act utilitarianism directs us to judge the morality of each action by whether or not it "will or is likely to produce the greatest balance of good over evil in the universe."[10] If "teleologism" means emphasizing intended goals, and "consequentialism" means emphasizing results, and "proportionalism" means emphasizing the ratio of good results to bad ones, these labels are all appropriate for act utilitarianism. However, forthright endorsements of act utilitarianism would be hard, if not impossible to find among the public statements of any Catholic moral theologians, whereas the three "isms" have often enough been applied to, and even accepted by Catholic moral theologians whom no informed ethicist could possibly confuse with act utilitarians, and who would certainly not repudiate the pope's doctrine as I have summarized it from the Vatican's official summary of the encyclical. For further light on whom the pope is opposing under these labels, and why he is opposing them, it is necessary to turn from the official summary of the encyclical to the encyclical itself. Unfortunately, while the encyclical abounds in footnote references to specific texts with which the pope agrees, not one specific text, or even a specific author, is cited as an unequivocal example of the "teleologism, consequentialism, and proportionalism" with which he so vehemently disagrees. Thus, of course, suspicions are generated: among the timorous, suspicions of persecution; among the censorious, suspicions of heterodoxy; among the cynical, suspicions of straw men.

Turning to the encyclical, we find that the material whose summary we have just analyzed is to be found in the second of the work's three chapters, where it comprises Section IV, headed "The Moral Act."[11] Here the matters under consideration are treated at much greater length. It is arguable whether or not they are treated with greater clarity.

"Teleology," we are told, is characteristic of the moral life, for moral life is life oriented towards its ultimate goal *(telos),* and morally good acts are those conducive to that ultimate purpose. Moral acts express and determine the moral quality of persons who perform them; they do not simply better or worsen the external world in which they produce their effects.

But actions cannot express and determine the positive moral quality of a life directed towards a divine goal unless they are kinds of acts that lead in that direction. That was what concerned the rich young man who asked Jesus what he must do to gain eternal life—a Gospel narrative about which the encyclical presents a lengthy commentary that actually comprises a fundamental moral theology.[12] And that was why Jesus directed the rich young man first to the commandments and then to self-denial and discipleship. The commandments are precisely God's warning against kinds of action that diminish moral character and divert human life from its divine goal.

Against this frankly theological background the pope considers modern efforts to answer traditional questions concerning what constitutes the morality of a free human act. He envisages the three alternatives outlined by Thomas Aquinas.[13] They are "the intention of the acting subject, the circumstances—and in particular the consequences—of his action, or the object itself of his act."[14] It is important to recall that the term "object" has here that technical scholastic significance explained previously—an esoteric usage unlikely to be even guessed at by modern readers whose education has not included medieval philosophical vocabulary!

The encyclical calls "teleological" theories that base the moral evaluation of acts on a "weighing of the nonmoral or premoral goods to be gained and the corresponding nonmoral or premoral values to be respected."[15] Thus the measures of being (morally) good would be the extent of doing (nonmoral) good—an idea of morality not without appeal for the common sense of conscientious people, regardless of their religious beliefs or disbeliefs. The pope acknowledges that many Catholic moralists who encourage this point of view do not themselves subscribe to utilitarian principles so completely as to disregard the ultimate divine goal of human life. And he recognizes that such theorizing in the direction of an "autonomous morality" is strongly motivated by a commendable desire to find, in pluralistic societies, authentic common ground for moral discourse. What, then, does the pope find ominous and reprehensible in the "teleological" theorizing of modern Catholic moralists?

The terms "consequentialism" and "proportionalism" seem always or nearly always to be used by the pope in a pejorative sense. The former relies on "a calculation of foreseeable consequences deriving from a given choice," the latter on "the proportion acknowledged between the good and bad effects of that choice"—a distinction that is intelligible but uneven.[16] But the pope further attributes to what he calls "proportionalism" and "consequentialism" an additional tenet that is the real basis of his opposition. For "while acknowledging that moral values are indicated by reason and by revelation," they "maintain that it is never possible to formulate an absolute prohibition of particular kinds of behavior which would be in conflict in every circumstance and in every culture with those values."[17] The crucial issue for the pope seems therefore to be the admission of at least the possibility of formulating negative moral norms that admit absolutely no exceptions.

Most negative moral norms are originally and familiarly formulated in ways that admit, and indeed demand numerous exceptions.

Thus the biblical prohibition, "Thou shalt not kill," is obviously understood within the Bible itself to admit several kinds of exceptions, including cases of self-defense, legitimate warfare, and capital punishment.
Biblical commentators sometimes recommend the rendering "Thou
shalt not commit murder." And thus reformulated, the prohibition might
well seem to be unexceptionable. But that is only because the word
"murder" precisely *means* illicit homicide—without shedding any light
on the practical question of just what kinds of homicide are illicit. One
must already know the exceptions to "Thou shalt not kill" in order to
know what counts and what does not count as murder. "Murder" implies
immorality. "Killing" does not. Hence "morally justified murder" is a
contradiction in terms whereas "morally justified killing" or "homicide"
is a coherent hypothesis. Strictly speaking, "Thou shalt not murder"
merely forbids us to commit whatever kinds of homicide are not morally
permissible!

But is it possible to formulate a prohibition of *all* and *only* those
kinds of homicide that could never be morally permitted? Such a prohibition would, no doubt, be very complex and lengthy, hard for most people to learn and harder to remember. Universal agreement with the
formulation would surely be too much to hope for. And yet it is by no
means evident that such a formulation is absolutely unattainable. And if
the pope could be satisfied with the mere admission of that sort of possibility, he could find little to object to among most even of those willing
to be labeled "consequentialists" and "proportionalists." Most ethicists
of even the most quibbling kind could, if pressed, come up with *some*
description of *some* kind of behavior that they could not in *any* circumstances imagine being justifiable. But the arguments of professional
ethicists would not likely be required to persuade normal people of the
moral wrongness of such behavior, nor indeed would divine revelation
or the authoritative teaching of a church.

Rather clearly, what is really bothering the pope is not the blanket
denial of any possibility of formulating an unexceptionable moral prohibition, but rather the denial that certain familiar and traditional moral
prohibitions, as they are usually stated, admit no exceptions. One must,
therefore, seek definite examples of what the pope regards as, in the
words of the Catechism, "specific kinds of behavior that are always
wrong to choose, because choosing them involves a disorder of the will,
that is, a moral evil,"[18] "objects of the human act which are by their nature

'incapable of being ordered' to God,"[19] "acts which, in the church's moral tradition, have been termed 'intrinsically evil,'"[20] "acts which per se and in themselves, independently of circumstances, are always seriously wrong by reason of their object."[21] Far from evading this question, the pope furnishes an actual list, taken from the Second Vatican Council, of what he calls "examples of such acts." It will be useful to cite this list in its entirety and to review it with some care. It needs to be noted, however, that the Second Vatican Council, in the passage that the encyclical cites, had no intention of addressing the issue that the pope wishes to address in citing it. Even without consulting records of the conciliar discussions, the text itself of *Gaudium et Spes* makes it entirely clear that the Council is not at this point addressing any issue of ethical theory or methodology, much less proposing any exemplary list of "acts which *per se* and in themselves, independently of circumstances, are always seriously wrong by reason of their object." In fact, what the Council does list is not confined to "acts" at all, but includes deplorable social conditions which are not acts but are very often *consequences,* and much more likely to be consequences of *in*action than of "acts." This is entirely consistent with the conciliar context, which had just previously urged the obligation of active neighborly intervention as contrasted with selfish disregard, but it contributes nothing whatever to the pope's argument in the encyclical, that certain acts can be categorically condemned without reference to their consequences. Oddly enough, the translation of this misappropriated passage in the official English version of *Veritatis Splendor* serves the pope's argument even less well than more familiar earlier translations of the Council document, as for example in preferring the term, "homicide" to "murder," and "voluntary suicide" to "willful self-destruction."[22] The following citation of the passage is from the official English version of the encyclical.

> Whatever is hostile to life itself, such as any kind of homicide, genocide, abortion, euthanasia and voluntary suicide; whatever violates the integrity of the human person, such as mutilation, physical and mental torture and attempts to coerce the spirit; whatever is offensive to human dignity such as subhuman living conditions, arbitrary imprisonment, deportation, slavery, prostitution and trafficking in women and children; degrading conditions of work which treat

laborers as mere instruments of profit, and not as free responsible persons: All these and the like are a disgrace, and so long as they infect human civilization they contaminate those who inflict them more than those who suffer injustice, and they are a negation of the honor due to the Creator.[23]

The Council's characterization of this list of social abuses is unexceptionable. The pope's characterization of it is exceptionable at nearly every point. And if all that the pope is saying is that *somewhere* in this list examples can be found of what he means by "intrinsically evil" acts, that information is hardly helpful unless he tells us *which* ones they are!

The same strange mystification reoccurs when the pope appeals to the Bible, producing again an unwieldy list, containing no "acts" whatsoever, but rather a loose itemization of what might be called "immoral" or "vicious types." "In teaching the existence of intrinsically evil acts, the church accepts the teaching of Sacred Scripture. The apostle Paul emphatically states: 'Do not be deceived: Neither the immoral, nor idolaters, nor adulterers, nor sexual perverts, nor thieves, nor the greedy, nor drunkards, nor revilers, nor robbers will inherit the kingdom of God.'"[24] Clearly, what Paul is teaching in this passage is what he states in introducing it, namely that "the unrighteous will not inherit the kingdom of God." The list comprises simply a conventional set of what might be called unrighteous types. The list contains no "acts," but rather habitual offenders in various areas of morality. To be sure, immoral persons are perpetrators of immoral acts, at least potentially. But that the characteristic behavior of each of the types cited is, in every instance, an act whose malice is independent of circumstances and consequences is patently absurd. To pinpoint the intrinsically evil act of "the immoral," or even of "the greedy" or "drunkards," would be a challenging task indeed. And as for "thieves," Thomas Aquinas himself responds affirmatively to his own question, "Is it licit to steal on account of need?" thus implying that the morality of thieves is indeed dependent on circumstances.[25] Here again, the text cited, even when torn from its context, contributes nothing whatsoever to support the argument to which it is applied.

In fact, there is only one example cited in this portion of the encyclical where an authoritative document definitely is referring to what John Paul II means by an "intrinsically evil act," here characterized as "something which of its very nature contradicts the moral order and which must therefore be judged unworthy of man, even though the intention is to protect or promote the welfare of an individual, of a family or of society in general." This is indeed what the pope is talking about and the authority he cites does indeed propose an example of "intrinsically evil acts." The authority is Pope Paul VI, referring in his famous encyclical *Humanae Vitae* to "contraceptive practices whereby the conjugal act is intentionally rendered infertile."[26] Thus the one unequivocal example the pope cites of an authoritatively specified "intrinsically evil act" turns out to be the most vigorously contested and widely rejected moral teaching in the entire modern history of the papacy. It is not easy to avoid a sense of profound anticlimax, combined with a strong suspicion that what purported to be a critique of certain moral theories was after all only one more assault against critics who find no real plausibility in certain official Catholic teachings about sex and, in particular, about contraception. It is certainly true that for a great many people who take morality very seriously the mere description of a bit of human behavior as, say, "sexual intercourse with the use of a condom" is morally significant; the statement, of itself, communicates nothing to elicit moral blame, moral praise, or even moral interest. To those people, of whom I am certainly one—and one who has read and pondered countless dreary pages on this subject—it is alternately funny and sad that an official doctrine of the Catholic church holds that anything identifiable as "contraceptive practices whereby the conjugal act is intentionally rendered infertile" can be denounced as "intrinsically evil" and "gravely disordered" behavior without knowing anything at all about the motives or results of these practices in individual cases. If one has any reason to question the morality of such practices, the questions will almost certainly be the kinds of questions associated with what the pope calls "teleologism," "consequentialism," and "proportionalism," questions like "Why are they doing it?" "Are there any bad effects?" And, "Do the good effects compensate sufficiently for the bad effects?" Questions of the most unsubtle kind, the answers to which can usually be reliably guessed before they are even asked.

It is no longer imaginable that any new arguments will be advanced either for or against the reasonableness of the Catholic church's official doctrine concerning the morality of contraception. At present it is extremely difficult to find any theologian, philosopher, or conscientious man or woman outside the Catholic church who finds that doctrine morally admirable or defensible. Inside the Catholic church the doctrine is rejected in practice by a great majority, in theory by an even greater majority, and accepted by most of those few who do accept it on grounds of authority alone. It is no contribution to this controversy, or to the issues with which it is concerned, to suggest or pretend that opposition to this official church teaching by moral theologians and philosophers is rooted in their adherence to one or several indistinct "moral theories." As observed at the beginning of this essay, the pope's clearest identification of these "theories" is to be found in the two statements he proposes in opposition to them: (1) "The moral evaluation of human acts is not drawn solely from the weighing of their foreseeable consequences or from the proportion of 'premoral' goods or evils resulting from them." (2) "Even a good intention is not enough to justify...a choice."[27] If an anonymous questionnaire were to be distributed among Catholic moral theologians and philosophers, requiring them simply to mark "True" or "False" on each of those two propositions, I do not believe the resulting tally of "Falses" would be even statistically significant. And I am certain that among the many, myself included, who accepted the two propositions as "True," would be vast numbers of those who regard the papal teaching about contraception as not only rationally untenable but a serious disservice to social morality. The intellectual adversaries whom the pope addresses in the portion of the encyclical under consideration in this essay are, in reality, straw men— and, to be sure, straw women! The pope's employment of these straw figures appears to be a rhetorical stratagem intended to imply that criticism of some of the Church's most dubious official tenets concerning sexual morality derives from certain broad theoretical premises which he defines under the labels "teleologism," "consequentialism," and "proportionalism." That implication is certainly false. If the pope believes it, his misinformation is dangerous. If it is merely a rhetorical exaggeration intended to support the greater good of what he deems to be moral orthodoxy, it would seem to exemplify the very kind of "results-dominated" moralizing that he deplores. In any case, it is scarcely an enhancement of the "splendor of truth." If these judgments are too severe, and the adversaries as the pope describes them are a real and present danger, it would not seem too much to ask that out of one hundred and eighty-two footnotes at least a few would identify in some bibliographically verifiable way, the persons and writings that explicitly profess the "moral theories" to which he objects. The recognition of "proportionate reason" as a significant factor in moral choice has been a part of Catholic moral theology since its earliest beginnings and among its most illustrious practitioners. Arguments about "proportionalism," variously defined and redefined, have been with us for about thirty years, associated most often during this period with practical issues of sexual morality.[28] What this period has actually witnessed in Catholic moral theology has been a progressive application to sexual morality of principles and patterns of argumentation that had long been common-place in treating virtually every other area of human morality. Some incautious and even rather foolish statements have been published during this controversy and on different sides of it. Most of them were subsequently modified in response to criticism. None of the participants in the controversy has, to my knowledge, consistently professed anything like the positions characterized by the pope's rejection of "teleologism," "consequentialism," and "proportionalism." Most of them have made considerable positive use of the teachings of Thomas Aquinas, including the Thomistic doctrine about the "sources of morality" which the pope employs against them.[29] It may be useful to conclude this essay with a brief review of that doctrine (itself by no means as clear as one could wish) and of its relevance to the issues here under consideration. Since the doctrine is restated in a form that is both contemporary and authoritative in the *Catechism of the Catholic Church* recently promulgated by the pope, I shall base my observation on that text, which is very faithful to that of Thomas Aquinas.[30]

"The object, the intention, and the circumstances form the 'sources' or constituent elements of the morality of human acts....The *object* chosen is a good towards which the will deliberately tends....The end is the first term of the intention and represents the purpose pursued in the action. The intention is a movement of the will towards the end....The circumstances, which include the consequences, are secondary elements of a moral act. They contribute to increasing or reducing the moral goodness or malice of human acts....The circumstances cannot of themselves modify the moral quality of the acts themselves; they cannot render good or just an action that is evil in itself."[31] The doctrine is evidently rooted in common sense, and focuses upon the questions common sense normally raises in attempting to judge the morality of human conduct, once it is established that the conduct is deliberate.

"What did he (or she, or they) do?" is the first such question. "Why did he (she, they) do it?" is the second. "Were there any aggravating or extenuating circumstances, including foreseeable effects?" is the third. Sometimes the answer to the first question sheds no light on the moral question, whereas the others leave no doubt as to the moral quality of the behavior under consideration. "Joe Doe extracted all Mary Roe's teeth" is meaningful but morally opaque. One kind of moral light dawns when we learn that John did it in order to appropriate Mary's gold fillings. And that moral light grows more intense when we learn additionally that the operation was performed without anesthesia, in a Nazi concentration camp, and that Mary was a Jewess. Moral judgment swings to the opposite pole if we learn instead that John was a dental surgeon by whose timely intervention Mary was spared the consequences of a progressive disease of the jaw, and that he provided the surgery and subsequent care without fee because Mary was a very poor woman. What such examples indicate is that sometimes, at least, to describe the object of a human act without any indication of its purpose or circumstances provides no basis for moral judgment. What it might further suggest is that the line of demarcation between "object," "intention," and "circumstances" is a line much sharper in abstract theory than in concrete application.

"Joe Doe copulated with Mary Roe" might also seem to be a meaningful but morally opaque statement. If we learn that they are a loving couple, eager for children, on their wedding night, we are unlikely to inquire further about their intentions or other circumstances. The circumstances and intentions would matter greatly if Mary were the victim of John, an armed rapist. The distinction between "object" and "intention," understood as simply the distinction between what one is doing and why one is doing it, is fairly clear-cut and often immediately usable. The same cannot be said of the distinction between "object" and "circumstances." Throughout the history of moral theology this confusion, in the very nature of things, between "object" and "circumstances" has been signalled by laborious redefinitions of actions deemed intrinsically evil, or evil from their very "object," in order to eliminate circumstances in which they seemed not to be evil. The first really celebrated example of this kind of thing was a tedious Augustinian discussion of the lie. The received doctrine was that lying is immoral, hence sinful. Common sense retorted that sometimes lying is not immoral, and sometimes it may be praiseworthy and even obligatory. Initially, to lie was understood as the dictionary still defines it, to "speak falsely." But progressively that definition, though sanctioned by usage, was subjected to a series of qualifications whereby at last what the "experts" meant by a lie could indeed be regarded as always immoral, while departing wildly from what ordinary people meant by a lie. "Thou shalt not kill" was similarly made an unexceptionable prohibition by simply defining away all permissible kinds of killing. Christian readjustments of the meaning of usury proved necessary in order to pay continued lip-service to the biblical condemnation of lending money at interest without weakening the foundations of modern capitalism.

In these and many other such instances, what the history of moral theology records is the consistent ethical condemnation of a named category of behavior while the description or definition of the behavior is subjected to endless revision, as circumstances are noticed in which it cannot reasonably be condemned. As a result, the Church's moral norms may undergo considerable evolution, but behind a facade of unchanging verbal formulation. Although it would be hard to deny that something very like sophistry enters this process, it has undoubtedly protected certain Catholic moral teachings from fossilization. Basically, it is a process of refining the classification of kinds of behavior considered to be immoral. One who freely indulges in such behavior may be said to perform a human act that is evil from its very object. One might express the same idea by calling it a kind of human act that is evil by moral definition. So long as one accepts the moral definition one cannot refute a moral judgment consistent with it. Commonly, once the moral definition wins acceptance, the behavior it describes is given a name that connotes the moral definition. And, of course, to attempt to defend the morality of a kind of behavior whose very name implies its immorality is logically absurd. Consequently, those who do wish to defend such behavior are likely to begin by replacing its morally pejorative name by one that is morally neutral. Thus, for example, persons who believe that morally innocent sexual intercourse can take place between an unmarried man and woman will naturally prefer to call such behavior not "fornication," but "pre-marital sex." "Fornication" has become an unpopular term with many people precisely because it seems to them to beg the very question they wish to argue. The rejections of a moral label typically reflects skepticism about a prevailing moral definition of some kind of behavior.

Nowadays, a number of traditional definitions, and the labels that imply them, are indeed widely rejected. Many others, however, are not. A great many people, for example, who would object to the morally pejorative term "fornication," do not in the least object to the morally pejorative term "rape." Nor, if they used that kind of vocabulary, would most of them object to calling rape intrinsically evil or evil from its very object. That is, whereas to identify a kind of behavior as sex between an unmarried man and woman seems to many people an insufficient basis for moral judgment, it is quite otherwise with behavior defined as sex forced upon an unwilling partner. Of the many people who are "proportionalist" in their assessment of pre-marital sex, very few are prepared to argue that rape might be quite all right as long as the rapist's satisfaction sufficiently exceeded the victim's distress! In other words, many people who would consider the pope's categorical condemnation of "fornication" shortsighted, would have no similar complaint about his categorically condemning rape. The difference is not between two general moral theories, but between two particular moral judgments.

In the same connection, it should not be overlooked that certain kinds of behavior that most modern Christians would readily define as immoral, would not have been so defined by such traditional authorities as Thomas Aquinas, for example enslavement and torture. In discussions of such behavior by moral theologians and by Christians generally, one would look far indeed to find those whom the pope stigmatizes as proportionalists. Once again, proportionalists, as the pope defines them, appear to be straw men. What the pope is really complaining about is the use of proportionately good and bad consequences to assess the morality of certain quite particular kinds of behavior, pertaining to sexuality, that have indeed been traditionally defined as immoral in Catholic teaching, but which many modern thinkers believe cannot be judged apart from considerations of intentions and circumstances. What most of these thinkers are in fact doing is applying to sexual behavior ethical theories and methods that have long been commonly applied, by Catholic philosophers and theologians and by church authorities, to other kinds of human behavior. And what the pope appears to be doing is resisting this critical enterprise under the confusing pretext of exposing an erroneous general moral theory called "proportionalism." Unfortunately, "proportionalism," as presented here by the pope, is quite simply a bugaboo.

Notes

1. "The Vatican's Summary of '*Veritatis Splendor,*'" *Origins* 23 (1993) 334–336, p. 336. [Hereafter abbreviated as *Summary VS*]

2. Ibid.

3. Ibid.

4. Ibid.

5. This traditional threefold distinction derives from Thomas Aquinas, *Summa Theologiae*, Iallae, q. 18.

6. *Summary VS*, p. 336.

7. To acknowledge that certain rights belong to human beings simply in virtue of the fact that they are human beings, and that these rights are inalienable, implies that any violation of these rights is, *ipso facto*, wrong. The point of affirming such rights is, of course, to indicate moral limits of the state's authority.

8. Petrus Abelardus, *Ethica* in J. P. Migne, ed., *Patrologia Latina*, vol. 178, pp. 640A, 650B.

9. See William K. Frankena, *Ethics* (Englewood Cliffs: Prentice-Hall, 1973), p. 35.

10. Ibid.

11. John Paul II, "*Veritatis Splendor,*" *Origins* 23 (1993) 298–334, pp. 313–322. [Hereafter abbreviated as *VS*.]

12. *VS*, 300–306.

13. *VS*, 321.

14. *VS*, 319.

15. Ibid.

16. *VS*, 320.

17. Ibid.

18. *Catéchisme de l'église catholique* (Paris: Mame, 1992), p. 374.

19. *VS*, p. 321.

20. Ibid.

21. Ibid.

22. See, e.g., Walter M. Abbott, ed., *The Documents of Vatican II* (NY: America Press, 1966), p. 226.

23. *VS*, 321.

24. Ibid.

25. Thomas Aquinas, *Summa Theologiae*, Iallae, q. 66, a. 7.

26. *VS*, 321.

27. *Summary VS*, 336.

28. For an historical resume, see Bernard Hoose, *Proportionalism: The American Debate and Its European Roots* (Washington: Georgetown, 1987).

29. For a synthetic account of a common trend of this recent work in moral theology, see John Mahoney, *The Making of Moral Theology* (Oxford: Clarendon, 1987), pp. 311–315.

30. *Catéchisme de l'église catholique*, pp. 373–375.

31. Ibid., p. 374.

6. Natural Law and Personalism in *Veritatis Splendor*

Janet E. Smith

This chapter first appeared in *Veritatis Splendor: American Responses,* eds. Michael E. Alsopp and John J. O'Keefe, in 1995.

For centuries natural law was the backbone of the Church's teaching on moral issues, but in the mid-part of this century it began to be mixed with natural rights language. Then with the pontificate of Pope John Paul II, a new language, the language of personalism, already in evidence in the documents of Vatican II, particularly *Gaudium et Spes,* dominated magisterial documents, to the point where natural law language nearly disappeared. Now, in the *Universal Catechism* and in *Veritatis Splendor* we encounter a knitting together of the language and concepts of personalism, natural law and natural rights.

Those trained in natural law and in Thomism (and others!) have been a bit befuddled by "personalism" and "phenomenology," not knowing exactly what they mean and what their principles are. This essay will attempt to offer a brief explanation of personalism while contrasting it with natural law. It will also attempt to show how personalism and natural law are compatible and skillfully integrated into *Veritatis Splendor* (a consideration of the place of natural rights language is beyond the scope of this essay).

Although for most of the English-speaking world, *Veritatis Splendor* was available prior to the *Universal Catechism,* the issuance of *Veritatis Splendor* was delayed so that it would follow and be seen as building upon the catechism. Thus, it seems appropriate to consult the catechism to contextualize some of the elements of *Veritatis Splendor.* The first part of this essay will highlight the personalistic approach of the moral section of the *Universal Catechism* by comparing it with the

Roman Catechism of the 16th century, a catechism entirely steeped in the natural law tradition. The second part of this essay will draw upon John Paul II's own explanations of how his phenomenological personalism draws upon but supplements the Thomistic metaphysical understanding of the person. He makes it clear that his anthropology and ethics are in no way incompatible with Thomism and indeed depend upon Thomistic metaphysics. The fourth and final portion of the essay will draw together the thematic concepts that distinguish a natural law approach to ethics and a personalist approach to ethics and show how they are integrated into *Veritatis Splendor.*

1.

A COMPARISON OF THE *ROMAN CATECHISM*
WITH THE *UNIVERSAL CATECHISM*

A useful way to illustrate the difference between a natural law approach to ethics and a personalist approach to ethics is to compare the treatment of morality in the *Universal Catechism* with its treatment in the *Roman Catechism.* Such a comparison illuminates certain shifts of emphasis that the Church has made over the centuries, especially as a result of the Second Vatican Council.

Cosmology vs. Christology

The new catechism expresses the christological and personalistic emphasis of the Council, rather than the cosmological and natural law emphasis of the past. To oversimplify matters, one could say that the Church has shifted from an emphasis on God the father as Lawgiver who has written his will into the laws of nature to an emphasis on Christ as our model of perfection and human dignity as the grounding of morality. The new catechism does not reject or abandon a view of the cosmos as ordered by God or of natural law as a guide to morality but it incorporates them in a secondary way in its presentation of morality. Furthermore, the dignity of the human person is seen as rooted not so much in his status as a rational creature whose mind is able to grasp reality but in his status as a free and self-determining creature who must shape himself in accord with the truth. (I shall develop these observations below.)

Ten Commandments vs. Dignity of the Human Person

The shift in emphasis from natural law to a christological and personalist emphasis is immediately apparent upon comparing the old and new catechisms. For instance, whereas the *Roman Catechism* began its moral section with the ten commandments, the *Universal Catechism* calls upon the Christian to "recognize your dignity" (n. 1691) and calls him to a life in Christ. Whereas the *Roman Catechism* focused almost exclusively on the commandments and the law, the *Universal Catechism* sketches a Christian anthropology, begins with the beatitudes, and touches upon such topics as freedom and the conscience, and includes a long section on man as a member of a community. Again, these new emphases and starting points are not to be taken as a rejection of the old. The natural law themes of the moral act, virtue, sin and grace and, of course, the natural law itself are also covered in the new catechism but they are imbued with a personalist cast—that is, with a focus on man's dignity as manifested in his power to determine himself freely in accord with the truth. Whereas the *Roman Catechism* stressed God as the author of nature and the author of all moral laws, the *Universal Catechism* stresses that all moral law is in accord with the dignity of the human person. These are emphases that began to emerge in the documents of Vatican II and come to a fuller flower in the *Universal Catechism.*

The moral section of the *Universal Catechism* begins with this passage:

> The dignity of the human person is rooted in his creation in the image and likeness of God *(article 1);* it is fulfilled in his vocation to divine beatitude *(article 2).* It is essential to a human being freely to direct himself to this fulfillment *(article 3).* By his deliberate actions *(article 4),* the human person does, or does not, conform to the good promised by God and attested by moral conscience *(article 5).* Human beings make their own contribution to their interior growth; they make their whole sentient and spiritual lives into means of this growth *(article 6).* With the help of grace they grow in virtue *(article 7),* avoid sin, and if they sin they entrust themselves as did the prodigal son to the mercy of

our Father in heaven *(article 8)*. In this way they attain to
the perfection of charity (n. 1700).

In this passage we can see several of the main concepts that
inform a personalist approach to ethics: man as made in the image and
likeness of God, man as determining himself by his deliberate and free
actions, a concern with the interior life, the need of conforming our
actions to the good that is made known to us by our conscience, and the
goal being attainment of perfect charity. These themes play a major
role in both the *Universal Catechism* and in *Veritatis Splendor.* These
concepts, of course, are also central to natural law ethics, but it is often
the emphasis that is placed upon identical themes that distinguishes the
two approaches.

2.

JOHN PAUL II'S EXPLANATION OF HIS OWN VIEWS

John Paul II, when he was the philosopher Karol Wojtyla, wrote
several essays explaining the compatibility between personalism and
natural law and the differences between them. In one essay, "The Human
Person and Natural Law," he asserts that any incompatibility between
them is illusory and that any notion that they are incompatible stems
from a faulty view either of what nature is or of what the person is.

Nature as Mechanistic vs. Nature as Rationality

The erroneous view of nature that Wojtyla combats is that held by
phenomenalists and phenomenologists (and, may I add, of many non-
phenomenological critics of natural law), that nature has nothing to do
with rationality and freedom; that it simply refers to the rather mechanistic laws of nature, that is, to the natural impulses and responses of
man's somatic and psychic nature; to what "happens in or to man" rather
than what he himself does. Whereas nature seems deterministic or
mechanistic to some extent, the person is free and thus it would seem
that the person should be above nature and perhaps even in conflict with
nature. (This is similar to the charge of biologism that is addressed in
Veritatis Splendor.) Wojtyla notes that this view of nature is not that held

by Aquinas. Rather he states that Thomistic philosophy speaks of "nature" in the metaphysical sense: "which is more or less equivalent to the essence of a thing taken as the basis of all the actualization of the thing." Wojtyla notes that the phrase "all the actualization of the thing" is important, for he ever has his focus on man's self-actualization by his free and deliberate choices. Wojtyla does grant that on the somatic and psychic level, man is dominated by nature as something "happening" to him and exercises little creative control over these happenings. But he also draws upon the Thomistic distinction of the *actus humanus* (human action) and the *actus hominis* (act of a man): the former being acts that engage the rational and free powers of the human person; the latter being such acts as breathing. Natural law pertains not to acts of man but to human action.

Wojtyla insists that Aquinas' view of natural law rests upon his understanding of the person as "an individual substance of a rational nature." He notes that Aquinas defines law as "an ordinance of reason for the common good, promulgated by one who has care of the community" and that Aquinas defines natural law as "the participation of the eternal law in a rational creature." From this he extrapolates that man's rational nature, which defines his personhood, intimately links man with the "ordinance of reason" that defines natural law. He contrasts Aquinas' view of reason with that of Kant, who would have subjective reason "impose its own categories on reality." (Wojtyla's interest in subjectivity is not the same as Kant's subjectivism.) Aquinas' reason has a "completely different orientation and attitude: that attitude of reason discerning, grasping, defining, and affirming, in relation to an order that is objective and prior to human reason itself." This objective order, this ordinance of reason, is no other than the eternal law; thus man through natural law, through his rational nature, participates in God's reason. With a proper understanding of nature, there should be no conflict between natural law and personalism. The person is not confined by natural law but indeed freely participates in God's governance; whatever subordination there is is to God. It is man's nature to be free and in that sense to transcend "nature"; he is not determined by any "natural law" to do the good; he may freely choose to do the good or not to do it.

The Person as Consciousness vs. the Person as Rational and Free

The definition of person that conflicts with natural law is the definition that elevates man's freedom unduly; it sees man as "some sort of pure consciousness" that makes the human being "a kind of absolute affirmed on the intellectual plane," subordinate to nothing. This definition of the person leads to the erroneous view of freedom that is rejected in *Veritatis Splendor;* this person is not subject to the "ordinances of reason" that point the way to objective, universal truths, but is free to form his own reality.

From this essay, we can discern what Wojtyla's understanding of the natural law is: it is the understanding that man's reason enables him to discover the "ordinances of reason" that govern the universe and that he is able to live in accord with it. Nature here does not have the mechanistic, determinative sense given to it by some modern philosophers. He also makes clear that his notion of person as a rational, self-determining creature does not entail that man's consciousness, and the subjective state is superior to objective truth; this notion is elaborated upon in other essays.

In the essay, "Thomistic Personalism," Wojtyla situates his own understanding of person *vis-à-vis* Aquinas and *vis-à-vis* the understanding of personalism devised by moderns such as Descartes and Kant. He accepts Aquinas' definition of the person, but integrates this definition into his ethics in a way significantly different from Aquinas. He notes that Aquinas develops his notion of the person largely in the theological context of an analysis of the Trinity and the Incarnation; as he notes, Aquinas' use of the term "person" is "all but absent from his treatise on the human being." In a theological context, the person is spoken of as being *perfectissimum ens,* the most perfect being, because it is a rational and free being. Despite its theological context, the definition of person used by Aquinas, taken from Boethius, is a philosophical one; it is that stated above, the person is an individual substance of a rational nature. Wojtyla restates the definition: "The person…is always a rational and free concrete being, capable of all those activities that reason and freedom alone make possible." Wojtyla notes that whereas Aquinas makes much use of the term "person" in his theological treatises, in his treatise on the human being, he adopts a hylomorphic view that sees man as a composite of form and matter. This definition does not, of course, conflict with the definition of man as a person, for man's form is a spiritual soul which is characterized by its rationality and freedom.

Wojtyla compares Aquinas' definition with that of Descartes, a definition which, like that of Kant mentioned above, tends to identify the person with consciousness and sees the body as a kind of mechanistic adjunct to the person. This view elevates freedom to a level of almost total independence. He observes that subjectivism is the most characteristic feature of such philosophy: "The person is not a substance, an objective being with its own proper subsistence—subsistence in a rational nature. The person is merely a certain property of lived experiences and can be distinguished by means of those experiences, for they are conscious and self-conscious experiences; hence, consciousness and self-consciousness constitute the essence of the person." Wojtyla notes that this is not the view of Aquinas, that he sees consciousness as something derivative of rationality.

Aquinas' Objectivity and Wojtyla's Subjectivity

While Wojtyla accepts Aquinas' view of the person, he supplements it. He summarizes Aquinas' view in this way:

> We can see here how very objectivistic St. Thomas' view of the person is. It almost seems as though there is no place in it for an analysis of consciousness and self-consciousness as a totally unique manifestation of the person as a subject. For St. Thomas, the person is, of course, a subject—a very distinctive subject of existence and activity—because the person has subsistence in a rational nature, and this is what makes the person capable of consciousness and self-consciousness. St. Thomas, however, mainly presents this disposition of the human person to consciousness and self-consciousness. On the other hand, when it comes to analyzing consciousness and self-consciousness—which is what chiefly interested modern philosophy and psychology—there seems to be no place for it in St. Thomas' objectivistic view of reality. In any case, that in which the person's subjectivity is most apparent is presented by St. Thomas in an exclusively—or almost exclusively—objec-

tive way. He shows us the particular faculties, both spiritual and sensory, thanks to which the whole of human consciousness and self-consciousness—the human personality in the psychological and moral sense—takes shape, but that is also where he stops. Thus St. Thomas gives us an excellent view of the objective existence and activity of the person, but it would be difficult to speak in his view of the lived experiences of the person.

Here is where Wojtyla moves beyond Aquinas. He shares the modern interest in consciousness and self-consciousness, though he does not share the modern view that the person *is* consciousness. Rather, in the *Acting Person* he uses an analysis of consciousness to unfold his notion of man as being free and self-determining. For it is his consciousness of himself as one who is an efficient cause of his own action and of his self-actualization that allows the human being to have a sense of responsibility for his actions and his character. In the *Acting Person*, particularly in chapters 3 and 4, Wojtyla maintains that to actualize himself properly the human person must have an authentic grasp of values or goods and must work to determine himself in accord with objective goods; only thus is his freedom truly exercised. (This, of course, is a major theme of *Veritatis Splendor.*) The dignity of the human person, for Wojtyla, lies in this determination of the self through the free choice of what is good.

Indeed, one of the chief differences between Wojtyla's interest in the human person and Aquinas is that Wojtyla begins with and returns to subjectivity and Aquinas focuses largely on objective truths. One might say that Aquinas' chief interest is in determining what acts are good and evil; for Wojtyla, the chief interest is in showing that man's very subjectivity and freedom require that he be concerned with the truth. For instance, in the *Acting Person* he states:

> For human freedom is not accomplished nor exercised in bypassing truth but, on the contrary, by the person's realization and surrender to truth. The dependence upon truth marks out the borderlines of the autonomy appropriate to the human person.

Aquinas' Metaphysical Interests and Wojtyla's
Phenomenological Interests

Another difference between Aquinas and Wojtyla emerges from
the above comparison. Whereas Aquinas is interested in developing a
metaphysical description of man, a description in terms of form and
matter, and rationality and animality, Wojtyla is interested in using
man's experience of himself, of his self-determining powers, to lead
him to an awareness of his dignity. Ultimately Wojtyla draws upon a
Thomistic metaphysics, for Wojtyla finds Aquinas' appropriation of the
Aristotelian concepts "potentiality" and "actuality" (metaphysical
terms) to be essential to a proper description of man's power to determine himself; man's life is a process of bringing into actualization various potencies that he has. But the fact remains that Aquinas aims at a
metaphysical description (one ultimately rooted in experience, but one
which seeks to arrive at ultimate principles, described in terms of universal categories), whereas Wojtyla aims at a phenomenological one,
one that remains as closely linked as possible to the lived experience of
the concrete human being of his own consciousness of himself as a self-
determining person. A metaphysical analysis would lead one to see that
man is capable of being self-determining because he is a person, that is
because he is rational and free, but for Wojtyla this metaphysical analysis is of secondary interest.

Man as a Social Animal vs. Man as Self-Giver

Wojtyla also emphasizes another feature of the human person that
links his view more closely with the documents of Vatican II than with
that of Aquinas, and this is the portrait of man as a "self-giver." Wojtyla
cites the lines of Vatican II that express concepts and use terms that were
characteristic of Wojtyla's thought before the council and that have
played a major role in his work after the council. He notes how these
lines are in accord with the tradition and with Thomism, but in a way
moves beyond them both:

> In Vatican II's Pastoral Constitution *Gaudium et Spes,* we
> read that "the human being, who is the only creature on
> earth that God willed for itself, cannot fully find himself or

herself except through a disinterested gift of himself or herself" (24). The document of the last Council seems in these words to sum up the age-old traditions and inquiries of Christian anthropology, for which divine revelation became a liberating light. The anthropology of St. Thomas Aquinas is deeply rooted in these traditions, while also being open to all the achievements of human thought that in various ways supplement the Thomistic view of the person and confirm its realistic character. The words of Vatican II cited above seem chiefly to accentuate the axiological aspect, speaking of the person as a being of special intrinsic worth who is, therefore, specially qualified to make a gift of self.

In the tradition man was defined as a social animal; much was made of his need to write human laws in accord with natural law to achieve harmony in the state. The Wojtylan view of man as one who must give of himself to perfect himself gives a much profounder cast to the traditional notion and approaches a more theological understanding of the person who can only perfect himself by imitating the total self-giving of Christ.

3.
Natural Law and Personalism in *Veritatis Splendor*

Now from the above analysis, let us draw together a list of the differences between natural law and personalism and see how the themes distinctive of each are integrated in *Veritatis Splendor.*

The Universal vs. the Concrete; the Objective vs. the Subjective

Natural law is interested in the abstract universal norm, whereas *Veritatis Splendor* is interested in the choices of the concrete individual. Natural law is interested in the objectivity of moral norms; personalism is interested in the subjectivity of the concrete individual, a subjectivity characteristic of all human beings.

The presentation of *Veritatis Splendor* begins with what might be characterized as a dramatization of a personalist moment; it is the encounter of one concrete individual, of one young man, with Christ, a young man who, conscious of his own faithfulness to the commandments, further seeks the truth about human action. *Veritatis Splendor* observes:

> For the young man, the *question* is not so much about rules to be followed, but *about the full meaning of life.* This is in fact the aspiration at the heart of every human decision and action, the quiet searching and interior prompting which sets freedom in motion. This question is ultimately an appeal to the absolute Good which attracts us and beckons us; it is the echo of a call from God who is the origin and goal of man's life (n. 7).

The emphasis here on the human heart and human interiority and its need for absolute truth for freedom are true to the emphases of personalism. In (n. 8), *Veritatis Splendor* invites us to enter into the question asked by the young man "allowing ourselves to be guided by [Jesus]." Here, in a sense, we are invited as concrete individuals to have our own personalistic moment.

Natural law is not left far behind. Christ is first interested in the young man's allegiance to the commandments, to the Law, which laws are considered to be the precepts of the natural law (n. 12). The person must not be guided by his own subjectivistic understandings of what is good and evil, but must submit to the objective truth. Throughout *Veritatis Splendor* the universality of natural law is stressed, while care is taken to acknowledge the dignity of the individual. A passage from (n. 51) speaks especially to this point:

> ...*the natural law involves universality.* Inasmuch as it is inscribed in the rational nature of the person, it makes itself felt to all beings endowed with reason and living in history...inasmuch as the natural law expresses the dignity of the human person and lays the foundation for his fundamental rights and duties, it is universal in its precepts and its authority extends to all mankind. *This universality does not ignore the individuality of human beings,* nor is it opposed to the absolute uniqueness of each person. On the contrary, it embraces at its root each person's free acts, which are meant to bear witness to the universality of the true good.

In this passage we see the parallel consideration of universality of natural law with the dignity of the human person and his individuality and uniqueness.

Refutation of Modern Interpretation of Natural Law as Biologistic

The rejection of natural law ethics because it is "biologistic" is handled in a distinctively personalistic way in *Veritatis Splendor.*

As we saw, Wojtyla was concerned to refute interpretations of natural law that portrayed man as slavishly subject to the mechanistic laws of nature. This view of natural law is addressed in *Veritatis Splendor* (n. 47). *Veritatis Splendor* mentions that modern theologians tend to reject many of the Church's teachings on sexual issues as based on a "naturalistic" understanding of natural law. They hold that man should be free to determine the meaning of his behavior and not be constrained by "natural inclinations." *Veritatis Splendor* argues that such an objection to natural law fails to correspond to the Church's teaching of the human being as unity of body and soul (n. 48). Indeed, *Veritatis Splendor* holds the view that man's very subjectivity is dependent upon his bodily state:

> ...reason and free will are linked with all the bodily and sense faculties. *The person, including the body, is completely entrusted to himself, and it is in the unity of the body and soul that the person is the subject of his own moral acts.* The person, by the light of reason and the support of virtue, discovers in the body the anticipatory signs, the expression and the promise of the gift of self, in conformity with the wise plan of the Creator. It is in the light of the dignity of the human person—a dignity which must be affirmed for its own sake—that reason grasps the specific moral value of certain goods towards which the person is naturally inclined. And since the human person cannot be reduced to a freedom which is self-designing, but entails a particular spiritual and bodily structure, the primordial moral requirement of loving and respecting the person as an end and never as a means also implies, by it very nature, respect for certain fundamental goods, without which one would fall into relativism and arbitrariness (n. 48).

In other writings, most notably in *Love and Responsibility, Familiaris Consortio* and his series of teachings on the theology of the body, John Paul II has laid out the connection between the dignity of the human person, the self-as-gift and the need to respect the life-giving power of the sexual act. In those writings, he holds that to reject the life-giving power of the sexual act is to reject a fundamental part of human dignity and to treat one's beloved as an object or a means rather than as an end. Here, he simply states in general terms his observation that natural law is not tied so much to the mechanistic laws of nature as it is to certain fundamental human goods that are embedded in certain natural inclinations.

God as Lawgiver vs. the Good as Perfective of Human Dignity

Natural law stresses that God is the source of what is good and that we ought to seek the good and obey the law because of God's authority. Sections 10 and 11 of *Veritatis Splendor* speak of the decalogue as having been delivered by God who declares, "I am the Lord your God," and *Veritatis Splendor* asserts that *"Acknowledging the Lord as God is the very core, the heart of the Law,* from which the particular precepts flow and towards which they are ordered" (sec. 11). The personalistic emphasis on morality as perfective of the dignity of the human person is seen in the comment on the commandment: "You shall love your neighbor as yourself" (Mt 19:19; cf. Mk 12:31). *Veritatis Splendor* states:

> In this command we find a precise expression of *the singular dignity of the human person,* "the only creature that God has wanted for its own sake." The different commandments of the Decalogue are really only so many reflections of the one commandment about the good of the person, at the level of the man, different goods which characterize his identity as a spiritual and bodily being in relationship with God, with his neighbor and with the material world (n. 13).

Throughout the document, it is stated that acts ordained to God are also acts that bring about the perfection of the person. For instance we read:

The reason why a good intention is not itself sufficient, but a correct choice of actions is also needed, is that the human act depends on its object, whether that object is *capable or not of being ordered* to God, to the One who "alone is good," and thus brings about the perfection of the person. An act is therefore good if its object is in conformity with the good of the person with respect for the goods morally relevant for him. Christian ethics, which pays particular attention to the moral object, does not refuse to consider the inner "teleology" of acting, inasmuch as it is directed to promoting the true good of the person, but it recognizes that it is really pursued only when the essential elements of human nature are respected. (n. 78).

Man as Rational Creature vs. Man as Self-Determined

It could be said that whereas natural law ethics emphasizes the objective goodness or evil of exterior acts and man's ability as rational creature to discern that objective goodness, personalism is concerned with subjectivity and the effect that one's choices have on the self that one is forming with one's choices. This statement of the difference between the two approaches to ethics is certainly fair to neither one, for natural law ethics has as its proximate end the formation of man in virtue so that he can achieve his ultimate end of salvation. And personalist ethics certainly does not downplay the necessity for man to act in accord with objective truths. Nonetheless, with natural law's emphasis on the rationality of man's personhood and its rootedness in the "ordinances of reason" that govern the world, and with personalism's emphasis on man's responsibility for his free determination, such a contrast can be pushed to some extent. A passage very true to a natural law emphasis is the following:

> The rational ordering of the human act to the good in its truth and the voluntary pursuit of that good, known by reason, constitute morality. Hence human activity cannot be judged as morally good merely because it is a means for attaining one or another of its goals, or simply because the subject's intention is good. Activity is morally good when it

attests to and expresses the voluntary ordering of the person to his ultimate end and the conformity of a concrete action with the human good as it is acknowledged in its truth by reason (n. 72).

A passage reflecting the personalist emphasis is the following:

> Human acts are moral acts because they express and determine the goodness or evil of the individual who performs them. They do not produce a change merely in the state of affairs outside of man, but to the extent that they are deliberate choices, they give moral definition to the very person who performs them, determining his profound spiritual traits (n. 71).

Man as Social Animal vs. Man as Self-Giver

The Aristotelian definition of man adopted by Aquinas defined man not only as a rational animal, but also as a social animal. His individual good was dependent upon the common good. Thus, in keeping with this view of man, *Veritatis Splendor* states: "The commandments of the second table of the Decalogue in particular—those which Jesus quoted to the young man of the Gospel (cf. Mt 19:19)—constitute the indispensable rules of all social life" (n. 97). The portion of *Veritatis Splendor* in which this statement appears speaks much of the state and civil authorities. *Veritatis Splendor* makes it clear that the good of society requires the recognition of absolute moral norms. The personalistic emphasis of *Veritatis Splendor* goes beyond this notion of obedience to the law being necessary for "social life"; it portrays man in his deepest onological core as being one who should make a "gift of himself." Talk of "gift of self" is nearly always linked to the imitation of Christ: *"Jesus asks us to follow him and to imitate him along the path of love, a love which gives itself completely to the brethren out of love for God..."* (n. 19, cf. 85, 87, 89). Indeed, Christ himself is the ultimate integration of the law and the gift of self: as *Veritatis Splendor* states:

> *Jesus himself is the living "fulfillment" of the Law* inasmuch as he fulfills its authentic meaning by the total gift of

himself: *he himself becomes a living and personal Law,*
who invites people to follow him; through the Spirit, he
gives the grace to share his own life and love and provides
the strength to bear witness to that love in personal choices
and actions (cf. Jn 13:34–35) (n. 15).

4.

THE CENTRALITY OF CONSCIENCE
TO BOTH NATURAL LAW AND PERSONALISM

Again, it would be a distortion to say that natural law is concerned
with rationality and truth whereas personalism is concerned with freedom, but such an assertion allows us to discern certain distinctive concerns and emphases of these two approaches to ethics. The point at which
these two approaches most manifestly overlap is in their understanding of
the centrality of conscience to the moral life. Both natural law and personalism find truth and freedom meeting in the human conscience. Conscience and its relation to truth and freedom is a major theme both in the
writings of Pope John Paul II and in *Veritatis Splendor*. Because the natural law is perfective of the human person, and because it is through his
free choices that man perfects himself, conscience is central to the moral
life. In "obeying" his conscience (a rightly formed conscience), which is,
indeed, his inner self, man is simultaneously living in accord with the
truth and freely determining himself. Paragraph 52 of *Veritatis Splendor*
states: "…universal and permanent laws correspond to things known by
the practical reason and are applied to particular acts through the judgment of conscience. The acting subject personally assimilates the truth
contained in the law. He appropriates this truth of his being and makes it
his own by his acts and the corresponding virtues." Paragraph 54 states:
"The relationship between man's freedom and God's law is most deeply
lived out in the 'heart' of the person, in his moral conscience." Paragraphs
57 and 58 make powerful statements of the subjectivity of the conscience
combined with its link with God himself:

According to Saint Paul, conscience in a certain sense con-
fronts man with the law, and thus becomes a *"witness" for
man:* a witness of his own faithfulness or unfaithfulness with
regard to the law, of his essential moral rectitude or iniquity.

Conscience is the *only* witness, since what takes place in the heart of the person is hidden from the eyes of everyone outside. Conscience makes its witness known only to the person himself. And, in turn, only the person knows that his own response is to the voice of conscience (n. 57).

The importance of this interior *dialogue of man with himself* can never be adequately appreciated. But it is also a *dialogue of man with God,* the author of the law, the primordial image and final end of man. Thus it can be said that conscience bears witness to man's own rectitude or iniquity to man himself but, together with this and indeed even beforehand, conscience is *the witness of God himself,* whose voice and judgment penetrate the depths of man's soul, calling him *fortiter et suaviter* to obedience.

Moral conscience does not close man within an insurmountable and impenetrable solitude, but opens him to the call, to the voice of God. In this, and not in anything else, lies the entire mystery and the dignity of the moral conscience: in being the place, the sacred place where God speaks to man.

The creativity of man, the freedom of man, is expressed not in inventing law, but in living out the law "written on his heart," conscious that in doing so he is either living in accord with his dignity or not, he is either forming himself in accord with his innate dignity or not.

CONCLUSION

Perhaps the passage of *Veritatis Splendor* that best brings together the themes of the encyclical while showing the overlap of natural law and personalism is the first paragraph of n. 90:

The relationship between faith and morality shines forth with all its brilliance in the *unconditional respect due to the insistent demands of the personal dignity of every man,* demands protected by those moral norms which prohibit without exception actions which are intrinsically evil. The universality and the immutability of the moral norm make manifest and at the same time serve to protect the personal

dignity and inviolability of man, on whose face is reflected
the splendor of God (cf. Gen. 9:5–6).

In all encyclicals written by Pope John Paul II, the theme of the
dignity of the human person, freedom, subjectivity, and self-determination are prominent. The above analysis has attempted to show that in the
most recent publications of the magisterium, particularly in the *Universal Catechism* and in *Veritatis Splendor,* we begin to see a blending of
natural law themes with those of personalism. One can only think the
Church is so much the richer for both approaches to ethics, approaches
that are, ultimately, thoroughly compatible.

7. Accent on the Masculine

Lisa Sowle Cahill

This chapter first appeared in *The Tablet* in 1993.

To be a feminist is to be committed to the equality of women and
men, and to cultivate a special sensitivity to the way women have been
marginalized in the world's cultures and religions. Christian feminists
draw on liberating strands within Christianity itself, especially in Scripture. Many have noted, for instance, that the creation stories present an
original equality distorted by sin, that Jesus interacted with women in
novel and affirmative ways, and that he made their roles in the religious
community dependent on personal faith rather than on marital and
maternal status.

In addition, Catholic Christian feminists both revise and renew the
"natural law" approach so strongly developed within their tradition. Natural law moral thinking, rooted in Aquinas and visible in different ways
in sexual teaching, bioethics, just war theory, and the social encyclicals,
works from reasonable and critical generalizations on shared human
experience. It is confident that moral common ground can be established
among people with different cultural and religious traditions. The
Catholic tradition has never stood for a narrow, sectarian morality, but
has based its moral conclusions on an interpretation of human well-being
in general. Thus, according to John Paul II's encyclical *Veritatis Splendor* "the natural law involves universality," is "inscribed in the rational
nature of the person," and "makes itself felt to all beings endowed with
reason and living in history" (51). Objectivity in matters of morality and
justice was highlighted by the Pope himself, when interpreting the
encyclical to a group of bishops from the United States in Rome

Many Catholic feminists supplement a liberating reading of biblical texts with an appeal to women's experience as disclosing the "full

humanity" and equality of women and men (in the phrase of Rosemary Radford Ruether). Pointing out that interpretation of the natural law has always been undertaken through specific historical and cultural perspectives, they argue that patriarchal definitions of human sexual nature and gender roles are distorted rather than built on what human experience demands. For instance, the fulfillment of human sexuality is through mutual love, not primarily through procreation; parenthood is as important a role for men as for women; and both sexes make contributions to the common good through public as well as domestic vocations.

Feminist critics frequently call attention to women's actual experience in order to challenge "universals" which, they claim, reflect the biases of those in power. Women's experience may not tally with female nature and roles as prescribed, especially when cultural and historical variations are taken into account. Feminists, in turning to the testimony of experience, often follow philosophers like Derrida and Foucault, who mistrust any appeal to an impartial rationality which can issue universal moral dicta. North American and European women zestfully dismantle culture-bound gender stereotypes by celebrating the "difference" and uniqueness of previously excluded voices. Feminists may rightly claim that many traditional Christian depictions of their natural or divinely mandated roles do not correspond to the reality and value of women's own lives.

Yet one problem that arises as a result of feminist theology's appeal to "experience" is the danger of replacing oppressive generalizations with bottomless particularity. If women's experience alone is exalted as the final moral standard, we run the danger of a feminist relativism which is ultimately unable to give any real reasons for preferring equality rather than hierarchy.

It is important to move back from particularity to the sense of shared human values which is so central to natural law. Women and men suffering economic and political repression, as well as sexism, appeal to values—justice, rights, and duties—which can be seen to hold true across eras, cultures, religions. *Veritatis Splendor,* then, may serve as a resource for feminist theology and ethics by affirming a moral foundation on the basis of which injustice of all kinds can be recognized and eradicated.

The question feminists will bring to this encyclical, however, is whether its defense of moral objectivity is not fatally wounded by a too visible male point of view, and by a tendency to resolve genuinely difficult questions by resort to authority. Although documents of the teaching authority are never notable for inclusive language, this encyclical accentuates patriarchal language and traditional gender imagery to a remarkable degree when contrasted even with papal writings such as *Familiaris Consortio* (the apostolic exhortation "On the Family" of 1981) and *Mulieris Dignitatem* (the apostolic letter "On the Dignity and Vocation of Women" of 1988). While both the latter still portray women's nature in maternal terms, *Familiaris Consortio* explicitly affirms greater social access for women (23), and *Mulieris Dignitatem* holds up Mary Magdalene as a leader and "apostle to the Apostles" (16). It thus comes as a disappointment that in *Veritatis Splendor* objective human morality—the encyclical's central theme—is relentlessly advocated as necessary to "man's" good.

Veritatis Splendor reasserts traditional sexual norms, which have in the past been tied to the role of women as wives and mothers. It makes no attempt to incorporate any special references to women's good, women's experience, or vocations of women beyond domesticity in its treatment of sexual norms which have a special impact on women (such as the ban on contraception). It condemns rape and prostitution, which have always been seen as sexual sins, yet does not specifically condemn sexual violence as a crime against women, nor social oppression of women.

Three important areas in which a feminist point of view will occasion criticism as well as appropriation of *Veritatis Splendor* are the body, intrinsically evil acts, and gender roles.

The moral meaning of the human body is both controversial and important across a number of issues today, many of which are central in Catholic teaching and for feminists. How does human (sexual) nature as embodied and physical relate to human nature as rational and free? When and how may freedom legitimately control the body in order to achieve "higher" human ends? In condemning artificial birth control, the teaching authority attaches great value to the physical structure of sexual acts as demanding an "openness" to procreation. On the other side, many feminists insist that women's self-determination requires them to be able to control their own reproductive powers.

A related issue is the development of reproductive technologies, which range from enhancing the conceptive potential of intercourse to *in vitro* fertilization and the use of donor gametes. What is the importance of physical relationships, both sexual and genetic, in evaluating the acceptability of these methods? Should the conception of a child be accomplished always and only through a sexual act, and never in a laboratory setting which compensates for infertility? Would conception by artificial insemination or *in vitro* fertilization be acceptable if the spouses provided the ova and sperm, enabling both to share a genetic relation to the child, and conferring on their marriage the fertility lacking to their individual sexual acts? To what degree does or should the body establish moral values, or limit the means we may use in removing obstacles to the realization of personal and social values we recognize as important?

Veritatis Splendor resists the idea that the body is simply freedom's "raw material" (46), and proposes that reason, freedom, soul, and body are linked in a unity (48, 50). This is an important corrective of some liberal feminisms which tend, at least theoretically, to make choice a moral absolute. Many feminists want to recover the integrity and worth of women's bodies over against patriarchal control, yet find it difficult to show exactly how embodiment functions as a positive moral value if it can never set limits on free choices. A profound affirmation of women's full moral agency requires more than the simplistic promotion of free choice, as most Catholic feminists recognize.

Yet the linkage which the encyclical makes of reason, freedom, soul and body leaves unresolved the critical question of whether the elements in this unity are all of equal importance. Church teaching holds that "love" is a foundational meaning of sex, but tends to revert to a sacralization of physical processes whenever sex is the moral issue. The precise value of the body and of bodily relationships in setting parameters for freedom needs better analysis from both a natural law and a feminist perspective. Catholic teaching will remain unable to address these issues effectively as long as it is perceived as raising them only in order to reassert sexual norms which had their origin in the primacy of procreation and in women's subordination to men through their procreative role.

What then, secondly, has a feminist to say about a central proposition of the encyclical, that there are in principle "intrinsically evil acts," which in themselves and apart from any circumstances and intentions are objectively sinful? The philosophical objections to this formulation are numerous and complex. From a feminist perspective, we may note two points.

First, traditional instances of intrinsic evil have higher visibility in the sexual category than in any other. Yet in the present encyclical masturbation, fornication, contraception, homosexuality, and abortion come in for mention only a couple of times (47, 80). This is certainly good in that it puts sexuality in perspective as one among other areas of moral concern. But it creates an ambiguous situation, in which traditional sexual norms can be played up or down as central to the meaning of the encyclical. Feminist sympathy for its message will obviously be higher if the encyclical can encourage creative reflection on the moral value of the body, rather than if it is used to shore up definitions of women's identity and roles that are based on the procreative function.

Secondly, the encyclical itself obfuscates the concept of intrinsically evil acts by giving examples on disparate levels, which are for the most part not under dispute by the so-called "proportionalists" it opposes (6, 80). Murder, adultery, stealing, genocide, torture, prostitution, slavery, "subhuman living conditions," "arbitrary imprisonment" and "degrading conditions of work" have few if any defenders among Catholic theologians. The point of course is that these terms and phrases do not, as the encyclical implies, define acts in the abstract, but acts (like intercourse or homicide) *together with the conditions or circumstances* in which they become immoral. Such acts are indeed wrong, because immoral circumstances have already been specified in the examples given. A single term like "murder" or "genocide" makes it clear that what might have been a justifiable "act in itself" (homicide) was done in wrong circumstances; or a phrase like "killing an innocent person," which spells out exactly what circumstances of homicide are meant, results in an absolute moral norm. About this there is little disagreement.

Is it really so easy to speak of "acts in themselves" as the defenders of that category and the opponents of it alike suggest? A key contribution of feminism is to highlight the social context of moral agency, and to be attentive to concrete human relationships. Upon reflection, it is evident that even an "act" like contraception is really intercourse-in-the-circumstances-of-birth-avoidance (by "artificial" means). Indeed, intercourse as the so-called "act" at the center of sexual debates could itself be broken down into male (or female) sexual response and performance, to be set "circumstantially" in a heterosexual or homosexual context. Where does "act" end and "circumstance" begin?

Feminist moral theologians, among others, might be led to conclude that when we speak of acts, we focus attention on a nexus of practical, physical, causal, and moral relationships, but do not mark off absolute boundaries around a moral event. Hence the whole discussion of the moral neutrality or evil of sexual acts in the abstract may depend on a category which a more relational philosophical approach reveals to be questionable. Perhaps the lesson to be learned is that we reject some decisions and practices as morally abhorrent not on the basis of properties they possess "in themselves" and apart from the dispositions and circumstances of agents, but because of their concrete and practical degradation of the human persons involved. Moral evil will not be recognized as such simply because an "intrinsic evil" flag is waved over it; substantive and reasonable arguments must be advanced about the specific nature of the acts in question.

The third area where a feminist approach has a special contribution to make concerns gender roles. Especially in Western, industrialized nations, women's and men's roles are fast changing. The suitability of women's gifts for public contributions to the common good is increasingly recognized, while men find rewards in family life and child-rearing. *Veritatis Splendor*'s neglect of these developments in the understanding of masculine and feminine nature casts a dark shadow over the Church's authority to specify truly the human goods of sex, gender and family.

Most problematic is the sexist language in which "man's" nature is defined. The opening line sets the tone: "The splendor of truth shines forth in all the works of the Creator and, in a special way, in man, created in the image and likeness of God." Exclusive language applied to a biblical text which explicitly associates both male and female with the divine image is unnecessary and even embarrassing. Five years earlier, *Mulieris Dignitatem* spoke of "the creation of the human being as male and female, made in the image and likeness of God" (11). How can we with any credibility make the case to a pluralistic (and confused) culture that the Catholic tradition has valid insights about sex, commitment, love and parenthood, when the most current official documents retrieve a male-oriented perspective as a prelude to asserting the Church's prerogative to interpret the Gospel and human nature?

The conclusion of the encyclical comes full circle with its eulogy of Mary as "Mother of Mercy." Following a 174-page promotion of negative moral norms, this section clearly was meant to encourage pastoral understanding of "human frailty and sin" (118). But gender stereotypes move into full view as Mary is exalted as the nurturing, loving and compassionate Mother of Jesus, a moral model for whom "freedom" meant "giving herself to God" and "accepting" God's will (120). "She understands sinful man and loves him with a Mother's love." Why not praise Jesus' compassion, forgiveness and obedience, while holding up Mary's courage and the leadership of other women like Mary Magdalene as contemporary models for both men and women?

From the perspective of a Catholic feminist moral theologian, *Veritatis Splendor* holds out promise for the reinforcement of our common moral foundations. Yet it also illustrates why those foundations must be laid more cautiously and critically, and why Catholic "natural law" ethics has been a particular target of feminist attack.

8. *Evangelium Vitae:*
The Law of Abortion

Leslie C. Griffin

This chapter was originally presented at the Georgetown Conference on *Evangelium Vitae,* November 9, 1995.

The Gospel of Life proclaimed by Pope John Paul II in *Evangelium Vitae*[1] opposes abortion with "dauntless fidelity" (no. 1). On the subject of abortion, the "good news" is old news.[2] The encyclical portrays its teaching on abortion as the standard that the church has always taught. The pope employs a traditional principle against direct killing of the innocent: *"I confirm that the direct and voluntary killing of an innocent human being is always gravely immoral"* (no. 57). He applies that principle to all abortions from conception onward: "Procured abortion is the deliberate and direct killing, by whatever means it is carried out, of a human being in the initial phase of his or her existence, extending from conception to birth" (no. 58). The embryo or fetus is by definition always an innocent human being. Finally, the principle is absolute: "[T]hese reasons and others like them, however serious and tragic, can never justify the deliberate killing of an innocent human being" (no. 58). The pope is "**unconditionally** pro-life" (no. 28). Although self-defense may be an exception to the general prohibition against taking human life, the self-defense exception does not apply to abortion. "In no way could this human being ever be considered an aggressor, much less an unjust aggressor! He or she is weak, defenseless, even to the point of lacking that minimal form of defense consisting in the poignant power of a newborn baby's cries and tears" (no. 58).

Within the church, the criticisms of this teaching are not new. The direct/indirect distinction has faced extensive criticism as an inadequate formulation of the church's theological tradition.[3] "No direct killing of the innocent" has been described as a rule, not a principle, and so subject to exceptions.[4] On the subject of abortion, the direct/indirect distinction has been criticized for its excess physicalism. The principle allows, e.g., the excision of the cancerous uterus and the ectopic pregnancy, but not other measures calculated to save the life of the mother. Moreover, in these two situations it requires that the woman's fertility not be spared.[5] In addition, theologians have questioned the abortion ban's extension to the time of conception. Some authors have argued, e.g., that implantation, not conception, is the significant developmental point, and so the prohibition against abortion should not apply to the pre-implantation embryo.[6] Moreover, theologians have argued that the church's own tradition does not support an absolute ban on abortion from the time of conception. The history of ensoulment suggests a shifting assessment of the morality of early abortion and undermines John Paul's claim of an unchanging Catholic teaching on abortion.[7] Finally, in the past, some authors have suggested that abortion is at times an act of self-defense for the woman whose life or health is threatened by her pregnancy, and so the general bar against abortion should not be absolute.[8]

Catholics have for years engaged in an extensive debate about the interpretation of the church's tradition on abortion and about the formulation of the moral principles that regulate abortion. The encyclical is not noteworthy for its contribution to that discussion; it reiterates the official teaching of the magisterium. What is significant about EV is not the substance but the style of its argument. The author prefers a distinctively Catholic, theological argument to a natural law style of reasoning. The analysis is predominantly scriptural and theological, not philosophical or scientific.

It is easy to identify both the advantages and disadvantages of this style. The theological focus will be valuable to Catholics who inhabit the "culture of death" decried by the encyclical. Such teaching may inspire and reinvigorate Catholic commitment to the church's moral teaching in a way that philosophical and scientific argument cannot. Theological language may serve as an important corrective to the excessively secular, anti-religious language of our public culture.[9]

However, the disadvantages of this approach are also evident in the encyclical's reasoning. By accentuating the theological argument, the encyclical urges Catholic moral principles upon all persons, non-Catholic as well as Catholic. It also recommends that Catholic moral teaching be inscribed into law. The result is a theory of civil law that is excessively entangled with theological doctrine. The retreat from natural law argument at the moral level undermines John Paul's arguments about the content of civil law in a democracy. Moreover, it burdens Catholic politicians with a moral obligation to vote their theological convictions into law.

NATURAL LAW

Even the title of EV, "The **Gospel** of Life," encapsulates its theological and scriptural emphasis. Scriptural quotations provide the framework of the document. Much of the encyclical's prose is in the style of reflection and meditation on scriptural texts. In the first chapter, the initial focus is the story of Cain and Abel, the story of an attack on human life. Such attacks must be condemned wherever they occur. The biblical story provides the basis for the encyclical's first extended treatment of abortion (nos. 13–17). As Cain attacked Abel, so abortion is an attack on human life. The brothers' story is an appropriate analogy because the locus of abortion's attack on human beings is the family.

The rest of the encyclical also emphasizes the scriptural and theological basis of the document's moral principles. Even the general prohibition against killing is cast in theological terms. It is "God's Holy Law" ("You Shall Not Kill") (no. 52). The prohibition against killing is a divine **command** (no. 52) revealed in **Scripture** (no. 54). Life is **sacred**; it comes from God, the "**Lord of Life**" (no. 53). The distinctively Christian nature of the prohibition against taking human life is evident in the encyclical's contrast between the teaching of the Old and New Testaments. Although "[t]he commandment regarding the inviolability of human life reverberates at the heart of the 'ten words' in the covenant of Sinai...we must recognize that in the Old Testament this sense of the value of life, though already quite marked, **does not yet reach the refinement found in the Sermon on the Mount**" (no. 40).

When the pope turns from Scripture, it is to the church's tradition against killing. The scriptural argument and the church's tradition are consistent. "[T]he church's tradition has always consistently taught the absolute and unchanging value of the **commandment**, 'you shall not kill'" (no. 54). Killing the innocent is a "serious **sin**" (no. 55). It is through "the very person of Jesus" that "man is given the possibility of 'knowing' the complete truth concerning the value of human life" (no. 29).

In the encyclical's second lengthy section on abortion (nos. 44–45) the pope's emphasis remains scriptural and theological. A verse from Psalm 139, *"For you formed my inmost being,"* provides the section heading. It is from Scripture that we learn that the ban on abortion extends to every fetus from conception. The pope concedes that "there are no direct and explicit calls to protect human life at its very beginning" (no. 44) in Scripture. Nonetheless the Old and New Testaments provide a normative argument against all abortion: "denying life in these circumstances is completely foreign to the religious and cultural way of thinking of the people of God" (no. 44). The pope's review of the relevant Old Testament texts demands: "How can anyone think that even a single moment of this marvelous process of the unfolding of life could be separated from the wise and loving work of the Creator?" (n. 44). Then the New Testament "confirms the indisputable recognition of the value of life from its very beginning" (no. 45). A passage in chapter three reiterates this argument:

> The texts of Sacred Scripture never address the question of deliberate abortion and so do not directly and specifically condemn it. But they show such great respect for the human being in the mother's womb that they **require as a logical consequence** that God's commandment 'you shall not kill' be extended to the unborn child as well (no. 61).

As in the case of Cain and Abel, another biblical story, of Mary and Elizabeth, is significant to the moral argument: "the value of the person from the moment of conception is celebrated in the meeting between the Virgin Mary and Elizabeth, and between the two children whom they are carrying in the womb" (no. 45). *Jeremiah, Job* and *Psalms* provide similar evidence that fetal life must receive absolute protection from conception onward because it is created by God at that "moment." When the pope turns from the Scriptural argument, it is to another ancient text. The prohibition on abortion is "repeated" (no. 54) in the text of the *Didache*.

Throughout these arguments on killing and abortion, the natural law is not abandoned. However, its role in the encyclical's argument is not important. Instead, the natural law serves a theological purpose. The numerous references to natural law throughout the text of EV reiterate the traditional description of the natural law, that it is shared by all human persons. For example, John Paul recognizes that "every person sincerely open to truth and goodness can, by the light of reason and the hidden action of grace, come to recognize in the natural law written in the heart…the sacred value of human life from its very beginning until its end" (no. 2). He states that "the voice of the Lord echo[es] in the conscience of every individual" (no. 24). He writes that the Gospel is "written in the heart of every man and woman," and "can also be known in its essential traits by human reason" (no. 29). By these natural law references, John Paul is asserting that the moral teaching of the Gospel of life is a teaching for all human persons, not for Catholics only.

In one sense, that is a traditional natural law argument. However, it is significant that John Paul argues that the **Gospel** is inscribed in all human persons. "The church knows that this Gospel of life, which she has received from her Lord, has a profound and persuasive echo in the heart of every person—believer and non-believer alike—because it marvelously fulfills all the heart's expectations while infinitely surpassing them" (no. 2). In other words, the pope is claiming that the Gospel of life proclaimed by him in this encyclical is a norm for all human persons. Yet the content of that Gospel is defined in theological, not philosophical or scientific, terms. There is, e.g., no inductive reasoning from human nature.[10] Instead, Scripture and tradition provide moral principles while the natural law provides reasons for the pope to urge all persons to follow those principles.

The role of the natural law in EV is limited in part because of the general theological agenda of the document. The encyclical is prophetic, counter-cultural. Commentators on the encyclical have with good reason focused on EV's central theme of opposition to the "culture of death."[11] Natural law reasoning is not always useful when one argues that culture is morally corrupt. In that context, it is more important to claim, as John Paul does in this encyclical, that the natural law continues to exist even when majorities of human persons do not recognize it.

Complementing the traditional assertion that the natural law applies to all persons is the reminder that culture may prevent individuals—indeed whole societies—from recognizing the natural law. The encyclical focuses on the deterioration in society's morals. In modern society, "conscience itself, darkened as it were by such widespread conditioning, is finding it increasingly difficult to distinguish between good and evil in what concerns the basic value of human life" (no. 4). There is a "progressive darkening of the capacity to discern God's living and saving presence" (no. 21). "Nature itself, from being *mater* (mother), is now reduced to being 'matter,' and is subjected to every kind of manipulation" (no. 22). For this reason, the encyclical states that "[w]hen the sense of God is lost, there is also a tendency to lose the sense of man" (no. 21). "Moreover, once all reference to God has been removed, it is not surprising that the meaning of everything else becomes profoundly distorted" (no. 22). This "eclipse of the sense of God" (no. 23) has bred individualism, utilitarianism and hedonism.

In an encyclical that emphasizes society's pervasive moral corruption, a natural law theory rooted in human experience is impractical. In response to this eclipse of natural law in the consciences of human persons, the encyclical offers the church's privileged moral insight. If cultural influence has blinded human beings to the natural law, the best response is not more reason, but more revelation.

Thus John Paul's steady references to the natural law do not mean that a natural law argument has been made. This does not mean, of course, that a natural law argument cannot be made. But it is noteworthy that the pope has chosen not to make it. The natural law is not significant to the moral argument of the encyclical. Instead, the natural law serves another purpose: it provides reasons to apply the pope's theological teaching to all human persons.

ABORTION AND NATURAL LAW

The theological role of the natural law is evident in the encyclical's treatment of abortion, where Gospel and nature are intertwined. Catholic theology, of course, has traditionally claimed that the natural law and the Gospel are consistent. But on the subject of abortion, the encyclical argues on the basis of the Gospel and then asserts the consistency of the natural law with this Gospel teaching. The natural law teaches us the "**sacred** value of human life" (no. 2). It is the "sacredness of life" that is the basis for life's invulnerability from attack (no. 40). We learn that "whoever attacks human life, in some way attacks God himself" (no. 9).

The teaching on abortion is "based upon the natural law and upon the written Word of God" (no. 62), church tradition and the magisterium. The teaching invokes the authority of the magisterium: "*I declare that direct abortion, that is, abortion willed as an end or as a means, always constitutes a grave moral disorder,* since it is the deliberate killing of an innocent human being" (no. 62).

These arguments are of great importance to Catholics. Without the natural law argument, however, the encyclical leaves the impression that non-Catholics should accept the document's theological and magisterial arguments that abortion is a violation of God's commandment not to kill. There are three areas where the inadequacy or absence of the natural law argument is striking, especially when viewed from the perspective of readers who are not Catholic. These topics are the linking of the prohibitions on contraception and abortion; the encyclical's absolute, exceptionless ban on abortion; and the argument that the fetus is a person from conception.

First is the linking of the prohibitions on contraception and abortion. Contraception and abortion are recognized as "specifically different evils: The former contradicts the full truth of the sexual act as the proper expression of conjugal love, while the latter destroys the life of a human being; the former is opposed to the virtue of chastity in marriage, the latter is opposed to the virtue of justice and directly violates the divine commandment 'you shall not kill'" (no. 13). Nonetheless, the ethics of contraception and abortion cannot be separated. They are "closely connected, as fruits of the same tree." "The close connection which exists in mentality between the practice of contraception and that of abortion is becoming increasingly obvious" (no. 13). To those who argue that more or better contraception will decrease the occurrence of abortion (and thus that the church should change its teaching on contraception), John Paul insists on the unity of the two teachings. He claims that the use of contraceptives leads to more abortion: "the pro-abortion culture is especially strong precisely where the church's teaching on contraception is rejected" (no. 13). The "negative values" of the "contraceptive mentality" "strengthen the temptation" to abortion (no. 13), and do not reduce its occurrence.

Moreover, John Paul rejects any demographic arguments for contraception. Overpopulation does not justify any artificial contraception. He states that it is better to share the world's resources than to encourage population control. The drop of birth rate in developed countries is "disturbing" (no. 16); the solution to overpopulation is not contraception, but redistribution of goods.

The magisterium's natural law argument against contraception has had a difficult reception among Catholics and Catholic theologians, many of whom have rejected *Humanae Vitae*'s artificial/natural distinction. There is no reason to expect that non-Catholics will accept the ban on artificial contraception as a universal moral principle. To argue that the bans on contraception and abortion are inseparable detracts from, rather than strengthens, a natural law argument about abortion.

There is a second area where the abortion argument of EV would be strengthened by some natural law analysis. The encyclical's ban on abortion is absolute, exceptionless. Possible exceptions to "no direct killing of the innocent" are not treated in any detail, but the mother's health and a decent standard of living are clearly rejected as justifications for abortion (no. 58). An absolute ban, of course, also prohibits abortions where maternal life is at stake as well as abortion in cases of rape and incest. Moreover, no fetal indications may justify abortion.

The moral principle that bans all these abortions may be correct. But in our American culture, whether of death or not, this strict position requires some reasonable explanation. Rape, incest and the life of the mother are commonly invoked as reasonable exceptions to prohibitions of abortion.[12] The theological rationale and the argument from papal authority may not be persuasive to those who do not share Catholicism's theological presuppositions.

The pope does address in greater detail the argument about conception and implantation, yet this remains a third area of the encyclical where more natural law reasoning is necessary. John Paul mentions the argument that allows abortion for some short time after conception. His response is that genetic science demonstrates that this life is human from the time of fertilization. He then states: "the results themselves of scientific research on the human embryo provide 'a valuable indication for discerning by the use of reason a personal presence at the moment of the first appearance of a human life; **How could a human individual not be a human person?**'" (no. 60).

The quotation is from the Congregation for the Doctrine of the Faith's *Donum Vitae*. This rhetorical question avoids the difficult questions. The pope does not address numerous arguments that the preembryo is not a human person. The philosophical and scientific challenges (e.g., on twinning or recombination or the nature of personhood) to the pope's position are not examined.

This claim about the presence of the person from fertilization also implicates the second issue of the absolute ban on abortion. The encyclical states that the "mere probability" of human personhood at fertilization justifies an *absolute* prohibition on abortion (no. 60). The encyclical does not address the obvious question of how the "mere probability" of human life outweighs the actual life of the mother in all circumstances. Absent a philosophical or scientific analysis of this question, the pope must return to the argument from the authority of the church's tradition: "over and above all scientific debates and those philosophical affirmations to which the Magisterium has not expressly committed itself, the church has always taught and continues to teach that the result of human procreation, from the first moment of its existence, must be guaranteed that unconditional respect which is morally due to the human being in his or her totality and unity as body and spirit" (no. 60). Catholic theologians have challenged, and will continue to dispute, whether the church has always taught this. What is indisputable is that the argument that the church has always taught something is not a compelling natural law argument.

Toward the end of the encyclical, the pope does make a natural law claim about the prohibition on killing. He states that "The Gospel of life is not for believers alone: It is for everyone....Life certainly has a sacred and religious value, but in no way is that value a concern only of believers. The value at stake is one which every human being can grasp by the light of reason; thus it necessarily concerns everyone" (no. 101). Once again, the pope has made a natural law claim that the Gospel teaching applies to everyone. However, he has not constructed a natural law argument.

This absence or weakness of the natural law argument need not detract from the encyclical's goals. The Catholic pope has good reason to encourage Catholics to heed Scripture, tradition and theology, and to remind Catholics that God cares for life in all its stages. However, the encyclical proposes a standard for civil law; civil law should be consistent with the encyclical's teaching. It is standard Catholic teaching that civil law should reflect the moral or natural law. A weak natural law argument will affect the quality of the discussion of civil law. The encyclical would be a better document if it had either presented the church's theological teaching or provided a natural law argument along with its implications for civil law. Instead, we receive in EV a theological rationale for changing civil law.

ABORTION LAW

EV concludes that the civil law must conform to the church's moral teaching, whether theological or natural. "The doctrine on the **necessary conformity of civil law with the moral law** is in continuity with the whole tradition of the church" (no. 72). On the subject of abortion, civil law must be in conformity with the moral conclusion that procured abortion is never permitted.

For abortion, as for the other life issues discussed in the encyclical, the pope argues that civil law must reflect the moral law because life is a fundamental value at the heart of every society. John Paul is sharply critical of legal systems that do not enforce the church's moral teaching. Earlier in this century, the popes lauded democracy for its encouragement of individual participation and its promotion of human rights.[13] This pope is ready to jettison democracy if it does not comply with the church's moral teaching. John Paul acknowledges that in the past the magisterium developed a "positive" view of democracy as a "sign of the times" (no. 70). However, once democracy permits moral relativism, it must be rejected: "the value of democracy stands or falls with the values which it embodies and promotes" (no. 70). Such values must not be relative because the values of democracy are based upon the "objective moral law which, as the 'natural law' written in the human heart, is the obligatory point of reference for civil law itself" (no. 70). The natural law is once again invoked as a reason to hold democratic institutions to the church's moral teaching.

Democracy's moral relativism is evident in the abortion law of many nations. The encyclical identifies a "disturbing" trend in countries that have legalized abortion. Legalization of abortion has meant not only the decriminalization of abortion. Instead, abortion has been recognized as a legal right. "Crimes against life" have become "rights of individual freedom" (no. 4). States now approve or authorize abortion "indeed with the free assistance of health-care systems" (no. 4). It is bad enough to decriminalize attacks on human life. It is worse to label these attacks "rights" and to include them as part of free health services. Once abortion is a right, proponents ask for "safe and free assistance of doctors and medical personnel" (no. 68), thus challenging the consciences of health care providers.

In response to these developments, EV argues that no law permitting any abortion, no matter how restricted the circumstances, is ever just. No democratic process, no democratic consensus, can justify any law that allows abortion. Abortion laws are per se totalitarian, not authentically democratic because they unfairly impose the majority's will in violation of the fundamental human right to life. The majority's recognition of a right to abortion can never legitimate abortion; instead, the existence of laws allowing abortion calls democracy itself into question. "In this way democracy, contradicting its own principles, effectively moves towards a form of totalitarianism" (no. 20).

The encyclical focuses on the "majority rule" aspect of democracy, suggesting that human rights are not protected in abortion laws because the majority has imposed its will upon the minority. Such majority rule encourages relativism:

> in the democratic culture of our time it is commonly held that the legal system of any society should limit itself to taking account of and accepting the convictions of the majority. It should therefore be based solely upon what the majority itself considers moral and actually practices...the only determining factor should be the will of the majority, whatever this may be (no. 69).

In the United States, of course, abortion law was not promulgated by a majority vote. EV adds that counter-majoritarian institutions may not legalize abortion. The constitutional recognition of a right to abortion is always wrong. Indeed the pope asserts that some countries have violated their basic constitutional principles in order to legalize abortion; this is evidence of "grave moral decline" (no. 4).

The encyclical thus vigorously rejects the arguments that the law in a democracy should respect moral disagreement about abortion by permitting individuals to choose in conscience that abortion is right or wrong. There is only one correct moral position on abortion: it is always wrong. The law must reflect that moral standard. If democracy leads to a different conclusion, it too is wrong. "The legal toleration of abortion or of euthanasia can in no way claim to be based on respect for the conscience of others" (no. 71) because the conscience that chooses abortion is wrong. Moral error has no rights. EV's conclusion is straightforward: "Abortion and euthanasia are thus **crimes** which **no** human law can claim to legitimize" (no. 73). Any law permitting abortion is "intrinsically unjust" (no. 73). "Laws which authorize and promote abortion and euthanasia are...completely lacking in authentic juridical validity" (no. 72).

Thus civil law must protect life from its conception. Not just civil law. The encyclical's identification of abortion as a crime against human life suggests that abortion should be subject to criminal prosecution. The encyclical does not address questions of criminal law. We do not learn the extent of criminal sanctions, e.g., to women who have abortions, to doctors, to all medical personnel who cooperate in abortions.

EV demands a radical change in the current abortion law of the United States. Moreover, abortion is not the only legal issue implicated by the encyclical's argument. If contraception and abortion are closely linked in their morality, and if democratic majorities and constitutional rulings have no legal status when they violate the moral law, then the logic of the encyclical demands a transformation of the law of contraceptives in the United States. If **Griswold** led to **Roe**,[14] then both should be overturned—for theological reasons. Such sweeping changes in the law demand a more compelling natural law argument than the one presented in EV.

Laws that are inconsistent with the church's teaching must be opposed by "conscientious objection" (no. 73), the duty left to Catholics in nations that permit abortion.

CATHOLIC COOPERATION WITH ABORTION

Given the discontinuity between Catholic moral teaching and laws that permit abortion, the only proper Catholic response to such laws is opposition, "conscientious objection." This duty of conscientious objection is cast in theological terms. "It is precisely from obedience to God...that the strength and the courage to resist unjust human laws are born" (no. 73). Catholics will need strength and courage because compliance with church teaching may "require the sacrifice of prestigious professional positions or the relinquishing of reasonable hopes of career advancement" (no. 74). Conscientious objectors may suffer but it is wrong that they suffer. They "must be protected not only from legal penalties, but also from any negative effects on the legal, disciplinary, financial and professional plane" (no. 74).

Some guidance to individuals who live in societies with unjust abortion laws is provided by the principle of cooperation. This principle gives Catholics "a right to demand not to be forced to take part in morally evil actions" (74). The encyclical distinguishes formal from material cooperation with evil; the former is never permitted and the latter is at times permitted. For the taking of life, formal "cooperation occurs when an action, either by its very nature or by the form it takes in a concrete situation, can be defined as a direct participation in an act against innocent human life or a sharing in the immoral intention of the person committing it" (no. 74).

In the manuals, the meaning of formal and material cooperation was illustrated in specific cases. EV provides a minimal casuistry, with limited examples, and so leaves many specific questions of individual conduct unresolved. It tells us that doctors and other medical personnel should not participate in any abortions. "Doctors and nurses [should not] place at the service of death skills which were acquired for promoting life" (no. 59). "'Causing death' can never be considered a form of medical treatment, even when the intention is solely to comply with the patient's request" (no. 89), and certainly not, as in the case of abortion, where there can be no patient request. In addition, "the opportunity to refuse to take part in the phases of consultation, preparation and execution of these acts against life should be guaranteed to physicians, health-care personnel, and directors of hospitals, clinics and convalescent facilities" (no. 74). Beyond these statements, EV does not provide any casuistry of cooperation to guide medical personnel as they conscientiously object to abortion. We do not know, e.g., if it is wrong for Catholics to work in hospitals or in the offices of doctors who perform abortions. We do not know if Catholics may refer their patients to providers who perform abortions.

More specific guidance is provided in EV's statement that: "In the case of an intrinsically unjust law, such as a law permitting abortion or euthanasia, it is therefore never licit to obey it, or to 'take part in a propaganda campaign in favor of such a law, or vote for it'" (no. 73). While all Catholic citizens face the moral obligation not to vote for abortion, the encyclical's focus falls upon the Catholic politician.

Politicians should in most cases not vote for abortion laws; moral "responsibility likewise falls on the legislators who have promoted and approved abortion laws" (no. 59). As a rule, Catholics are never supposed to vote for "intrinsically unjust" abortion laws. However, the encyclical identifies one exception to this rule; the pope states that in some circumstances Catholic politicians may vote for laws that permit some abortion.

EV examines a "particular problem of conscience...where a legislative vote would be decisive for the passage of a more restrictive law, aimed at limiting the number of authorized abortions, in place of a more permissive law already passed or ready to be voted on" (no. 73). EV concludes: "[W]hen it is not possible to overturn or completely abrogate a pro-abortion law, an elected official whose absolute personal opposition to procured abortion was well known could licitly support proposals aimed at limiting the harm done by such a law and at lessening its negative consequences at the level of general opinion and public morality" (no. 73). Such a vote is not "illicit cooperation" with evil. It is material and not formal "to cooperate to pass less restrictive abortion laws." Here in the political realm is one exception to EV's absolute moral stance.

Catholic politicians will be left to calculate what "absolute personal opposition" is; what "limiting the harm" of abortion means; what "lessening its negative consequences" entails. For example, former governor Mario Cuomo made known his personal opposition to abortion ("I accept the bishops' position that abortion is to be avoided....For me, life or fetal life in the womb should be protected, even if five of nine justices of the Supreme Court and my neighbor disagree with me").[15] He supported legislation that would prevent abortion by "present[ing] an impoverished mother with the full range of support she needs to bear and raise her children."[16] He also stated that "legal interdicting of abortion by either the federal government or the individual states...wouldn't work" because these laws could not be enforced.[17] The pope appears to reject this last argument about enforcement (no. 68). But it is possible on one reading of this encyclical that Cuomo's political stance, so criticized by the American bishops,[18] has been vindicated by the current pontiff.

Such vindication should not be consoling to many American Catholic politicians, however. While the encyclical recognizes the possibility of their casting a pragmatic vote for less restrictive abortion laws without violating their Catholic consciences, EV imposes on them a more difficult dilemma of conscience. EV forsakes the natural law and asks Catholic politicians to enact a theological teaching into law. Despite the absence of the natural law argument, the encyclical asks Catholic politicians to impose the church's teaching on non-Catholics. For pragmatic reasons, Catholics may vote for less restrictive abortion laws when their absolute ban on abortion cannot be passed. Catholics may vote only to restrict abortion rights or to ban abortion altogether. Their goal must be for Catholicism's teaching on abortion to become the law for all citizens of the United States, so that no abortion is permitted. Moral error has no rights.

Without a natural law argument about abortion, American Catholic politicians (and, one presumes, justices) are asked to inscribe their religious beliefs into the law of the United States. In the past, American Catholic politicians have balked at this suggestion. So they should. Joseph Donceel has stated that: "The church may in certain cases impose a philosophical doctrine upon her faithful, when that doctrine is essential to safeguard a revealed truth. But she has no right to impose it on non-Catholics and to expect the state (and therefore the politicians) to impose it."[19] EV imposes a theological doctrine upon the church's faithful, but theological doctrine should not be imposed on non-Catholics by the state and politicians, not even by Catholic politicians. It is not clear why EV does not ask politicians to show their conscientious objection to unjust laws, or to a democracy without moral foundation, by leaving politics altogether. In the United States, that would be a better moral option than to ask them to object to the law by making the law theological and not secular. After all, as EV reminds us, "laws are not the only means of protecting human life" (no. 90).

CONCLUSION

In the years before the Second Vatican Council, Roman pontiffs asked American Catholics to oppose their First Amendment because Catholicism as the one true religion was entitled to establishment. In EV, the Polish pontiff asks American Catholics to oppose the constitutional protection of abortion because Catholicism as the one true morality is entitled to legal enforcement. In the former case, the magisterium was eventually dissuaded from its opposition to the separation of church and state by its acceptance of a natural law right to religious freedom. In the latter case, in EV the magisterium has chosen not to address natural law arguments about abortion, but instead to argue that the natural law requires that the church's moral teaching become the civil law of all human persons.

Notes

1. Hereinafter EV. References to numbered sections of the encyclical are included in the text. I have used italics where the encyclical uses them. Words set in boldface show my own emphasis.

2. See, e.g., Bryan Hehir, "Get a (Culture of) Life," *Commonweal* 122.10 (May 19, 1995): 8–9, at 9 ("Neither the vision [chapter 2] nor the moral argument [chapter 3] breaks new ground; the power and value of the encyclical lie in its synthetic quality.").

3. See generally Bruno Schuller, S.J., "Direct Killing/Indirect Killing," in *Readings in Moral Theology No. 1,* eds. Charles E. Curran and Richard A. McCormick, S.J. (New York: Paulist Press, 1979), pp. 138–57.

4. Richard A. McCormick, S.J., "The Consistent Ethic of Life: Is There an Historical Soft Underbelly?" in *Consistent Ethic of Life*, ed. J. Bernardin (Kansas City, MO: Sheed and Ward, 1988), pp. 109–22; Richard A. McCormick, "The Gospel of Life," *America* 172.15 (April 29, 1995): 10–17.

5. See generally Susan T. Nicholson, "The Roman Catholic Doctrine of Therapeutic Abortion," in *Feminism and Philosophy*, eds. M. Vetterling-Braggin et al. (Totowa, NJ: Rowman & Allanheld, 1977), pp. 385–407.

6. John Mahoney discusses these arguments in *Bioethics and Belief* (Westminster, MD.: Christian Classics, 1984), pp. 62–67.

7. See generally Joseph F. Donceel, S.J., "Immediate Animation and Delayed Hominization," *Theological Studies* 31 (1970): 76–105; Joseph F. Donceel, S.J., "Mediate v. Immediate Animation," in *Abortion: The Moral Issues*, ed. Edward Batchelor, Jr. (New York: Pilgrim Press, 1982), pp. 110–14.

8. For the history of the self-defense argument, see generally John Connery, S.J., *Abortion: The Development of the Roman Catholic Perspective* (Chicago: Loyola University Press, 1977), pp. 124–224.

9. See generally Stephen L. Carter, *The Culture of Disbelief: How American Law and Politics Trivialize Religious Devotion* (New York: Basic Books, 1993).

10. For discussion of the inductive method in Catholic social ethics, see generally Marie-Dominique Chenu, *La "Doctrine Sociale" De L'Eglise Comme Idéologie* (Paris: Les editions du Cerf, 1979); Charles E. Curran, "The Changing Anthropological Bases of Catholic Social Ethics," in *Moral Theology: A Continuing Journey* (Notre Dame: University of Notre Dame Press, 1982), pp. 173–208.

11. Many news reports highlighted the culture of death theme. See, e.g., Paul Baumann, "The Pope vs. the Culture of Death," *The New York Times*, Oct. 8, 1995, at 4:13; Cal Thomas, "In America, Pope's 'Gospel of Life' Battles 'Culture of Death,'" *The Dayton Daily News*, Apr. 7, 1995, at 19A; James D. David,

"'Culture of Death' Encyclical Stirs Pope-Conscience Debate," *Sun-Sentinel*, Apr. 1, 1995, at 7D; Paul Galloway, "John Paul Condemns 'Culture of Death,'" *Chicago Tribune*, Mar. 31, 1995, at 1; Celestine Bohlen, "Pope Condemns a 'Culture of Death,'" *International Herald Tribune*, Mar. 31, 1995; Judith Lynn Howard, "'Culture of Death, Decried," *The Dallas Morning News*, Mar. 31, 1995, at 1A.

12. See, e.g., Utah Code Ann. § 76–7–301.1(4) (1995); La. Rev. Stat. Ann. § 40:1299.34.5(B) (West 1955); *Harris v. McRae*, 448 U.S. 297 (1980) (ruling on 1980 version of the Hyde Amendment, Publ. L. 96–123, §109, 93 Stat. 926); the Hyde Amendment, Departments of Labor, Health and Human Services, Education, and Related Agencies Appropriations Act of 1994, § 509, 107 Stat. 1082; *Little Rock Family Planning Services, P.A. v. Dalton*, 60 F.3d 497 (8th Cir. 1995).

13. See, e.g., Pius XII, "Christmas Message, 1944," in *The Unwearied Advocate: Public Address of Pope Pius XII*, ed. V. Yzermans (St. Cloud, MN.: St. Cloud Bookshop, 1956), vol. I, p. 54.

14. *Griswold v. Connecticut*, 381 U.S. 479 (1965); *Roe v. Wade*, 410 U.S. 959 (1973).

15. Mario Cuomo, "Religious Belief and Public Morality: A Catholic Governor's Perspective," in *Abortion and Catholicism*, eds. P. Beattie Jung & T. Shannon (New York: Crossroad, 1988), p. 209.

16. Mario Cuomo, "Religious Belief," p. 214.

17. Mario Cuomo, "Religious Belief," p. 212.

18. See, e.g., Kenneth A. Briggs, "Fight Abortion, O'Connor Urges Public Officials," *The New York Times*, Oct. 16, 1984, at A27; Robert D. McFadden, "Archbishop Asserts that Cuomo Misinterpreted Stand on Abortion," *The New York Times*, Aug. 4, 1984, at A1, A7.

19. Joseph F. Donceel, "Catholic Politicians and Abortion," *America* (Feb. 2, 1985): 81–83, at 82. See also John Rawls, *Political Liberalism* (New York: Columbia University Press, 1993), pp. 224–26: Public reason "means that in discussing constitutional essentials and matters of basic justice we are not to appeal to comprehensive religious and philosophical doctrines—to what we as individuals or members of associations see as the whole truth...." Instead, public reasoning should "rest on the plain truths now widely accepted, or available, to citizens generally."

9. The Mystery of Easter and the Culture of Death

Marc Ouellet

This chapter first appeared in *Communio* in 1996.

"Death and life were locked together in a unique struggle. Life's Captain died; now he reigns, never more to die."[1]

As the third Christian millennium approaches, the Church is becoming increasingly immersed in an extraordinary fight for life. The publication of the encyclical *Evangelium Vitae* (1995) represents an important stage in this battle for the affirmation of the value and inviolability of human life. It aims at countering a certain nihilism of values which threatens what we may call the spiritual ecology of mankind. John Paul II's solemn intervention assumes all the more significance from the fact that it continues and realizes the moral teaching reaffirmed by the *Catechism of the Catholic Church* and the encyclical *Veritatis Splendor,* published in 1992 and 1993, respectively. One infers a long-term strategy to mobilize the conscience of believers and people of good will in the fight against the "culture of death," which has more and more established itself on a planetary scale.

Nevertheless, the message of *Evangelium Vitae* does not principally concern the denunciation of threats against life. It first and above all proclaims the good news of life in a way that makes explicit the theological foundations of human dignity: "The Gospel of life is not simply a reflection, however new and profound, on human life. Nor is it merely a commandment aimed at raising awareness and bringing about significant changes in society. Still less is it an illusory promise of a better future. The Gospel of life is something concrete and personal, for it consists in the proclamation of *the very person of Jesus*" (*EV,* n. 29).

This christological proposition is affirmed as the spearhead of the project of new evangelization promulgated by John Paul II. It is inscribed within a doctrinal development which integrates more profoundly fundamental morality and the precepts of natural law into a christological and trinitarian vision. The categorical moral imperative "You shall not kill," which inspires the Church toward a preference for life in the face of cultures of death, proceeds more clearly than ever from the paschal Christ, the victor over sin and death. It is important to emphasize this fact, which renews the magisterial approach to ethical problems. Indeed, it is true that the inviolable dignity of the human person rests upon the natural law issued by the Creator; but its ultimate foundation arises from God's engagement in history. The awareness of this engagement must more than ever nourish the Church's hope and the message of life she addresses to secularized cultures.

The Culture of Death

To those young people gathered from around the world in Denver in 1993, the pope from the East exclaimed: "Do not allow the makers of the culture of death to manipulate your consciences!" The "culture of death" is a paradoxical expression with a more profound significance than simple rhetoric, since it is taken up systematically in *Evangelium Vitae* to stigmatize the massive attacks upon life. This paradoxical expression provides a dramatic complement to the rather optimistic developments of *Gaudium et Spes* on the blossoming of culture (nn. 53–62). Confronted with the changes characteristic of the modern world (industrialization, urbanization, means of communication) which have generated new forms of culture (mass culture), the Council reconsidered the Church's mission with respect to cultures in the most positive way possible. However, with the passing of time and the evolution of societies, a certain number of critical questions raised at the Council have today acquired a more dramatic relevance. For example: "how can we recognize as legitimate the autonomy a culture claims for itself, without thereby reverting to a humanism which is purely worldly and even hostile to religion?"[2]

John Paul II returned to the discourse on the dignity of the human person in the light of the cultural developments concerning the respect for life in the last thirty years. His intervention assumes the form of a warning cry, because he witnesses a veritable "conspiracy against life" at work on every level (*EV,* n. 17). Beyond territorial armed conflicts and civil wars occasionally bordering on genocide, he sees with a great unease that the threats against life have broadened and multiplied as far as the eye can see. Particular interest groups have joined forces with national and international institutions to spread contraception, sterilization, abortion, and even euthanasia as conquests of freedom. The phenomenon has grown to such magnitude that John Paul II does not hesitate to denounce it as "scientifically and systematically programmed threats" (*EV,* n. 17), the fruit of a secularist mentality become hostile to the significance of God in ethical debates.

The problem is articulated in terms of "culture" because it goes beyond the recognition of personal situations more or less in conflict with universally recognized values. We observe, rather, an upheaval of values on the social, cultural, and political level. The crimes against life thus come to be presented as "legitimate expressions of individual freedom, to be acknowledged and protected as actual rights" (*EV,* n. 18). What follows is an astonishing contradiction, which the pope unambiguously unmasks: "Precisely in an age when the inviolable rights of the person are solemnly proclaimed and the value of life is publicly affirmed, the very right to life is being denied or trampled upon, especially at the more significant moments of existence: the moment of birth and the moment of death" (*EV,* n. 18).

As the pope indicates, lying at the roots of this "culture of death," legitimized through legal dispositions and democratic practices, is the severing of the link between freedom and truth in the consciences of people today. Such was the object of a detailed analysis in *Veritatis Splendor:* "The saving power of truth is contested, and freedom alone, uprooted from any objectivity, is left to decide by itself what is good and what is evil" (*VS,* n. 84). This culture of autonomous choice, liberated from God's commands, only accelerates "the fearful plunging of the human person into situations of gradual self-destruction" (*EV,* n. 84); it also destroys the basis that safeguards just relations among people. In effect, the absence of a sure moral reference based on truth opens the door to an exploitation of ideas and convictions for the sake of power. This applies not only to totalitarian ideologies which have systematically manipulated public opinion, but also to pluralistic societies in which the *"risk of an alliance between democracy and ethical relativism"* threatens civil concord (*VS*, n. 101): "As history demonstrates, a democracy without values easily turns into open or thinly disguised totalitarianism."[3]

Thus, at the heart of the drama lived by modern man, there lies the "eclipse of the sense of God and of man" (*EV*, n. 21), which leads individual consciences toward a systematic violation of the moral law and a loss of the awareness of God's vivifying and saving presence. The consequences of this touch not only private relations among persons and the foundations of communal life, but they reach moral judgment and man's capacity to hear God's voice in his conscience. Bereft of its vital grounding in the Judeo-Christian tradition, "the moral conscience, both individual and social, is today subjected, also as a result of the penetrating influence of the media, to an *extremely serious and mortal danger: that of confusion between good and evil* precisely in relation to the fundamental right to life" (*EV*, n. 24). Such is the warning that emerges from the pope's critique of the culture of death.

Alarmism? Intolerance? Pessimism? Does this critique of modern culture rely too much upon a vision tied to a passé Christianity, long since transformed? Does it not ignore the signs of noticeable progress, even at the moral level, in the awareness of human rights, democratic values, and the spirit of solidarity that characterizes the evolution of cultures? It is important to note that the brushstrokes John Paul II vigorously applies to this portrait also include positive signs inspiring hope. The growth and development of biomedical research, the rise of a sensitivity increasingly opposed to war as a means of conflict resolution, the continual broadening of public opinion's aversion to the death penalty, pro-life movements which, without recourse to violence, give witness to society to the value of life, as well as countless voluntary commitments to the service of life figure among the positive signs that complete and nuance the dark painting of negative signs (*EV*, nn. 26–27).

It would not be inappropriate to remark in passing that the pope's diagnosis of the deplorable state of health of secularized societies echoes the warning cries coming from specialists in the human sciences: "An atmosphere of death and the idea of a universe deprived of perspective seem to characterize our times. Society inwardly unravels and implodes as political and moral causes prove, with the passing of time and the encounter with reality, to be illusions."[4] Attentive observers of the psychological evolution of individuals and societies marvel with increasing concern at the breakdown of personal communication, the emergence of increasing and uncontrollable violence, the spreading phenomenon of depression, and the rising suicide rate, especially among young people. This specialist of social psychology dares to confess that the legal practice of abortion and euthanasia releases an atmosphere of death into society: "The mother and the doctor—symbols of life—thus become a symbol of selection and negation of life. This deadly reversal serves only to express society's need for self-destruction: 'No future!'"[5]

According to the same author, we must search for the remedies for a "depressive society," which no longer offers any ideal to young people, in a clear affirmation of the relation to God and the moral values grounded in it: "We must admit it, the relationship to the transcendent makes possible a deepening of meaning in life, a development of interiority, and the humanization of individuals and societies."[6] The Church's message of life goes much further. It does not aim first at raising again the moral level of society. It proclaims the gospel of life in Jesus Christ, which transcends the horizon of earthly life in order to embrace that of eternal life. That which psychologists—those who do not accept secularist presuppositions—recognize as a need for structuring the psychological identity of individuals, the Church proposes as a grace and mission of salvation accomplished in Jesus Christ. In short, the proclamation of hope lies at the heart of the gospel of life.

THE HOPE OF THE CHURCH

The reasons for living that so many young people so cruelly lack cannot be found outside of the truth affirmed by Vatican Council II and taken up as a refrain by John Paul II: "by his Incarnation, he, the son of God, has in a certain way united himself with each man" (*GS*, n. 22). The Church's response to the challenges of secularized cultures is not limited to reaffirming the basic truth that any person of good will can understand. To be sure, the Church recalls the created character of human freedom and thus its dependence on the Creator and its need to obey the precepts of the natural law affecting the inviolable value of life. However, something more decisive wholly permeates the message about the value of life: a christological development which places the ethical discourse in a more concrete relation to the grace of Christ. In other words, the natural law discourse does not suffice on its own. It is integrated as an important element in a more comprehensive christological whole. In the style of *Gaudium et Spes,* the developments of each chapter are articulated around the paschal mystery of Christ who joins together the worldly responsibility for life and the participation in the eternal life of God.[7]

When the Church observes the ravages of the culture of death upon so many innocent victims, she lifts her eyes toward the crucified One whose passion and death assume all of the anxieties and tragedies that form the fabric of human history. The *Catechism of the Catholic Church* expresses this in a profound way: "All the troubles, for all time, of humanity enslaved by sin and death, all the petitions and intercessions of salvation history are summed up in the cry of the incarnate Word. Here the Father accepts them and, beyond all hope, answers them by raising his Son" (*CCC,* n. 2606). The Church's first attitude with respect to the culture of death consists in confessing the mystery of Easter, proclaiming the reversal of every tragedy and the granting of every prayer. "No one saw the hour of your victory. No one is witness to the birth of a world. No one knows how the night of that Saturday's hell was transformed into the light of the Easter dawn. Asleep it was that we were all carried on wings over the abyss, and asleep did we receive the grace of Easter. And no one knows how it happened to him. No one knows which hand it was that caressed his cheek so that suddenly the wan world beamed with a thousand colors, and he had to smile involuntarily over the miracle that was realized in him."[8]

The moment the son of Man hands over his spirit to the Father in the extreme abandonment of death a stream of eternal life trickles from the pierced side, prefiguring the river of life of Easter and Pentecost. The Son's obedience vanquished every disobedience of all the sons and daughters of Adam and Eve and sealed the new covenant, the mutual and fruitful covenant, in his blood. From here comes the Church's imperative, her boldness in affirming the inviolable value of human life (*EV,* nn. 50–51): "The blood of Christ, while it reveals the grandeur of the Father's love, *shows how precious man is to God's eyes and how priceless the value of his life*" (*EV,* n. 25). Divine love paid the price of blood to win back human freedom gone astray. Who has sung this better than Péguy?

It was yours to reckon the eternal account
How much those abandoned it cost me to save.
Here's ink and here's table to figure it out
At what rate I borrowed the blood that I gave.

It was yours to reckon, O tireless bursar,
Space, site, and time, how much it cost.
To what extent man drew from my purse
The blood of a God, to ransom the lost.[9]

The blood of Christ gives a priceless value to all human life by virtue of the indestructible bond that links all men to the theanthropic obedience of the Son of God. This redemptive obedience brings the human being into the realm of the trinitarian exchanges. John Paul II's christological meditation thus opens into the trinitarian foundation of the supreme dignity of human life. "To know God and his Son is to accept the mystery of the loving communion of the Father, the Son and the Holy Spirit into one's own life, which *even now* is open to eternal life because it *shares in the life of God*" (*EV*, n. 37). Already infinitely precious because he is loved for his own sake by an infinite God, the human person receives an unfathomable excess of dignity from the fact that he belongs henceforward to the sacred enclave in which the intra-trinitarian love is expressed. He is infinitely precious not only in himself but also for God himself who has invested his Glory in this unique creature created in his image and likeness.

If each person is a gift from the Father, not only for his own sake but also for the Son—a gift received, enriched and returned to the Father in the Spirit— then it becomes sacrilegious to violate the life that is called to express and serve the greater glory of God. "Father, I wish that, there where I am, those that you have given me be also with me, and that they fulfill the glory that you have given me for you have loved me before the foundation of the world" (Jn 17:24). Irenaeus's comment is appropriate in this context: "The Glory of God" is certainly "the living man" but "the life of man consists in the vision of God,"[10] that is, in communion with God, something already begun in this world. Here, the human person finds himself enriched by God himself—which is to say divinized—becoming a participant in the trinitarian relations. The profound identity of each person is thus hidden in Christ in the theanthropic

Person of the incarnate Word, the *vinculum substantiale,* who joins mankind and the Trinity together in a nuptial and indissoluble fashion. Trinitarian life and human life are forever more inseparable. In the paschal Christ, their destinies are joined and wedded for a common fruitfulness that the Scriptures call Glory. As the sacrament of this covenantal mystery, we see that the Church is engaged in the first person in the mission of him who has come so that men may have life and have it abundantly (Jn 10:10).

That is why the sovereign ideal that the Church proposes to humanity is the total gift of self in the image and likeness of the Trinity. This total gift through love in the following of the crucified Christ designates the path of true freedom. *"The Crucified Christ reveals the authentic meaning of freedom, he lives it fully, in the total gift of himself,* and he calls his disciples to share in his freedom" (*VS,* n. 85). Because his blood was spilled as a sign of love, he has changed the sign of death and definitive separation into a sign of communion and eternal life. "In this way Jesus proclaims that *life finds its center, its meaning and its fulfillment when it is given up"* (*EV,* n. 51). "Death has been swallowed up in victory. Death, where is your victory? Death, where is your sting?" (1 Cor 15:54–55). The battle for freedom which stands at the heart of the Church's mission leads through the witness borne to the Truth who "sets free" for eternal life (Jn 8:32; Gal 5:1).

ENGAGED IN GOD'S BATTLE

The Holy Father's christological meditation marks all of the developments concerning the Church's mission in the service of life and the promotion of a "culture of life." Whether it be to bring to light the inviolable dignity of the person, the sacred character of his belonging to God in Christ, to confirm the natural law of the fifth commandment, or to awaken the conscience of believers and galvanize their energies toward the battle for the respect for life, we find ourselves in the presence of a divine drama, to use Balthasar's term, which includes mankind in Christ's Easter. In this respect, the encyclical's conclusion adds a Marian dimension which far surpasses the framework of a pious and exemplary reference. This reference to the Mother of sorrows clearly illustrates the prophetic character of the Polish pope, mindful of illuminating people's consciences from the standpoint of the Marian message of the Apocalypse. Under the "great portent" of the "Woman" chased by "an enormous red fire Dragon" who wants to "devour the newly born Infant" (Rev 12:1–4), he sees the hostility of the forces of evil at work in history which strike the Mother before striking the children. "Mary thus helps the Church to *realize that life is always at the center of a great struggle* between good and evil, between light and darkness" (*EV,* n. 104; emphasis added).

Mary teaches the Church to give birth, amidst great pains, to the Savior throughout the centuries by standing with her at the foot of the cross (Jn 19:25). Her spiritual maternity "fully ripened on the day of the cross, when the time came for Mary to welcome as a son every person who had become a disciple, bearing them the Son's redemptive love" (Jn 19:26). It is thus that Mary, the sorrowful yet victorious Mother, is the living word of consolation and strength for the Church in her battle against death and the culture of death.

The figure of Mary, set in relief in such an expressive manner, remains emblematic. She leads the Church into God's battle, which the book of the seven seals describes in apocalyptic images. The victory of the Lamb over the forces of darkness that wash human history in blood is not a pious consolation of the "happy-ending" sort. It is an exhortation to battle and to faithfulness to the end, in the midst of adversity and persecution. John Paul II assumes this apocalyptic vein in a more forceful and incisive way here than in any other document of his pontificate. We sense in this encyclical a passion that echoes that of a Charles Péguy, who praises the mystery of the charity of Joan of Arc: "A soul, a single soul, bears an infinite worth. What, then, would be the worth of an infinity of souls?"[11] At the spectacle of impiety that unfolds over the kingdom of France, the Orléans maiden is moved with compassion, as well as with impatience and bravery, for God's battle in his saints: "Jeanette: Saint Geneviève, Saint Aignan, Saint Loup were not afraid to go before the pagan armies....In the folds of their coats they carried the glory of God and the body of Jesus...Never would they have abandoned it...."[12] "Christianity must go on"—a phrase tirelessly repeated by the poet theologian, the peasant soldier Péguy, whose passion for justice was equalled only by the breadth of his hope. Christian culture must go on.

By taking up an account of the familiar commandment "You shall not kill" in the light of Easter, John Paul II sides with the poorest, the most innocent and the defenseless, following the Master's example. Now more than ever, the disillusioned world awaits a similar witness from Christian men and women. Something of the infinite worth of a human life shines through a doctor's refusal to perform an abortion; through a nurse's dedication in comforting the suffering of one dying, without shortening his days; through the charity of a social worker who directs a helpless young pregnant woman to a clinic of life and not death; through the courage of a delegate who opposes a majority wishing to legalize the attacks on human life. With an admiration mixed with respect and astonishment, the whole world saluted King Baudouin, who stepped down from the throne rather than countersign his country's parliamentary law legalizing abortion. Christianity must assert itself as a "culture of life" in the service of a world disoriented by the "culture of death."

In the encounter with the nihilist drift leading democracies to level sacred values, the Church, the expert in humanity and the servant-spouse of the Lamb, recalls the truths and the values that form the basis of a civilization of love; obedience to the Creator and his law inscribed in the moral conscience of mankind; respect for life from the moment of conception to the moment of death; the priority of the family in social politics; union with Jesus in the "call for a 'sincere gift of self' as the fullest way to realize our personal freedom" (EV, n. 81). As a compassionate mother, the Church patiently accompanies the meandering steps of her children, and she casts a hopeful look at the human tragedies arising from sin. She thus points to the crucified and risen One who unveils the ultimate truth: the unfathomable freedom of trinitarian love, able to change darkness into light so that his Glory will shine in man.

By the way of conclusion, we once again leave the word to the poet of hope, blessed for having died in battle in the sight of God:

> Now every man has the right to bury his own son.
> Every man on earth, if the great misfortune befalls him
> Not to have died before his son. And I alone, God,
> My hands tied by this adventure,
> I alone, father at that moment like so many fathers,
> I alone was unable to bury my son.
> It was then, O night, that you arrived.
> O my daughter, my most precious among them all, and it is
>   still before my eyes and it will remain before my eyes for
>   all eternity.

It was then, O Night, that you came and, in a great shroud,
 you buried
The Centurion and his Romans,
The Virgin and the holy women,
And that mountain, and that valley, upon which the evening
 was descending,
And my people of Israel and sinners and, with them, he who
 was dying, he who had died for them
And the men sent by Joseph of Arimathea who were already
 approaching
Bearing the white shroud. [13]

                —Translated by David Louis Schindler, Jr.

Notes

1. The Roman missal, Easter Sunday sequence.

2. Cf. *GS,* n. 56. See also the very critical passage denouncing the attacks upon life (*GS,* n. 27).

3. John Paul II, encyclical *Centesimus Annus* (1 May 1991), n. 46; cited in *VS,* n. 101.

4. T. Anatrella, *Non à la société dépressive* (Flammarion, 1993), 9.

5. Ibid., 289.

6. Ibid., 305.

7. See, for example, the Introduction, 1–2; chap. I, n. 25; the whole of chap. II, but most especially nn. 29–30, 50–51; chap III, nn. 52, 76–77; chap. IV, nn. 78–81; and the Conclusion, nn. 101–5.

8. Hans Urs von Balthasar, *The Heart of the World*, trans. Erasmo S. Leiva (San Francisco: Ignatius Press, 1979), 157.

9. Charles Péguy, *Eve* (Paris: La Pléiade, 1975), 988, quatrain 426, and 989, quatrain 430.

10. St. Irenaeus of Lyon, *Adversus Haereses* IV, 20, 7 (SC 100/2:648–49), cited in *EV,* n. 38.

11. Charles Péguy, *Le mystère de la charité de Jeanne d'Arc* (Paris: La Pléiade, 1957), 522.

12. Ibid., 500–501.

13. Charles Péguy, *Le porche de la Deuxième Vertu* (Paris: La Pléiade, 1986), 669–70 [Eng. trans., *The Portal of the Mystery of Hope* (Grand Rapids: Eerdmans, 1996)].

10. *Evangelium Vitae* and Its Broader Context

Charles E. Curran

This chapter first appeared in the author's *History and Contemporary Issues: Studies in Moral Theology* in 1996.

On March 25, 1995, Pope John Paul II issued the eleventh encyclical of his pontificate, *Evangelium Vitae.*[1] The encyclical's issuance constituted no surprise. The college of cardinals in 1991 requested such a document reaffirming life which is now seen as a more practical follow-up to the earlier (1993) and more theoretical encyclical, *Veritatis Splendor.*[2]

The basic positions taken in *Evangelium Vitae* are well known—the condemnations of murder, direct abortion, euthanasia, and the death penalty (its justification is practically nonexistent). The method is similar to the approaches John Paul II's encyclicals have employed in the past—the assumption of the traditional natural law teaching of the Catholic tradition on particular points, an explicit scripturally based understanding of fundamental themes and principles with a concentration in this case on the Cain and Abel story, and a commentary on contemporary cultural trends. There is little that is new in the encyclical. On the major points of murder, abortion, and euthanasia the pope expressly claims to confirm the existing teaching. The position on the death penalty is stronger and more negative than found in past papal documents but consistent with recent emphases of John Paul II.

What effect will this document have on Catholics in the United States? In my judgment, not much. As mentioned, much of the encyclical is not new. Probably the majority of Catholics and of theologians are in fundamental agreement with the thrust of the teaching on abortion and euthanasia from the moral perspective, although I have some modifications and see more grey areas and nuances and less certainties than the pope. Those who have disagreed with the teaching on these points will probably continue to do so. The opposition to the death penalty will be somewhat upsetting to some Catholics. The encyclical constitutes a practical follow-up dealing with these particular questions in the light of the more theoretical points made in *Veritatis Splendor,* the 1993 encyclical. Some of the same points are developed here, but *Veritatis Splendor* often caricatured the positions taken by revisionist Catholic theologians, which generally speaking does not occur in this document.

The first part of this essay will comment on the document itself and develop three points—the aspects of the encyclical, two problematic aspects, and the teaching on law and public policy.

COMMENTARY

Positive Aspects

John Paul II's basic thesis about a failure to respect the sacredness and dignity of human life in our contemporary society is shared by many people today. Our age has experienced much violence, killing, and disrespect for human life. Life is a gift of God and, although not absolute, a very fundamental and sacred value. Every human and political community rests on this fundamental right to life (nn. 1–3). *Evangelium Vitae* points out many of the same problems mentioned in *Veritatis Splendor*—a notion of freedom which exalts the isolated individual in an absolute way and gives no play to "solidarity"; the self "understood in terms of absolute autonomy"; "the shifting sands of complete relativism" (nn. 19–20).

The encyclical perceptively recognizes other problems in our contemporary society. Materialism and the possession of things often become all-important. Having is more significant than being. Life in this understanding can easily be reduced to just another thing or possession (nn. 22–23). An overemphasis on efficiency and technology constitutes a danger for us. The pope points out the penchant for trying to have complete control over our lives. However, we are finite creatures and will never have such full control. There are many things that happen to us in this life that we do not want and cannot control. As human beings we cannot avoid some suffering in our lives. The technological can never be totally identified with the fully human. Technology can be helpful to truly human advancement, but at times we must say no to technology and its possibilities in the name of protecting the human and our environment (n. 15).

The pope speaks up for the poor, the weak, the defenseless, the marginalized, the oppressed, and the aged and calls upon human society to help and empower these people. Too often today in our society such people are forgotten about or not respected, but human dignity does not depend on what one does, makes, or accomplishes (n. 18). Likewise the encyclical points out the danger to the ecological and environmental aspects of the earth that can come from an absolute freedom, individualism, and relativism (n. 10).

The encyclical compassionately addresses women who have had an abortion and recognizes the many factors and influences often mitigating such a decision. Although what has happened remains terribly wrong, the mercy and forgiveness of God exist in the sacrament of reconciliation (n. 99). (One phrase in this section would have caused great consternation only a few years ago—the pope considers that the aborted child is now living with the Lord. Whatever happened to limbo?)

The striving for consistency in the life issues across the board constitutes a positive aspect of the document, although the pope does not explicitly refer to the consistent ethic of life championed by Cardinal Joseph Bernardin.[3] War would be too big a topic to include, but in a passing reference the pope notes the growing tendency not to resort to war if at all possible (n. 27).

One striking aspect of the present document comes from the pope's insistence on the collegial nature of this teaching. He refers explicitly to the 1991 Consistory of Cardinals in Rome and the personal letter he sent to all bishops asking for their input (n. 5). In his solemn proclamation of the teaching on murder, abortion, and euthanasia, the pope insists on his communion with other bishops in confirming and declaring these traditional teachings (nn. 57, 62, 65). However, this collegial aspect of the document is only a very small beginning and much more needs to be done. Papal documents must have much more regular and structured input from the bishops of the world and from the people of the church.

Problematic Aspects

The primary problem comes from the document's oppositions and certainties that combine to deny the grey areas and nuances that have been a part of the Catholic moral theology tradition. The pope frames the issues in terms of the struggle between the culture of life and the culture of death. John Paul II compares this dramatic conflict between the culture of death and the culture of life with the conflict of the cross and the massive conflict between good and evil (nn. 28, 50, and throughout the encyclical). However, such a thoroughgoing opposition between the church and the world of the gospel and culture has not been the typical Catholic approach. Some Protestant approaches have seen the world primarily in terms of the opposition between grace and sin, but the Catholic tradition did not see sin as destroying the human and its basic goodness, but only infecting it.[4]

The Catholic position has traditionally seen the divine as mediated in and through the human. The glory of God is the human person come alive.[5] The human person is an image of God precisely because like God she has intellect, free will, and the power of self-determination. The Catholic tradition has insisted on the basic goodness of the human and of human reason. The church in its history has supported and encouraged human truth, beauty, and goodness. If anything, the danger of the Roman Catholic tradition has been its failure at times to criticize the surrounding culture.

History shows that at times the church has learned from the world—for example, the condemnations of slavery and torture and the support of political rights and the role of women. At other times the church has rightly condemned the pride, materialism, greed, and individualism too often found in the world. The pope himself recognizes the limits of his own oppositional approach by briefly pointing out some signs in our cultures that point to the victory over death even though these cultures are strongly marked by the culture of death (nn. 26–27).

The oppositional approach allows one to put one's own position under the good or the positive aspect of life while assigning those who disagree to the negative camp of the culture of death. But this is not fair. First, it tends to create a triumphalism of the church as identified with the forces of good and life and fails to recognize the church's own failures in promoting life. Second, many proponents of some abortions would not see themselves as part of the culture of death. Their position is that the early embryo or fetus is not yet a truly individual human being or person. The differences in the debate about abortion cannot be conceived so simply as a struggle between the culture of life and the culture of death.

The oppositional approach identifies one's total position with the good and does not explicitly recognize the nuances and the different levels of certitude with regard to parts of one's own position. The pope explicitly deals with exceptions to killing in the Catholic tradition as illustrated by the legitimacy of killing an unjust aggressor as a last resort in self-defense. Human life is not an absolute value and in some conflict situations human life can be taken. The official hierarchical position as phrased by the pope is, "The direct and voluntary killing of an innocent human being is always gravely immoral" (n. 57). The Catholic tradition has solved conflict situations on the basis of the principle of double effect with its condemnation of direct killing.

However, as mentioned earlier the ethical theory of direct killing depends on an epistemological understanding of the human act which is far removed from the core gospel values. Today many Catholic theologians disagree with it and would admit more conflict situations than the concept of direct killing allows.[6] The present Catholic hierarchical teaching on direct abortion has only been in place for one hundred years. Prominent theologians in the nineteenth century admitted more justifications for abortion than the present teaching allows.[7] Recall that the ultramontanist Aloysius Sabetti approved the removal of an ectopic pregnancy, a position later condemned by the Holy office.

The life-death, good-evil oppositional approach covers over the lack of certitude that the Catholic tradition has always recognized with regard to the theoretical understanding of when individual human life begins. For the great part of its existence, the Catholic Church held for delayed animation according to which the human soul was infused sometime (e.g., forty to ninety days) after conception. However, even before animation, abortion was not accepted.[8] John Paul II alludes to this tradition without explicitly recalling it (n. 60). The Catholic position has maintained that in practice one must act as if the human person is present from the moment of conception. However, this is a prudential judgment that cannot claim an absolute certitude. Some in good faith and with some reason on their side could disagree with that judgment.

Even with regard to euthanasia, there are more nuances and less certitude than the life–death oppositional approach recognizes. The pope proposes the traditional Catholic understanding that one does not have to use means to keep a person alive that are disproportionate to any expected results or means that impose an excessive burden on the patient and the family (n. 65). But one cannot positively interfere to bring about death. Again, the issues involve a philosophical discussion about the difference between withdrawing a means and positively interfering to bring about death.[9] In all these cases (meaning of direct, beginning of human life, difference between withdrawing a means and positively interfering), the hierarchical magisterium's teaching rests on philosophical understandings that are removed from the core of faith. Many theologians and Catholics agree with these approaches, but others disagree without thereby becoming part of the culture of death.

A second problem concerns the continued insistence on the teaching condemning artificial contraception, even though this is not a major topic in the encyclical (nn. 13–66), and the well known papal positions on the role of women. Many of us believe that these teachings have seriously harmed the credibility of the hierarchical magisterium as a moral leader and teacher. Granted that the positions on abortion and euthanasia are based on different reasons, but such a context makes it hard for many to pay attention to what the pope says on these life issues.

Law and Public Policy

Perhaps in the United States the section on law and public policy (especially nn. 68–74) will receive the most sustained public attention. John Paul II maintains that civil law must respect and promote the basic right to life. The will of the majority or public opinion cannot override basic human rights. The present situation of permissive abortion laws in many countries shows the presence of ethical relativism, individualism, and the separation of freedom from truth. Although the pope frequently calls attention to the distressing situation of such permissive laws as a sign of the culture of death, he does not propose his teaching on civil law in the same authoritative way as he does on the moral issues themselves.

The document briefly refutes a number of reasons that have been proposed to justify permissive abortion laws. The pope claims it is never licit to vote for or obey an intrinsically unjust law such as a law permitting abortion or euthanasia (n. 73). However, the encyclical recognizes the prudential aspect in lawmaking and the difficulty in changing permissive laws. Christians must take account of what is realistically attainable. One thus can support legislation that will lessen the harm done even if some abortions are still permitted. Where permissive laws exist, the pope calls for conscientious objection for those who disagree with the law; however, recourse to violence is excluded (n. 74).

There are two different Catholic approaches today to the understanding of the proper relationship between law and morality—what was called the Thomistic approach and the John Courtney Murray–Vatican II approach. "The doctrine on the necessary conformity of civil law with the moral law is in continuity with the whole tradition of the church...(and) is the clear teaching of St. Thomas Aquinas" (n. 72). Democracy cannot be reduced just to the will of the majority "but depends on conformity to the moral law, to which it, like every other form of human behavior, must be subject" (n. 70).

The Thomistic approach can be contrasted with the Murray–Vatican II approach. The latter approach begins not with the moral law but with the freedom of the person, which, however, is limited not by the common good but by the narrower concept of the public order. Likewise the Vatican II approach recognizes freedom as a very important part of the common good. "For the rest the usages of society are to be the usages of freedom in their full range. These require that the freedom of man *[sic]* be respected as far as possible and curtailed only when and insofar as necessary."[10]

John Paul II has obviously chosen not to employ the Murray–Vatican II approach. He always begins with moral law and not freedom. He insists often on the common good as being the criterion for law and never mentions the public order (nn. 70–72). The encyclical does not develop the role of freedom in the broader common good. However, the encyclical does cite the crucial paragraph seven of the Declaration on Religious Freedom of Vatican II, which proposes the different approach to law and morality. The pope cites this paragraph to show that the purpose of civil law is "that of ensuring the common good of people through the recognition and defense of their fundamental rights and the promotion of peace and of public morality" (n. 71). In the original these three elements comprise the public order which is narrower and less than the common good. Without doubt the Thomistic approach makes it easier for the pope to show that civil law should prohibit abortion and euthanasia. This might explain why he chose such an understanding.

The Vatican II approach definitely gives a greater role to freedom and a somewhat lesser role to law in public society. However, one could employ the Vatican II theory and maintain that civil law should not allow abortion and euthanasia. The three elements of public order include the protection of the rights of all. One could argue that freedom in these cases must be restricted to protest the fundamental right to life. On the other hand, I have maintained that one could employ the Vatican II approach to come to a different conclusion about abortion laws. In the light of the differences within a pluralistic society the presumption in favor of freedom and not the moral law can argue for a more permissive law. The practical difficulties of overturning a permissive law and of enforcing a restrictive abortion law buttress the argument not to work to change the existing abortion laws in the United States. Thus I maintain that Catholics who hold the hierarchical moral teaching on abortion do not have an obligation to work to change the permissive abortion laws now existing in the United States.

One final point on this issue. Those who disagree with the encyclical on the legal issue of abortion should not accuse the pope and other church leaders of violating the separation of church and state by working for civil laws prohibiting abortion and euthanasia. In the United States, if you believe for whatever reason that basic human rights are violated, you can legitimately work for a law to protect them—but of course you must convince others. Those making such an accusation would reduce all religion to the personal and private sphere with no ability to affect public and common life. According to these principles Martin Luther King could not have worked for civil rights on the basis of his biblical understandings.

A Broader Context

The second section of this chapter will discuss the two encyclicals *Veritatis Splendor* and *Evangelium Vitae* in the light of the totality of papal moral teaching. I have maintained that papal social teaching has employed a different methodology from papal teaching on personal and sexual issues.[11] The two encyclicals just studied deal primarily with personal morality. A comparison with Pope John Paul II's 1995 address to the United Nations shows four very significant differences in approach.

1) The two encyclicals tend to downplay historical development and even see it as threatening the existing teaching. The emphasis is on what has been true always and everywhere. According to *Veritatis Splendor,* these new approaches to Catholic moral theology reject the traditional doctrine regarding the natural law and the universality and permanent validity of its precepts (n. 4). *Evangelium Vitae* proclaims and reaffirms the older Catholic teaching about life in all its dimensions because of the extraordinary increase and growth of threats to life in the modern world. This disturbing state of affairs is expanding with a new cultural climate which gives crimes against life a new and even more sinister character (nn. 3–4).

How different is the address to the United Nations.[12] John Paul II wants to reflect on "the extraordinary changes of the last few years" (n. 1) with the "global acceleration of that quest for freedom which is one of the great dynamics of human history" (n. 2). Many people at the end of this millennium are fearful for themselves and of the human future. We must learn to conquer fear through a new flourishing of the human spirit based on an authentic culture of freedom and a rediscovery of the spirit of truth (n. 16).

2) *Evangelium Vitae,* as mentioned, develops its theme by contrasting the culture of life with the culture of death existing in the world today, adopting an "either-or" or "we versus them" approach. At the United Nations, the pope took a very different tack. The answer to the present fear about the future is "neither coercion nor repression, nor the imposition of one social 'model' on the entire world. The answer to the fear which darkens human existence at the end of the twentieth century is the common effort to build the civilization of love, founded on the universal values of peace, solidarity, justice, and liberty" (n. 18). There is no "we versus them" approach here.

3) *Veritatis Splendor* insists on the universal and the uniform. What is presented here is the same for all persons in all places and at all times. The "central theme" of *Veritatis Splendor* is "the reaffirmation of the universality and immutability of the moral commandments, particularly those which prohibit always and without exception intrinsically evil acts." (n. 115).

At the United Nations, John Paul II was much more open to

particularity, differences, and diversity. "The human condition thus finds itself between these two poles—universality and particularity—with a vital tension between them; an inevitable tension, but singularly fruitful if they are lived in a calm and balanced way" (n. 7). "To cut oneself off from the reality of difference—or, worse, to attempt to stamp out that difference—is to cut oneself off from the possibility of sounding the depths of the mystery of human life" (n. 10). Consider what would happen if the above sentence were applied to homosexuality.

4) *Veritatis Splendor* and *Evangelium Vitae* both presume that moral truth is easy to find and that the hierarchical magisterium has this truth and proclaims it authoritatively to all others. The entire thrust of *Veritatis Splendor* rests on the splendor of truth and that people are "made holy by the 'obedience to the truth' (1 Pt 1:22)" (n. 1). At the root of the present crisis in the church lie "currents of thought which end by detaching human freedom from its essential and constitutive relationship to truth" (n. 4). The first chapter tells the story of the rich young man asking Jesus what good he must do to have eternal life. "Jesus' conversation with the rich young man continues in a sense in every period of history, including our own....The task of interpreting these prescriptions was entrusted by Jesus to the apostles and to their successors, with the special assistance of the Spirit of truth: 'He who hears you hears me' (Lk 10:16)" (n. 25). The church, "the pillar and bulwark of the truth," continues the teaching role of Jesus with "the task of authentically interpreting the word of God... entrusted only to those charged with the church's living magisterium whose authority is exercised in the name of Jesus Christ" (n. 27).

How different is the understanding of truth and the search for it in the address to the United Nations. "The truth about man *[sic]* is the unchangeable standard by which all cultures are judged; but every culture has something to teach us about one or other dimension of that complex truth. Thus the 'difference' which some find so threatening can, through respectful dialogue, become the source of a deeper understanding of the mystery of human existence" (n. 10).

There can be no doubt that significant differences in approach exist between *Veritatis Splendor* as well as *Evangelium Vitae* and the 1995 papal address to the United Nations. Significant continuities also exist, but the thrust of this chapter is to recognize the differences.

What explains these significant differences in the two approaches? One possible explanation concerns a basic difference between personal and social ethics. For example, Catholic social thought has always been willing to tolerate evil, which is not true in personal morality. Society rightly needs a statute of limitations, but such a statute does not exist in the moral order. The end or purpose of society is somewhat different between personal and social morality.[13] However, this difference does not seem to account for the more significant differences between the two approaches in papal moral teaching especially because the Catholic tradition, while recognizing some differences between the two areas, has tended to emphasize the continuities between them.

Perhaps the very nature of the documents under consideration explains the differences. Both *Veritatis Splendor* and *Evangelium Vitae* by definition are apologetic documents, defending the present teaching against those who disagree with it. On the other hand, the address to the United Nations speaks to the whole world about the need for human cooperation in working for a better humankind. Without doubt the two different genres involved here have had some influence on the different methodologies invoked in the documents themselves. However, I do not think this constitutes the total or the most basic explanation for the differences between them.

In my judgment the primary difference between the two approaches comes from the fact that in general the social documents employ a more historically conscious approach whereas the sexual and personal papal teachings employ a more classicist approach. The classicist approach tends to stress the eternal, immutable, and unchanging and adopts a more deductive methodology; whereas the historically conscious approach gives more importance to change, development, and historical differences, while employing a more inductive approach. The four differences mentioned above can be explained in a great measure by these two different methodological approaches.

All recognize the change that has occurred in the last one hundred years in hierarchical and papal social teaching.[14] The nineteenth-century papal teaching strongly condemned individualistic liberalism, the Enlightenment, and democracy. However, in the light of the growth of totalitarianism of the right, and especially of the left, in the twentieth century, papal teaching began to defend the dignity, freedom, and rights of the person. However, this does not mean that such papal and hierarchical teaching no longer had some problems with individualism or the Enlightenment. Only in the 1940s did Pius XII recognize democracy as the best form of government. Only in 1963 did John XXIII for the first time develop in a systematic way a Catholic understanding of human rights. Only in 1965 did Vatican II accept religious freedom. Significant change has occurred in hierarchical social teaching in the twentieth century.

Corresponding to the recognition of historical development and change, the hierarchical documents adopted a more historically conscious approach that begins with the concrete historical realities and not with abstract definitions or essences that are always and everywhere true. The Pastoral Constitution on the Church in the Modern World of Vatican II begins its discussion of five different areas of social morality with a consideration of the signs of the times.[15] Paul VI's *Octogesima Adveniens* adopts a very historically conscious approach. "In the face of such widely varying situations it is difficult for us to utter a unified message and to put forward a solution which has universal validity. Such is not our ambition, nor is it our mission."[16] His predecessors before Vatican II would not recognize themselves in this description. In addition, Vatican II employed a historically conscious hermeneutic to justify the change in church teaching. In many ways the primary issue in the religious liberty debate at the council was the change that had obviously occurred in church teaching. The problem was solved by invoking a historically conscious hermeneutic. The historical circumstances changed and so the teaching on religious freedom has changed.[17]

There has been less change and development in personal and sexual ethics over history, but significant developments have occurred especially in sexual morality. At one time the intention of procreation was necessary to avoid mortal sin in marital sexual relations, but with the acceptance of rhythm and natural family planning one could intend not to procreate and still have marital sexual relations. However, in the last fifty years no change has occurred in the concrete norms governing personal and sexual morality. Since the issue of contraception for spouses was taken out of Vatican II, the council did not have to confront the question of change and development in this area. Hence an historically conscious methodology was not required nor was an historically conscious hermeneutic needed to justify change. Thus the recent history explains the different approaches and methodologies existing in papal teaching on social morality and on personal or sexual morality.

One final point. The invocation of an historically conscious hermeneutic to explain the change in the church's teaching on religious freedom is not adequate. There was some error involved at least at some time in the official teaching. Unfortunately, even Vatican II was unwilling to explicitly admit error in church teaching. If the council had recognized such error in past church teaching, Catholicism might have developed quite differently in the last thirty years. Consider the case of artificial contraception. Paul VI took this issue out of the council (where it might have been solved in a different way) and finally reaffirmed the ban on artificial contraception in *Humanae Vitae* primarily because he could not accept the fact that the past teaching was in any way erroneous.[18]

The point of this chapter has been to show that different methodological approaches exist in papal teaching on social and personal morality and to explain why this has occurred. To explore the implications of these differences would require not only another chapter but at least a volume or two. I have tried to deal with these implications in earlier chapters and in many of my own writings in moral theology. Here I can only summarize my approach.

The different approaches in methodologies definitely raise problems of consistency and coherence for papal moral teaching. A more historically conscious approach with all that entails should also be employed in personal and sexual morality. However, such an approach by no means excludes the existence of some absolute moral norms (e.g., unjustified killing of human beings, adultery) and very significant continuities in the teachings. But it does call for some changes and the recognition that certitude and truth are much harder to come by on specific moral issues.

Notes

1. Pope John Paul II, *Evangelium Vitae*, in *Origins* 24 (1995): 689–727. Subsequent references in the text will be to the paragraph numbers of the document.

2. "Communique: College of Cardinals Meeting," *Origins* 20 (1991): 747.

3. For a discussion of Cardinal Bernardin's theory see Joseph Cardinal Bernardin, *Consistent Ethic of Life*, ed. Thomas G. Fuechtmann (Kansas City, Mo.: Sheed and Ward, 1988).

4. For a classical discussion of the different models of relationships

between Christ and culture, see H. Richard Niebuhr, *Christ and Culture* (New York: Harper, 1956).

5. *Evangelium Vitae* actually quotes the famous saying of St. Irenaeus of Lyon, "*Gloria Dei vivens homo*" (n. 34). But the pope fails to develop the important understanding that the divine is mediated in and through the human.

6. See for example *Readings in Moral Theology No. 1: Moral Norms and Catholic Tradition*, ed. Charles E. Curran and Richard A. McCormick (New York: Paulist Press, 1979).

7. John R. Connery, *Abortion: The Development of the Roman Catholic Perspective* (Chicago: Loyola University Press, 1977), 213–69.

8. Ibid., 88–123.

9. Alastair Norcross and Bonnie Steinbock, eds., *Killing and Letting Die*, 2d ed. (New York: Fordham University Press, 1994).

10. Declaration on Religious Freedom, n. 7, in *The Documents of Vatican II*, ed. Walter M. Abbott (New York: Guild, 1966), 687.

11. Charles E. Curran, *Tensions in Moral Theology* (Notre Dame, Ind.: University of Notre Dame Press, 1988), 87–109.

12. Pope John Paul II, "U.N. Address: The Fabric of Relations Among People," *Origins* 25 (1995): 293–99. Subsequent references in the text will be to the paragraph numbers.

13. John Courtney Murray, *We Hold These Truths: Catholic Reflections on the American Proposition* (Kansas City, Mo.: Sheed and Ward, 1960), 286.

14. For my development of this point, see my *Directions in Catholic Social Ethics* (Notre Dame, Ind.: University of Notre Dame Press, 1985), 5–69.

15. Pastoral Constitution on the Church in the Modern World, nn. 47, 54–56, 63, 73, 77, in *Documents of Vatican II*, 249–50, 260–62, 271–72, 282–83, 289–90.

16. Pope Paul VI, *Octogesima Adveniens*, n. 4, in *Catholic Social Thought: A Documentary Heritage*, ed. David J. O'Brien and Thomas A. Shannon (Maryknoll, N.Y.: Orbis, 1992), 266.

17. Richard J. Regan, *Conflict and Consensus: Religious Freedom and the Second Vatican Council* (New York: Macmillan, 1976).

18. Robert Blair Kaiser, *The Politics of Sex and Religion: A Case History in the Development of Doctrine 1962–1984* (Kansas City, Mo.: Sheed and Ward, 1985).

Part Two

SEXUALITY, GENDER, MARRIAGE AND FAMILY

The many earlier talks and addresses given by Pope John Paul II on these subjects have been published in four volumes by the Daughters of St. Paul: *The Original Unity of Man and Woman: Catechesis on the Book of Genesis* (Boston: St. Paul Editions, 1981); *Blessed Are the Pure in Heart* (Boston: St. Paul Editions, 1983); *Reflections on Humanae Vitae* (Boston: St. Paul Editions 1984); *The Theology of Marriage and Celibacy* (Boston: St. Paul Editions, 1986).

Other later pertinent documents include:

Familiaris Consortio, 1983
Mulieris Dignitatem, 1988
Letter to Families, 1994
Letter to Women, 1995

11. Recent Ecclesiastical Teaching

Richard Grecco

This chapter first appeared in *The Sexual Revolution,* eds. Gregory Baum and John Coleman, in 1984.

POPE JOHN PAUL II'S THEOLOGY OF THE BODY

Pope John Paul II has used more than one hundred General Audiences to present a "theology of the body."[1] He develops his theological anthropology in three phases.[2]

1. The Pre-Historical Phase: "From the Beginning": Matthew 19:3–9

Twenty-two addresses from 5 September 1979 to 2 April 1980 outline John Paul II's meditation on Matthew 19:3–9. Jesus refers all those who would argue the indissolubility of marriage to return to "the beginning." John Paul II tries to follow Jesus' advice. He attempts to rediscover the original meaning of man as female and male. Establishing a theological anthropology which incorporates sexual polarity is the key, says John Paul II, to understanding indissolubility.

For John Paul II re-constructing the primordial meaning of sexuality is a universal, intuitive pursuit: first, because the redemption of the body "guarantees continuity and unity between the hereditary state of man's sin and his original innocence" (26 Sept. '79); second, because,

> our human experience is, in this case, to some extent a legit-
> imate means for theological interpretation, and is, in a cer-
> tain sense, an indispensable point of reference which we
> must keep in mind in the interpretation of the "beginning"
> (26 Sept. '79).

Revelation, an intuitive pursuit of the meaning of sexuality, and human experience characterize the method of John Paul II's theology of the body.

John Paul II interprets Genesis 1 as an objective description of sexuality. Its context is "free from any trace whatsoever of subjectivism" (12 Sept. '79). However, the second account of creation, contends John Paul II, reflects the subjective definition of man as male and female. Nineteen addresses based on the Yahwist tradition paint John Paul II's unique picture of primeval subjectivity. It is the subjective meaning of original solitude, communion, nakedness, innocence and shame which significantly distances this teaching from a rigid act-oriented approach to sexual morality. The nuptial meaning of the body for today, concludes John Paul II, depends partly on how well the person consciously appropriates the return to this pristine experience of the body. In his view, it is impossible to understand our present historical state (i.e., sinfulness) without referring first to our fundamental state of innocence, our image of God as female and male (26 Sept. '79). John Paul II's analysis of "the beginning" starts with the phenomenon of solitude. Solitude is the original act of self-consciousness. How is Adam made aware of being alone? Through a test before self and God, Adam examines the visible world of bodies and identifies them by name (Gen. 2:19). Through his dissimilarity he recognizes the self as apart, as namer, alone. Naming the creatures emphasizes subjectivity. Bodily visibility conveys the experience of dissimilarity but solitude is the meaning which the experience constitutes for the subject.

Recognizing solitude in the world is "self-knowledge." But what in the world is one's self? Consciousness of solitude inaugurates the search for identity.

> For created man finds himself right from the first moment
> of his existence *before God as if in search* of his own entity;
> it could be said: in search of a definition of himself. A con-
> temporary would say: in search of his own identity (10 Oct.
> '79).

For John Paul II human sexuality is set within the context of the person's search for identity.

It is significant, argues John Paul II, that the search for identity occurs in the world. It implies that consciousness and corporality grow through mutual interaction.

> Self-knowledge develops at the same rate as knowledge of the world, of all the visible creatures, of all living beings to which man has given a name to affirm his own dissimilarity with regard to them. In this way, therefore, consciousness reveals man as the one who possesses the cognitive faculty as regards *the visible world.* With this knowledge which, in a certain way, brings him out of his own being, *man* at the same time *reveals himself to himself in all the peculiarity of his being.* He is not only essentially and subjectively alone. Solitude, in fact, signifies man's subjectivity, which is constituted through self-knowledge. (10 Oct. '79).

Another constituent of subjectivity is the meaning of the body itself.

> Man is subject not only because of his self awareness…but also on the basis of his own body. The structure of the body is such as to permit him to be the author of a truly human activity. In this activity the body expresses the person (31 Oct. '79); (see also 24 Oct. '79).

Who one is, is expressed through the body. The person does not simply *have* a body. The body is constitutive of the subject and expresses interiority. Both the structure of consciousness and self-determination, says John Paul II, are constituted through the body. This is a fact "which cannot but be discovered when analyzing solitude" (31 Oct. '79). Although the search for identity begins in solitude, still there awaits "the new consciousness of the sense of one's body: A sense which, it can be said, consists in a *mutual enrichment*" (14 Nov. '79). It was not good for Adam to be alone, records the Yahwist. Alone he could discover much, yet…

> Man becomes the image of God not so much in the moment of solitude as in the moment of communion.…We can deduce that man became the "image and likeness" of God not only through his own humanity, but also through the

community of persons which man and woman form right
from the beginning (14 Nov. '79).

Sexuality, therefore, is not an attribute of the person but a constituent of
subjectivity (21 Nov. '79).

From a consciousness of solitude to an awareness of communion
through the sense of nakedness, innocence and shame, John Paul II
develops his understanding of the constituent elements of subjectivity.
He concludes that "from the beginning" the meaning of the body was
nuptial: a freedom to discover totally the giftedness of the body, sexuality, and consciousness so that the person gives freely and totally of self
in a mutual acceptance of the other as subject (16 Jan. '80).

On account of subjectivity the search for self-identity must
include a conscious effort to realize the meaning of one's sexuality. That
meaning is known through intimacy, interiority and communication:

> They see and know each other, in fact, with all the peace of
> the interior gaze, which creates precisely the fullness of the
> intimacy of persons...they "communicate" on the basis of
> that communion of persons in which, through femininity
> and masculinity, they become gift for each other. In this way
> they reach in reciprocity a special understanding of the
> meaning of their own body. Now the original meaning of
> nakedness corresponds to that simplicity and fullness of
> vision, in which understanding of the meaning of the body
> comes about, as it were, at the very heart of their commu-
> nity—communion. We call it nuptial (2 Jan. '80).

This search must begin with a return to primordial experience for "only
by returning to the beginning can man resist seeing man as object and
realize himself as subject" (2 Apr. '80).

2. The Historical Phase: "In the Heart": Matthew 5:27–28

Jesus' reference to the lustful look as adultery "in the heart" is the
second key to understanding the experience of sexuality. Objective acts
are not as important as who the person is becoming. "Moral value is
connected with the dynamic process of man's intimacy" (16 Apr. '80).

From 16 April 1980 until 6 May 1981, Matthew 5:27–28 is central to the development of phase two of his anthropology: the search for self-identity which necessarily includes the primordial experience of the body as female and male must give priority to the process of interiority. When Christ qualified a lustful look as adultery "in the heart," he appeals to the interior man (16 Apr. '80).

To unpack the historical meaning of man, John Paul II explains fear, shame, lust, disquiet, sin, struggle, adultery, eros and ethos. These do not reside in the heart. They ferment there. They shape the subject to be this or that kind of person. However, the historical experience of man is not as hopeless as these terms imply. John Paul II's anthropology and views on sexuality are neither Manichean nor pessimistic. The human heart is not totally corrupt. The power of redemption completes the work of creation (29 Oct. '80). The interior dynamic of man as female and male is being transformed by the spirit.

The following examples of the interiority of historical man highlight John Paul II's approach.

Adam's response, "I was afraid because I was naked and I hid myself," says John Paul II, represents a new state of consciousness. Previously they had sense knowledge of nudity yet suddenly they are conscious of fear and shame. "It is not a question here of passing from 'not knowing to knowing' but a radical change of the meaning of the original nakedness of the woman before the man and of the man before the woman" (12 Dec. '79).

Physically Adam tries to cover a reality that is much deeper, personhood. The fear is of the loss of the personal. This subjective loss of meaning is a cosmic shame as well. "It contains such a cognitive acuteness as to create a fundamental disquiet in the whole of human existence" (28 May '80).

Historically, man (as female and male) is alienated from self. This affects the *communio personarum.*

> The shame which according to the biblical narrative induces man and woman to hide from each other and their bodies, and in particular their sexual differentiation confirms that the original capacity of communicating themselves to each other...has been shattered (4 June '80).

The alienation of the body from personhood implies a reduction of the meaning of the body to the objective. Subjective meaning is reduced. This, argues John Paul II, is what lust, in all three of its forms, is all about (30 Apr. '80). By limiting the body to object, freedom is limited. This constraint prevents the personal gift of subject: "The relationship of the gift is changed into the relationship of appropriation" (23 July '80). Lust limits the nuptial meaning of the body (25 June '80).

The legalistic approach to adultery tends to objectify sexuality (20 Aug. '80). The objective meaning of adultery refers to a legal violation. The prophetic approach to adultery concerns subjective meaning. Adultery is a violation of the person (27 Aug. '80). It is a breakdown of a personal covenant which signifies the communion of two people. Besides fear, shame, lust, adultery, disquiet and sin "in the heart" there is also purity. John Paul II identifies "purity" with Paul's life in the spirit (14 and 28 Jan. '81). Purity of heart is striving to align the heart with the ethos of redemption, to confirm integral subjectivity (3 Dec. '80). John Paul II notes that the facts, situations, and institutions of Jewish society at that time provided an ethos of "hardened hearts" (Matt. 5:27–28). According to. P. Ricoeur, says John Paul II, Nietzsche, Freud and Marx were masters of suspicion of the human heart. Their philosophical, psychological, and social theories all converged on the corruption of the human heart as the fundamental principle for interpreting man. John Paul II takes extra care to insist that the Christian cannot do this. The reason is in Matthew 5:27–28. Jesus makes an appeal precisely to the heart to rise above the evil in the heart. The basis for an appeal to the heart and the foundation of hope is "the ethos of redemption."

> Man cannot stop at putting the heart in a state of continual and irreversible suspicion due to the manifestations of lust of the flesh and libido....Redemption is a truth, a reality in the name of which man must feel called, and called with efficacy....

> Man must feel called to rediscover, nay more, to realize the Nuptial meaning of the body and to express in this way the interior freedom of the gift...(29 Oct. '80).

Interiority is the subjective dynamic by which the experience of frailty and sin come to be accepted (i.e. as components of subjectivity) in order to be transformed; only then does bodily expression signify moral uprightness, self-fulfillment and spiritualization. Only as subjective *gift* does the body convey and constitute the meaning of "the beginning."

3. The Eschatological Phase: Matthew 22:23–33

John Paul II finds the final key to a holistic vision of man as female and male in Jesus' blunt reply to the Sadducees about marriage after death; "You don't know the scriptures or the power of God; they will be like angels…men and women will not marry."

The Resurrection, states John Paul II, completes the revelation of the body. Life in the "other world" has an impact on the meaning of who I am and who we are as subjects. Since the Resurrection affects the person, whether celibate or married, consideration must be given to the redemption of the body. From 16 November 1981 to 10 February 1982 Matthew 22:23–33 and 1 Corinthians 15 is the focus of John Paul II's attention.

The Resurrection reveals the completion of subjectivity and intersubjectivity.

> This concentration (of knowledge; vision) will be above all man's rediscovery of himself, not only in the depth of his own person, but also in that union which is proper to the world of persons in their psychosomatic constitution. This is certainly a union of communion.

> We must think of the reality of the "other world" in the categories of the rediscovery of a new perfect subjectivity of everyone and at the same time of the rediscovery of a new perfect intersubjectivity of all (16 Dec. '81).

This perfection of subjectivity includes the body.

> The resurrection will consist in the perfect participation of all that is physical in man in what is spiritual in him…it will consist in the perfect realization of what is personal in man (9 Dec. '81). The resurrection constitutes the definitive accomplishment of the redemption of the body (27 Jan. '81).

Because of the meaning of pre-historical and historical man John Paul II
is anxious to deny that the spiritualization or divinization of the body
has anything to do with disincarnation or dehumanization (2 Dec. '81
and 9 Dec. '81). Christ's words, says John Paul II "seem to affirm...that
human bodies, recovered and at the same time renewed in the Resurrection, will keep their masculine or feminine peculiarity" (2 Dec. '81 and
13 Jan. '82). The person retains her or his psychosomatic nature. Yet,
John Paul II is equally anxious to point out that the resurrection "signifies a realization of the primacy of the Spirit" (9 Dec. '81). The person
exists in a new way. The body is both dominated and permeated by the
Spirit (9 Dec. '81). He says the person is divinized or spiritualized. "The
Resurrection means a new submission of the body to the spirit" (2 Dec.
'81).

The Resurrection is an experience available to historical man on
account of "the beginning" and on account of Christ. Relying on Pauline
texts, John Paul II connects the phases of anthropology. "Every man
bears in himself the Image of Adam and every man also is called to bear
in himself the Image of Christ, the Image of the Risen One" (3 Feb. '82).
The reality of the Resurrection is connected therefore to the experience
of historical man in an existential way. "It is a reality ingrafted in the
man of 'this world,' a reality that is developed in him toward final completion" (3 Feb. '82). Each person experiences eschatological reality.
Each person is in touch with "eschatological man" (9 Dec. '81), because
the human body bears in itself

> the "potentiality for Resurrection," that is, the aspiration and
> capacity to become definitively "incorruptible, glorious, full
> of dynamism, spiritual," this happens because, persisting
> from the beginning in psychosomatic unity of the personal
> being, he can receive and reproduce in this "earthly" image
> and likeness of God also the "heavenly" image of the second
> Adam, Christ (3 Feb. '82). (See also 13 Jan. '82.)

About revelation, John Paul II is explicit. It not only conveys conceptual
information, but on account of the body enables "the historical body to
go beyond the sphere of its experience of the body" (16 Dec. '81).
Christ reveals truth but the truth of a humanly experienced reality. Fur-

thermore, adds John Paul II, the truth about both dimensions is unavailable to empirical and rationalistic methods (13 Jan. '82).

John Paul II then proceeds to discuss celibacy and virginity. He bases thirteen addresses from 10 March 1982 to 21 July 1982 on Matthew 19:11–12 and 1 Corinthians 7. Then from 28 July 1982 to 15 December 1982 sixteen audiences delve into the sacrament of marriage. He bases these meditations on Ephesians 5:21–33. Both marriage and celibacy must be understood in the context of a Christian anthropology which takes a holistic view of pre-historical, historical and eschatological experience.

John Paul II concludes with three very interesting presentations on the language of the body. The person embodies the language of the Spirit. "He has already been constituted in such a way from the 'beginning,' in such wise that the most profound words of the Spirit—words of love, of giving, of fidelity—demand an adequate 'language of the body.' And without that they cannot be fully expressed" (12 Jan. '83). Relying on the Prophets and Paul, John Paul II identifies the body as the primordial sacrament of creation, of the person and of God. Its feminine and masculine structure expressed the complexity of meaning which is called Covenant. Conjugal behavior involves a language of tenderness expressing love, fidelity, uprightness and union. This language corresponds to the meaning authored by God in the very constitution of man "from the beginning" (26 Jan. '83).

> If the prophetic texts indicate conjugal fidelity and chastity as "truth" and adultery or harlotry, on the other hand, as "non-truth," as a falsity of the "language of the body," (then) this happens because…the subject (that is, Israel as a Spouse) is in accord with the spousal significance which corresponds to the human body (because of its masculinity or femininity) in the integral structure of the person (12 Jan. '83).

For John Paul II it is not so much a question of authoring one's own body language. It is a language "which God originated, by creating man as male and female, which Christ renewed" (19 Jan. '83). The issue is to rediscover and re-read the language which once bespoke the subject. Re-reading this language in truth is an "indispensable" condition of the sacrament (19 Jan. '83).

REMARKS

One reviewer ardently characterizes John Paul II's theology of sexuality as "revolutionary."[3] Probably this is an exaggeration. Nevertheless, John Paul II's originality does compel a degree of enthusiasm.

First, John Paul II is offering theological understanding, not simply rules about sexual behavior. There is here the potential to modify the ethical model of official Church teaching. Whereas a legalistic model for sexual ethics emphasized the objective meaning of sexuality,[4] John Paul II's theology of the body attends to the subjective dimension. This anthropological development is the most salient feature in recent ecclesiastical teaching. It promotes a personalistic model for ethical theory.

Second, instead of a natural law theory expressed in a Neo-scholastic language, John Paul II's method is experiential. An extensive reliance on biblical texts, a conviction about the intuitive pursuit of the meaning of sexuality and the attempt to connect these to human experience typify John Paul II's methodology.

Third, his new emphasis on subjectivity and experience steers a course away from rationalism towards a wider and more relational appreciation of the ways of knowing. Intimacy, tenderness, spontaneity, body language and interiority are non-rationalistic modes of learning and growing.

Originality can tease the imagination, inspire the mind, challenge the spirit and move the heart, yet leave the person free. It is one indicator that motivation, not indoctrination, is the objective of the educator. Because originality tends to motivate there is a pedagogical reason for enthusiasm. Because this quality is especially important in moral matters, there is pastoral cause for further study of John Paul II's work.

Finally, there are a few questions that need exploration.

(a) About subjectivity. John Paul II pays relative inattention to the social sciences and this has consequences. For example, of man and woman he says, "their conjugal union presupposes a mature consciousness of the body" (21 Nov. '79). The way to such "maturity" entails a search in all three dimensions of experience. But developmental theories of consciousness indicate that many, if not most people never achieve the high degree of authentic subjectivity that he describes.[5] Can Church teaching realistically presuppose such keenly developed levels

of subjectivity? If empirical data show that it cannot, then is not the implication a revision to the Church's teaching on indissolubility?

(b) About terminology. What do the terms "experience," "eschatological man" and "ethos" mean? Sometimes "experience" refers to sense-knowledge, at other times to aspects of self-consciousness or intuition. "Eschatological man," despite John Paul II's three phase approach, seems to refer exclusively to a thoroughly unrealized eschaton. "Ethos" at times refers to the state of redemption and at other times to cultural norms opposed to the Gospel. These terms are a few examples which indicate an ambiguity[6] in John Paul II's approach.

(c) About the structure of consciousness. John Paul II's approach to the meaning of the body seems to be overly structured, almost mechanistic or pre-programmed. His emphasis, for example, on re-creating, re-constructing, re-discovering the meaning and then re-reading the language of the body appears somewhat exaggerated. What does such an emphasis say about the spontaneity of human expression and about human creativity and individuality?

The ecclesiastical teaching identified in this report as Pope John Paul II's theology of the body is original on account of its emphasis on subjectivity, its methodology, and its avoidance of rationalism. This uniqueness raises many interesting questions. Both the originality and the questions it poses may indicate a shift in ecclesiastical teaching. Undoubtedly, they are cause for further study.

Notes

1. All references are to the date of the audience itself. The quotations are taken from the English edition of the *Osservatore Romano*.

2. The "total vision of Man" must integrate all three dimensions of anthropology, past, present, future (2 Apr. '80).

3. Marcel Clément, "Une Théologie de la Sexualité" in *L'Homme Nouveau*, no. 797 (1 Nov. '81), p. 1, published in France, Belgium and Canada. This is his first in a series of fifteen commentaries: 798 (15 Nov. '81), 799 (6 Dec. '81), 800 (20 Dec. '81), 801 (3 Jan. '82), 802 (17 Jan. '82), 803 (7 Feb. '82), 804 (21 Feb. '82), 805 (7 Mar. '82), 806 (21 Mar. '82), 807 (4 Apr. '82), 808 (18 Apr. '82), 809 (2 May '82), 810 (16 May '82). It is preceded by "Les fondements de la théologie de Jean-Paul" par Aline Lizotte, 796 (18 Oct. '81).

4. The "Declaration on Certain Questions Concerning Sexual Ethics" is a good example of such an approach. For a precise summary of theological opinion on this see Richard A. McCormick, S.J., *Notes on Moral Theology 1965 through 1980* (Washington, 1981), pp. 668–682.

5. For example, the six stages of moral development theorized by Lawrence Kohlberg; see "Education for Justice: A Modern Statement of the Platonic View" in *Moral Education: Five Lectures* (Cambridge Mass: Harvard Press, 1970), 57–83. For a theological attempt to connect the developmental theories of Piaget, Erikson, and Kohlberg with a transcendental theory of conscience, see Walter E. Conn, *Conscience: Development and Self-Transcendence* (Birmingham, Alabama, 1981). James W. Fowler has utilized a developmental approach to explain the process of faith. "Faith Development Theory and the Aims of Religious Socialization" in *Emerging Issues in Religious Education*, ed. Gloria Durka and Joanmarie Smith (New York, 1976), pp. 187–208, and his *Life Maps: Conversations on the Journey of Faith* (Waco, Texas, 1978); see also his "Stages in Faith, the Structural-Developmental Approach" in *Values and Moral Development*, ed. Thomas C. Hennessy, S.J. (New York, 1976), pp. 173–223.

6. Ronald Modras explores the ambiguity of John Paul II's personalistic ethics in "The Moral Philosophy of Pope John Paul II," in *Theological Studies* 41 (Dec. 1980) 683–697.

12. Pope John Paul II's Theology of the Body

Ronald Modras

This chapter first appeared in *The Vatican and Homosexuality,* eds. Jeannine Gramick and Pat Furey, in 1988.

The Vatican letter on the pastoral care of homosexual persons may have been signed by Joseph Ratzinger, cardinal prefect of the Congregation for the Doctrine of the Faith, but its contents and terminology bear the marks of Pope John Paul II. Not only approved but obviously also authorized by the pontiff, the letter is infused with his thinking and constitutes but one more item on the already considerable list of pronouncements that have emanated from this pontificate relating to sexuality. It contributes but one more reason for puzzlement as to the cause for what appears at first glance as almost an obsession with the subject.

Not only the existence of the letter but its language and ideas can be clarified when perceived within the framework and from the background of Pope John Paul II's theology of the body and human sexuality. Time and again the letter speaks of "the truth" about the human person, a phrase that has become a hallmark of his discourse. The letter maintains that homosexuality is to be properly understood from the standpoint of the first chapters of the biblical book of Genesis, the subject of a lengthy series of papal addresses. Both in those addresses and the Ratzinger letter, reference is made to the "spousal significance" of the body, now "obscured by original sin." The letter, like the pope, identifies love as self-giving born of self-denial. Most telling of all, however, nowhere does the letter speak of homosexuality in terms of nature nor are homosexual acts described as being contrary to natural law or as sins against nature. Instead, the letter makes the highly controversial and problematic claim that the homosexual condition itself, although not a sin, is an "objective disorder."

Space does not allow a lengthy let alone exhaustive elaboration of the pope's anthropology as it impinges on sexual morality. Only the more salient features can be outlined as they relate to the Vatican letter. Even so modest an essay, however, may serve to clarify the foundations and fuller implications of the often obscure, sometimes ambiguous references in the pope's theology of the body and human sexuality.

THOMISTIC PERSONALISM

If the pope's theology of the body is sometimes ambiguous, it is because it can appear so revolutionary and original at first. He uses the language of personalism and the phenomenological method of description in his analyses of sexuality. He speaks rarely about nature and often about persons, personal dignity and responsibility, and so appears to have broken with his neo-Thomistic training with its insistence upon immutable natural laws. Upon a closer examination, however, the pope is a skillful and energetic exponent of the neo-Thomistic natural law ethic, as he translates it into personalist categories and calls it "Thomistic personalism."

Karol Wojtyla wrote an article under that title in 1961.[1] In it he described personhood as the "highest perfection" in the created order, but time and again spoke of human emotions and feelings as something to be dominated and subordinated by the rational will. So too in his book, *The Acting Person*,[2] Wojtyla describes human transcendence and spirituality in terms of self-domination. Although he constantly refers to personhood with its connotations of unity and integration, Wojtyla still maintains the old Platonic dualism with its suspicion of the body and its passions. The soul, for him, is the principle which allows us to possess and govern our bodies like a "compliant tool."

Wojtyla espouses a stratified concept of the human person. Like the pagan Stoics and medieval schoolmen, he views the emotions as dangerous if not evil. They are part of our "lower" sphere, requiring control by the "higher" sphere, the intellect and will, in an "absolute manner" if need be (p. 315, n. 72). Such self-control constitutes, for Wojtyla, authentic spiritual power and is, he writes, "probably the most fundamental manifestation of the *worth* of the person" (p. 264). It is difficult to conceive of a higher valuation of the category of control.

His stratified, dualistic body-soul anthropology lies at the basis of Wojtyla's *Love and Responsibility,*[3] the fullest exposition of his thinking on sexual ethics before he became pope. Here too, although he uses words like "person" and "love" liberally, his understanding of those terms is hardly that of his readers. Like his arguments, his definitions refer constantly to nature. Like his neo-Thomistic teachers, he describes the sexual urge as a specific force of nature whose natural end is procreation. True love, he argues, is not an emotion. It is the virtue or habit of goodwill *(benevolentia),* whereby the rational will affirms the value of a person. Such affirmation requires "subordination" to the laws of nature. "In the order of love a man can remain true to the person only in so far as he is true to nature. If he does violence to 'nature,' he also 'violates' the person by making it an object of enjoyment rather than an object of love" (p. 229). With love so linked to nature, one can see why Wojtyla attacks artificial birth control so aggressively. Procreation is not distinct from love, nor love from procreation. Contraception has "a damaging effect on love" (p.53), and "the correct attitude toward procreation is a condition for the realization of love"(p. 226).

Karol Wojtyla has never been one for offering empirical evidence for such claims. Instead, his argument is philosophical, an appeal to the moral imperative first formulated by Immanuel Kant: a person must not be *merely* the means to an end for another person. Artificial contraception, he contends (and a fortiori homosexual activity), is a matter of two people using one another for "mutual, or rather, bilateral 'enjoyment.'" This is not love, he concludes, but utilitarianism. If there is a weakness in Wojtyla's argument, it hinges upon the word *merely.* Although he states the Kantian imperative correctly the frist time he quotes it, he thereafter regularly omits the crucial word *merely.* We cannot help but make use of other persons as means, as we deal with each other. The pope uses cardinals the way the rest of us use mechanics and grocery clerks. Kant's principle forbids using persons "merely" as means without recognizing their value "at the same time as an end." Wojtyla simply asserts without further argumentation or qualification that "anyone who treats a person as the means to an end does violence to the very essence of the other" (p. 27).

In treating of the erotic and emotional aspects of sexuality, Wojtyla says at first that the benevolence or goodwill that is genuine love can "keep company" with the love that is desire, so long as desire "does not overwhelm all else" (p. 84). Further into his exposition, however, the language becomes more negative: the will "combats" the sexual urge and "atones" for the desire to have the other person. Genuine love is the antithesis of emotional desire, and a couple "must free themselves from those erotic sensations which have no legitimation in true love." Wojtyla describes love as a "duty" whereas sexual desire or concupiscence "means a constant tendency merely to 'enjoy'" (p. 160).

Assisting us in performing our duty is the virtue of chastity, which "implies liberation from everything that 'makes dirty.' Love must be so to speak pellucid." Wojtyla does not explicitly describe sexual feelings as dirty, but he does imply it when he writes that "sensations and actions springing from sexual reactions and the emotions connected with them tend to deprive love of its crystal clarity" (p. 146). Sexual emotions or enjoyment are not evil in themselves, but only if dissociated from procreation. God's attitude toward contraception is comparable to that of a father when his child, to whom he gave bread and jam, throws away the bread and eats only the jam (p. 309, n. 66).

Long before becoming pope, Karol Wojtyla evinced an unremitting interest in sexuality. In 1971 he wrote about concupiscence, which we may here define as spontaneous sexual desire, as destroying human dignity and impoverishing the world. Even concepts like salvation are more fully intelligible in the context of "overcoming concupiscence."[4] Clearly, birth control and homosexual acts are not peripheral matters of secondary importance to him. Sexual ethics, he wrote in 1978, possess "such powerful anthropological implications" that it has become the battlefield for a "struggle concerning the dignity and meaning of humanity itself."[5]

SEXUAL DESIRE AND DISORDER

Less than a year after becoming pope, Karol Wojtyla began a remarkable series of addresses on the first chapters of Genesis.[6] Pilgrims and tourists who had come to a general audience to catch a glimpse of the pope were accorded an erudite theological exposition on marriage, sexuality, and original sin. The addresses, accompanied by elaborate footnotes, bear all the features of a book the pope had been writing prior to his election. The work is not one of biblical scholarship; the pope does not pretend to be a biblical scholar and only infrequently relies upon modern biblical exegesis. The talks comprise a "catechesis," as they are subtitled, on the Book of Genesis, or rather on a particular school of interpreting Genesis, namely, that of Saint Augustine. (Jewish, Eastern Orthodox, and contemporary historical-critical interpretations are quite different.)

Although he acknowledges that the first chapters of Genesis have a "mythical character" (p. 28), the pope treats the creation stories as if they were history, or, as he calls them, "revealed theological pre-history" (p. 37). The reader may be confused at first, since one is not altogether sure whether Adam ("humankind") is regarded as a historical individual engaged in historical events or a symbolic representation of ourselves in our present human condition. In either case, the pope uses the creation stories not so much for substantiation as for inspiration or a jumping-off point for his own personal reflections. Those reflections in no way contradict his earlier ideas but rather restate them. Once again he affirms the importance of self-control but now in terms of the ability of a person's self-gift to another, described by the pope as the "nuptial" or "spousal" meaning of the body.

The pope can be profound as he expounds upon our call to a "community of persons" achieved by self-giving. More problematic, however, is his discussion of the spontaneous sexual desire that Catholic theological tradition has come to call concupiscence.[7] Together with the Genesis story of Adam and Eve, the pope conjoins the words of Matthew 5:28 ("Everyone who looks at a woman lustfully has already committed adultery with her in his heart") and of 1 John 2:16 ("For all that is in the world, the lust of the flesh, and the lust of the eyes, and the pride of life, is not of the Father but is of the world"). The pope interprets these texts not within their own distinct historical contexts but in the light of one another, assuming that they share a common theological vision and attitude toward the body and its sexuality. The attitude is very much that of Augustine as the Pope describes the sin of Adam and its sexual consequences in terms of "cosmic shame" (p. 48).

Absent are any references to "mythical character" as the pope draws an historical "state of original innocence" from the first chapters of Genesis (p. 71). Adam is obviously not a symbol but a historical individual and his sin an event whose "cosmic shame" is indicated by our sexual shame. The pope not only interprets the Genesis story historically but assumes that the nakedness of Adam and Eve implies their original "self-mastery" and "self-control" over their sexual organs (p. 51). They were created "above the world of living beings or 'animalia'" (p. 52), capable of "disinterested" self-giving without any taint of the selfish "enjoyment" that is the negation of the "nuptial meaning" of the body (p. 83.). The loss of original innocence resulted in a "constitutive break within the human person, almost a rupture of man's original spiritual and somatic unity" (p. 50). As a consequence of that first sin, our bodies are marked by the "humiliation" that is spontaneous sexual desire or concupiscence (p. 50).

The pope uses words like "imbalance" and "distortion" (p. 72) to describe the concupiscence or "lust of the flesh" that is now a permanent element or "disposition derived from man's sinfulness" (p. 145). The human heart has become a "battlefield" between the "sincere giving" that is love and the lust that seeks to "appropriate" another as an object of enjoyment (pp. 75–77). Because of that first sin, "'the desire of the body' is more powerful than 'the desire of the mind'" (p. 84). We can become gifts to and for one another (the "nuptial meaning" of the body) only if we have self-control. Concupiscence "limits" and "reduces" self-control (p. 77) and makes us "ashamed" of our bodies (p. 53).

Here, within the context of concupiscence as the pope under-stands it, we can properly understand the controversial reference in the Vatican letter to homosexuality as a "disorder." The word should not be taken to mean a psychological or even a moral disorder, since the letter makes clear that the homosexual condition is not a sin. Within the framework of the pope's theology, however, homosexuality is the result of sin. God simply could not, would not, and did not create homosexuals as such. The homosexual condition is a result of the first sin, an aspect or form of the concupiscence that is the condition of us all. Unwilled, spontaneous sexual attraction or desire for someone of the same sex is a "disorder" in the same way that unwilled, spontaneous sexual attraction or desire for anyone is an "imbalance" and "distortion."

According to the pope's theology of the body, it is a disposition "derived from man's sinfulness" that we do not have our sexual inclina-tions and desires completely under our rational control. It is a "disorder" and "distortion" since, for the pope as for Augustine, sexuality was cre-ated for procreation, not enjoyment. Homosexual persons are bound to combat and control their erotic impulses the same way that heterosexual and even married persons are. Disinterested self-giving is the only love that is genuine, and homosexual acts, like birth control, are the antithesis of such love.

Pope John Paul II's language is abstract, at times turgid, and often ambiguous. He created an outcry when he stated that it was possible for a husband and wife to commit adultery with one another "in the heart" (8 October 1980). Apologists hurried to point out that such adultery "in the heart" results from spouses using one another for "mere satisfaction" of their sexual needs. To quote the pope completely: "Man can commit this adultery 'in the heart' also with regard to his own wife, if he treats her only as an object to satisfy instinct" (p. 145). What the apologists usually fail to point out is that, for Pope John Paul II, birth control is precisely an example of spouses using one another for "mere satisfaction" and therefore is a matter of adultery "in the heart."

Pope John Paul II is an attractive and charismatic evangelist of Thomistic personalism and the theology of the body and sexuality he derives from it. The idea, however, of a historical Adam in complete control of his sexual organs cannot help but pose some difficulties for contemporary biblical scholars. Psychologists will question whether a completely self-giving love is possible, and if complete rational self-control to the detriment of spontaneity is altogether desirable. Karl Rahner, the foremost Catholic theologian of our century, has pointed out that concupiscence is natural, since, according to Catholic tradition, freedom from it is preternatural and so not required by human nature. If Adam in the Genesis story was free from concupiscence, it did not stop him from sinning. It follows, moreover, that if concupiscence limits our self-control and thereby our totally free self-giving to virtue, it also limits our totally free self-giving to vice. If it keeps us from being angels, it keeps us from being demonic as well.[8]

But it is not biblical scholars, theologians, or psychologists who pose the greatest resistance to the pope's theology of the body. The pope speaks to the masses of Catholic faithful, and it is the masses of the faithful he will have to convince. His persuasive powers are considerable, but he will have to confront more thoroughly something to which homosexual persons and married couples practicing birth control both appeal. The pope is intelligent and articulate, but he has to contend with something more formidable than ideas. Whether it is a matter of describing birth control as adultery "in the heart" or the homosexual condition as a "disorder," the greatest challenge to the pope's theology of the body and its sexuality is people's experience. What the pope approaches from the outside and calls lust, they live on the inside and call love. More than anything else, it is the experience of their lives, reflected on in the faith and sustained by the sacraments, which lead them respectfully to disagree.

Notes

1. "Personalizm Tomistyczny," *Znak* 13 (1961): 664–76.

2. *The Acting Person* (Dordrecht, Holland/Boston: D. Reidel, 1979).

3. *Love and Responsibility* (New York: Farrar, Straus & Giroux, 1981).

4. "Notatki na Marginesie Konstytucji 'Gaudium et Spes,'" *Atheneum Kaplanskie* 74 (1970): 3–6.

5. "Antropologia Encykliki 'Humanae Vitae,'" *Analecta Cracoviensia* 10 (1978): 13.

6. The addresses first appeared in English translation in *L'Osservatore Romano*, English Edition. They have been subsequently compiled and reprinted as a series in book form by the Daughters of St. Paul: *Original Unity of Man and Woman, Catechesis on the Book of Genesis*, with a preface by Donald W. Wuerl (Boston: St. Paul Editions, 1981).

7. *Blessed Are the Pure of Heart, Catechesis on the Sermon on the Mount and Writings of St. Paul*, with a preface by Donald W. Wuerl (Boston: St. Paul Editions, 1983).

8. K. Rahner, "The Theological Concept of Concupiscentia," *Theological Investigations,* vol. 1 (Baltimore: Helicon, 1961).

13. The Family and Sexuality

Richard M. Hogan
John M. LeVoir

This chapter first appeared in the authors' *Covenant of Love: Pope John Paul II on Sexuality, Marriage, and Family in the Modern World* in 1985.

A. MAN AND WOMAN (IMAGES OF GOD) AND LOVE

After twenty-five years of thought and reflection on marriage and the family, Karol Wojtyla was called to the chair of Saint Peter. As a theologian in his own right, he developed a new understanding of the moral precepts of Christ. This development can already be seen in his early work, *Love and Responsibility.* Later, as archbishop of Kracow and as a participant in the Second Vatican Council, he proposed his new moral theology to the other conciliar fathers. His new understanding was received by the council and became part of its teaching in the *Pastoral Constitution on the Church in the Modern World.* Now, as the Vicar of Christ, John Paul II has offered the world his fully matured moral theology in his papal addresses entitled *Theology of the Body* and in his *Apostolic Exhortation on the Family.* Since this new development is found in the conciliar documents, John Paul II is teaching us what the Second Vatican Council intended.

The central idea in the new theology of John Paul II is the subjective turn founded on the revelation in Genesis that we are made in God's image. Endowed with a likeness to God, we have been created to act as He does, i.e., to love, to give ourselves as He does within the Holy Trinity. Our dignity lies in our similarity to God. When we fail to act as He does, we destroy ourselves and our dignity. As John Paul wrote in his first encyclical, "Man cannot live without love. He remains a being that is incomprehensible for himself, his life is senseless."[1] Continuing the same theme in his document on family life, the Pope says, "Love is therefore the fundamental and innate vocation of every human being."[2] Thus, the Holy Father insists that we must love. This necessity flows from within ourselves. God does not compel us to love. Rather, the obligation to love is derived from the kind of creatures we are, i.e., persons made in the image of God.

However, God must show us how to love because love is primarily a divine activity in which we, through God's creative act, are called to share. (Thus, Christ, the God-man, is absolutely central to each and every human being. Only in Him can we see how God loves, i.e., how we should love.) We know from revelation, i.e., from the Old Testament and most perfectly from Christ, that God loves through a complete self-donation of Himself. This love is perfectly present in the Holy Trinity where each divine Person totally surrenders Himself to the others. This total self-gift of each Person within the Trinity, while preserving the distinct features of each Person (Father, Son, Holy Spirit), establishes a complete union of wills. The love of each divine Person is a personal choice, a will-act, made by each based on knowledge of the truth. The self-donation of each divine Person to the others unites all three in a *communion of persons.* In effect, there is an attitude, a choice, to act as one. This is what love is: an act of the will to do what another wills.

God's self-gift of Himself is extended to us and made known to us in the creation and most especially in the redemption. In creation, God shared Himself with us and all creation because He shared what He is: existence. He gave Himself to what He created. Of course, in a unique way, He gave Himself to man and woman when He created Adam and Even in His own image. But His creative act, as much of a self-surrender as it was, is infinitely less precious than the total abnegation of self that is manifested in the incarnation. As Saint Paul wrote, "Though He was in the form of God, [Jesus] did not count equality with God a thing to be grasped, but emptied Himself, taking the form of a servant being born in the likeness of men."[3] The incarnation, God taking the nature of one of His creatures, shows us how God loves. But even the assumption of a human nature did not completely reveal the full extent of God's love. Only on the cross do we see how far the self-surrender of God extends. He gave Himself for our sakes that we might have life. He gave until He had nothing more to give and He did it totally for us. This is love! Since we are made in God's likeness, we are made to love as He did and does:

an all-encompassing self-surrender for the sake of others. Only when we mirror the love of the Trinity in our love do we fulfill ourselves as God created us. Only then is life meaningful.

Wojtyla points out that the vocation to give ourselves in love is a call given to us because we are persons: creatures endowed with minds and wills. In other words, as personal beings, we can know the truth and we can choose to give ourselves to another person or persons. Thus, like the Trinity, we have the capability of entering a *communion of persons.* We are first called to enter a *communion of persons* with God and then with other human beings. Failure to form a *communion of persons* is an attack, an aggression, against our very persons. We must love. It is a subjective need which every human being has.

Of course, a *communion of persons,* a relationship of love, cannot be established unless there are at least two persons who individually choose through a personal will-act to give themselves to each other. Thus, we cannot, properly speaking, love a thing or even an animal. These beings do not have wills; they do not have the ability to give themselves to others. They cannot love and since love is a reciprocal gift of at least two persons, we cannot love them.

Love is an activity proper to persons. Love is also the *only* way to relate to persons. In one of his early works on love, John Paul teaches that a "person is a good towards which the only proper adequate attitude is love." "This [personalistic] norm, in its negative aspect, states that the person is a kind of good which does not admit of use and cannot be treated as an object of use and as such the means to an end."[4] The dignity of persons as created in God's image makes them superior to the remainder of creation. That superiority gives them a right to be treasured for their own sakes, not as means to an end. We must, then, relate to other persons only through love, i.e., in and through a *communion of persons.* The dignity of other persons and our own dignity require such a stance. Should one person treat another as a means to an end, as someone to be used, the second becomes, for the first, less than a personal being. The first person is reducing the second to a thing. Of necessity, because the first person is equal to the second, the first is also reducing himself/herself to a thing. The dignity of persons, our own and that of others, requires that the personalistic norm always be observed.

As human persons, we are not merely spirits. We have bodies and they, as we have seen, are given to us by God as part of the gift of life so that our persons might be expressed in a physical way. Of all the persons in the universe, the three Persons in God, the angels, and humans, only human persons have bodies. Of all the bodily creatures in the world, only we are persons. Thus, we are unique. Only we can express in the physical world how a person loves. Only we can manifest a *communion of persons* in a physical way. The body is the means by which our love is expressed. But it is also a means by which the love of others may be received. As such, it can only be viewed as an object of love. The body is not an appendage which a person carries around with him/her. To treat the body as a thing is to treat the person as a thing. The body is the expression of the person and it should be loved as the person should be loved. The personalistic norm is not limited to the spiritual aspects of persons. It includes the bodies of persons. We may never exclude the body from the dignity proper to personal beings. Many different practices traditionally taboo in most societies could be justified if the body were divorced from the person. But we dare not permit such an opinion to gain acceptance because it would irreparably harm human dignity.

B. The Family Is a *Communion of Persons*

In His creative act, God specified two particular communions which should exist for us when He said to Adam and Eve, "Be fruitful and multiply, and fill the earth and subdue it."[5] We are called, by creation and "from the beginning," to enter into a *communion of persons* so that we may increase and multiply and to enter into a communion so that the earth might be subdued. Of course, the first communion is the family. The second is that found in the workplace. In both communions, the activity of man and woman reflects the acts of God, not only in the self-gift which establishes the communions, but also in the effects of the self-gift. When God loves, it is life-giving. When man and woman love within the family, new life is brought forth. When people work, they dominate creation. They are acting in a way analogous to God, who, as the Creator, has total dominion over the world. Still, the first communion is the more fundamental. It is the one which reflects God's trinitarian life more closely because it is a total self-surrender of one person to another. In the workplace, we do not give ourselves completely to one another. Second, the *communion of persons* of the family is life-giving whereas that of the workplace is not. The love of a man and a woman is usually fertile as God's love is fertile. Thus, in this way, the *communion of persons* which is the family reflects God's love more closely. It is appropriate to consider the family as the first and most important *communion of persons* and then to examine the relationships which should exist in the workplace.

"Male and female He created them."[6] If we are called to love one another, as God loves, i.e., to surrender ourselves completely to one another, and if our bodies are to express our persons, it is most appropriate that there be bodily differences which allow us to express our love for one another. By God's holy will, there are such differences: God created us as men and women (although both male and female bodies equally express the human person). The physical gift of a man and a woman to each other is the outward sign, the sacrament, of the familial *communion of persons.* The body, then, is the means and the sign of the gift of the male-person to the female-person. The Holy Father calls this capacity of the body to express the total self-surrender of one person to another the nuptial meaning of the body. In this total physical surrender based on *communion of persons,* the married couple becomes, physically, an image of God. When a married couple acts in accordance with their vows and God's will, they are a sign (a sacrament), a physical manifestation, of the love of persons. They are an image of God in their bodily gift to one another.

The Pope also stresses that the communion of two persons expressed through their bodies is a mutual giving and acceptance. The gift of each spouse mirrors God's gift of Himself in creation. Each spouse gives himself/herself as the Creator did when He created the world. He/She gives himself/herself for the sake of the other. Similarly, the acceptance of the other's gift on the part of each spouse is an act of gratitude to the Creator for the gift. The entire physical creation participates in the gratitude of the man and the woman to the Creator for the gift each has received. The married couple gives as God gives and each responds with gratitude and in that response, all creation responds to the Creator thanking Him for the gift of being. At one and the same time, the couple is an image of God and a sign of creation's response to the Creator.

In his *Theology of the Body* series, the Holy Father defended the ancient biblical terminology for the sexual union of a man and a woman: to know. Of course, since we gain self-knowledge through our acts, the self-gift of a husband and a wife to one another does reveal to each of them more about themselves. But the knowledge gleaned from the gift of a husband and a wife to one another transcends the truth they know about themselves from their other acts because this act of self-surrender is more God-like. The gift of love, acting as God does, expressed through the body, touches the central mystery of the human person in a way in which most of our other acts do not. Therefore, the verb, to know, is most accurate for the self-gift of a man and a woman to one another.

The knowledge gleaned from this act may be specified in three areas. First, there is the knowledge of oneself and the other in the mutual *communion of persons.* In this mutual giving, one experiences and knows oneself as well as the other in a much fuller way than would otherwise be possible. Second, the hidden treasures of humanity are revealed in motherhood and fatherhood. The woman, whose femininity is hidden, is revealed to herself and to others (especially to her husband) in motherhood. Similarly, the new relationship of the male to the child, fatherhood, reveals to the husband and to others (especially to his wife) an aspect of humanity not previously experienced. Third, in the child, both the man and the woman see and know themselves.

Of course, true love, the surrender of oneself to another, is a freely chosen act of a person. Acts of human persons have (or should have) their origins in the faculties of mind and will. The physical union of a man and a woman is not simply an act of their bodies. It is founded on their marriage vows. These vows are choices or will-acts grounded in the dignity of the beloved by which an irrevocable union—a *communion of persons*—is established. This communion can then be expressed in the physical order through their bodies because God gave their bodies a nuptial meaning when He created them male and female.

Marriage vows, then, are freely chosen will-acts. In the vows, each spouse promises to give himself/herself to the other. These vows are not (or should not be) exchanged solely on the basis of sensuality or sentiment. Rather, they should be exchanged because each, perceiving the dignity which God gave the beloved in His creative act, wishes to give himself/herself to the other. Unlike some sensual or sentimental feelings, marriage vows are always under the control of the ones making them. Each spouse promises to love the other forever, i.e., to give himself/herself to the other until death. He/she can always be faithful to that promise, can always give himself/herself to the other, no matter what feelings he/she has or what the other does. Good feelings might cease, but marriage must be founded on a firmer basis than transient emotions. If marriage were only constituted by the feelings of each spouse, there would be a violation of the personalistic norm. In this case, implicitly, each spouse would marry because the other makes him/her feel good. If that good feeling should cease, the marriage would end. In other words, the spouse would have been there to make the other feel good. With such a union, there would be no assurance for either spouse that the marriage would endure. Neither spouse could be sure that he/she would feel good in two months, five years, let alone forty or fifty years. It is quite clear that a union founded on a selfish desire to achieve an emotional high through the spouse is directly contrary to the commitment of marriage, which is based on a God-like self-donation of each spouse to the other. Marriage, if it is to be a *communion of persons,* must originate in the will, must be rooted in the personalistic norm, and must be an imitation of the Trinity. Sensuality and sentiment will then accompany the marital communion instead of determining it.

Marriage reflects God's love within the Trinity and His love for us, because marriage is constituted by the irrevocable choice in the wills of the spouses. In the Trinity and in creation, love is a choice in the wills of the divine Persons. The familial *communion of persons* reflects the trinitarian *communion of persons* because the irrevocable will-acts of the married partners, establishing a mutual self-surrender, mirror the unbreakable fidelity of God to Himself (within the Trinity) and to those whom He loves (us) outside the Trinity. He never will cease loving Himself or us because He has chosen to do so and His will-acts are, as those of married partners ought to be, irrevocable.

An act of the will is within the control of the one who makes it. Neither the spouse, nor even the angels, including the devil, can cause us to alter our own choices. It is within the power of the fallen angels to tempt, i.e., to suggest possible choices contrary to God's will, but they can never actually make us choose what we do not choose ourselves. Only God has such power and He will never choose for us. If He were to do that, it would destroy us because we would be reduced to the status of animals, lacking free will. Of course, through lack of cooperation, sickness, or a variety of other causes, the expression of mutual self-donation in marriage may be hampered. However, that does not alter the gift itself.

Since the love of a husband and a wife should be a *communion of persons* based on the truth of the infinite dignity with which the Creator endowed both of them, it is not offensive, as Sacred Scripture has it, to ask wives to be obedient to their husbands. Nor is it too demanding to ask husbands to be willing to die for their wives as Christ died for the Church. In the exchange of marital vows, both the man and the woman give themselves completely to each other. They each promise, "Not my will, but thine be done."[7] To ask obedience of wives is simply to remind wives of what they have already promised. Obedience, if it is a human act based on a relationship between persons, must be an act of love (personalistic norm). Otherwise, the demand for obedience would be an act of tyranny and the one who is obedient would be acting as a slave. Obedience is the willing cooperation of one with the other because both are united through their freely chosen will-acts. Of course, wives should obey their husbands, i.e., they should be united with them in their wills. That is what was promised on the marriage day through the vows. Similarly, when Saint Paul asks husbands to be ready to die for their wives, he is only reminding them of what they promised. They, in the vows, promised everything they had to their wives: a total self-surrender. In that total gift, they function as creatures made in the image of God. They act as Christ acted. If necessary, husbands must be ready to do what Christ did, surrender everything for the sake of the other. What Saint Paul affirmed of husbands is equally true of wives and what he said of wives is equally true of husbands. Husbands and wives have promised obedience, i.e., a union of wills, to one another. They have voluntarily given themselves totally to one another and each should be ready to die for the other. Seen in the light of John Paul's personalism, Saint Paul's teaching is not sexist. It is the obvious corollary to the total union which husbands and wives are called to form with one another.

The gift of a man and a woman to one another in marriage must be indissoluble as long as both live. Each surrenders himself/herself to the other and receives the gift of the other in return. Once given, the gift may never be withdrawn. Once received, the gift of the other may never be rejected. As the *Apostolic Exhortation on the Family* argues, "The indissolubility of marriage...[is] a sign and a requirement of the absolutely faithful love that God has for man and that the Lord Jesus has. for the Church."[8] In other words, God's love is always characterized by perfect fidelity. Human love, since it is to be a reflection of God's love, must also be faithful forever. God is always faithful in His love because anything less would not be a total self-surrender. A gift, if it is total, is not bounded in degree or in time! To give oneself only for a period of time and not forever (at least, for as long as marriage is possible, i.e., until the death of one of the spouses) is to limit the gift. But anything less than a total surrender of oneself for the other is, as we have seen, a violation of the requirement of love, a violation of the personalistic norm. It is, in effect, to use someone rather than to love him/her.

A husband or a wife who has divorced his or her spouse and remarried has treated his or her first spouse as a thing. When the offended spouse ceased to please, he/she was rejected. One may treat cars, boats, and even animals as objects to be used, but never may a human person be so humiliated (personalistic norm). Since the offended spouse was presumably sincere in his/her total self-surrender, he/she cannot help but feel totally devastated. First, he/she, believing in the gift of the other party, fell victim to a broken covenant (which is, in itself, devastating) and, as a result, unwittingly allowed himself/herself to become an object of use, a "thing." Second, and even more humiliating, the offended spouse is now rejected even as a "thing" to be used! Objects are at least useful, but the abandoned spouse is not even considered to have a use! No wonder there are such psychological difficulties for those who have been set aside by their spouses! The Pope continually stresses that marriage should be an affirmation of the value of the person. However, when it is no longer indissoluble, it not only ceases to confirm the personal dignity of the individual spouses, it actually has the potential of destroying the sense of self-worth and dignity in the offended spouse. Once that awareness of one's own value is destroyed, it is most difficult to recover it. The spouse has been used as a thing and he/she may believe himself/herself to be just that: a thing (perhaps even a worthless thing).

The indissolubility of marriage is not harmed either by separation of the spouses without remarriage or by the death of one of the spouses and a subsequent second marriage by the surviving spouse. Separation (in practice in the United States, civil divorce without a second marriage) is an evil, but sometimes justified. As John Paul says so descriptively, one or both spouses "may cease to feel that there is any subjective justification for this union, and gradually fall into a state of mind which is psychologically or both psychologically and physiologically incompatible with it. Such a condition warrants separation from 'bed and table,' but cannot annul the fact that they are objectively united, and united in wed-lock."[9] Even living apart, they are wedded and bound to one another. Their separation, as all other decisions, should be mutually agreeable. But, even if one unilaterally separates, i.e., moves out, that does not change the union in which they are joined. In separation, the self-surren-der of both parties remains intact, but it is not expressed. A second mar-riage after the death of the spouse does not prejudice the self-surrender in marriage because marriage is both a spiritual and a bodily reality. When one of the spouses dies, i.e., when the body and soul separate, the marital union ceases. A widow or widower is free to remarry.

It should be clear that the conclusions of the foregoing discussion regarding the indissolubility of marriage are founded on the principle that marriage is a total *communion of persons* established by the will-acts of the spouses. Once the self-gift of the man and the woman is made in the marriage vows, it is irrevocable. Even if both cease to feel any stirrings of sensuality or sentiment in the presence of the other, they are still united as husband and wife. They chose one another forever.

C. Revisionist Sexual Morality: An Attack on the Family

The familial *communion of persons* was established by God in Gen-esis. Through this union of love, man and woman were to fulfill their call-ing to love as God loves. However, original sin intervened and prevented Adam and Eve from surrendering themselves to each other as God had planned "from the beginning." Indicating that our first parents, by sinning, tottered on the precipice of total self-destruction, the Pope teaches that with the loss of God's grace and the concomitant loss of the dominion of the mind and will over the body, there was a "constitutive break within the human person, almost a rupture of man's original spiritual and somatic unity."[10] Further, there was an "ending of the capacity of a full mutual communion."[11] It is "as if the body, in its masculinity and femininity, no longer constituted the 'trustworthy' substratum of the *communion of per-sons*"[12] After sin the other (usually of the opposite sex) is often looked upon not for his/her own sake, but for selfish reasons: what can he/she do for me? How can he/she satisfy my selfish desires and inclinations? But, "man indeed, as a person is 'the only creature on earth that God has willed for its own sake' and, at the same time, he is the one who can fully discover his true self only in a sincere giving of himself."[13] Thus, original sin attacked man in his most essential activity, his sincere giving.

Offenses against the sincere giving in the family, i.e., against the first and primary *communion of persons* established by God in His creative act, have been committed by men and women since the fall. For example, in divorce and remarriage, as we have seen, the offended spouse is treated as an object. This is a violation of the familial *communion of persons* caused by selfishness. Selfishness also attacks the family in many other ways, e.g., pre-marital intercourse, polygamy, adultery and lust, abortion, contraception and artificial conception (test-tube babies), and homosexuality. In our age, most of these practices are not only commonplace (as they have been in past ages), but they are even defended. Many would like to justify these acts and cease making an effort to resist them.

Four different positions are often advanced in favor of this revisionist morality. The first is proposed by those who misunderstand freedom. They mistakenly equate it with a selfish independence, precluding all forms of self-donation. But this attitude, as well as the actions flowing from it, destroys true freedom because only in an unselfish gift of love is our freedom realized. God made us to love and He also made us free. The two are not in conflict and cannot be because we are made in God's image. Just as God loves and is at the same time perfectly free, when we love unselfishly we are perfectly free. Furthermore, failure to love unselfishly destroys us and consequently our freedom. This is the experience of people who have accepted the "do your own thing" attitude. They ruin themselves, leading miserable lives, because they fail to love, the "fundamental and innate vocation of every human being."[14]

Others would justify these selfish violations of the familial *communion of persons* by divorcing the body from the human person. This is a fundamental misunderstanding of how God made us. They would argue that if the body is meant to express the person, then the individual should be able to choose how his/her body should express his/her person. In their eyes, the christian sexual ethic makes people slaves to the biological functions of their bodies. If we are to be the masters of nature, why can we not govern our own bodies, freely choosing to express whatever we want through them?

But the human person is not the arbiter of nature! The order of nature is the same as the order of existence and depends upon God, the first cause. On the other hand, the biological order is a scientific abstraction from nature. Showing incredible insight, Karol Wojtyla stated twenty-five years ago that our sexuality "owes its objective importance to its connection with the divine work of creation....and this importance vanishes almost completely if our way of thinking is inspired only by the biological order of nature" which "as a product of the human intellect... abstracts its elements from a larger reality."[15] The Holy Father insists that the body expresses the person as it is because God made the body as well as the soul. In other words, people do not govern their bodies absolutely because their bodies belong by God's creative act to the order of nature, not only to the biological order. There is an integral view of the human person in John Paul's thought, i.e., the body, in all of its functions, is a gift from God just as life itself. As we may not tamper with our lives, so we may not tamper with our bodies.

Still others might argue that since the christian norms are ideals which can never be attained, God would not ask us to live by them. They might point to the seeming unnatural demands made by the christian ethic on men and women. Therefore, in their view, acts contrary to these teachings are not sins, i.e., sub-human, but rather are normal (read: permissible) for us. Of course, the commandments are impossible for fallen man without God's grace. With God's grace, however, anything is possible. What is natural for man and woman is the state of original innocence where lust and selfishness were not a problem. In a sense, then, our present state is unnatural. Christ calls us to return to our original state. In response to the questions the Pharisees asked Him about divorce, He taught, "Have you not read that He who made them from the beginning made them male and female, and said, 'For this reason a man shall leave his father and mother and be joined to his wife, and the two shall become one.'"[16] The phrase, "the beginning," is a clear reference to the first words in Genesis, to the time before the fall. In other words, Christ told the Pharisees that married people must live the way Adam and Eve did before the fall in a total *communion of persons* without any tinge of selfishness. This is clearly impossible for fallen man left to his own devices. But Christ would never ask us to do the impossible. His victory on the cross makes God's grace available to us and with that it is possible to live as Adam and Eve did.

A fourth objection to the moral teachings of the Church begins with the same premise as the third one: the christian moral life is comprised of ideals impossible for us to reach. Since we often fall short of these ideals while striving through our best efforts to live by them, some would argue that we must not be burdened with the full force of the moral ideals, but rather congratulated for what we have attained. Thus, they claim there are differences in the application of the law to individuals, what the Pope calls a gradualness of the law.

However, the Holy Father teaches, as we have seen, that the christian life is possible with God's grace. It is always attainable. Therefore, we are always bound by the moral teachings. But it is quite clear that we find it easier to do things we have done before. As we practice the christian life, we grow accustomed to it. There is a growth in virtue. The moral precepts always bind, but they become easier for us to practice. This is not a gradualness in the application of the law to an individual. Rather, it is a gradual perfection of the person in his/her practice of the christian life (or as John Paul labels it, the law of gradualness in human behavior).

The Church is *for* man. It has the optimistic view of man. The Church repeats to each human person the message of Christ, "Yes, you can live as God's image!" Those who wish to justify acts opposed to the teachings of the Church and the nature of man and woman see the difficulties and hardships many people have in living according to christian norms. Although those opposed to Church teaching seem to be motivated by compassion, in effect they are pessimistic about our possibility of ever overcoming the effects of sin. If their position were to be accepted, we would be reduced to a level beneath that planned for us "from the beginning." The Pope counters the arguments of the critics by an insistence that true compassion is that shown by Christ on Calvary. Through the blood of His cross, we can live as Adam and Eve before the fall, if we are only willing to cooperate with God's grace. As the Pope teaches, "to diminish in no way the teaching of Christ constitutes an eminent form of charity for souls."[17] There is no compassion without the truth. Let us always offer the truth compassionately.

D. VIOLATIONS OF THE FAMILIAL *COMMUNION OF PERSONS*

1. Pre-Marital Sex

The physical union of a man and a woman before they are married (pre-marital sex) is an attempt to express with their bodies a union which is not as yet present in their minds and wills. If the body is the expression of the person and if a person is characterized by a mind and a will, then nothing can be expressed with the body which is not in some way known and chosen through the mind and the will. In pre-marital intercourse, the marital union is not yet present, but the man and the woman are uniting as though they were married. Such is less than a personal act for each because their wills have not yet chosen the union. The self-surrender has not been made, but their bodies are (as though they were independent) surrendering themselves.

Of course, putting the case this way begs the question. As those engaged in pre-marital sexual contact will argue, the union is present. "I do love her; I do love him. Why must we wait for the symbolic [read: empty and meaningless] marriage vows?" The union of a man and a woman in marriage is, as we have seen, a total self-surrender of each spouse to the other. Marriage is reciprocal. There is no *communion of persons* without at least two persons. The gift of each spouse is dependent on the other. No one may risk such a total donation without knowing with as much certainty as is possible that the other is truly making the same self-donation.

It is not possible to know with certainty that the other intends to donate himself/herself in a lasting irrevocable union unless it is a public act. Marriage is a reciprocal self-donation. Private promises are hardly sufficient for each to be sure of the other's self-donation. Even in the lesser self-gift which constitutes employment agreements, most would not trust a private, and therefore, non-binding agreement. How much more, then, when it is one's total self which is being surrendered, is it necessary to know with certainty that the other is truly giving himself/herself?

The public act makes the community the witness and the guarantor of the mutual agreement. Society is willing to secure the marital union because without such an assurance for the spouses, the dignity of its members who enter marriage is at great risk. Further, society is necessarily concerned about its future members, i.e., the children of marital unions who are also put at great risk if the marriage is not surrounded with safeguards. With the public as witness, both spouses are quite aware of the seriousness of the commitment. With that knowledge, each may be reasonably certain of the intention of the other. Each will have given his/her decision more careful consideration than they would a non-binding private act.

Of course, the preceding comments prescind from the marriage of baptized Christians. When two baptized people marry, a sacrament of union is brought into existence. Through the sacrament, the two spouses are united in Christ, not only in a *communion of persons* between themselves. Christ seals their love, i.e., their self-gift, and unites them in Himself. It is as though Christ writes the name of each person on the soul of the other. Christ elevates the spousal *communion of persons* to a union in the Trinity. If the *communion of persons* of the non-baptized requires a public act, how much more should the sacrament of Matrimony, an act of the Church, require a public act before a priest or, by special dispensation, before another official. Obviously, Christians cannot express this union before it is present. Pre-marital sex is thus gravely wrong because it is a violation of the sacramental union as well as a violation of the call given by God in His creative act to form a familial *communion of persons.*

2. Polygamy

In the *Apostolic Exhortation on the Family,* the Holy Father writes that the familial *communion of persons* "is radically contradicted by polygamy. This, in fact, directly negates the plan of God which was revealed from the beginning, because it is contrary to the equal personal dignity of men and women, who, in Matrimony, give themselves with a love that is total and therefore exclusive."[18] Polygamy, the union of one man with more than one woman, or polyandry, the union of one woman with more than one man, is contrary to the personalistic norm because the one individual divides himself/herself among many (does not give himself/herself totally to any one). When one man has several wives, each of them may surrender herself to him, but he does not give himself totally to each of them. "Polygamy...is in practice conducive to the treatment of women by men as objects of enjoyment and so at once degrades women and lowers the level of morality amongst men....The abolition of polygamy, and the re-establishment of monogamy and the indissolubility of marriage are necessary consequences of the command to love."[19] Few in our society would quarrel with these conclusions.

3. Adultery and Lust

Adultery, a married person giving himself/herself physically to someone who is not his/her spouse, is a betrayal of the familial *communion of persons*. Just as with divorce and remarriage, the husband or wife guilty of adultery offends his/her spouse in two ways. First, the married adulterous man or woman presumes to offer what is no longer his or hers to give. A married person has already surrendered himself/herself to the spouse. It is impossible for a husband or a wife to take back this gift from the spouse and bestow it on another because the gift of love must be forever. Second, the adulterous spouse rejects the self-donation of the legitimate spouse to him/her. Not only does the man or woman guilty of adultery presume to take back his or her own gift, but he or she also scorns the self-donation of the legitimate spouse. By presuming to take back his/her own gift and by rejecting the self-gift of his/her spouse, the adulterer/adulteress treats the spouse as a thing. It is also clear that the adulterer/adulteress is treating his/her present sexual partner as a thing. But the sexual partner is at least a useful thing whereas the legitimate spouse is treated as a useless and worthless thing.

Adultery has always been one of the gravest sins not only because of the terrible wound to the dignity of the offended spouse which it causes, but also because it is a falsification of the familial *communion of persons,* which should be a reflection of the trinitarian *communion of persons.* In the familial communion the spouses have pledged themselves until death. Their love should be faithful as God's love is faithful. Adultery is directly contrary to such a union. Adultery is also a grave sin because, as all sin, it is self-destructive. Through this sin, the adulterous spouse fails to act as God acts, as the image of God which he/she is. Adultery offends the spouse, the familial communion, and the adulterer.

Christ extends the definition of adultery to a lustful look. Christ teaches, "You have heard that it was said, 'You shall not commit adultery.' But I say to you that every one who looks at a woman lustfully has already committed adultery with her in his heart."[20] Commenting on the words of Christ, the Pope says that a lustful look is an "interior act of the heart," but "a look expresses, I would say, the man within."[21] In this look, the other person is reduced to an object which is viewed as a means to one's own personal gratification. The man or woman who looks lustfully wishes to gratify his or her physical desires without the sincere giving of himself or herself that would be present in a true *communion of persons*. There are, however, further problems with this behavior. The lustful look violates the dignity of the one who looks and the one who is desired. The one who is desired becomes an object, a thing. But the one who looks lustfully is, at the same time, reducing himself/herself to a thing. If a person seeks union with a thing, then how is he/she superior to it? The look violates the infinite dignity of both persons.

Of course, Christ's expansion of adultery to include an interior act of one's heart indicates that even two spouses may commit "adultery" with one another. Adultery is the reduction of another human being to a thing. When one spouse thinks of the other as an object (lustful look) or uses his/her spouse in an act, e.g., forced intercourse, he/she is committing "adultery." If the dignity of both spouses is to be preserved, neither may use his/her spouse in these ways. In other words, the personalistic norm must be observed or adultery is committed.

Lust also "entails the loss of the interior freedom of the gift."[22] Since a gift ceases to be a gift when it is the result of compulsion, lust makes the self-surrender, the gift of one spouse to the other, impossible. When lust dominates one of the spouses, the mutual, selfless, free giving necessary to the expression of the *communion of persons* is missing. Only God's grace allows the spouses to gain control over themselves and makes it possible for them to give themselves to each other freely without any tinge of selfishness stemming from lust or any other cause.

It is important to note the difference between a lustful look and an admiration of God's beauty as manifested in the human body and in art. "There are works of art whose subject is the human body in its nakedness, and the contemplation of which makes it possible to concentrate, in a way, on the whole truth of man, on the dignity and the beauty—also the 'suprasensual' beauty—of his masculinity and femininity. These works bear within them, almost hidden, an element of sublimation, which leads the viewer, through the body, to the whole personal mystery of man."[23] In the hands of great artists, the naked human body is painted, sculpted, or otherwise depicted truly as the expression of the person. Thus, in Michelangelo's works we are not led to lustful looking. With *Playboy,* the purpose is quite different. The same principles apply to our own admiration of the physical beauty of another. Providing we are focusing on the whole mystery of man, the full truth about the other, then we will not be led to adultery in the heart.

4. Abortion

The familial *communion of persons* is founded on the self-dona-tion of each spouse and in this way is an imitation of the Holy Trinity. When God loves, it is life-giving. He loved us in creation and gave us life. In the redemption, He surrendered Himself totally for us and this love brought forth life, divine life, in us. Since we are made in His image, our love, the love of persons, is also life-giving. In the familial *communion of persons,* the gift of a man and a woman to each other in their bodies does serve life, new life. This is plainly stated by John Paul when he writes, "Thus, the couple, while giving themselves to one another, give not just themselves but also the reality of children, who are a living reflection of their love, a permanent sign of conjugal unity."[24] "A relationship between spirits which begets a new embodied spirit is something unknown in the natural order."[25] Procreation is the most pro-found blessing which can be bestowed on the love of a couple. They have cooperated with God in giving life to a person, a spiritual being. With this gift, there are responsibilities. Married love, the willingness to bear burdens for the sake of the spouse and children, makes these responsibilities a joy.

Abortion, the killing of a yet unborn child, is evidence of a deep-rooted selfishness. If, in the physical union of a man and a woman, either is seeking his or her own desires, he or she will not hesitate to use the other's body as a thing to achieve some other end. If the other's body is treated and used as a thing, it is a small (but logical) step, when plea-sure is the goal, to regard the child as merely so much tissue, a product of conception. Paralleling the attitude toward the other, the selfish man or woman views the child as just a thing, a biological growth, which he or she may cut out or manipulate (e.g., fetal experimentation) in any way he or she chooses. The removal of this growth through abortion might seem to be especially appropriate if the self-centered man or woman does not like it because the child is handicapped or even because the child's gender is not the one desired. The possibility (or so someone with such an attitude might think) of new growths which he or she might like better is always present. Unborn children then become things (like the sexual partner) which the person rooted in selfishness can make and use to suit him or her. This is selfishness carried to an extreme. With such an attitude, the human race cannot survive because God made us to love, to give, not to be selfish.

Abortion, as an extreme manifestation of selfishness, is a radical contradiction in the familial *communion of persons.* Moreover, in the pre-marital or adulterous union, abortion is an even more extreme indication of selfishness than the relationship itself. In all cases, abortion is a sign of the total rejection of the child's mother or father. When the partners in marriage truly make a self-donation to one another, i.e., when they love one another, they are open to life. A rejection of life is a rejection of love. On the other hand, the giving and acceptance of new life is the most profound realization of the familial *communion of persons.* But even outside of marriage, a baby is always flesh of the parents. To reject that person, a new life and the fruit of love, is to reject the sexual partner. Thus, abortion is not only destructive to children (undoubtedly the most terrible aspect of the war on the unborn), it also destroys mothers and fathers. Short of the murder of the spouse or of one's sexual partner, abortion, the taking of life, is the greatest possible rejection of another.

5. Contraception and Artificial Conception

As we have seen, the personalistic norm is violated by divorce and remarriage, pre-marital intercourse, polygamy, adultery and lust, as well as abortion. Contraception also attacks the total gift of a man and a woman to one another. Husbands and wives cannot give themselves to each other completely when they refuse to surrender themselves at least potentially as mothers and fathers. In one of the clearest and most forceful statements on contraception, Wojtyla writes that couples who practice contraception "'manipulate' and degrade human sexuality—and with it themselves and their married partner—by altering its value of 'total' self-giving. Thus, the innate language that expresses the total reciprocal self-giving husband and wife is overlaid, through contraception, by an objectively contradictory language, namely, that of not giving oneself totally to the other."[26]

A human person, created in God's image with a body and a soul, should reflect God, i.e., he/she should love by giving himself/herself unreservedly to others. Since we are embodied spirits and the body is the expression of our persons, it is appropriate that there be a bodily means of giving ourselves to one another, i.e., of loving one another. The bodily differences between a man and a woman are the physical means by which the unselfish donation in love is made. The sexual act should be the total physical surrender of each spouse to the other in all of his or her potentialities. As such, it should be a sign and expression of the fundamental union the spouses enjoy in the familial *communion of persons* established through the marriage vows. By God's design, the self-donation of a man and a woman to one another includes the possibility of procreating new life. Since we are made in the divine image, it is fitting that our love be fruitful as God's love is fruitful. Contraception alters the sexual act and makes it something other than a self-surrender. For the contracepting couple, the sexual act is a lie because the spouses refuse to give themselves to one another as potential mothers and fathers. They engage in what is only an apparent act of self-surrender. In other words, since the sexual union is no longer the expression of a total gift, it does not mirror the spousal *communion of persons.*

But even for the pre-marital or adulterous couple, contraception cannot be defended. Adultery and pre-marital intercourse are offenses against the familial *communion of persons* because in such acts the man and the woman attempt to surrender themselves to each other without having properly chosen each other in their wills. In effect, they presume to divorce their bodies from their persons and still to give themselves to each other in a bodily way. However, in contracepting, they even refuse to give themselves fully to each other in their flesh. Even the bodily union is not a gift. It is only an apparent gift, i.e., a lie.

In an act of love, husband and wife should give themselves to each other and should be open to the transmission of life. The denial of either good, conjugal love or procreation constitutes a falsification of the act. With conjugal love or procreation denied, the act no longer reflects God's fruitful love. Most would grant that a husband seeking only children from his wife without any thought of her welfare is using her. Such a man denies the value of conjugal love. However, the husband who denies the possibility of procreation also is using his wife. (The wife, of course, would be using her husband if she denies either conjugal love or the procreation of children.) For God, life and love are not separated and thus, for us, as images of God, life and love should not be separated, i.e., conjugal love and life should always be united.

Contraception and the other abuses against the familial *communion of persons* are violations of the personalistic norm and therefore aggressions against human dignity. They occur because of original sin and its effects, especially selfishness as manifested in lust. But other forms of selfishness, in addition to lust, are equally damaging to the *communion of persons* and human dignity. For example, some couples may selfishly wish to have a large number of children although they cannot care for all of them. Such children can become mere objects possessed by their parents. This is a grave violation of human dignity. Another form of selfishness is apparent in some couples who experience difficulties in conceiving a child. They desire children more than any other gift God could give them. Desperately seeking to conceive a child, they might turn to their physician for advice. The doctor may suggest that they visit one of the clinics where babies are conceived in test tubes.

This practice, however, cannot be tolerated. The couple's selfish desire for children leads them to violate their own dignity by manipulating and using their bodies. The practice of artificial conception reduces procreation to a merely biological, laboratory act when it must be, by God's will, the fruit of a covenant, a *communion of persons,* as expressed in the conjugal embrace of a man and a woman joined in marriage. A new spirit, a baby, must be conceived within a union of spirits, i.e., the spousal union. Artificial conception is a manipulation because it divorces the life-giving potential of the body from the person. Similar to the contracepting couple, the test-tube baby couple refuses to accept God's will in their own lives and claims total control over their bodies. But the body is not a machine and it is contrary to human dignity to manipulate it.

When a couple contracepts or conceives artificially (or when these practices are defended by others), sexuality is reduced to a merely biological function. With this understanding of sexuality in place, there is no reason to object to surrogate mothers, artificial insemination, and many other serious abuses which are now proposed and even practiced. Such a view destroys both love as it is expressed physically, and life as the fruit of the love of spirits, i.e., persons. The widespread acceptance of artificial conception and these other abuses shows how the contraceptive mentality has accustomed us to view our bodies as machines. If human dignity is to be preserved, we must abandon this false understanding of ourselves.

6. Homosexuality

The bodily differences between a man and a woman given by God in His creative act are the physical means of expressing a familial *communion of persons*. Further, the bodily expression of love serves life, new life, because God willed that our love be fruitful as His love is fruitful. Homosexual activity can never be a physical expression of familial love. Familial love is precisely the union of a man and a woman in a total self-donation, which is physically expressed through their masculine and feminine bodies. Since it is impossible for two men (or two women) to give themselves physically to one another, any attempted union between them ceases to be a gift. It becomes a using of each other, or, at least, a using of each other's bodies. Again, such use is a violation of the personalistic norm and not an expression of the familial *communion of persons*. A further indication that homosexual acts cannot be the expression of a true self-donation of each to the other is that such acts are always and in every case sterile. They do not serve life. Two men (or two women) can never form a familial *communion of persons*.

Still, if both homosexual and heterosexual orientations are transmitted by genes, neither is consciously chosen. Even if homosexual tendencies are learned or acquired in some other way, they are not usually the result of a free personal choice. The person with a homosexual orientation has not chosen to violate the vocation to love. But, of course, a homosexual act is the result of a choice in the will. When a homosexual chooses to act on his/her tendencies, he/she chooses to use himself/herself and others. Therefore, specific homosexual acts are contrary to our call to love. On the other hand, the homosexual orientation, even though it may make a true self-donation to a person of the opposite sex difficult, does not directly contradict our vocation to imitate God's love.

The less difficult road is the one of least resistance: to surrender to selfishness and then to justify the actions. In the present era many have followed this path. Not only have some people used other people, but they have also justified such actions. The false ideas employed to justify such abuses have established thought patterns for our entire society. Thus, they are even more destructive than individual lapses against human dignity. Those who wish to reject the abuses and the arguments favoring them have difficulty because they, in doing so, are rejecting their own culture. They are acting counter-culturally, which is always most difficult.

It is clear that many who attack human dignity either in their behavior or, more seriously by justifying selfish acts, misunderstand human dignity or believe the christian norms to be impossible ideals. The Pope teaches that our dignity rests on the divine image in each one of us. Knowing the destruction which the false concepts of human dignity have caused, how can we refuse to accept the truth of the papal understanding of ourselves? The Pope insists that our lustful and other selfish inclinations are gravely harmful to human dignity and that they can be overcome in Christ. Christ calls each and every one of us "to the beginning," to live as Adam and Eve did, despite original sin and its effects, and He makes this possible through His grace won for us by the blood of His cross. Christ desires every human person to share His life, His grace with Him. Therefore, He makes Himself present to us in the sacraments. However, even blessed with grace we may fail in our effort to act as we were made "in the beginning," but His forgiving love, available in the sacrament of Penance, restores us and allows us to make the effort again. Nonetheless, this optimistic view of the human person rests on the acceptance of the papal view of our dignity and the equally important principle that the effort to live in accordance with that dignity is worthwhile. We must acknowledge that the alternatives to the christian norms are gravely injurious to our dignity, i.e., to our very selves.

E. Natural Family Planning

The Holy Father proposes that natural family planning be the means for teaching the world to observe the personalistic norm. This mandate from John Paul II is extraordinary. He advocates knowledge of the fertility cycle for everyone, even those not yet married. In the *Apostolic Exhortation on the Family,* the Pope writes, "The necessary conditions [for marriage] also include knowledge of the bodily aspect and the body's rhythms of fertility. Accordingly, every effort must be made to render such knowledge accessible to all married people and also to young adults before marriage, through clear, timely and serious instruction and education given by married couples, doctors, and experts."[27] Obviously, the Pope sees that the understanding of one's fertility, as taught in natural family planning courses, is essential to married life and even to one's life before marriage.

Natural family planning is a tool for understanding and examining human fertility. Through this tool, both married and unmarried adults learn about their fertility. Then they make use of this knowledge depending, of course, upon their state of life. Many have identified the knowledge of fertility with the decision of couples to avoid or to have children. However, the distinction between the knowledge of fertility and the application of that knowledge within the sexual act is vital. Natural family planning is used here to mean the tool for understanding human fertility. But the tool is distinct from how a couple applies it in their sexual relationship. In other words, natural family planning is a method. As a method for understanding one's own fertility, it is universally approved.

In applying the method of natural family planning in marriage, couples are to exercise responsible parenthood. This means that husband and wife are to have a definite family and procreative attitude. They are to be *for* children because their love should reflect God's love which is always life-giving. In the normal situation, a married couple must decide each month whether to seek a pregnancy or not. They must have sufficient reasons for either decision. If "there exist reasonable grounds for spacing births, arising from physical or psychological condition of husband or wife, or from external circumstances,"[28] then a couple may have recourse to periods of infertility and may abstain from the sexual embrace during their fertile times. Outside of marriage, young adults apply the knowledge of their fertility responsibly when they exercise chastity.

The underlying reason why young adults, engaged couples, and married couples should know natural family planning is that this method teaches them that the body, as God made it, is the expression of the person. For example, when husband and wife accept the natural cycle of fertility and infertility as a gift from God, not subject to artificial manipulation, they usually assent to the principle that the body is the expression of the person. They experience themselves as spirits endowed with a body and they know that those who would divorce the body from the person misunderstand human beings.

An unmarried female might begin to observe the signs of fertility and infertility of her own body and thus come to a greater appreciation of the mystery and wonder of herself as a woman. This greater appreciation of her dignity, gained through natural family planning, would foster in her the virtue of chastity because she in no way would want to compromise her dignity.

Pope John Paul has issued a universal and unrestricted call for all men and women to learn natural family planning, i.e., to know their own fertility. In John Paul's view, natural family planning is a means to counteract the entire sexually permissive mentality which encourages a manipulation of the body and a contempt of self-mastery. It is a means to teach the theology of the body. Natural family planning is thus the means by which many men and women learn to affirm human dignity by observing the personalistic form.

F. Virginity

It is possible that the papal emphasis on the familial *communion of persons* could obscure the equally important principle that virginity and celibacy are treasured gifts from God as well. Those who have voluntarily remained unmarried for the sake of the kingdom of God have entered a *communion of persons* (the Church), albeit not a familial one (in the usual sense, at least), which is expressed through their bodies. "In virginity or celibacy, the human being...in a bodily way...anticipates in his or her flesh the new world of the future resurrection."[29] Bodily this communion is expressed in the celibate's self-mastery, not unlike that expected of married couples. Further, the celibate or virgin does not view sexuality as something worthless. "When human sexuality is not regarded as a great value given by the Creator, the renunciation of it for the sake of the kingdom loses its meaning."[30] If love (a *communion of persons* founded on a total self-donation of one person to another) is not valued in marriage, it will not be held in high esteem in its other expression, celibacy and virginity.

G. Conclusion

"The future of humanity passes by way of the family"[31] because it is in the family that the incomparable dignity of each human person is first affirmed. Each family member should donate himself/herself to the others. There can be no greater affirmation of one's own dignity than receiving the infinitely precious gift of other human persons. The self-donation,

certainly on the part of the husband and the wife, must be total and it must be given as a response to the dignity of each family member. The children then learn to love from their parents, who are the teachers in this school of love called the family.

However, it is equally true that no institution can do more harm to individuals than the family. For, if the dignity of each is not affirmed because one or more (but, again, especially the husband or the wife) are acting for selfish reasons, the results are devastating to the members of the family.

Notes

1. See RH, no. 10.
2. See FC, no. 11.
3. See Phil. 2:6–7.
4. See LR, p. 41.
5. See Gen. 1:28.
6. Ibid., 1:27.
7. See Luke 22:42.
8. See FC, no. 20.
9. See LR, p. 215.
10. See TB, no. 28.
11. Ibid., no. 29.
12. Ibid.
13. Ibid., no. 32.
14. See FC, no. 11.
15. See LR, p. 57.
16. See Matt. 19:4–5.
17. See FC, no. 33.
18. Ibid., no. 19.
19. See LR, p. 213.
20. See Matt. 5:27–28.
21. See TB, no. 39.
22. Ibid., no. 32.
23. Ibid., no. 63.
24. See FC, no. 14.
25. See LR, p. 55.
26. See FC, no. 32.

27. Ibid., no. 33.

28. See Karol Wojtyla (Pope John Paul II), "A Discipline That Ennobles Human Love," *L'Osservatore Romano* (English edition), vol. 17, no. 36, (September 3, 1984), p. 6

29. See FC, no. 16.

30. Ibid.

31. Ibid., no. 86.

Abbreviations

RH = *Redemptor hominis*
FC = *Familiaris consortio*
TB = *Theology of the body*
LR = *Love and Responsibility,* by Karol Wojtyla, translated by H. T. Willetts. New York: Farrar, Straus and Giroux, 1981.

14. *Familiaris Consortio:*
A Review of Its Theology

Michael D. Place

This chapter first appeared in *The Changing Family: Views From Theology and the Social Sciences in the Light of the Apostolic Exhortation Familiaris Consortio,* eds. Stanley L. Saxton, Patricia Voydanoff, and Angela Ann Zukowski, in 1984.

One of the givens of contemporary Roman Catholic theology is that just as scripture cannot be read uncritically or literally, so too magisterial statements are in need of contextualization and interpretation.[1] The reason is clear. Magisterial statements do not exist in a vacuum but are situated within a history of thought and action and often are part of an ongoing dialogue. This is especially true of magisterial statements related to the Synod of Bishops.[2] The topic of the synod is chosen because it reflects an ecclesial need. The synod is prepared for through a variety of consultative processes that occur nationally and internationally. The synod itself elicits a multitude of interventions, and issues a concluding report or document. And in the case of the 1980 synod, the synodal process was brought to a close with the papal exhortation *Familiaris Consortio.*

But what would be the best way to critically examine the theology of this document? One could compare it to other magisterial statements, or to the synodal interventions, or to the concluding propositions of the synod, or to the allocutions of John Paul II.[3] All of this could and should be done. However, in reflecting on the setting of this symposium—an American Catholic center of higher learning and education—it struck me that a more appropriate way to analyze the theology of *Familiaris Consortio* would be to set it in the context of another part of the dialogue of which it is a part; namely, the work of contemporary Catholic theologians. And in such a context, it is fair to say that Catholic theologians and canonists from the United States have made a significant contribution to the contemporary ecclesial discussion about marriage and family.[4] Because of the breadth of issues addressed both in the exhortation and in the work of the theologians, it will be necessary to limit this analysis.[5]

It is evident that there are three issues which in themselves do not directly pertain to the theology of marriage but which involve presuppositions that will affect significantly the development of a theology of marriage. They are theological methodology, an ecclesiological perspective, and an understanding of moral values or norms. After a review of the manner in which the exhortation discusses these issues, four theological topics relating to marriage will be reviewed: the meaning of Christian marriage, the significance of human sexuality, the sacramentality of Christian marriage, and the church's response to marital failure. The format of each consideration will be a summary of the manner in which certain theologians have been addressing the issue, a presentation of the papal position, and a comparison of the two. The conclusion will contain some observations about where the dialogue can go from here.

THEOLOGICAL METHODOLOGY

Perhaps one of the most important but subtle debates within Roman Catholic theology has centered on the manner in which the theological enterprise is approached. Recent writing has reflected on the impact of the scholastic method and in particular that of the nineteenth century neo-scholastic revival on the formulation of theological positions.[6] Both Bernard Lonergan and David Tracy have raised the question whether there is not a need to shift from what is described as a "classicist" perspective to an "historicist" perspective.[7]

The classicist perspective involves a methodology that is primarily deductive in nature. It begins with certain eternal and immutable truths that are accepted as the basis for any statements that might follow. In such an approach, there is little room for history or change to be of significance. The historicist perspective is more inductive in nature. Though it does not deny the ability to arrive at meaning or truth, it does make greater provision for the significance of the concrete, historical moment and does not see change as peripheral to the discovery of meaning or truth.

On first reading, it would appear that the exhortation has embraced this shift. The pope affirms that, "...the call and demands of the spirit resound in the very moments of history, and so the church can also be guided to a more profound understanding of the inexhaustible mystery of marriage and the family by the circumstances, the questions, and the anxieties and hopes of the young people, married couples, and parents of today" (FC§4). This recognition of the movement of the spirit in time is coupled with an image of the human person as one who advances "gradually with the progressive integration of the gifts of God and the demands of His definitive and absolute love..."(FC§9).

A more careful reading would suggest that while this recognition of the historical and this acknowledgment of the exigencies of change are real, they stand side by side in the papal reflections with the older methodology. At critical moments in the line of argumentation, there is a return to a description of a "divine plan," which gives a specificity to the inductive reasoning far beyond its own inner logic. A specific example can be found in the discussion on the meaning of sexuality. Sexuality is seen as an expression of a total self-giving, but that self-giving is immediately qualified by the phrase "through acts which are proper and exclusive to spouses" (FC§11). I do not say that this might not be the case, but rather suggest that this is asserted without any justification.

Thus it is that the text shows a sensitivity to a new perspective, but the adherents to that perspective might suggest that it does so in a manner that often returns to an older methodology in order to arrive at its conclusions.

ECCLESIOLOGICAL PERSPECTIVE

Intimately related to the question of theological methodology is the perspective from which one understands the meaning of church and the role of its various members in the discernment of the meaning of Christian living. Historical studies have revealed that the present self-understanding of the church and the relationships between the various offices and ministries is a "time-bound" understanding. There have been suggestions that the present dominant image of ecclesial life is too readily defined by a juridical or legalistic perspective which fails to recognize the diverse gifts of the ecclesial fellowship.[8] Of particular concern is the proper relationship of the theologian to the magisterial teaching of pope and bishops. The writings of theologians on these issues today make it clear that many of them ascribe a greater competency to the life and experience of the individual Catholic in matters of faith and morals than formerly was the practice.[9] Likewise, the role of the theologian is recognized as having a unique magisterial competency of its own—without denying the authoritative nature of the episcopal-papal magisterium.[10]

This shift in perspective is very much evident in the first part of the exhortation. Consistent with an approach that is more inductive in nature, the pope does not speak of a process of imposition of truth but rather of an "evangelical discernment" that offers an orientation toward the world which will preserve and realize the dignity of marriage (FC§§4, 5). This discernment is done through a sense of faith "which is a gift that the Spirit gives to all the faithful." Because of this giftedness, "the church...does not accomplish this discernment only through the pastors...but also through the laity." And the laity engage in this discernment in order to interpret the history of the world in the light of Christ (FC§5).

In this initial recognition of the various movements of the Spirit, the pope does not lose sight of the authoritative role of the church's pastors. He is quick to point out that this sense of faith does not consist "solely or necessarily" in the consensus of the faithful. Sociological and statistical research is "not to be considered in itself an expression of the sense of faith" (FC§5). It is for that reason that there is an apostolic ministry that promotes the sense of faith, examines and authoritatively judges the genuiness of its expression, and educates the faithful in evangelical discernment.

This discussion of ecclesiological questions in general is sensitive to the theological posture outlined above. As the document develops, however, there seems to be a return to an ecclesiological language, if not perspective, that is more akin to a pre-Vatican II mentality or at least to a form of articulation that is problematic for many. Particularly striking is the description in the section on "Agents of Pastoral Care" of the relationship between pastors and the laity in the exercise of the prophetic mission of Christ. The laity are viewed as witnessing to the faith by their words and Christian lives. The pastors exercise their mission "by distinguishing in that witness what is the expression of genuine faith from what is less in harmony with the light of faith..."(FC§73). In this expression the nuanced complexity of the earlier articulation is lost, and the previous theological posture of the pastors teaching and the people listening seems to return.

This reaffirmation of an older ecclesiological perspective, which seems to minimize any possibility of legitimate tension or dialogue arising from a pluralism of charisma, is also found in the document's description of the role of the theologian. Rather than acknowledging the honest divergence of opinion on various questions which are addressed in the exhortation, the pope re-echoes Pius XII's description of the proper function of the theologian when he asks theologians to commit themselves "to the task of illustrating ever more clearly the biblical foundations, the ethical grounds, and the personalistic reasons behind this doctrine" (FC§31).[11]

Thus it would seem that while the pope is anxious to affirm a more nuanced and developed ecclesiology emerging from the work of Vatican II, he also is still able to repeat an earlier ecclesiology. How the two postures are to be reconciled is difficult for many theologians to see.

MORAL VALUES OR NORMS

Integrally related to the questions of theological methodology and ecclesiological perspective is the problem of how to articulate and understand moral guidelines and the correlative question of the relationship of the individual to such guidelines.

Recently, a significant part of the theological community has experienced a qualitative development in its understanding of the role and function of moral guidelines and the place of individual responsibility.[12] While not denying that there is an objective order of morality to which all human beings and believing Christians are called to conform, today the articulation of that moral order is understood as being more complicated than before. For these theologians, the reality of human finitude and sinfulness are not seen as having destroyed the human condition but as having made conflict between "goods," or values, inevitable. As a result, it is not possible for the human person to achieve all goods in all situations, and at times various goods can be in conflict.[13]

The acceptance of this conflictual state of the human condition by some theologians has resulted in a disagreement between those theologians who see the human vocation as being "the maximizing of the good and the minimizing of the bad" and those who hold to an older perspective which asserts that in some situations there is a particular good that must be realized no matter what the conflict. Or to put it in more technical language, there are those who recognize the complexity of the human situation and assert that one must evaluate the appropriateness of moral activity by analyzing all of the components of the situation: the act, the circumstances, and the end. Those who hold this opinion believe that no single component can determine the rightness or wrongness of a human action. The other position proposes that while this might be acceptable in some moral situations, there are others where the rightness or wrongness of an activity is determined by the nature of the act itself. Thus it is that some acts are considered to be "intrinsically evil."

While this disagreement is on the level of how moral values are described, it also has bearing on the living of the Christian life. While adhering to the traditional Catholic belief that one is called to grow in the meaning of a Christian life that has a specific content to it, many moral theologians recognize the unique role of the individual conscience and the fact that growth in the moral life is a lifelong process.[14] Of its nature, the present human condition precludes the possibility of a full realization of the ideals which were preached and lived by Christ. The recognition that the human family is living in the eschatological tension of searching for an ideal that is not yet, provides room for a pastoral response in certain situations that would differ from that of theologians of another perspective. Whether justified by the theory of compromise or through other categories, an individual could be seen as being in "good faith" and not living in complete conformity with certain Christian ideals.[15]

It is obvious that some of the insights of this moral perspective have been recognized in the writing of the papal text. The conflictual nature of human existence is described as an interplay of light and darkness. History is not a fixed progression "toward what is better, but rather an event of freedom, and even a struggle between freedoms that are in mutual conflict…" (FC§6). In this vein, the condition of the human person is seen as historical and in process; thus it can be said that the human person "is an historical being who day by day builds himself up through his many free decisions; and so he knows, loves, and accomplishes moral good by stages of growth" (FC§34).

This recognition of conflict and growth by the Holy Father is limited, however. He clearly separates himself from the newer perspective on the conflictual nature of moral values when he reasserts the teaching of Vatican II on birth control, which says that "…the moral aspect of any procedure does not depend solely on sincere intentions or an evaluation of motives. It must be determined by objective standards" (FC§32). By objective standards, he means the nature of the act of intercourse. The same approach will be seen later in his discussion of marital failure.

This disagreement also is evident in his consideration of the implications of moral growth. Moral law is not "an ideal to be achieved in the future." Rather, it is "a…command of Christ to overcome difficulties with constancy." He goes on to say "what is known as the 'law of gradualness' or step-by-step advance cannot be identified with 'gradualness of law,' as if there were different degrees or forms of precept in God's law for different individuals and situations" (FC§34). While recognizing the reality of conflict and the difficulty of achieving the ideal, he suggests that it is not possible to achieve the resurrection without the cross and that sacrifice cannot be removed from life. It is the task of church to call people to such sacrifice and nourish and strengthen them in their struggle.

It is this disagreement about the meaning of moral values and their relationship to the life journey of each Christian that will serve as a foundation for other variances between the position of some Catholic theologians and the teaching of this papal exhortation. It would be unfair to focus on the particularity of some of the other discussions because the real debate is in this area of moral norms and absolutes.

The Meaning of Christian Marriage

Previous to the time of Vatican II, the Catholic perspective on marriage was very much defined by a legal or canonical interpretation. Much of the foundational theology on the sacrament of marriage was developed during a time in the life of the church that was dominated by its "jurist" popes.[16] Moreover, the manuals, which communicated moral and sacramental teaching in the fifty years before Vatican II, were written under the guidance of church law. The result was that the church spoke of and understood marriage in terms of a contract. For the contract to be valid, there had to be: competent parties, apt matter, the proper intention, the ability to fulfill the terms of the contract, and an appropriate signing of the contract.[17]

In recent years there has been a movement away from this view. Influenced by the personalist and existential thought of Western Europe, Catholic theologians came to speak of marriage as a covenant rather than a contract. The purpose or meaning of that covenant was seen as the establishment of a community of life and love between the couple; and this was expressed and celebrated in an openness to life. Gone was the extensive debate over primary or secondary ends of marriage and the impression that the only purpose for marriage was the bearing of children.[18]

Similar to the move to a non-juridical understanding of marriage itself was the questioning of the historical belief that marriage had about it a unitive dimension which was to last for life. Many began to suggest that while the value of such permanence was an essential ingredient of Christian marriage, the concept of indissolubility, which expressed that permanence, was as inadequate to the mystery of marital permanence as the concept of contract was to the mystery of marital union. The suggestion was made that a movement away from the physical imagery of the *vinculum,* or bond of indissolubility, toward the idea of a moral ideal or ethical imperative would be more faithful to the Christian belief.[19]

In some of these areas the papal exhortation clearly reflects the movement which has taken place in theological circles. The primary source of reflection on the meaning of Christian marriage is not a legal category but the very mystery of the Godhead. The reasoning is easy to follow. Humans are made in the image of God and thus share in the meaning of a divine plan (FC§§11, 17). It is the meaning of the divine that gives shape and direction to what is human. And that meaning is: "God is love, and in Himself He lives a mystery of personal loving communion" (FC§11). The human person is given the capacity and responsibility of such love and communion.

Setting aside for the moment the detailed analysis of the question of sexuality, it is necessary to point out that, according to the text, this vocation to the love and communion of the Godhead can be expressed either in marriage or celibacy. In marriage, the total physical self-giving of conjugal love is akin to the intimate community of life and love that is willed by God. The only place in which love is possible is in marriage. Marriage is the interior requirement for the covenant of conjugal love that is publicly affirmed as unique and faithful.

While this covenanted love, which requires marriage as its necessary conclusion, reflects the inner life of the Godhead, there is another dimension to the Godhead: its relationship with the human family. In this relationship, God is seen as being ever faithful. This fidelity is especially revealed in the covenant of God with the people of Israel and becomes the "model of the relations of faithful love that should exist between spouses" (FC§12). Because marriage is a reflection of the inner and outer life of the Godhead, it naturally is a covenanted and faithful love that unites two persons together in life.

This inner meaning is brought to fulfillment in Christ and his sacrificial union with humankind and the church. In Christ, man and woman are given the capacity to live as he did, and the plan "which God has imprinted on the humanity of man and woman since creation" is revealed (FC§13). Conjugal love reaches a fullness to which it is ordered, conjugal charity; and because it is a participation in the spousal love of Christ, it is sacramental in nature. For that reason, marriage between two Christians has been considered one of the seven sacraments of church life and understood to be indissoluble.

In this discussion of the basic meaning of Christian marriage, the pope again has caught the flavor of contemporary theological discussion. By moving into the interiority of the life of the Godhead, in fact, he has given greater depth to the communitarian dimension of marital love. The clear association of marriage with the movement of divine faithfulness gives a firm foundation to the permanency and sacramentality of Christian marriage.

In the same way, the document goes a long way to rectify an exaggerated view of the relationship of childbearing to marital life. On the one hand, the pope proposes that the fruitfulness, which is to be part of marital life, is not to be restricted solely to the procreation of children, but "is enlarged and enriched by all those fruits of moral, spiritual, and supernatural life which the father and mother are called to hand on to their children, and through the children to the church and to the world" (FC§28). On the other hand, in speaking of physical sterility, he says that "even when procreation is not possible, conjugal life does not for this reason lose its value" (FC§14). In fact, it can be the occasion for other important services to the life of the human person.

Though these correctives are present, the more traditional emphasis on the procreative aspect of marriage is not lost. Early in the document, he proclaims that "the very institution of marriage and conjugal love is ordained to the procreation and education of children, in whom it finds its crowning" (FC§14). Though this unnuanced assertion is later contextualized by the Vatican II concern not to make "the other purposes of matrimony of less account," he affirms with Vatican II that "the true practice of conjugal love and the whole meaning of family life which results from it, have this aim: that the couple be ready with stout hearts to cooperate with the love of the creator and savior, who through them will enlarge and enrich His own family day by day" (FC§28).

Reviewing the papal theology, one sympathetic to the recent theological concerns would raise certain questions. For example, because of the clear and repeated affirmation in the past of the unique ordering of marriage towards childbearing, has there been any attempt to reconcile the tension between a communion of life and love, which is the pope's basic image of marriage, with the demands of childbearing? After reading the full text, one wonders whether the prior category of the primary end of marriage as procreation has really been replaced by the primacy of a community of life and love.

Similarly, though the argumentation for the unity and permanence of marriage originates in the faithfulness of God toward all people, is it clear that the concept of indissolubility is the most apt expression of that unity and permanence? Or is the use of indissolubility in part influenced by the primacy of childbearing? The reason for the question is that if we accept the primary meaning for permanence as being rooted in divine fidelity, then the justification for indissolubility contains a second reason: the good of children (FC§20). Without denying that children need a stable familial setting, is that need of the same significance as the fidelity of Christ to his church? Is it possible that there could be other needs on the part of the children that are equal to or at times greater than such stability? If so, how do they relate to the concept of indissolubility? Finally, in the context of marriage that is understood in personal and communal terms, how can one use the impersonal and juridical category of indissolubility to describe interpersonal fidelity? These and other questions reflect a significant distance between this part of the papal exhortation and the work of contemporary theology.

THE SIGNIFICANCE OF HUMAN SEXUALITY

It is no secret that for many centuries the Catholic tradition in regard to human sexuality was marked by dualism and negativity. Within much of Catholic writing there was a suspicion of a dichotomy between the corporeal and spiritual dimensions of a person. It was the spiritual dimension which was more divine-like, therefore it was implied that corporeality was less than good. Because sexuality is experienced as something very much related to the body, it was often viewed as a necessary evil of the human condition and was justified only in the context of the procreation of offspring. The specific ethic which developed this perspective was equally negative in orientation and actuality. The only appropriate context of sexuality and sexual activity was that of marriage. In line with this approach, celibacy was viewed as a better or higher vocation than marriage. [20]

Consistent with the other developments in Catholic theology, there has been a move away from this dualism and negativity. The human person is now viewed as a totality whose life project is to integrate all parts of one's being. Human sexuality is no longer identified with the genital function but is essentially related to the distinctively human capacity for, and drive toward, intimacy. In such a context, sexuality is a basic human good and is devoid of all taint of evil. (Though like all human goods, it is capable of misuse.)[21]

When viewed in this manner and placed in the context of the newer understanding of moral values or norms, sexuality and sexual activity are evaluated in a very different fashion. Though there is no consensus on the terms of the analysis, many moral theologians have come to ethical conclusions on issues such as masturbation, pre-marital sexuality, birth control, and homosexuality that are at variance with earlier stances. Likewise, the meaning of celibacy or virginity is expressed differently.

Once again, the papal document reflects an awareness of this newer understanding of human sexuality. In unequivocal terms it moves away from the exaggerated dualism of the past when it describes the human vocation to love as the vocation of a "unified totality" (FC§11). "Love includes the human body, and the body is made a sharer in spiritual love." Sexuality is not something tainted by its embodiment, but "concerns the innermost being of the human persons as such" (FC§11). While not speaking directly of intimacy, the pope describes sexuality as only being truly human if it is "an integral part of the love by which a man and woman unite themselves totally to one another until death" (FC§11).

Where the document diverges from contemporary writing is in its apparent identification of sexuality with marriage, and in particular with fertility. Though all people are called to a vocation of love, the pope only mentions "two ways of realizing" this vocation: "marriage and virginity or celibacy" (FC§11). But sexuality is only realized "in a truly human way" in the marital union. The obvious question of the newer theological stance described above is: What does this say about the sexuality of those who are not in a marital union? Is their sexuality to be expressed or experienced in a less than human way? If the only "place" in which this self-giving "in its whole truth is made possible is marriage," then is the love of a celibate or non-married person less than the whole truth? (FC§11).

When the logic of this first discussion is placed alongside the explicit discussion of celibacy or virginity, the papal answers to the above question become more apparent. In comparing marriage and celibacy, the pope says that "when human sexuality is not regarded as a great value given by the creator, the *renunciation of it* for the sake of the kingdom of heaven loses its meaning" (FC§16). Though the Holy Father goes on to suggest that the meaning of celibacy is to give witness to and support of marriage, because celibacy gives witness to the "eschatological marriage of Christ with the church…," it would seem that the celibate or consecrated virgin is one who left sexuality behind. In suggesting this renunciation, the document has returned to an understanding of sexuality that is rather physical in nature and specifically identified with the genital. This assumption is complicated, however, by the later assertion that celibacy is "the supreme form of that self-giving that constitutes the very meaning of sexuality" (FC§37). At the very least, the relationship between sexuality and intimacy with the celibate life is not self-evident.

Besides being concerned about this rather "asexual" notion of celibacy, some theologians wonder whether this line of reasoning provides any explanation of the place of sexuality in the life of the unmarried who are not called to celibacy or consecrated virginity. Especially in the United States and other Western nations, the numbers of such people are growing. And the document provides no theoretical foundation for the meaning of their lives.

At the same time, the document continues the historical affirmation that, because of its eschatological witness, the charism of celibacy is superior to that of marriage "by reason of the wholly singular link which it has with the kingdom of God" (FC§16). Many theologians would be uncomfortable with the identification of one charism as superior to another, especially when the very nature of marriage has been identified in this document as reflective of the inner life of the Godhead. Is it not possible to say that both charisms are divine calls, without the prioritization which seems to resurrect the old dualism?

Turning to the specific ethical imperatives that flow from this theoretical posture, the exhortation unequivocally affirms the teaching of *Humanae Vitae*. This begins with an affirmation of the values which are to be present within marital love and marital sexuality. The love "between husband and wife must be fully human, exclusive, and open to new life" (FC§29). The proper expression of these values requires that there can be no breaking of the "inseparable connection willed by God…between the two meanings of the conjugal act: the unitive meaning and the procreative meaning" (FC§32). For that reason, he reasserts that an act is intrinsically immoral that "either in anticipation of the conjugal act, or in its accomplishment, or in the development of its natural consequences, proposes, whether as an end or as a means, to render procreation impossible" (FC§32).

This affirmation of the intrinsic evil of birth control and sterilization not only affirms the papal adherence to a vision of moral norms and values that were mentioned above, but it also gives implicit support to the specific ethical conclusions which have been applied to the question of masturbation, pre-martial sexuality, and homosexuality. Such conclusions have been, and will remain, a source of tension between papal teaching and the writings of many moral theologians.

THE SACRAMENTALITY OF CHRISTIAN MARRIAGE

As we noted above, the present theology and discipline of marriage is very much a product of an age when the ecclesial experience and cultural experience were one—the age of Christendom. In that world, all who were baptized were assumed to be believers, and all who believed were capable of, and intended to do, what the church intended.

Within this perspective, the church's belief—that all those who were baptized and celebrated a marriage had necessarily contracted a valid sacramental union—made perfect sense.[22]

In recent years, however, many theologians have questioned this assumption. It should be clear that the theologians have not questioned whether a true Christian marriage is sacramental, but only *when* a marriage is sacramental. (The manner in which the permanency is associated with that sacramentality is questioned, however.) The reason for the recent concern is that in many parts of the Western world baptism has become more of a social event than a celebration of faith. And so baptized Catholics may approach marriage without what many theologians would consider to be a true faith in the Christian mysteries. Without such faith, theologians ask whether there can be a sacramental and permanent union. Implicit in this discussion is a re-examination of the meaning of Christian faith. Consistent with the movement to think of the human person in a wholistic and developmental fashion, there has been a move to understand faith not in mechanistic terms but as a lived reality in which a person is called to move from an immature to mature possession.[23]

The pastoral conclusions of this thinking have been significant. First, there is the acknowledgement that there can be a baptized person who, in fact, is not a believer and therefore is incapable of a sacramental union. Second, there can be baptized Catholics who wish to get married but who are not at a level of faith possession that would allow them to live a Christian sacramental union in its full meaning. Third, marriage should be prepared for with a care and pastoral strategy that will help the couple move from a less mature to a more mature understanding of its meaning and toward the ability to celebrate marriage in its Christian fullness. Where such movement does not occur, then marriage should be delayed.[24]

The Holy Father, in his reflections on the pastoral care of the family, recognizes the change in emphasis which these discussions have precipitated. Noting that we live in a secularized society, he acknowledges that the "faith of the person asking the church for marriage can exist in different degrees..." (FC§68). For that reason, he strongly urges that there should be a time of preparation for marriage, which is a type of "journey of faith which is similar to the catechumenate" (FC§66). Such a journey is a gradual and continuous process with three main stages: remote, proximate, and immediate. Though this preparation is primarily meant to prepare the couple for entering the marriage union, it is also to assist the couple in seeing that their union is an interpersonal relationship that is "to be continually developed."

Though recognizing the developmental nature of faith and the various levels of peoples' readiness for marriage, the pope draws some conclusions that would challenge certain pastoral strategies. While he calls for a period of preparation, saying that one "must not underestimate the necessity and obligation of immediate preparation for marriage," he goes on to say that such preparation should be put in practice "in such a way that omitting it is not an impediment to the celebration of marriage" (FC§66).

Similarly, though he recognizes the different levels of faith possession, the pope tells pastors that they must also understand "the reasons that lead the church to admit to the celebration of marriage those who are imperfectly disposed" (FC§68). The reasoning behind this conclusion is interesting. In line with his earlier description of marriage, he suggests that marriage is part of the very economy of creation and the decision of a couple to marry "in accordance with this divine plan...really involves, even if not in a fully conscious way, an attitude of profound obedience to the will of God, an attitude which cannot exist without God's grace." This possibility of right intention enlightened by grace means that those who are baptized "at least implicitly, consent to what the church intends to do when she celebrates marriage" (FC§68). The conclusion of this reasoning would be that ordinarily it is impossible to have a union of two baptized persons that is not sacramental in nature. This is affirmed in a later section when the pope speaks against trial marriages, saying that "between two baptized persons there can exist only an indissoluble marriage" (FC§80).

Implicit in this stance is a rejection of the pastoral practice, which has developed in some areas, of distinguishing between different types of unions which Christians might celebrate. In this practice, only those who are fully prepared to celebrate the integral meaning of marriage would be allowed to enter a sacramental union. For those not so prepared, a different non-sacramental ceremony would be celebrated. Though his focus is on the reality of Catholics who celebrate a merely civil marriage, the pope opposes this practice when he speaks against baptized Catholics entering into any union that is not fully sacramental. Though he recognizes that such unions reflect the desire of a couple to accept not only the advantages but also the obligations of marriage, he says that "nevertheless, not even this situation is acceptable to the church" (FC§82). It should be noted, however, that while he affirms the impropriety of a Catholic entering into a non-sacramental union and discourages any other unions for the baptized, he does say that whenever a couple "reject explicitly and formally what the church intends to do when the marriage of baptized persons is celebrated, the pastor of souls cannot admit them to the celebration of marriage" (FC§68).

As in other sections of the exhortation, it is difficult for many theologians to reconcile the pope's recognition of certain theological and pastoral developments with his refusal to accept consequent changes in pastoral practice. Many of those who are actively involved in parochial ministry would question the necessity of maintaining the identification of sacramentality with the union of two baptized Christians regardless of their level of faith. Likewise, the resorting to an "implicit" or unconscious faith is viewed as not being consistent with the principles of faith development and maturation that is called for in the new Rite of Christian Initiation of Adults. They would argue that it would be better to respond with a pastoral practice that would recognize the diversity of those approaching marriage, rather than insisting on a sacramental marriage or no marriage at all. In this instance, the pope is rather clear in why he wishes to affirm his view:

> As for wishing to lay down further criteria for admission to the ecclesial celebration of marriage, criteria that would concern the level of faith of those to be married, this would above all involve grave risks. In the first place, the risk of making unfounded and discriminatory judgments; second, the risk of causing doubts about the validity of marriages already celebrated, with grave harm to Christian communities and new and unjustified anxieties to the consciences of married couples; one would also fall into the danger of calling into question the sacramental nature of many marriages of brethren separated from full communion with the Catholic Church, thus contradicting ecclesial tradition (FC§68).

Whether the citing of these risks will convince those who have raised the concern noted above is not evident.

RESPONSE TO MARITAL FAILURE

Many of the developments outlined above come to a very concrete articulation in the way in which the church responds to those who experience marital failure. The understanding of the meaning of church and the nature of moral norms, the articulation of marriage, its sacramentality and indissolubility, all coalesce into a pastoral practice regarding marital failure and the remarriage of divorced Catholics.

In theological and canonical circles the approach to such people has undergone a significant evolution. Previously, there was one and only one response to someone who had contracted a church wedding: If you cannot keep the marriage together and if a church court does not grant an annulment, then you may live apart but never remarry. If someone acted contrary to that discipline and did remarry, but later sought to return to full participation in the life of the church, they were required to leave the invalid union. In those instances where such a separation would cause extreme harm, then a couple could be allowed to live together as "brother and sister."[25]

The first change that has occurred is in the procedures and theory which guide the church tribunal system. Responding to the growing number of Catholics who have experienced a breakdown of their marriages, the theological and canonical tradition has developed so that more Catholics are able to have recourse to the external forum of church tribunals in order to find the freedom to remarry.[26]

But these developments were soon found to be inadequate to the complexity of the situation. What could be done for those who had been in a previous union that they believed to be invalid, but which for a variety of reasons could not be submitted to a tribunal? What of those who had been in a previous union they believed to be valid, but who now are in a second union that is permanent and stable? Is there no way in which they might return to the life of the church? In either or both of these situations, is there any way in which the couple could have some public recognition of this second union?

At the same time as these questions were being raised, a related issue was being debated: What is the relationship between full participation in the Eucharist and indissolubility? Is it possible for one who has celebrated a valid union where both parties are still alive, and is in a second union, to receive the Eucharist?

The discussion of these questions has been extensive, and it would be inappropriate to say that there is a clear theological consensus on all issues. It is possible to give an outline of what many would suggest is a "probable" opinion on certain of these questions and what, in fact, has become the pastoral practice in many parts of the church in the United States and which, in some local churches, exists with episcopal approval.[27]

First, there is a large number of theologians who hold that there is no necessary union between indissolubility and reception of the Eucharist. There are valid reasons to argue that in certain situations it is possible for one who is living in a second but irregular union to receive the sacraments. Once this has been determined as possible, then the question of "when" becomes foremost.[28]

Second, there is a recognition that the pastoral response to marital failure should recognize the different types of situations which are present. For those who in good conscience believe their previous union was invalid, should they not be allowed to share in the sacramental life of the church? The answer to this question for many is a rather firm yes. Because their problem cannot be solved in the external forum of the tribunal, it is proposed that an internal forum solution is possible. In this context of conscience and in light of certain general guidelines for the pastoral care of such situations, a return to full participation in the life of the church is possible. Such situations are described as "hardship" cases.[29]

While there appears to be a fair amount of theoretical and pastoral consensus on these cases, it is not as clear in the instance of one who knows that the previous union was valid. These situations are known as "conflict" cases, and some theologians would approve a cautious readmission to the sacraments on a case-by-case basis.[30]

There is even less consensus on whether there can be any kind of liturgical or para-liturgical recognition of these second unions. There has been no serious suggestion in print that such unions be regarded in the same manner as an external forum sacramental union. To do so would be to compromise the meaning of such union. There has been discussion about, and in pastoral practice there have been attempts to provide, some kind of a celebration that while not being the same as a sacramental marriage would celebrate in an ecclesial and prayerful setting the goodness of the second union.[31]

The papal response to these developments continues the pattern which has emerged previously. There is a recognition of, and sensitivity to, the pastoral issues, but at the same time there is a firm disagreement over the response or resolution. The Holy Father recognizes that "various reasons can unfortunately lead to the often irreparable breakdown of valid marriages" (FC§83). He asks the ecclesial community to "support such people more than ever."

The document also recognizes that many Catholics who experience divorce "usually intend to enter a second union." Though calling this an evil, the pope says that the church "cannot abandon to their own devices those who have been previously bound by a sacramental marriage and who have attempted a second marriage" (FC§84). He goes on to say that pastors must carefully discern the situation because there is a difference between those who are suffering after having tried to save a marriage and those who, through their own fault, have destroyed a canonically valid marriage. In the spirit of this discernment, pastors and the whole community are called upon to help such people feel at home in the church and its life of prayer.

There are limits, however, to this participation. This is because "...the church reaffirms her practice, which is based upon sacred scripture, of not admitting to Eucharistic communion divorced people who have remarried" (FC§84). The reasons for this decision are two. First, the condition of the second union objectively violates the union which is signified by the Eucharist. Second, if this were to happen, "the faithful would be led into error and confusion regarding the church's teaching about the indissolubility of marriage" (FC§84). The only way possible for there to be participation in the sacramental life of the church would be for the couple to "take on themselves the duty to live in complete continence, that is, by abstinence from the acts proper to married couples" (FC§84).

For the same reasons, the pope says that it is forbidden for "...any pastor for whatever reason or pretext, even of a pastoral nature, to perform ceremonies of any kind for divorced people who remarry" (FC§84).

The full force of this discipline also would seem to apply to those who enter a second union and are "subjectively certain in conscience that their previous and irreparably destroyed marriage had never been valid" (FC§84).

With these words, the pope once again places himself at variance with a large number of theologians. While many theologians would be uncomfortable about suggesting that there is clarity on all of these issues, there would be a strong feeling that there have been enough historical, theological, and pastoral questions raised to suggest that there is need of a more nuanced reconsideration of the present discipline. The papal affirmation of the existing discipline with the firmness of its assertion would be considered premature and unfortunate.

CONCLUSION

The focus of these considerations has been a comparison of the theology of marriage found in the papal exhortation *Familiaris Consortio* and the manner in which some theologians are considering the same themes or topics. The results of the comparisons have been striking. It is obvious that the papal thought in many ways is similar to the thought of the theologians. This is especially true in what could be considered the more theoretical aspects of his thought. The pope acknowledges the theological significance of the "signs of the times," recognizes the diverse charisms within the ecclesial community, senses the complex nature of values and the need for growth in virtue, regards marriage as a community of life and love, affirms that sexuality is a dimension of the entire person, notes the need for adequate preparation within the journey of faith preparatory to marriage, and calls the church to a pastoral sensitivity towards those who experience marital failure.

Though there is this notable similarity or agreement, there is a striking disparity when it comes to the development and application of these concepts. The pope and theologians have very different postures on the role of the laity and theologians in discerning truth, on the meaning of moral norms, on the import of childbearing in marriage, on the nature of indissolubility, on the rejection of artificial birth control, and on denying access to the Eucharist for the divorced and remarried.

Such diversity in itself is not something to be feared. The life of the Christian community has seen such diversity throughout the centuries. What is disconcerting is the absence of the ways in which dialogue on these questions can be opened so that a consistent or integrated vision can be offered to the church. Three factors appear to be working against such a dialogue. First, there is the papal description of the role of the theologian. The theologians seem to be restricted to the explanation of what has already been decided. There is no clear theology of how the theologians may participate in the development of doctrine. Until there is agreement on this issue, there does not seem to be much opportunity for real dialogue.

Second, there is the almost dichotomous nature of the theology found in the exhortation. On the one hand, the pope seems to embrace the themes and values of the post-Vatican II enterprise. But, on the other hand, when those themes or values are brought to bear on more concrete or applied questions, the pope arrives at a very different set of conclusions than those of many theologians. It is not easy to discuss how such apparently common presuppositions can render such different conclusions.

Third, though the theologians have arrived at a different set of conclusions, most of them do so with a tentativeness that reflects a desire to reconcile the insights of the tradition with the results of contemporary thought and practice. The underlying assumption is that in areas of Christian practice, which are known to have been highly influenced by historical and cultural conditions, there is the possibility of change or development. The tenor of this exhortation, however, with its consistent reaffirmation of pastoral strategies which some would suggest have not been the perennial position of the church, appears to be opposed to such openness. If the implicit assumption of any conversation is that the mode of presentation can change but the conclusions cannot, then there is very little room for future dialogue.

Rather than being restricted by these factors which appear to complicate the possibility of dialogue, would it not be better for the theological community, in cooperation with the other sciences, to pursue those fundamental questions, the answers to which might provide the environment for a future conversation? Three such topics might be:

What is the relationship between developing human experience and the meaning of the category "truth"? Can there be qualitative change in human understanding without losing any sense of objectivity or meaning?

What is the meaning of human intimacy, its relationship to sexuality, procreation and marriage?

What is the meaning of church? Is it a pilgrim community of sinners or an eschatological incarnation of divine ideals?

Hopefully, the good will of all and hard work of scholarship, combined with a great deal of patience, will insure that the dialogue takes place.

Notes

1. For a description of the complexity of the contemporary theological enterprise, see the chapter entitled "The Pluralist Context of Contemporary Theology," in David Tracy's *Blessed Rage for Order* (New York: Seabury Press, 1975).

2. The Synod of Bishops is a post Vatican II development. In an attempt to express the collegial nature of the office of bishop and the intimate relationship between the college of bishops and bishop of Rome, the Synod of Bishops was established. It does not sit, however, as a legislative body. It meets at the summons of the pope, and it is not free to establish its own agenda. The results of its deliberations are advisory to the Holy See.

3. It is not possible to cite all of the material related to the activities of this Synod. A valuable resource is the NC Documentary Service *Origins*. Some pertinent material would be: the working paper prepared by the Synod Secretariat found in *Origins* 9 (1979) pp. 113–28; the working paper which was submitted to the Synod when it began its deliberations, found as excerpted in *Origins* (1980) pp. 227–33; various interventions of the Synod participants published during and after the Synod; and the Synod's final "Message to Christian Families" *Origins* 10 (1980) pp. 321–29.

4. For detailed references see: Edward Schillebeeckx, *Marriage: Human Reality, and Saving Mystery* (New York: Sheed and Ward, 1965); William Bassett and Peter Huizing, eds., *The Future of Christian Marriage*, Concilium, volume 87 (New York: Herder and Herder, 1973); Franz Bockle, ed., *The Future of Marriage as an Institution*, Concilium, volume 55 (New York: Herder and Herder, 1970); Charles E. Curran, "Divorce in Light of a Revised Moral Theology," *Ongoing Revision: Studies in Moral Theology* (Notre Dame: Fides, 1975), pp. 66–106; Charles E. Curran, "Divorce: Catholic Theory and Practice," *New Perspectives in Moral Theology* (Notre Dame: University of Notre Dame Press, 1976), pp. 212–76; Robert T. Kennedy and John T. Finnegan, "Select Bibliography on Divorce and Remarriage in the Church Today," *Ministering to Divorced Catholics*, James J. Young, ed. (New York: Paulist Press, 1979), pp. 260–76; Richard A. McCormick, "Notes on Moral Theology," *Theological Studies* 32 (1971) 107–22; 33 (1972) 91–100; 36 (1975) 100–117; and Seamus Ryan, "Surveys of Periodicals: Indissolubility of Marriage," *The Furrow* 24 (1973)

150–59, 214–24, 272–84, 356–74, 524–39. A more recent bibliography can be found in Thomas P. Doyle, O.P., ed., *Marriage Studies* (Toledo: Canon Law Society of America, 1980), pp. 78–101.

5. The selection of topics obviously reflects the theological interests of the writer. Several topics of significance are not considered both for want of space and lack of competence. Their exclusion is not a comment on their merit. In the same way, there is an obvious editorial judgment involved in the decision as to which theological positions will be presented. Without engaging in the impossible task of attempting to label the ideological postures that are presented, it is possible to say that these are the positions which a review of recent proceedings of the Canon Law Society of America or of the Catholic Theological Society of America would find being discussed or cited.

6. For the development of the neo-Thomist paradigm, see Gerald McCool, *Catholic Theology in the Nineteenth Century* (New York: Seabury, 1977). This research and the work of other theologians have suggested that there have been a variety of ways in which the church has experienced itself. Various forces have contributed to these developments. For an analysis of these forces and an extended bibliography, see "A Social Portrait of the Theologian," in David Tracy, *The Analogical Imagination* (New York: Crossroad, 1981) pp. 3–46.

7. The best description of this position can be found in Bernard Lonergan's "The Transition from a Classicist World View to Historical Mindedness," *Law for Liberty*, James Biechler, ed. (Baltimore: Helicon, 1967) pp. 126–33. The consequence of this model for the theological enterprise is developed by David Tracy in his revisionist model of theology. See Tracy, *Blessed Rage for Order*, pp. 43–64.

8. The ground-breaking work in this area of ecclesial models was that of Avery Dulles, *Models of the Church* (New York: Doubleday, 1974). Similarly, Richard McBrien, in his *Catholicism* (Minneapolis: Winston, 1980) pp. 691–728, develops his own notion of ecclesial models. The theological and historical sources of much of this work have been the writings of Yves Congar and Karl Rahner.

9. Avery Dulles summarizes this development when he says in his book, *Resilient Church* (Garden City: Doubleday, 1977), p. 100: "Among the living voices that have authority in the Church I would mention, in the first place, the general sense of the faithful. This is to be obtained not simply by counting noses but by weighing opinions. The views of alert and committed Christians should be given more weight than those of indifferent or marginal Christians, but even the doubts of marginal persons should be attentively considered to see if they do not contain some prophetic message for the Church. The sense of the faithful should be seen not simply as a static index but as a process. If it becomes clear that large numbers of generous, intelligent, prayerful, and committed Christians

who seriously study a given problem change their views in a certain direction, this may be evidence that the Holy Spirit is so inclining them. But there is need for caution and discernment to avoid mistaking the influences of secular fashion for the inspirations of divine grace."

Intimately related to the role of the laity in the development of Catholic tradition is the question of dissent. For discussions of dissent from the magisterium see Richard McCormick in *Theological Studies* 29 (1968) pp. 714–18; 30 (1969) pp. 644–68; and 38 (1977) pp. 84–100; and in *Proceedings of the Catholic Theological Society of America* 24 (1969) pp. 239–54.

10. The relationship between the theologian and the magisterium has had a complex history. For a summary of a great deal of recent research, see *Chicago Studies* 17 (1978), which is devoted to the theme "The Magisterium, the Theologian and the Educator." The question of there being a "magisterium of doctors" is explored by Yves Congar, "Bref Histoire des Formes du 'Magistére' et ses relations avec les docteurs," *Rev. des sciences phil. et theol.*, 60 (1976), p. 104. Also see Avery Dulles, S.J., "What Is Magisterium" *Origins* 6 (1976) pp. 81–87. For a recent commentary on the role of the moral theologian in the church, see Edward A. Malloy, C.S.C., "The Christian Ethicist in the Community of Faith," *Theological Studies* 43 (1982) pp. 399–427.

11. For the teaching of Pius XII on the role of the theologian, see his encyclical *Humani Generis*, AAS 42 (1959) pp. 561 and 562.

12. Writers such as Curran, Dedek, O'Connell, Keane and McCormick would exemplify this approach.

13. The debate over the role of conflict and its consequences for the ethical enterprise has been central to Roman Catholic moral theology for almost twenty years. For a collection of some of the most important writings within the debate, see *Doing Evil to Achieve Good* edited by Richard McCormick and Paul Ramsey (Chicago: Loyola Press, 1978). To follow the history of this debate, the writings of McCormick in his annual "Moral Notes" in *Theological Studies* are an invaluable resource. Fifteen years of his articles have been published in a collection entitled *Notes on Moral Theology, 1965 through 1980* (Washington, D.C.: University Press of America, 1981). For a systematic presentation of the theological posture which incorporates a full recognition of the role of conflict, see Timothy O'Connell, *Principles for a Catholic Morality* (New York: Seabury Press, 1978).

14. This position is developed by O'Connell, *Principles*, pp. 83–97.

15. Though the question of compromise has been discussed by many others, it has been treated explicitly by Charles Curran. For examples of his thought, see his *A New Look at Christian Morality* (Notre Dame: Fides, 1968) pp. 169–73, 232–33 and his *Catholic Moral Theology in Dialogue* (Notre Dame: University of Notre Dame Press, 1976) pp. 216–19. For a discussion of his theory, see my

article "The Pastoral Implications of Charles Curran's Theory of Compromise," *Chicago Studies* 17 (1978) pp. 225–41.

16. Recently there has been a great deal of scholarly work on the history of, and theological developments surrounding, the Christian understanding of marriage. Inspired by Edward Schillebeeckx's *Marriage: Human Reality, Saving Mystery* (New York: Sheed and Ward, 1965), other theologians and historians have traced the development of the church's understanding of marriage. Two such works are Walter Kasper, *Theology of Christian Marriage* (New York: Seabury, 1980) and Theodore Mackin, S.J., *What Is Marriage?* (New York: Paulist Press, 1982). For a popular review of the history of Christian marriage, see Michael D. Place, "The History of Christian Marriage," *Chicago Studies* 18 (1979) pp. 311–26. As a reference point, citations pertaining to the development of an understanding of marriage will be from Mackin. The impact of the middle ages can be found in Mackin's *What Is Marriage?* pp. 145–76.

17. Mackin, *What Is Marriage?* pp. 176–224.

18. The shift in perspective on the meaning of Christian marriage involved a major transition in Catholic thought. The acceptance of marriage as being covenantal in nature has had an effect on the theological and canonical life of the church. An overview of this movement can be found in Mackin, *What Is Marriage?* pp. 225–327. For a sampling of the theological journal writing on this subject and a fuller bibliography of some of the early writing on this question, see Paul F. Palmer, "Christian Marriage: Contract or Covenant," *Theological Studies* 33 (1974) pp. 617–65, and Mackin, "Conjugal Love and the Magisterium," *The Jurist* (1976) pp. 263–301. To understand how this change in perspective has affected the canonical tradition and the practices of the American tribunal system, as well as for an extensive bibliography on this subject, see Thomas P. Doyle, O.P., "Matrimonial Jurisprudence in the United States," *Marriage Studies* 2 (1982) pp. 111–59.

19. The literature on the question of the meaning of indissolubility and whether it is the best expression of the notion of marital permanence is vast. Certain works have contributed significantly to the dialogue. They are Bernard Häring, "A Theological Appraisal of Marriage Tribunals," *Divorce and Remarriage in the Catholic Church*, Lawrence G. Wrenn, ed. (New York: Newman Press, 1973) pp. 18–21 and Lawrence G. Wrenn "Marriage—Indissoluble or Fragile," in the same work, pp. 134–47. Also see Charles E. Curran, "Divorce: Catholic Theory and Practice," *New Perspectives in Moral Theology* (Notre Dame: University of Notre Dame Press, 1976) pp. 212–76 and Richard A. McCormick, "Indissolubility and the Right to the Eucharist: Separate Issues or One?" *Canon Law Society of America Proceedings* 37 (1975) pp. 26–37. For a review and commentary on this discussion, see McCormick, *Notes on Moral Theology* pp. 544–63.

20. For a brief overview of this approach to sexuality, see Philip S. Keane, S.S., *Sexual Morality, a Catholic Perspective* (New York: Paulist Press, 1977) pp. 5–13.

21. There are two works in English which exemplify this change in understanding. They are the work of Philip Keane cited in the note above and the controversial Anthony Kosnik, et al., *Human Sexuality: New Directions in American Catholic Thought* (New York: Paulist Press, 1977). The literature surrounding the publication of *Human Sexuality* is extensive. For an initial survey, see McCormick, *Notes on Moral Theology*, pp. 737–45.

22. The historical setting of this understanding is found in Mackin, *What Is Marriage?* pp. 145–224.

23. A sampling of the writing which has contributed to this new theology of marriage would include: Karl Rahner, "Marriage as a Sacrament," *Theological Investigations, Vol. 10* (New York: Herder and Herder, 1973) pp. 199–221; Edward Killmartin, "When Is Marriage a Sacrament?" *Theological Studies* 34 (1973) pp. 275–86; William J. LaDue, "The Sacrament of Marriage," *Canon Law Society of America Proceedings* 36 (1974) pp. 25–35. An article by Ladislas Orsy, S.J., "Faith, Sacrament, Contract and Christian Marriage: Disputed Questions," *Theological Studies* 43 (1982) pp. 379–98 reviews the current state of the discussion and proposes a contemporary understanding of faith in his footnote 6.

24. For a description of this evolving pastoral practice and its complexity, see Orsy, "Christian Marriage: Disputed Questions" cited above and James A. Schmeiser, "Welcomed Civil Canonical Marriages," *Studia Canonica* 14 (1980) pp. 49–88; also Walter Cuenin, "The Marriage of Baptized Non-Believers," *Origins* 9 (1978) pp. 321–28. For one description of a program that prepares the Catholic couple for marriage, see *A Special Kind of Loving* (Chicago: Buckley, 1980), which summarizes the work of the Marriage and Family Life Office of the Archdiocese of Chicago.

25. For a summary of the previous discipline and the developments which have taken place in recent years, as well as a popular review of the subject matter of this section, see Thomas J. Green, "Canonical-Pastoral Reflection on Divorce and Remarriage," *Living Light* 13 (1976) pp. 560–76.

26. For extensive discussions on the present state of the law and tribunal practice as well as possible future changes resulting from the promulgation of a new Code, see Thomas J. Green: "The Revised Schema De Matrimonio: Text and Reflections," *The Jurist* 40 (1980) pp. 57–137; "Marriage Nullity Procedures in the Schema *De Processibus*," *The Jurist* 38 (1978) pp. 311–414, and "The Revision of the Procedural Law Schema: Implications for Tribunal Practice," *The Jurist* 40 (1980) pp. 349–83. All three of these articles contain excel-

lent bibliographical references to the literature on the theology of marriage as well as the revision of church law and procedures.

27. Two articles which summarize much of the recent discussion are James H. Provost, "Intolerable Marriages Revisited," *The Jurist* 40 (1980) pp. 141–96 and Anthony Diacetis and Michael Place, "Alternative Possibilities for Pastoral Care for the Remarried," *Canon Law Society of America Proceedings* 43 (1981) pp. 270–84. Also see McCormick, *Moral Notes*, pp. 332–48, 372–80, 544–61, 826–40.

28. The most articulate statement of this position can be found in McCormick, "Indissolubility and the Right to the Eucharist."

29. A suggested set of guidelines for hardship situations was proposed by a committee of the Canon Law Society of America (Committee on Alternatives to Tribunal Procedures, *Canon Law Society of America Proceedings* 37 [1975] pp. 170–74). They were: "(1) the previous marriage (or marriages) is irretrievably broken and reconciliation is impossible; (2) obligations incurred by virtue of the previous marriage are accepted and responsibly discharged; (3) obligations arising from the present union are accepted and responsibly discharged; (4) a willingness to live the Christian faith in the ecclesial community is apparent." For a study of the canonical implication of internal forum solutions, see Robert W. Thrasher, "Reflections on Canon 1014," *Marriage Studies*, Thomas P. Doyle, ed. (Toledo: Canon Law Society of America, 1980) pp. 144–45. For a popular presentation of this matter and other related questions, see Thomas J. Green, "Ministering to Marital Failure," *Chicago Studies* 18 (1979) pp. 327–44.

30. The discussion of these two types of situations has not been confined to theological or canonical journals. For a review of discussions and actions taken by bishops and the Holy See, see Provost, "Intolerable Marriages Revisited," pp. 174–93.

31. One of the clearest discussions of this possibility can be found in Curran, "Divorce: Catholic Theory and Practice," pp. 246–47.

15. Economic Justice for Whom?
Women Enter the Dialogue

Pamela K. Brubaker

This chapter first appeared in *Religion and Economic Justice*, ed. Michael Zweig, in 1991.

The primary conceptual reason for the marginality of women's needs and experiences within Roman Catholic papal teaching and liberation theology is the perpetuation of a static, natural law view of women's nature. Even recent pronouncements, such as those of the Latin American bishops at Puebla, the encyclicals of John Paul II, and the United States bishops' pastoral letter on the U.S. economy, which show increasing concern for women's marginality, have not moved beyond these conceptions. For instance, the Puebla documents speak of woman's fundamental role as that of mother and charge that this role must shape women's social participation. Such understandings are not brought to bear on fathering or men's social participation.[1]

Earlier papal teaching, which Pope John Paul II has recalled, legitimates and perpetuates women's economic vulnerability and dependency by insisting that nature destines women to be mothers and that this role is incompatible with participation in the labor force.[2] Women's economic dependency is perpetuated by this stand, as is women's exclusive responsibility for unpaid household labor. For instance, John Paul II contends that it is "wrong from the point of view of the good of society and of the family" to abandon the care and education of children for "paid work outside the home" if doing so contradicts or hinders the primary goals of the mission of a mother.[3] John Paul II is echoing Pope Pius XII, who taught that "every woman is destined to be a mother....The Creator has disposed to this end the entire being of woman, her organism, and even more her spirit, and above all her exquisite sensibility."[4]

211

In this view of womanhood the ability to give birth totally defines a woman's personhood. "Motherhood" becomes a woman's entire identity and purpose in life. In actuality, such a view obscures the social construction of this role. Mothering is presented as a natural function, given women's biological capacity for childbearing. Responsibilities such as full-time child care and the physical and emotional care of home and family, which are not necessarily connected to childbirth at all, are linked "naturally" to this capacity. As Giglia Tedesco, an Italian Catholic legislator, points out, this teaching transforms maternity "from a human relationship into a social role which then becomes a social handicap for women."[5]

Furthermore, neither the economic value nor the physical character of household labor and child care is generally recognized. In part this is due to conceptualizations of work in economic theory. But it is also related to the tendency of most religions to sacralize the family, which we have already seen in World Council of Churches' teaching. In Catholic teaching, domestic work is also spiritualized or idealized as "nurturing" or "creating the family hearth," as in this statement from Pope John XXIII: "At all times and in all circumstances they [employed women] are the ones who have to be wise enough to find the resources to face their duties as wives and mothers calmly and with their eyes wide open; to make their homes warm and peaceful after the tiring labors of daily work; and not to shrink from the responsibilities involved in raising children."[6]

It is significant that the responsibilities of raising children and making a home "warm and peaceful" are not seen as part of the "tiring labors of daily work." But how else can one describe food preparation, cleaning, laundry, and the many other tasks involved in domestic labor? This sacralization of family life also obscures the fact that Pope John was legitimating women's double day. Even recent teaching that highlights women's marginality and economic vulnerability has not seriously challenged the double day and thus justifies social relations that contribute to women's socioeconomic marginality and exploitation.

The contributions—usually unpaid—of women to agricultural work, particularly in Third World countries, are not acknowledged in church pronouncements on international development or the food crisis in Africa, where women produce 80–90 percent of food for domestic consumption. Nor are women's specific needs and concerns—such as their access to land, credit, and support services—taken into account by the suggested strategies.

The mystification of women's work is particularly ironic in light of the consistent advocacy of "the just wage" as a central norm of Catholic social teaching. For example, John Paul II insists that the just wage is "the concrete means of verifying the justice of the whole socioeconomic system," because wages are the practical means through which most people have access to goods intended for common use.[7] Catholic social teaching has gotten around this omission by defining the just wage as a family wage. But it has never specified that women are to have a say in the allocation of the family wage received by the male, so there is no guarantee that women will have access to the goods that the just wage is to ensure.

Such views prevent Roman Catholic social teaching from recognizing women's economic inequality, because women's economic dependency is seen as "natural." Presuppositions about "woman's nature" are more clearly illuminated in other papal pronouncements. An examination of some of these documents shows that natural law assumptions about woman's nature not only obscure women's economic vulnerability but also distort women's capacity for moral agency.

Samuel Bowles and Herbert Gintis consider moral agency in Chapter 9, where they characterize social action as "the individual constituting him- or herself by developing personal powers through acting in the world." Moral agency is the ability to act in the world and thereby to become fully responsible. Feminist liberation theology believes that our ability as women to constitute ourselves fully as self-determining members of human communities is critical to our liberation. Feminist ethicist Ruth Smith explains why this is so: "Becoming the subject of one's own action is a social and historical process key to liberation politically, socially, and psychologically so that we no longer collude in our own oppression and so that we can attempt to change conditions of life negation and alienation into conditions of affirmation and fulfillment."[8] If Catholic social teaching is committed to human liberation, it must also liberate women. This requires, among other things, supporting rather than distorting women's capacity to act as moral agents.

Roman Catholic social teaching has affirmed the equal dignity and worth of women and men since Pius XI, but never without qualification. In his encyclical *Casti Connubii* (On Christian Marriage), Pius XI affirmed "a true equality" in the dignity of women and men, in contrast to a "false equality": any change in the civil rights of a married woman must always give regard to "the natural disposition and temperament of the female sex, good morality, and the welfare of the family."[9] Women's equality and participation are consistently limited—in later papal teaching, Vatican Council II documents, and statements of regional bishops— by "her nature" and "her proper role." This approach denies women's full moral personhood through what Canadian philosopher Kathryn Morgan calls a "difference in kind": theories are generated "about the nature of woman which claim that women differ from men either in degree or kind such that women are not entitled to full moral agency."[10]

A brief review of some of the main points of John Paul II's letter *Mulieris Dignitatem* (On the Dignity and Vocation of Women) clearly indicates how traditional notions of femininity limit women's ability to act as adult human beings. The Pope affirms the mutuality and equality of male and female, but he also maintains the notion of "that dignity and vocation that result from the specific diversity and personal originality of man and woman." Consequently, "even the rightful opposition of women to what is expressed in the biblical words 'he shall rule over you' (Gen. 3:16) must not under any condition lead to the 'masculinization' of women. In the name of liberation from male 'domination,' women must not appropriate to themselves male characteristics contrary to their own feminine originality." Precisely what John Paul II means by this becomes apparent in his definition of femininity: "receiving so as to give of self, *always in response to the love of God or of husband*."[11] The implication is that a woman is not to take initiative. Thus her ability to act as a full moral agent is denied because of her assumed "difference in kind" from the male, and one is left to wonder how women may rightfully oppose being ruled over by men.

The conceptualization of femininity as "receiving" also informs Catholic teaching against artificial contraception and against women's ordination to the priesthood, positions that some see as oppressive to women. In his encyclical *Humanae Vitae* (On Human Life), Paul VI discusses "the generative process" without ever mentioning women as the bearers of life,[12] thus rendering women's reproductive labor as invisible here as their actual domestic labor is in most other social teaching. John Paul II also uses this understanding of femininity as the basis for the denial of ordination to women, as they cannot represent Christ who first gave of himself.[13]

Notes

1. See "Evangelization in Latin America," nn. 841, 846, in *Puebla and Beyond: Documentary and Commentary*, ed. John Eagleson and Philip Scharper (Maryknoll, N.Y.: Orbis Books, 1979).

2. See Michael Zweig (Chapter 1) and Gregory Baum (Chapter 3) for discussion of this earlier teaching, in Michael Zweig, ed., *Religion and Economic Justice* (Philadelphia: Temple University Press, 1991).

3. See John Paul II, *Laborem Exercens*, n. 19, in Gregory Baum, *The Priority of Labor: A Commentary on Laborem Exercens* (New York: Paulist Press, 1982).

4. *The Pope Speaks: The Teachings of Pius XII,* ed. Michael Chinigo (New York: Pantheon Books, 1957), p. 58.

5. Giglia Tedesco, "Laborem Exercens: A Handicap for Women," *NTC News* (Rome) 8, nos. 11–12 (1981): 1.

6. John XXIII, "The Woman of Today," in *The Pope Speaks* 7 (1961): 172–73.

7. John Paul II, *Laborem Exercens*, nn. 16–19. I am not arguing here that "wages for housework" is a necessary or adequate norm for economic justice for women. Rather, I am using the just wage in relation to domestic work as an example of the invisibility of women's economic contribution in Catholic social teaching. This is also true of World Council social teaching, and in both such invisibility is due in part to the economic theory they are using.

8. Ruth L. Smith, "Feminism and the Moral Subject," in Andolsen, Gudorf, and Pellaver, *Women's Consciousness, Women's Conscience*, p. 250.

9. Pope Pius XII, *Casti Connubii*, n. 77, in *Seven Great Encyclicals* (New York: Paulist Press, 1963).

10. Kathryn Pauly Morgan, "Women and Moral Madness," *Canadian Journal of Philosophy,* supp. vol. 13 (n.d.): 204; reprinted in *Feminist Perspectives: Philosophical Essays on Method and Morals*, ed. Lorraine Cole, Sheila Mullett, and Christine Overall (Toronto: University of Toronto Press, 1988), pp. 146–67.

11. John Paul II, *Mulieris Dignitatem*, August 15, 1988, *Origins* 18 (1988): 261–83, nn. 10–11 (emphasis added).

12. Paul VI, *Humanae Vitae*, n. 14, in *The Gospel of Peace and Justice: Catholic Social Teaching since Pope John*, ed. Joseph Gremillion (Maryknoll, N.Y.: Orbis Books, 1976).

13. John Paul II, *Mulieris Dignitatem*, nn. 26–27.

16. Sincere Gift: The Pope's "New Feminism"

Léonie Caldecott

This chapter first appeared in *Communio* in 1996.

In *Evangelium Vitae* (1995), Pope John Paul II calls for a "new feminism"—just as in earlier encyclicals he has called for a new evangelization and a new theology of liberation. He writes: "In transforming culture so that it supports life, *women* occupy a place in thought and action which is unique and decisive. It depends on them to promote a 'new feminism' which rejects the temptation of imitating models of 'male domination,' in order to acknowledge and affirm the true genius of women in every aspect of the life of society, and overcome all discrimination, violence and exploitation." Through motherhood, he goes on, women who are mothers "first learn and then teach others that human relations are authentic if they are open to accepting the other person: a person who is recognized and loved because of the dignity which comes from being a person and not from other considerations, such as usefulness, strength, intelligence, beauty or health. This is the fundamental contribution which the Church and humanity expect from women. And it is the indispensable prerequisite for an authentic cultural change" (*EV,* n. 99).

Evangelium Vitae sets out the pope's prophetic vision of today's "dramatic conflict between the 'culture of death' and the 'culture of life'" as the context for this attempt to enlist women on the side of life (*EV,* n. 50). The consequences of the gospel are plain: "Human life, as a gift of God, is sacred and inviolable. For this reason procured abortion and euthanasia are absolutely unacceptable. Not only must [innocent] human life not be taken, but it must be protected with loving concern" (*EV,* n. 81). "As far as the right to life is concerned, every innocent human being is absolutely equal to all others. This equality is the basis of all authentic social relationships which, to be truly such, can be founded only on truth and justice, recognizing and protecting every man and woman as a person and not as an object to be used" (*EV,* n. 57).

The defense of life is intimately connected with the *celebration* of life. We can "reverence and honor every person" only if we rediscover a "contemplative outlook" (*EV,* n. 83). It is an outlook that affects our attitude not only to human life, but to the entire cosmos—as the pope has made clear on other occasions.[1] "Such an outlook arises from faith in the God of life, who has created every individual as a 'wonder' (cf. Ps 139:14). It is the outlook of those who see life in its deeper meaning, who grasp its utter gratuitousness, its beauty and its invitation to freedom and responsibility. It is the outlook of those who do not presume to take possession of reality, but instead accept it as gift, discovering in all things the reflection of the Creator and seeing in every person his living image" (*EV,* n. 83).

This defense and celebration of life, this "contemplative outlook," the pope sees as entrusted primarily to women. Here lies the great task and the starting point for a new feminism.

I.

The pope's brief but weighty remarks on the role of women in the encyclical on life can be expanded with reference to the 1994 *Letter to Families,* the Message for the 1995 World Day of Peace ("Women: Teachers of Peace"), the Letter to Priests for Holy Thursday 1995, and the 1995 *Letter to Women,* together with the many talks and addresses given around the occasion of the UN's Beijing Conference. The main theological and exegetical work, of course, had already been done for the apostolic letter *Mulieris Dignitatem* (1988), on the "Dignity and Vocation of Women on the Occasion of the Marian Year." What the 1990s have brought is clearly a keener sense of the injustices to which women have been subjected throughout history, and which persist in large parts of the world. Many of the pope's remarks in 1995—and even aspects of the Holy See's official representations at the Beijing Conference itself—took the secular media by surprise.

Pope John Paul's respect and concern (indeed love) for women is evident in almost everything he writes, and many women respond to him with equal respect and affection. But "old-style feminists" are not so happy. The pope's respect for women may be genuine, but they suspect it is based merely on an intensely nostalgic love for his own mother, transferred to the Blessed Virgin and to an idealized image of femininity. Is "motherhood" somehow intrinsic to being a woman, as the pope always seems to imply? Is there such a thing as "femininity"? Was the decision to restrict the priesthood to men in reality just a way of ensuring that women will never be allowed an influence in the running of the Church, despite all the rhetoric about equality? In trying to answer some of these concerns, I draw on my own experience of the women's movement, some manifestations of which I had the opportunity to observe both before and after my reception into the Catholic Church.

Even before the present pope came on the scene, there were always many types of feminists, and differences between them that no amount of "sisterhood" could paper over. There were moderate feminists, and radical, separatist feminists. There were feminists who denied any intrinsic difference between men and woman (the extrinsic physical divergences being something that technology was expected eventually to overcome). But there were others, the "eco-feminists" (among whom I more or less counted myself) who believed in very radical differences, and thought that women—by virtue of their femininity, their closeness to nature, and other distinctive qualities—could "save the earth" which men had almost succeeded in destroying by violent assault. However, one aspect of eco-feminism that struck me as incoherent even within the framework of the movement was its lack of concern for one particular kind of "violent assault" on life, namely, that represented by abortion. Amidst all the rhetoric about the insidious power of masculine technology, the long-term dangers of nuclear power and male indifference (or worse) to the female sphere of experience in the home or in personal relationships, there was a conspicuous silence about the significance of the central fact in most women's lives—the capacity to conceive and bear a child. The eco-feminists, in short, wavered in front of the ideological stronghold of mainstream feminism on the issue of "reproductive rights." (Here I was not alone in my concern, and it is important to note the presence on the American scene of "pro-life feminists," of whom Juli Loesch Wiley would be an outstanding example.[2]) Ironically, the same eco-feminists were often quite sympathetic to "natural family planning," purely on the grounds of respect for the nature of a woman's cycle. (This of course did not preclude using this most effective "alternative technology" with a contraceptive mentality.)

Another aspect of eco-feminism that concerned me was its reliance on pagan spiritualities, often leading to some form of goddess-worship. At the time of my contact with the movement I was researching a book on women and Christianity. The hostility to this subject evinced by most eco-feminists at that time was absolute. Yet I felt intuitively that it was within Christianity that the answer to the problems so eloquently expressed by the eco-feminists truly lay, and it was this intuition that eventually led to my seeking admission to the sacramental life of the Church in 1983, and distancing myself from what I had come to feel was a hopelessly shallow analysis of humanity's problems. For me as for many other women, the Holy Father, in asking for a new feminism, is bringing to fruition a question which in many respects is not so new. What is "new" is the fact that the pope has succeeded in integrating pro-life with the best aspects of eco-feminism, in a way that has its roots firmly in the fertile soil of the Catholic tradition, rather than the ideological newspeak and psychobabble of much of modernity.

The synthesis is made to seem possible, even "natural," thanks to the pope's highly developed Christian anthropology. As a personalist philosopher from his days in Lublin, he locates the intrinsic and constant value of every human life in the fact that it is the life of a *person* in the order of love and grace. Man and woman are fundamentally equal in that sense. As a Christian, he further locates the meaning of human life in *love*, defined as the giving and receiving of the self. Marriage and parenthood, both human and divine, he sees as revealing love in its most intense and archetypal form. Thus he affirms the importance of a natural complementarity between men and women as such, intended by the Creator as the means by which the loving relations of the Trinity could be mirrored in the cosmos.

II.

To illustrate this further, let us look at a particularly beautiful and moving expression of the pope's view of women, taken from a Lenten message to the Brazilian Church in 1990. "Woman...is a person as much as man is; the person is the sole creature which God wanted for its own sake; the sole creature to be made expressly in the image and likeness of God, who is Love. Precisely for this reason, a person cannot find complete fulfillment except by making a sincere gift of self. Herein lies the origin of 'community,' in which the 'unity of the two' and personal dignity must be expressed, as much for man as for woman." Woman, he goes on:

> finds her fulfillment and vocation as a person according to the richness of the attributes of femininity, which she received on the day of creation and which is transmitted from generation to generation, in her special manner of being the image of God, tarnished by sin and redeemed in Jesus Christ....

> The hardness of the human heart, wounded by the consequence of original sin in the passing of history, was harming and upsetting the Creator's plan for woman as well, the image of God. It is necessary for us now to walk down the paths of conversion, to return to the original vision of the Lord.

> Here now I make my appeal to the Brazilian woman and on behalf of her, neither slave nor queen, just woman:

> —*Woman as child:* a being with the look of a simple but rare flower; blooming at the dawn of her life, she wants to receive and reflect God's light;

> —*Woman in youth:* sun of spring morning, seen clearly radiating hope, in need of respect, trust and dignity;

> —*Adult woman:* midday sun, with her simple dignity, sincerity and purity, giving light and warmth with serene reflection, with rectitude of spirit, with harmony which is her wardrobe and adornment;

> —*Elderly woman:* a welcoming shadow which falls, with natural maternal affection and particular wisdom and prudence, living in self-gift, with the desire to serve the happiness of others, the happiness of her fellow creatures.

Certainly the pope holds a very "romantic" view of woman. But is it an "unrealistic" view? He is speaking here of "the Creator's plan," in full awareness of the damage wrought by sin. It is useless to protest that the pope is "idealizing" the feminine. John Paul II believes that God has revealed his own plan for human nature in revealing himself through Mary and Jesus, and that any Christian who reads the book of Scripture and the book of nature with the eyes of faith—in the light of the Holy Spirit dwelling in the Church—will be able to discern there the features of man and woman as originally created and as presently redeemed. The descriptions he gives of the ideal Brazilian woman at each stage of her life are not mere wishful dreams, but accurate depictions of those women who, joining themselves to Christ, have become saints.

In his *Letter to Women,* the pope reflects on the complementarity of men and women, and the "genius" or specific contribution of woman to this partnership in life and salvation. He writes, indeed, that it "is only through the duality of the 'masculine' and the 'feminine' that the 'human' finds full realization" (*LW,* n. 7). Basing himself on Genesis 2:18–20, he explains that woman is created by God to be a "helper" for man not only in a physical or psychological sense—for the sake of reproduction or comfort—but *ontologically,* and for the task of transforming the earth through culture (*LW,* nn. 7–8). Even in the task of salvation, this cooperation is evident: Mary complements Christ by the active receptivity of her *fiat.* By grace, she is raised (and in her the Church) to union with God in that love which is the eternal dance of the Blessed Trinity. In the Church, as Balthasar writes and the pope echoes, the "Marian" principle complements the "Apostolic-Petrine" (*LW,* n. 11). But it is Mary, not Peter, who is supreme: as representative of humanity, she is "Queen of the Apostles without any pretensions to apostolic powers: she has other and greater powers."[3]

Given the pope's "nuptial" understanding of human nature as a "unity of the two," the first key to his new feminism must lie in the exegesis of the marriage covenant as one of *mutual subjection,* over against the simple subjection of wife to husband. There is still subjection, still obedience, still a distinction of roles, still complementarity, but it is a *mutual* subjection and therefore not "oppressive." This is how the pope introduces the concept in *Mulieris Dignitatem,* drawing out the implications of Ephesians 5:21:

The text is addressed to the spouses as real women and men. It reminds them of the "ethos" of spousal love which goes back to the divine institution of marriage from the "beginning." Corresponding to the truth of this institution is the exhortation: *"Husbands, love your wives,"* love them because of that special and unique bond whereby in marriage a man and a woman become "one flesh" (Gen 2:24; Eph 5:31). In this love there is a fundamental *affirmation of the woman* as a person. This affirmation makes it possible for the female personality to develop fully and be enriched. This is precisely the way Christ acts as the bridegroom of the Church; he desires that she be "in splendor, without spot or wrinkle" (Eph 5:27). One can say that this fully captures the whole "style" of Christ in dealing with women. Husbands should make their own the elements of this style in regard to their wives; *analogously, all men should do the same in regard to women in every situation* [emphasis mine]. In this way both men and women bring about "the sincere gift of self." (*MD*, n. 24)

Later on, the pope concludes: "In relation to the 'old' this is evidently something 'new': it is an innovation of the Gospel." It is indeed "new," a "call which from that time onwards does not cease to challenge succeeding generations," including our own. In its light we may locate the basis for the "new feminism." As we shall see, this notion of "the sincere gift," which in this context is seen as the central goal of the marriage union, is also at the heart of the new feminism, demonstrating that a fresh understanding of the married state must play a vital role in the renewal of culture towards which the new feminism tends.

John Paul II's writings on women, in all their essential points, echo the contents of a classic piece of feminist (or perhaps I should say "post-feminist") writing by the "grandmother of European Orthodoxy," Elisabeth Behr-Sigel.[4] No doubt independently, working from within their respective traditions, this man and this woman have come to similar conclusions about the role of women and the need for cultural change. Elisabeth Behr-Sigel calls for us to replace the "Cartesian humanism" of the male as "master and possessor" of woman and the earth with a new humanism of tender and compassionate respect for the other. Women's legitimate roles are infinitely varied: the choice need not and should not be between the domestic and the monastic life. Marriage itself, according to St. Paul, is a mystery of "reciprocal love" and of "submission each to the other." We need a dialogue between theology and anthropology, an understanding of gender that is faithful both to the lived experience of women and to the account of man's creation in Genesis. The loving unity to which we are called will be achieved not by suppressing all distinctions, but by ending the "quarrel" between the *bad masculine* and the *bad feminine* that has developed in the state of sin. Feminism, she concludes, must be freed from the mentality of a society dominated by "perverted masculine values."

Elisabeth Behr-Sigel emphasizes "respect for the other"; the pope integrates this with "respect for life." His is the fuller and more urgent appeal. The "civilization of love" is also a "culture of life." The special genius of women is concerned with the fact, not that all women are or should be mothers in the physical sense, but that womanhood is "designed" with motherhood in mind, and therefore feminine strengths and sensibilities are orientated towards the welcoming and nurturing of life. "A mother welcomes and carries in herself another human being, enabling it to grow outside her, giving it room, respecting its otherness" (*EV*, n. 99). All women as women share this capacity to welcome the life of the other and to create the conditions for it to grow and flourish, whether in physical motherhood or spiritual motherhood; in the home or the office, the factory or the university or the convent; in political life, economic life, in the city or the country.

The particular "genius" (as the pope terms it) of the woman who has not surrendered her womanhood and yet operates in the working world has been traced by a long line of Catholic writers such as Edith Stein, Gertrud von Le Fort, Caryll Houselander, and Adrienne von Speyr. In an exemplary way, von Le Fort brings the sensibility of a poet to her philosophical and theological reflections, and although she was writing in the 1930s, her prophetic insights remain relevant today. For instance, on the primacy of men and women working alongside each other in the hierarchy of social interaction she writes: "Every sort of co-operation, even the most insignificant, between man and woman is, in its bearing upon the wholeness of life, of far greater import than associations that are purely masculine or purely feminine. Naturally, such associations have their definite purposes inasmuch as they are dedicated to a common struggle or ideal and serve for the development of certain new thoughts, but for limited scope only. In fact they risk sterility because of narrowness or one-sidedness and therefore are of little import in the wider cultural field."[5]

Her insights into the inner landscape of "women's work" and its connections with the maternal principle are also fascinating:

> The world has need of the motherly woman; for it is, for the most part, a poor and helpless child. As man comes feebly into the world, so in profound weakness he departs from it; to the hand that wraps the child in its infant clothes corresponds the merciful hand of the woman who supports the aged man and wipes the sweat from the brows of the dying. Between birth and death lies not only the achievement of the successful, but the unending weariness of the way, the workaday monotony, all that belongs to the needs of the body and of life.

> The motherly woman is appointed the quiet stewardess of this tremendous inheritance of necessity and distress. Under this aspect of mother, woman does not represent, as she does as bride, only the one half of reality. Here her part is more than half. People know why the man calls his wife "Mother." In doing so he does not address only the mother of his children, but the mother of everyone, which means above all, the mother of her own husband.[6]

III.

The pope's most compelling exposition of the social, spiritual and eschatological significance of human motherhood can be found in *Mulieris Dignitatem* (nn. 18 and 19). After taking a stand against the very biological reductionism falsely attributed to Catholic teaching by feminists,[7] he embarks on a profound exegesis of the maternal condition, an exegesis which illuminates all the essential points of Catholic moral teaching in this area, from the defense of life to the need for stable and faithful marriages. Rejecting any "exclusively bio-physical interpretation of women and motherhood," he links motherhood "to the personal structure of the woman and to the personal dimension of the gift: 'I have brought a man into being with the help of the Lord' (Gen 4:1)." And, whereas parenthood is something that belongs to both men and women, "It is the woman who 'pays' directly for this shared generation, which literally absorbs the energies of her body and soul. It is therefore necessary that the man be fully aware that in their shared parenthood he owes a special debt to the woman. No program of 'equal rights' between women and men is valid unless it takes this fact fully into account." Men in some sense *learn their fatherhood from the mother of their children,* so that as the child grows, the contribution of both parents can come into play.

Mary's *fiat* signifies "the woman's readiness for the gift of self and her readiness to accept a new life" (*MD*, n. 18). Through the perfection of her self-gift, made possible by the absence of original sin in her unclouded and lovely soul, the New Covenant is established between God and man. Though imperfect in comparison, each fresh instance of motherhood in human history is nonetheless related to this central act on the part of Mary. The "*fiat* mentality" is the essential key to the fulfillment of a mother's vocation, not only at conception, but throughout the life of the child. For we must remember Jesus' response to the women in the Gospel of Luke: "Blessed rather are those who hear the word of God and keep it" (11:27–28). This means that "The motherhood of every woman, understood in the light of the gospel, is similarly not only 'of flesh and blood': it expresses a profound *'listening to the word of the living God'* and a readiness to 'safeguard' this Word....For it is precisely those born of earthly mothers, the sons and daughters of the human race, who receive from the Son of God the power to become 'children of God' (Jn 1:12). A dimension of the New Covenant in Christ's blood enters into human parenthood, making it a reality and a task for 'new creatures' (cf. 2 Cor 5:17). The history of every human being passes through the threshold of a woman's motherhood: crossing it conditions 'the revelation of the children of God' (cf. Rom 8:19)" (*MD*, n. 19).

The entire passage about motherhood concludes with a meditation on Our Lord's use of the imagery of childbirth in John 16:21. "The first part of Christ's words refers to the 'pangs of childbirth' which belong to the heritage of original sin; at the same time, these words indicate the link that exists between the woman's motherhood and the Paschal Mystery." There is a hint here of the mysterious parallel between the feminine vocation of motherhood and the masculine vocation of the priesthood. In any case, the pope goes on to enumerate some of the sufferings which women go through for the sake of this vocation, before focusing our attention anew on the Resurrection. The key word here is "joy"—"the joy that a child is born into the world," and Jesus' words before his passion: "I will see you again and your hearts will rejoice, and no one will take your joy from you" (Jn 16:22–23).

IV.

I have quoted from *Mulieris Dignitatem* at such length because I believe we have here all the essential elements for the creation of the "new feminism," which is intrinsically linked to the maternal capacity of women, a capacity which, it is worth repeating, goes much further than the fact of biological childbearing. In addition to the point about mutual subjection, there are four key concepts to be noted:

(1) The "sincere gift of self," of which the Blessed Virgin's *fiat* is the summit.

(2) The "debt" owed by men to women, who pay the heaviest price for the bearing of life.

(3) The "keeping of the Word" by women in their vocation, no matter what it is.

(4) The conditioning of "the revelation of the children of God" as the effect of the relationship between child and mother.

All four are inextricably linked, and necessary for the process of cultural transformation envisaged by the Holy Father. Firstly, the acquiescence of women to what is asked of them must be *sincere,* that is to say, arising out of a deep conviction and sense of purpose. It must have a personal authenticity, the subject being defined in terms of her divine destiny, the will of God for her life, and not in terms of the status quo. Mainstream feminism is frequently objecting to the falsity of the feminine consciousness—for example the 1950s-style suburban housewife "married to her house," or the lack of integrity in the (Strindbergian) martyred or devouring mother. The woman of the sex-war, be she collaborator or guerrilla, manifestly lacks both sincerity and the ability to give of her true self. This poor "unrepentant Eve" should hardly be mourned by anyone.[8]

It is worth quoting Edith Stein on this all-important principle of the "sincere gift of self," which links the spousal impulse clearly to the maternal vocation, the married state to that of consecrated virginity. She shows how it is only in the profound communion with her Lord that a woman can find the strength to be truly herself.

> The deepest longing of woman's heart is to give herself lovingly, to belong to another, and to possess this other being completely. This longing is revealed in her outlook, personal and all-embracing, which appears to us as specifically feminine. But this surrender becomes a perverted self-abandon and a form of slavery when it is given to another person and not to God; at the same time, it is an unjustified demand which no human being can fulfill. Only God can welcome a person's total surrender in such a way that one does not lose one's soul in the process but wins it. And only God can bestow himself upon a person so that He fulfills this being completely and loses nothing of Himself in so doing. That is why total surrender which is the principle of the religious life is simultaneously the only adequate fulfillment possible for women's yearning.[9]

The second point gives us the absolutely necessary precondition *on the part of men* to the sincere gift of self on the part of women. If their surrender (whose true object is God) is met with ingratitude, or even a dishonorable and inappropriate complacency on the part of men, an offense is committed against both woman and her Creator, and disaster ensues. Misogyny is a very real phenomenon (even if it is exaggerated for the sake of the propaganda war between the sexes), and it is particularly crushing for a woman who presents herself with an attitude of good will and generosity. She may not resort to aborting the child in her womb (either literally or figuratively), but she can be so drained of strength by the encounter that she becomes incapable of effectively nurturing that which God has entrusted to her. The sincere gift of self on the part of the woman is thus guaranteed and protected by a sincere rendering of the debt—a debt of gratitude and all the actions which ensue—on the part of our brothers in Christ.

So the third point concerns the necessity of long-term continuity in the woman's vocation, a continuity which has perforce to be rooted in the eternal. One of the Christian ideas which secular feminists object to is the emphasis on sacrifice. Yet there is no birth (or re-birth) without a certain blood-letting; there is no unconditional love without the preparedness to suffer. Is it worth speculating, however, on the distinction between the *preparedness* for sacrifice and the grim *determination* to carry it out? Could it be possible that there is a grain of truth in the secular crusade against an alleged Christian "obsession" with suffering? We are apt to slide into a kind of complacency with regard to Christ's passion and death which mirrors some men's complacency about female suffering. The redeemed Eve does not mind suffering torments to bring a child (or any other of God's works) into the world, and at her most sublime will accept that her labors not bear fruit until after her own death. Yet if God has called woman into being in order to *keep and protect* the Word, what shall we say of those who render this continuity through time difficult or even impossible? "Troubles will come," said our Lord, "but woe to him through whom they come." The Holy Father himself has exemplified this logic in his compassion for women who have wounded themselves through abortion.[10]

The image of abortion (literally "putting out of its place") is an apt one. For woman can be said to have a womb-shaped vocation.[11] She is a space-maker, a protector of growth, an enabler of life, a place of safety where others can encounter Christ and know themselves to be loved. Hers is the mission to behold the world and all its confusing travail in a very particular way: to make use of her very weakness (cf. St. Thérèsa) to obtain the privileged place of the lamb which is carried upon the shoulders of the Shepherd, and thus see things from the perspective of His gaze. "I love you as you are, for I see you as you are destined to be." The eyes of a woman are a precious thing: they should not be put out.

"One of the privileges of the maternal woman," wrote Gertrud von Le Fort, "is the quiet, extremely important function of knowing how to wait and be silent, the ability sometimes to overlook, indulge in, and cover up a weakness. As a work of mercy this is no lesser charity than clothing the naked. It is one of the most ominous errors of the world, one of the most essential reasons for its lack of peace, to believe that all that is wrong must always be uncovered and condemned."[12]

The final point is perhaps the most intriguing and profound ever made about the mystery of motherhood by Pope John Paul II: "The history of every human being passes through the threshold of a woman's motherhood: crossing it conditions 'the revelation of the children of God.'" Surely here we see the weighty implications of our theme. Nobody passes into the world without as it were passing through the "ambience" of a woman. Woman therefore has, even if only *in potentia,* an immense influence on the history of mankind. Her attitudes and outlook are paramount. So is her welfare, both physical and spiritual. We see the effects of the sex war in the devaluing of motherhood, degeneration of life-giving attitudes in the home, and the assault on the concept of a love faithful unto death. However, it is useless to point back to the "Victorian values" as the panacea: the problem goes much further back than that. Von Le Fort ascribed the rise of the feminist movement, with all its imbalance, to this legitimate sense of cultural loss:

> The feminist movement had it spiritual roots in the dullness
> and narrowness of the middle-class family. Its economic
> backgrounds do not concern us here. From the stress of their
> starving souls, the women of that period cried out for a spir-
> itual purpose in life and for an activation of their capacity
> for love. It was a tragic motivation, for these women sought
> out a share of responsibility in the man's world, and sought
> it outside the family which could no longer shelter and sat-
> isfy them.

As G.K. Chesterton put it, writing at the same period as von Le Fort, and with the same prophetic acuity, even in the Victorian household the hearth was already cold.

V.

How then shall we rekindle the flame in that "hearth" which is embodied by the woman? How shall we reach the hardened heart of those who have sacrificed the hope of children and the love of life on the altar of mammon? How shall we cradle the waifs and strays "liberated" by an illusory revolution for a false freedom? What comes to mind is a prayer card I kept to commemorate my own conversion, a prayer card for the Holy Year of 1983, showing the Holy Father in prayer. His sincerity and "aliveness" radiate through the photograph. It is prayer like this that changes things. That prayer is the human contribution which the Lord desires as our response to his love, a prayer that represents at its own level the profound communion of wills between his Sacred Heart and the Immaculate Heart of his Mother.

Excursus

There is a particular subject of prayer, concerning the locus of interaction between creature and Creator, which I feel bound to bring up here, on the way to a conclusion. The recent permission for girls to serve on the altar is an issue which pertains not only to the role of women, but to the space where prayer is made most possible: the liturgical space, the sanctuary at the heart of the Church. It is, of course, the Church's right to legislate on all such matters, and I accept whatever she may decide. This particular permission, however, appears to remain open to further debate in a way that (for example) the defined inability of the Church to ordain women to the sacrament of Holy Orders does not. And so it is in a desire to serve the Church that I present the following argument, a response to which would at least help to clarify the principles underlying the decision.

It is an unfortunate fact that some of the arguments deployed by liturgical conservatives against the permission for girls to serve on that altar seem (especially to a woman's eyes) to imply a profoundly negative view of women. The message that comes across, even if unintentionally, is that women must be kept out of sight because they are liable to be viewed by men in terms of sexual provocation. I cannot help wondering whether it is not precisely such attitudes that affected the decision to *allow* girls onto the altar—as if it were necessary to prove that the Church, whilst reserving priesthood to men, is no misogynist, and is not afraid to entrust a certain role to women even in the sacred mysteries. Nonetheless, in spite of my objections to some of the conservative reactions, from a woman's point of view there remain—apparently unaddressed—some important reasons why it is not a good idea to have girls or women serve at the altar.

These concern the symbolic sphere, which a "masculinized" society naturally tends to discount as insignificant, but which should mean a great deal more to those of us who have a sacramental view of the world. According to this viewpoint, the male priest represents the Bridegroom, the altar the Bride, the cross with its vertical and horizontal dimensions the marriage of the two. Or, from a slightly different symbolic perspective the priest represents the Son, the sanctuary the Mother's mystical womb, the rest of the church the visible body of the Mother. If the gender of the priest is indeed a significant element in the "iconographic" representation of Christ at the altar (as is persuasively claimed by opponents of women's ordination[13]), then an analogous argument would suggest that the sanctuary itself, at least during the eucharistic rite, should remain as much as possible a male preserve. For if you take away or blur the distinction between the sanctuary and the rest of the church, you risk (to use an image from the feminine sphere) unraveling the exact tension which knits together the fabric of the sacramental liturgy, and thus obscuring the life-giving nuptial mystery at the core of our faith. The role of women in the liturgy is in part to preserve that mystery, so that the cross may not be rendered vain but is able to bear "fruit that will last." It is not therefore "women as a distraction from the higher things" that is the danger, but losing the principle of the feminine presence, *Mater Ecclesia,* Daughter of Zion, protectress of all that is sacred and beautiful, offering herself in the temple on behalf of the people of God—letting herself be offered *with the people, by the priest.*

Mary is the Church, not the cross. Christ's body was given back into her arms after the deposition. Certainly, during his passion, Mary and other women stood by the cross; but the *foot of the cross* is the symbolic equivalent not of the sanctuary but of the church where the congregation is gathered. The Virgin Mary represents the whole of humanity before God, from the *fiat* of the Annunciation to the *fiat* of the *Mater Dolorosa.* This renders the sublimest moment of our contact with God a uniquely "feminine" one, and yet it is easy to forget that Mary never drew attention to herself, but only to her Son. This does not mean that she was merely passive, as an earlier anthropology often suggested; but her activity was orientated towards him, not herself.

In short, it is for the sake of promoting the truth and beauty of the human condition, and the disciplined poetry of liturgical action, that I believe the space around and pertaining to the priest during the act of sacrifice should be kept for men and boys. All the baptized share in the *royal* priesthood of Christ, and young girls can make the offering of themselves in countless ways apart from service at the altar. It is far from inappropriate, for example, for them to read the Word before the Gospel, since the Jewish race (feminine in relation to God throughout the Scriptures) prepared the ground—culminating in Mary—for the reception of Christ. The continuous presentation of the gifts of themselves could surely be epitomized in the offertory procession. Is it not redolent of the most stifling clericalism to say that girls can make a proof of their dignity only in the role which is necessarily the most visible service of the altar?

This reasoning may also affect the physical position of the priest during the celebration of the Mass. There is an important contrast between the moments when he is greeting the people, reading the words of the Word, giving them the Host *in persona Christi,* and those moments at the heart of the eucharistic mystery in which the priest is much more involved in representing the feminine principle at the altar of sacrifice, offering the human contribution (bread and wine, the prayers of the faithful) and receiving the divine response: the eucharistic miracle, Christ's self-gift.

I say all of this as a "conservative," for the new feminist would naturally wish to *conserve* not only ecological harmony, but everything that is precious and vulnerable and perhaps not readily understood by the world. I say it also as a "radical": that is, out of a desire to get to the *root* of problems which currently affect the Church, problems that I am convinced are linked to those between the sexes. The new feminist is committed to the defense of life, and that includes the life of the Church, in which the growth and protection of priestly vocations is a vital element. The delicate balance of relationships within the space-time of the liturgy, and the subtle process of initiation into a potentially priestly vocation, can be neglected only at the expense of future generations. It is a travesty of the truth to present this concern in a light which links it with a fear of women, or a loathing of the feminine.

* * *

As far as women are concerned, a profitable way forward to the "new feminism" may lie in an authentic meditation on the rich and varied attributes of Our Lady celebrated in the Litany of Loreto. If justice is required, Mary is the mirror of that justice, not the judge. If devotion is required, she is the singular vessel of that devotion, not herself the object of worship. Women can be tempted to turn themselves into goddesses, heroines of the hour in cosmic proportions. It matters not whether she plays Gaia or Kali, it all amounts to the same: the sin of Eve, who listened to the serpentine words "You shall be as gods." "Women for Life on Earth" is a lovely ideal, but women are powerless to do more than wreak more havoc on earth, unless they are rooted in heaven. "I will lift up mine eyes unto the hills, from whence cometh my help." With this help, through the covenant made in Christ Jesus— sealed in the heart of a real human woman, in one real moment of human history—everything is assured for us. Yes, even those sacred spaces, those churches and homes where the divine will is borne to fruition, those little sanctuaries of heaven on earth scattered through time, are assured and protected by those women who follow the Second Eve, whose transcendent humility called down the power of God upon earth—and by those men who, like St. Joseph, exercise unceasing and loving vigilance over their interests.[14]

And what are their interests, these daughters of Zion? Indeed, their ambition, being in the world but not of it, knows no bounds. It is a divine conspiracy in which they collaborate: that of Justice for the sake of Love. The new woman is busy lowering her consciousness, not raising it, since it is humility which calls down the action of almighty God upon earth. "Be it done to me according to thy Word...." It is the Lord who does the raising, giving his own beauty in return for the sincere offering of her identity. The new feminist is truly a daughter of the "Mother of Fairest Love," as the Holy Father dubbed her in his *Letter to Families.* She is truly free to do the will of the One who sent her, free to give without counting the cost. For she has inherited from her Mother the assurance of true motherhood, in which the economy of the virginal *fiat* is constantly renewed.

> Every mother puts a surplus at her child's disposal, a kind of unlimited credit. Every mother has so much maternal love that even the most loving child cannot give it back to her—certainly not now, during the time of expectation. She keeps this surplus ready for the child, for his coming good and bad days. The Mother of the Lord also knows this secret. But over this, too, the grace of her Son has already disposed. So the Mother holds this surplus ready not only for her Child, out of her natural motherliness, but for all the plans, thoughts and concerns of the Child, not only in the measure of their worldwide extension, but also according to their divine, supernatural depths. The Mother's surplus of love in the expectation is already, even in concealment, flowing over onto the Church and the whole world.[15]

Notes

1. For example, in his Message for the World Day of Peace, "Peace with God the Creator: Peace with All of Creation" (1 January 1990).

2. See, e.g., *Pro-Life Feminism,* ed. Gail Grenier Sweet (Toronto: Life-Cycle Books, 1985). Also, more recently, Naomi Wolf's cogent criticism of the

internal inconsistencies in the moral reasoning and rhetoric of the pro-choice position.

3. Balthasar's expression, quoted approvingly by the pope in *Mulieris Dignitatem,* fn. 55.

4. See *The Ministry of Women in the Church* (Oakwood Publications, CA). I am quoting with approval from her earlier writing, but I emphatically part company with Behr-Sigel in her later stages, where she gravitated towards accepting female ordination. This evolution seems to me to show up, among other things, a certain weakness in her style of reasoning about tradition and adaptation.

5. *The Eternal Woman* (Milwaukee: Bruce Publishing Co., 1962), 39.

6. Ibid., 74.

7. See the alarming satirization of this attitude in Margaret Atwood's *The Handmaid's Tale.*

8. It would require many pages of analysis to portray the permutations on this theme. Karl Stern's *The Flight from Woman* contains some interesting, if not definitive, material.

9. Edith Stein, *Woman,* trans. Freda Mary Oben (Washington: Institute of Carmelite Studies, 1987), 62.

10. See *EV* (n. 99) where, interestingly enough, his thoughts pass immediately from the role of women in bringing about general cultural change, to the spiritual condition of women who have had abortions.

11. On this theme, see Robin Maas's excellent appreciation of Caryll Houselander in *Crisis* (October, 1995).

12. *The Eternal Woman,* 75.

13. And see *Inter Insigniores.*

14. The theology of St. Joseph and the meaning of fatherhood need development, but for one prophetic attempt, see Andrew Doze, *Discovering St. Joseph* (New York: Alba House, 1991). See also my husband's article in this same issue of *Communio.*

15. Adrienne von Speyr, *Handmaid of the Lord* (San Francisco: Ignatius Press, 1985), 70.

Part Three

SOCIAL TEACHING

Pertinent Encyclicals of Pope John Paul II

Laborem Exercens, 1981
Sollicitudo Rei Socialis, 1987
Centesimus Annus, 1991

17. An Ethical Critique of Capitalism: Contributions of Modern Catholic Social Teaching

Gregory Baum

This chapter first appeared in *Religion and Economic Justice,* ed. Michael Zweig, in 1991.

Critiques of capitalist economic structures have been elaborated at all levels within the Catholic hierarchy, including national and regional assemblies of bishops. In response to the appalling conditions of life that hundreds of millions of Catholics and others experience in the modern capitalist world, and in the presence of powerful mass movements to confront these conditions, church leaders have sought ways to bring Catholic teaching to bear on the daily needs of the common people.

Liberation theology is the most recent and vibrant development of Catholic social doctrine. It has emerged in Latin America, where mass suffering has been particularly acute, but its influence and vision have extended into North America as well. The link between liberation theology and the popular masses is well known. But it is no less important to understand that liberation theology finds sources of support in the teachings of Pope John Paul II as well.

It is surprising to many that John Paul II should be associated with liberation theology. As Pamela Brubaker so clearly shows [see Chapter 15], John Paul's teachings concerning women are profoundly reactionary. His antipathy to Marxism has been abundantly expressed, and he has consistently opposed the leading proponents of liberation theology in Latin America and elsewhere.

Nonetheless, there is much in papal teaching that lends weight to liberation theology. Whatever one's evaluation of John Paul's other theological pronouncements or his record in the papacy, his critique of capitalism is a crucial tool for activists within and without the Church who are working for justice and equality. Catholics should study it to discover how it applies to their concerns for economic justice. Others, including Marxists, can use papal teaching to evaluate and enhance their own critiques of capitalism. Through such broad-based reflection and praxis, the genuine insights of papal teaching will be deepened. Furthermore, the process will broaden the common ground on which different religious and secular currents advocating economic and social justice can meet and link their efforts.

THE SOCIAL CONTEXT OF CHURCH TEACHING

Since Vatican Council II (1962–65), Catholic social teaching has turned toward a deeper and more pointed critique of modern capitalism, elaborating and extending earlier critical reflections. The process has been a contradictory one, reflecting the conflict of interests in the larger society to which the Church has been responding. In this regard, the historical development of church teaching, including the writings of John Paul II, has exemplified the dynamic interaction between social conditions and religious doctrine.

The Catholic Church has never fully reconciled itself with modern capitalist society. The revolution of the burgher class threatened the feudal-aristocratic society from which capitalism emerged, including the place occupied in it by the Catholic Church. To resist the spread of modern society, the Catholic Church identified itself with the conservative sectors of European society and defended the old order against the new.

As capitalism became the dominant order in the world, the Church struck a long peace with the system and its rulers. According to revised church teaching, the market was a useful economic and social institution, but since it did not protect the common good or the poor from exploitation by the rich, the market had to be limited by government regulation and humanized by an ethical culture of fraternity.

From the time of Leo XIII at the end of the nineteenth century, Catholic social teaching condemned the abuses and excesses of capitalism but not capitalism as such. The Church defended private property, even though it understood private property, contrary to liberal opinion, as an institution that included social responsibility. In its defense of private property, the Church strongly and unambiguously condemned socialism.

Leo XIII led the Church to criticize modernity, especially the individualism, utilitarianism, and secularism promoted by the philosophy and the institutions of liberalism. But unlike socialist doctrine, which criticized capitalism with an eye to the future possibilities of human development, the Church criticized modern liberal society by contrasting it with an idealized picture of the past. Against the contractual basis of the recently emerged capitalist society and its strong individualism, church teaching defended the older, organic concepts of feudal society, the traditional notion of the common good, and the ancient virtues of social solidarity and respect for hierarchy.

The surprising shift to the left that has taken place in the Church's teaching since the 1960s preserves a good deal of continuity with the past. There remain the resistance to liberal philosophy and liberal economics, the emphasis on the common good and social solidarity, and the call for an ethical culture of justice and compassion. What is new is "the preferential option for the poor," the reading of society from the perspective of the disadvantaged. But modern Catholic teaching is often contradictory, not least the pronouncements of John Paul II. The new injunction to identify and overcome structures of oppression often comes into conflict with continuing strands of more conservative thought.

The experience of the Latin American Church in the 1960s and 1970s was especially important in the evolution of Catholic social teaching. Thanks to the influence of liberation theology it became clear to the Latin American bishops that the organic, corporatist concept of society did not apply to their societies, divided as they were between a small sector of wealthy and middle-class people and the great majority, impoverished and excluded from all social participation.

In two important church documents, the "Conclusions" of the 1968 Medellín Conference and the "Final Document" of the 1979 Puebla Conference, the Latin American bishops chose a conflict model to describe their own society. They recognized the division of society between the rich and the poor and argued that human justice and God's justice demanded "the preferential option for the poor": that is, solidarity with the poor and their struggle for emancipation.[1]

But Catholic social teaching is not without its ambiguities. Because of the effort to preserve a certain continuity with past teaching, there are passages in the contemporary documents that continue to promote a corporatist approach to society. Conflict and struggle then appear as brief interruptions of an underlying harmony, to be repaired by concessions on the part of the powerful, compromises on both sides, and the creation of a new consensus.

Another ambiguity is the fact that in most situations the Catholic Church applies its own social teaching in neither its internal organization nor its social counsel. Many bishops nominated by John Paul II in Third World countries and in the developed countries have tended to be conservative personalities, defenders of the status quo, indifferent or hostile to the new social teaching. Despite his trenchant critique of capitalism, which in many ways parallels the insights of liberation theology, John Paul II has been unwilling to allow the critique to become the basis of truly revolutionary practice.

Still, it is important that these and other reactionary aspects of church teachings do not obscure the progressive aspects that are emerging. These can be seen even in two important encyclicals of Pope John Paul II, *Laborem Exercens* (On Labor) of 1981 and *Sollicitudo Rei Socialis* (On Social Concern) of 1987, as well as in the pastoral letters of the Canadian and American bishops.[2] The shift to the left in these church documents is supported with religious enthusiasm by a significant minority in the Church, the Christian left, manifested in a faith-and-justice movement embodied in a network of groups, centers, and individuals committed to emancipation and sustained by frequent meetings and an appropriate literature. In some parts of the world, these Christians constitute the core of the political resistance against oppression. In fact, it is due to this movement, especially in the Third World, that a change has taken place in the Church's official teaching. The shift to the left has come from below.

The radical church documents offer an ethical critique of capitalism that has modified Catholic social teaching and drawn it closer to left-wing politics. Three ideas in John Paul II's encyclicals, for example, have a close affinity with ideas developed by Karl Marx in his early manuscripts, at a time when he too engaged in ethical reflection on liberal institutions.

In these early writings Marx introduced the concept of alienated labor.[3] Wage labor in the factory system robbed workers of the fruit of their labor and estranged them from their own humanity. Workers were meant to be the subjects of production. It was capitalism that made them into objects of production. We note in passing that Marx offered here an ethico-philosophical critique of capitalism, not a scientific one, for to speak of human alienation and the human destiny to be subject presupposes a normative concept of human nature.

In one of his first essays, Marx proposed an even more radical concept of alienation.[4] He argued that people became estranged from their human nature whenever they were prevented from assuming collective responsibility for society and the institutions to which they belonged. People were meant to be the subject of their society. This was democracy. Political democracy in capitalist countries, Marx argued with some vehemence, was not very democratic: it proudly proclaimed that all citizens were equal before the law, and in doing so disguised the crass economic inequality between workers and owners and the total absence of democracy in the economic institutions.

In his early manuscripts Marx also defined the human as a "species being" *(Gattungswesen),*[5] a term derived from German idealism. Humans differ from animals inasmuch as the human struggle for survival and well-being is oriented toward the entire species, the whole of humanity. Against John Locke and the liberal philosophers, who promoted individualism, Marx defined the human as a social animal.

These three ideas in Marx are developed from a Christian perspective in the papal encyclicals. First, John Paul II argues that the dignity of labor is such that workers are entitled to participate in the decisions affecting the work of their hands and the organization of the work process. Workers are meant to be subjects, not objects of production. The Pope calls this "the priority of labor over capital."[6]

Workers are alienated from their human nature when they are excluded from ownership and co-responsibility, as they are both in capitalism and in Communism as represented by the Soviet and East European collectivism of the post-World War II era. In capitalism the fate of the workers depends on decisions made by the owners and directors of the industries, and in Communism on the decisions of the appropriate agency of the state bureaucracy. In both systems, wages are the important reality for the workers, and the struggle for just wages must continue for the time being. But eventually wage labor must be replaced by worker co-ownership; eventually workers will be the owners of their giant workbench.

For John Paul II, worker ownership is no unfailing guarantee of social justice. What is required for justice is that the industries be run to serve the well-being of the whole society. Workers who make decisions regarding the industries must therefore be responsible to a government that protects and promotes the common good.

In this context, John Paul II has also elaborated the Catholic position on property. As has been done since Leo XIII, he defends the rights of property, but only conditionally. The title to property, whether it be private, cooperative, or public, is valid only if the industries or the land actually serve the common good of society.[7] But more than any pope before him, John Paul II recognizes that it may not be possible to hold privately controlled property to standards of public interest. In such a situation, he has extended Catholic teaching to countenance collective, public ownership of means of production as a way to bring the fruits of labor's effort to bear in workers' interest.

But public ownership offers no guarantee that production will serve the needs of society. As in capitalism, where private ownership tends to serve the accumulation of private profit, a government may run the economy to enhance its power at home or expand its power abroad without regard to the welfare or needs of the workers. As is his custom, John Paul II formulates his ideas as critiques of both capitalism and collectivism. Because of oppression and sociopolitical marginalization of workers and the poor in both systems, protest movements and organized efforts to change the economic structure have an ethical foundation in capitalist societies no less than in socialist ones.

In his encyclicals John Paul II also defends the theory, formulated by the young Marx, that humans are meant to be subjects of their society and decision-making participants in all the institutions to which they belong.[8] In the past, Catholic social teaching opposed egalitarianism. The Catholic conservative tradition distinguished between the *majores,* the responsible leaders, and *minores,* the simple people, and demanded that "the leaders" serve the common good of society and "the simple people" obey their laws and regulations. Perhaps it was his experience in Poland that made John Paul II put great emphasis on what he calls "the subjectivity" of peoples.[9] Societies are just only if they allow the responsible participation of their members.

Governments may serve or claim to serve the well-being of their societies, but from an ethical perspective they are just only if they recognize the "subjectivity" of the people, their right to share responsibility in defining their culture and shaping their society. John Paul II does not suggest, however, that this necessarily calls for parliamentary democracy. One can imagine other institutional forms that respect the subjectivity of a people.

It is unfortunately both characteristic and remarkably inconsistent that John Paul II does not introduce the principle of subjectivity into the one institution over which he has power: namely, the Catholic Church. In ecclesiastical matters the Pope has all the instincts of a conservative, frightened of democracy as the beginning of chaos. In 1988 he went so far as to silence Leonardo Boff, one of the leading voices of liberation theology in Latin America, when Boff insisted publicly that the Church open itself to the active and creative participation of the common people.

Yet in his encyclicals John Paul II advocates the concept of universal solidarity. With Hegel and the young Marx and Abraham Lincoln as well, he argues that freedom is indivisible: if some remain oppressed, all remain imprisoned in one way or another. The alienation inflicted on some has adverse effects on the whole of society. If the wealthy nations of the North promote their own economic development to the detriment of the poor nations of the South, then even the northern nations will suffer. Why? Because the economic mechanisms that widen the gap between rich and poor countries also widen the gap between rich and poor classes in the North. Human development, the Pope argues, is "a duty of all towards all."[10]

The ethical discourse of universal solidarity is not always free of ambiguity. Universal solidarity is sometimes used as an ethical argument against class struggle and thus in favor of a corporatist concept of society. Many ecclesiastical texts, however, clearly recognize that universal solidarity begins with the poor and oppressed. Solidarity is not extended to the oppressor. Solidarity is preferential; it embraces those who struggle for justice. We note that the social perspective is here conflictual, not organic. Preferential solidarity aims at the reconstruction of the social order so that then, with the establishment of justice, solidarity may be extended to all. Preferential solidarity is the means; universal solidarity is the end.

In the encyclical *Laborem Exercens,* John Paul II argues that the workers are the dynamic element in both capitalist and Communist societies. Their exclusion from ownership and responsibility makes them the agents of social transformation in both societies. What counts in these struggles is that the workers develop solidarity in their own ranks and that those who are not workers, including the leadership of the Church, extend their solidarity to the workers' movement. The ethical imperative formulated by John Paul II is "the solidarity of labor and solidarity with labor."[11] For less developed countries, the Pope speaks of solidarity of the poor and with the poor. Universal solidarity here clearly begins with the poor and oppressed.[12]

In the mind of John Paul II, these innovative social ideas have nothing to do with Marxism. The Pope looks upon Marxism as an economistic and deterministic set of ideas that falsely claims the status of demonstrable science, that is devoid of humanistic reflection and insensitive to the aspirations of working people, a conservative, unimaginative ideology protecting the interests of the holders of power in so-called Communist regimes.

Even Western "scientific" Marxism does not appear attractive to the Pope. Against positivistic science on the left and the right, the papal encyclicals strongly emphasize the element of freedom and responsible choice that continues to be present in economic institutions. There are no economic "laws," only strong economic "trends." Economic systems are never completely internally determined. They always operate through specific, concrete institutions—industries, banks, decision-making boards—which people establish and for which they are responsible. Through human action, these institutions might be set up differently, even in the given system. In his analyses John Paul II always brings out both the "structuration" and the "human agency" present in the historical situation, even if he does not use this terminology.

Of special interest in this context is the concept of "structural sin," which John Paul II has reiterated in Catholic social teaching.[13] In another striking parallel with liberation theology, he argues that it is impossible to understand the present economic and political crisis simply as the multiplication of personal sins, the malicious acts of individuals. In the past, the churches used to "moralize." They created the impression that the problems in society were caused by pride and selfishness, and that if people only became more generous and loving, these problems would straighten themselves out.

Against this former trend, John Paul II speaks of "structures of sin," of mechanisms and institutions—created by people—which, following a logic built into them, inflict heavy burdens on certain sectors of society. As examples he gives colonialism and imperialism.

Even though people are shaped by the socioeconomic institutions through which they produce and live their lives, John Paul II brings out the agency and hence the responsibility that remains with individuals. Structural sin is always linked to personal sin, and individuals cannot escape responsibility by hiding behind generalized institutional or historical forces. Since systems always operate through specific, concrete mechanisms, decision-makers do make some choices and so have some responsibility for increasing or lightening the burden on people's backs. Increasing the unjust burden is sinful.

More than that, systems that create oppression also generate opposition and provoke critical ideas. In this situation, the Pope argues, personal sin is present in people who refuse to listen to criticism, who defend social injustice, and who oppose social change or seek to slow it down in order to protect their own privileges.

Against any form of determinism, the Church defends human agency and responsibility. Christian theology is suspicious of totalizing systems and evolutionary theories that predict the direction of history. History remains open. In times of great anguish such as our own, this openness of history to human agency and the unexpected is a source of hope.

THE CHURCH AND GLOBAL CAPITALISM

Recent church documents also provide an ethical critique of present-day global capitalism. The social analysis of the present economic crisis as presented in the papal encyclicals has been endorsed and developed by the Canadian bishops and, less consistently perhaps, by the U.S. bishops as well. According to these documents, world capitalism is entering upon a new and brutal phase which, unless stopped, will dispossess and disenfranchise ever widening sectors of the world population.[14]

After World War II, at different speeds in different countries, capitalism became a somewhat more benign economic system in the advanced countries. The Great Depression convinced people that capitalism was an essentially unstable system subject to economic cycles and that for this reason governments should extend a helping hand to industries and the general population during periods of decline. And the war demonstrated that greater government control actually made the national economy thrive.

Capitalists became willing to enter into an unwritten contract with society: in return for government assistance and broad popular support for capitalism, they promised to favor high levels of employment, support welfare legislation, and respect labor organizations that did not threaten the capitalist domination of society. This more benign phase of capitalism was successful for a time. It produced great wealth in the industrialized countries and created the hope of upward mobility among ordinary people. People believed that if they themselves did not make it, at least their children would.

This phase has come to an end. The capitalists' unwritten contract with society is coming apart. Unemployment is steadily rising, welfare legislation is slowly being dismantled, and labor organizations find themselves attacked from all sides. The gap between the rich and the poor, and more especially between rich countries and poor countries, is ever widening.

What is taking place is a giant reorganization of the economy on an international basis around privately owned, giant transnational corporations. These macrocorporations are not concerned with the well-being of the society in which they were originally located. On the contrary, they have become so powerful that they are able to blackmail national governments to do their will: to introduce neoconservative economic policies at home and adopt foreign policies that will protect their overseas interests and allow them to compete more successfully with transnationals based in other parts of the world. The national economy thus becomes a slave of the international market.

The Canadian bishops have described this process in some detail.[15] They point to the changes taking place in the structure of Canadian capital as a symptom of the reorientation of the global economic system. They show that capitalism, following its own logic and no longer restrained by government policies, creates industrial and financial centers of power that become wealthy at the expense of the less developed hinterland. This process impoverishes the developing countries of the South, and in the North the same process creates unemployment and regional disparity and thus widens the gap between rich and poor.

John Paul II refers to this trend as "economic imperialism." During a visit to Canada he said, "Poor people and poor nations of the South— poor in different ways, not only lacking food, but also deprived of freedom and other human rights—will sit in judgment of those people of the

North who take these goods away from them, amassing to themselves the imperialistic monopoly of economic and political supremacy."[16]

Without saying so explicitly, papal teaching seems to recognize that capitalism has become a global economic system, with centers of power in North America, Western Europe, and East Asia, each competing with the others. These centers are surrounded by the dependent regions of the rest of the world, including the countries of Eastern Europe, which suffer from the domination of the major capitalist powers.

In his encyclical *Sollicitudo Rei Socialis,* John Paul II deals specifically with the inequality between the developed North and the slowly developing South. Why is the South sinking into ever greater poverty and powerlessness? Why is the gap between rich and poor widening all over the world? John Paul offers two reasons for this. The first one is the organization of world capitalism in a manner that enhances the wealth of the industrial and financial centers in the North.[17] The economic mechanisms that regulate the flow of capital, resources, and goods have been set up by the powerful and wealthy to the detriment of the poor nations in the South.

Writing in the 1980s, before the fall of the Berlin Wall and the transformations of Eastern Europe and the Soviet Union, John Paul II identified a second major cause of increasing Third World misery. The Cold War had divided the North into two hostile and competing camps, a division detrimental to the nations of the South and harmful to the entire human family. The two blocs constituted empires that promoted antithetical ideologies—liberal capitalism and Marxist collectivism— each claiming to have universal validity.[18] The competing superpowers fostered regional wars by proxy and spent hundreds of billions of dollars in preparation for total war.

The division of the North into two hostile blocs, each pursuing an end it regarded as absolute, had a devastating impact on the South.[19] Countries in the South that wanted to free themselves from colonial bondage and start their own development were forced to choose between one and the other side. And in choosing, they tragically entered into the destructive East-West dynamics of the Cold War.

The two empires in the North understood the South not in terms of its own problems and aspirations but in geopolitical terms, in terms of the power struggles of the East-West conflict. Because countries of the South had to choose between the two blocs, their populations became divided over the choice. The countries were thus weakened by internal conflicts that sometimes even led to civil war. In some cases one country found itself adjacent to another that had opted for the opposite bloc, a situation often leading to hostility, armed struggle, and impoverishment.

More profoundly still, by opting for one of the two blocs, these countries were drawn into one or another ideology, liberal capitalism or Marxist collectivism, each one in its own way discontinuous with their own cultures, values, and mores. Such economic development produces human alienation and inevitably leads to failure. The difficult task of these regions is to create structures of economic development that respect their own cultural and religious heritage and thus strengthen the people in their sense of self-identity and self-respect.

John Paul II has raged against the ideological bipartition of the North as one of the principal causes of the world's ills.[20] Even with the end of the Cold War and the collapse of Soviet and East European collectivism, the prospect for humane progress for the world's peoples is far from assured. Widespread restoration of more or less full capitalist markets is bringing great misery to working people in formerly collectivist societies and intensifying capitalist rivalries among the major powers. Meanwhile, the ideological hold of capitalist individualism is tightening everywhere.

These are the very evils that have been the principal targets of Catholic social teaching since Vatican Council II, even as the evils of collectivism have also been criticized. With the collapse of the socialist alternative, if the Church maintains its critique of capitalism, it will become a more prominent global pole of opposition, no longer a mediating force between capitalism and socialism. In this period of capitalism triumphant, Catholic social teaching will be severely challenged as it continues to focus on the inhuman side of capitalist society.

Liberation theology has already begun to blaze this oppositional path, but it is under attack. Papal teachings, while in many ways supportive of radical social action, are ambiguous in their substance and hostile to liberation theology as such. It remains to be seen whether liberation theology will be able to continue within the framework of Catholic teaching as a doctrine of empowerment whereby poor and working people can effectively challenge and overcome the capitalist system.

The ethics of solidarity, as we have seen, holds a central position in the Church's social teaching. This is not an "idealistic" position, not the ethical approach scathingly designated by Marx and Engels as "utopian socialism." The ethics of solidarity does not imply that if all people become more loving, then social injustice will disappear and present structures will not have to be changed. On the contrary, the ethics of solidarity begins with the preferential option for the poor, feeds the social struggle for reconstruction, and aims at the creation of a more just society on the global level.

In my opinion it was the great weakness of Marxism to have so little to say on the motivation for social struggle, apart from the collective self-interest of economic classes. Making use of a distinction introduced by Max Weber,[21] we can say that movements for social reconstruction are successful if they are driven by a complex set of motivations: "purpose-rational," referring to the self-interest, personal and collective, of the people involved; "value-rational," referring to the alternative vision of society entertained by the people; and "emotional," referring to cultural factors such as national resistance or religious conviction.

The Catholic ethics of solidarity incorporates these three motivations. The ethics of solidarity has a purpose-rational dimension for all concerned, for masters and slaves alike, because without bold social change, world society is seriously threatened; it has a value-rational dimension because it is based on an alternative vision of society; and it has an emotional component because it is filled with religious yearning.

Toward Economic Justice

My analysis of Catholic social teaching makes it seem clearer and more precise than do the ecclesiastical documents themselves. The reason is that church documents are usually not perfectly consistent: they do not pursue the same perspective throughout; they often repeat phrases taken from an earlier perspective without acknowledging the difference. Even bold church documents want to preserve continuity with past teaching. Nor do the radical principles affirmed in one papal document necessarily appear in the appropriate place of the next papal pronouncement. These inconsistencies reflect also the conflicting social interests expressed in the process by which the documents are drafted.

Some readers wonder whether radical principles deserve to be taken seriously when they are uttered only once or twice and fail to reorient the entire approach to social theory. As I mentioned above, John Paul II does not apply his own social theory to the self-organization of the Catholic Church or to the political orientation of the Vatican administration. On the contrary, at this very time the Vatican makes every effort to tame the progressive bishops of Brazil whose "preferential option for the poor" has shaped their entire pastoral approach, while the same Vatican did not reproach the reactionary bishops of Argentina for their alliance with the political right and their silence during the years of terror in the 1970s and early 1980s. Nor has John Paul II ever recognized the ethical foundation of the women's movement. There are many reasons to be skeptical.

Still, in my opinion the evolution of Catholic social teaching encourages an important social movement within the Christian churches and makes a significant contribution to contemporary social theory. The recent shift in the official teaching has been brought about through a multiple dialogue: dialogue with the prophetic texts of the Bible, with the voices of oppressed groups and classes, and with critical political and social science, including Marx and Weber. Catholic social theory has come to entertain a conflictual understanding of society which challenges both the traditional organic concept found in conservative thought and the pluralistic concept embraced by liberalism. In this new strand of theological reflection, the struggle for justice is understood as calling for preferential solidarity. Church teaching provides strong arguments against the present "neoconservative" economic trend that the "neoconservative" culture associated with it.

From my point of view, however, the greatest merit of the more recent Catholic social theory is its contribution to the critical dialogue taking place among social thinkers of the left.

First, Catholic social theory, as mentioned above, consistently rejects institutional determinisms of any kind. Despite the logic and the pressure of institutions, a certain human freedom remains. Catholic social theory defends the agency and the creativity of consciousness, even though the collective self-understanding of people is largely shaped by the economic institutions in which they labor and live. Because of this dimension of freedom, social theory should not understand itself as an exact science. It cannot predict the future. History remains ever open. Catholic social theory has little sympathy for evolutionary or revolutionary theories of history that anticipate the final outcome. It rejects all this-worldly eschatologies, including the Marxist expectation of the classless, reconciled society.

Yet the openness of history is itself a source of hope. The contradictions of society always generate critical thought and countervailing movements. Sometimes unexpected historical events—wars, severe economic crises, or ecological disasters—create conditions that allow these countervailing movements to acquire political power.

Second, Catholic social theory emphasizes the abiding importance of ethics. Despite their passionate ethical convictions, Marxist theorists too often refrain from ethical reflection. They lack an ethical discourse and provide no norms for the interaction of comrades in the movement. Nor have they formulated adequate values to guide the new societies they have sought to build where they have had power. Catholic social theory can make a contribution to these movements by contributing its sense of the importance of ethics, in particular the abiding relevance of love and compassion.

Third, the preferential option for the poor, we note, is not the equivalent of the option for the proletariat. In Catholic social theory, preferential solidarity embraces the workers and the poor; that is, the popular sector of low-income people, casual workers, the unemployed, people on welfare. The marginalized sector includes the native peoples, major sectors of the other despised races, and poor women.

The social struggle against the unjust order calls for the building of a solidarity network, possibly around a political party, that brings together labor unions and representative organizations of other disadvantaged groups. Such a network could receive the active support of all citizens who love justice, including church and synagogue groups.

What emerges here is a more pluralistic concept of the left. Each of these concerned groups will have a slightly different perspective, and only as the solidarity among them is strengthened through joint action and the give-and-take of negotiations will a single political orientation emerge. Unity of social analysis is not the starting point but the end result. Each group will have to compromise a little in relation to its own collective self-interest in order to support a more universal political movement, one representing all the poor and oppressed and aimed at transforming the unjust social order.

Finally, Catholic social theory recognizes the importance of social passion in the struggle for economic justice. While the great religious traditions of humanity have been compromised by their entanglement with ruling classes and ruling-class culture, they are nonetheless heirs of an original religious yearning for love, justice, and peace.

Religion has an ideological and a utopian dimension. At present we observe both right-wing and left-wing movements in the world religions. In the Christian churches, Catholic and Protestant, the left-wing movement has affected official teaching. Even the political left is beginning to recognize that it must allow its supporters to retain their cultural and religious traditions, to find in them spiritual resources for the social struggle. Secular people have a great humanist tradition to draw upon, and religious people have their own inheritance, which, though marked by ambiguity, is able to nourish the yearning for justice and strengthen political commitment.

Such Christians believe that the infinite and incomprehensible source of all life, love, and justice, which they call God (and see revealed in Jesus Christ), is operative in human history, especially in people's struggles against injustice and oppression. To stand against the established powers in solidarity with workers and the poor is for Christians a place of new religious experience.

Notes

1. The preferential option for the poor was endorsed and explained by the Latin American bishops in the "Final Document" (nn. 1134–40) of the 1979 Puebla Conference, reprinted in *Puebla and Beyond: Documentary and Commentary,* ed. John Eagleson and Philip Scharper (Maryknoll, N.Y.: Orbis Books, 1979).

2. John Paul II, *Laborem Exercens,* in Gregory Baum, *The Priority of Labor: A Commentary on Laborem Exercens* (New York: Paulist Press, 1982); John Paul II, *Sollicitudo Rei Socialis,* in *The Logic of Solidarity: Commentaries on Sollicitudo Rei Socialis,* ed. Gregory Baum and Robert Ellsberg (Maryknoll, N.Y.: Orbis Books, 1989); Canadian Conference of Catholic Bishops, "Ethical Reflections on the Economic Crisis," in *Ethics and Economics,* ed. Gregory Baum and Duncan Cameron (Toronto: Lorimer, 1984); National Conference of Catholic Bishops, "Economic Justice for All: Catholic Social Teaching and the U.S. Economy," *Origins* 16, no. 24 (1986). See also Gregory Baum, *Theology and Society* (New York: Paulist Press, 1987).

3. Karl Marx, "Alienated Labor," in *Karl Marx: Early Writings,* ed. T. B. Bottomore (New York: McGraw-Hill, 1964), pp. 120–34.

4. Karl Marx, "On the Jewish Question," in *Early Writings,* pp. 3–31. See also Bertell Ollman, *Alienation: Marx's Conception of Man in Capitalist Society* (Cambridge: Cambridge University Press, 1970).

5. Marx, "Alienated Labor," pp. 126–28.

6. John Paul II, "The Priority of Labour," in *Laborem Exercens,* n. 12. See also "Work and Ownership," n. 14.

7. "The means of production cannot be possessed against labor, they cannot even be possessed for possession's sake, because the only legitimate title to their possession—whether in the form of private or collective ownership—is that they should serve labor" (ibid., n. 14).

8. John Paul II, "Man as Subject of Work," in ibid., n. 6. "We can speak of socializing the means of production only when the subjectivity of society is ensured, that is to say, when on the basis of his work each person is fully entitled to consider himself a part owner of the great workbench at which he is working with everyone else" (n. 14).

9. John Paul II, *Sollicitudo Rei Socialis,* n. 15: "No social group, for example a political party, has the right to usurp the role of sole leader, since this brings about the destruction of the true subjectivity of society and of the individual citizens."

10. Ibid., nn. 38–40, 32.

11. John Paul II, *Laborem Exercens,* n. 8.

12. John Paul II, *Sollicitudo Rei Socialis,* n. 39.

13. Ibid., nn. 36–37.

14. Baum and Cameron, *Ethics and Economics,* pp. 52–54.

15. See Canadian Conference of Catholic Bishops, "Ethical Reflections on the Economic Crisis," pp. 5–18. This document created a nationwide debate in Canada. Many critics accused the bishops of being Marxists. Of course they were not, but their analysis was undoubtedly influenced by the positions adopted by the Latin American bishops and liberation theology, which had been formulated in dialogue with the neo-Marxist dependency theory elaborated by such scholars as André Gunder Frank and Samir Amin.

16. Quoted in Baum, *Theology and Society,* p. 96. The theory of imperialism, first developed by the liberal J. A. Hobson and modified by V. I. Lenin, has been reformulated by more recent neo-Marxist scholars. See, e.g., Harry Magdoff, *Imperialism: From the Colonial Age to the Present* (New York: Monthly Review Press, 1978); and I. M. Zeitlin, *Capitalism and Imperialism* (Chicago: Markham, 1972). In some form, the theory appealed already to Pope Pius XI, who made use of it in his 1931 encyclical, *Quadragesimo Anno,* nn. 105–9, in *Seven Great Encyclicals,* ed. William Gibbons (New York: Paulist Press, 1963), pp. 153–54.

17. John Paul II, *Sollicitudo Rei Socialis,* nn. 16–17.

18. Ibid., nn. 20–21.

19. Ibid., nn. 22–23.

20. See Gregory Baum, "The Anti-Cold War Encyclical," *The Ecumenist* 26 (July–August 1988): 65–74.

21. Max Weber, *Basic Concepts in Sociology* (New York: Citadel Press, 1969), p. 59.

18. Decoding the Pope's Social Encyclicals

Richard T. DeGeorge

This chapter first appeared in *The Making of an Economic Vision: John Paul II's "On Social Concern,"* eds. Oliver F. Williams and John W. Houck, in 1991.

Pope John Paul II's social encyclicals, *On Human Work* and *On Social Concern*[1] have not caught the conscience of the American people despite the fact that they enunciate sound moral principles and challenge fundamental aspects of the U.S. economy and of U.S. international relations. The encyclicals contain more than enough to think about, fight over, and learn from, yet they have not received much attention in either the popular press or the scholarly community, especially when compared with the pastoral letter of the American Catholic bishops on the economy. Why not? Some American commentators who have paid attention to the encyclicals have even seen in them the making of a counterculture. This reaction, as well as the absence of much other reaction, is all part of a piece. The reasons the encyclicals have not caught on here also explain in a paradoxical way the countercultural interpretation of the encyclicals.

First and most important, the two encyclicals were not written primarily for or aimed at a U.S. audience. Some Americans might take this as an affront, even though there is little reason for such a reaction. Even though encyclicals are in a certain sense universal and addressed to all Catholics, they address particular issues and are written with a certain aim. The Pope's major concern in both encyclicals is not with the United States and what it should do, but with the Church's need to counter the appeal and continuing threat of Marxism. The Pope's Polish heritage makes him understandably sensitive to and aware of this appeal and this threat. For the Church, the main ideological struggle is not between Communism and Capitalism—a struggle toward which it can be neutral, if not indifferent—it is between Marxism and Catholicism. The encyclicals, I shall argue, attempt to seize the global moral initiative from Marx. The Pope's primary target audience, thus, is people in areas where Marx's writings are well known and influential—Eastern Europe (including Poland), much of Western Europe, and Latin America. In his social encyclicals the Pope seizes Marxist themes and Christianizes them. Here, perhaps, lies their appeal as a counterculture.

Second, the encyclicals fail to speak to Americans because the style, the diction, and the rhetoric are not American; they are at best European. The encyclicals are rife with subtle and not so subtle allusions to Marx and are filled with Marxist diction, vocabulary, and jargon. Although most Americans miss these references, they help explain what some perceive as the countercultural tone of the encyclicals. Of course, Pope John Paul II is not a Marxist. He is anything but a Marxist. Yet Marx is his antagonist on social issues in the world. No revolutions are fought currently in the name of free enterprise. They are fought in the name of Marxism in Latin America, in Africa and in Europe. That is the ideology that opposes Catholicism and that threatens it. In a style familiar to those who live in a repressed society, the words of the encyclicals are not always the message. One must read between the lines. This style is well known in Poland. References rarely are direct. The thesis is not stated openly; the reader must divine it. Pope John Paul II was raised on that style and knows it well. The style is lost on most Americans who are not used to it, trained in it, or taught to read that way.

Third, the two encyclicals, but especially the second, have a strong anti-U.S. flavor. They show little awareness of, much less appreciation for, anything American—a point not lost on Americans. The encyclicals are more negative about the wealthy than about any other group, including those in the Second World or the Eastern Bloc. The target of Marxism is capitalism and, in struggling against Marxism, Pope John Paul II's strategy is to seize Marx's moral critiques of capitalism, and revise them just enough to capture the high moral ground of human rights and concern for the poor. Although he acknowledges the right to private property, he joins with it the obligation to share the wealth to such a degree that he breaks with the traditional natural law defense of private property, say, of John Locke.[2] He attacks wealth as strenuously as does Marx, and for somewhat the same reasons. This is the third reason why some read his encyclicals as a call for a counterculture in the United States.

No one can call Pope John Paul II soft on Soviet communism. Yet he is clearly not a fan of capitalism. He allows for some private property, yet calls for centralized control and "rational" government planning. Both of these resonate with Marx's claims. Marx contrasts rational planning to what he sees in capitalism, namely, the anarchy of the marketplace, which is guided not by reason but by self-interest, and which is wasteful—another theme the Pope adopts. His heart lies with socialism of some sort, although exactly of what variety he never says. If one pieces together what Pope John Paul II does not attack, what he allows, and what he calls for, the result is probably something like self-management socialism of the mixed Yugoslavian type which permits some small private ownership as well as state and worker ownership. The fact that no such economic structure has been successful—Yugoslavia comes closest to having tried, with less than impressive results—seems to him beside the point.

The two encyclicals are not letters on economics but on theology and morality. Yet the attacks on wealth show little understanding of production and what makes countries wealthy. The belief that wealth must come from exploitation is a disputed Marxist claim, which John Paul II implicitly accepts. The Pope, like Marx, emphasizes distribution. What there is to distribute, how it was created, and how it can continue to develop so that people may benefit are not beside the point—either economically or morally. That has been the concern of Americans. Because the encyclicals ignore that dimension and underline only the obligation to distribute what one has, it is little wonder they have not moved the American people.

My claim that the encyclicals were not primarily addressed to Americans, even though they were, in fact, addressed to all people, in no way implies that Americans were singled out. For instance, the Pope did not have the Japanese or the Koreans or the Australians in mind any more than he did the Americans. The moral principles he enunciates apply to all, because they are universal. But the rhetoric he uses is no more Japanese than it is American. The emphasis is not on excluding any group, but on purposely addressing a specific audience. The fact that the encyclicals may have less to say to some other parts of the universal Church is a price that anyone who writes for a particular audience must pay. To expect any encyclical to be addressed to all equally and to be written in a style and diction that will appeal to all equally is either to expect the impossible or to be content with vacuous prose that in effect appeals to no one.

John Paul claims that his encyclical *On Social Concern* is not ideological. To Americans, this is a strange claim to find in an encyclical. But the Pope knows full well that the Marxist-Leninist tradition sees Christianity as the most dangerous counterideology to Marxism. He knows that in adapting Marx's critique of capitalism he runs the risk of being charged with adopting an ideological perspective. He claims not to present an ideology to replace liberal capitalism or collectivist Marxism, but he knows that in attacking them both he is open to the charge. He speaks the language of morality, conscious of the fact that, for Marx, morality was as ideological as religion or philosophy or politics. Denying that one's position is ideological does not automatically make it so.

CHALLENGING THE YOUNG MARX

The actual target of the encyclicals' attack, I claim, is Marxism, and the primary audience is those for whom Marxism might be an option, namely, the people of Eastern and Western Europe and of Latin America. A remarkable fact about the encyclical *On Human Work* is that, with the exception of the citations from religious sources, the last chapter, and a brief critique of Soviet communism, it could have been written by the young Karl Marx. In fact, much of it was. A brief comparison between the Pope's text and those of the young Marx shows this to be the case. From this we should not conclude that Marx and the Pope think alike, or that each has more going for him than his followers respectively acknowledge about the other, or that they both misunderstand the phenomenon they both call capitalism. The point, if you see the closeness of language and hence the unattributed allusions, is that the Pope is challenging Marx on his own ground.

Marx is the defender of labor; the leader of the labor union movement; the originator of the call for all working men of the world to unite (read: "solidarity"); the defender of human liberation; the champion of the oppressed, the poor, the downtrodden; the attacker of alienation and exploitation. Pope John Paul II knows this all too well. He knows the moral power of that message. By making many of the same claims about labor that Marx does, the Pope attempts to show that the Catholic message contains all that and more; that Christianity, not Marxism, is the real humanism; that Christ was the friend of the poor before Marx. In Christianizing Marx's analysis, the Pope emphasizes that justice and morality must infuse the critique of labor. In this encyclical the Pope fights to reappropriate the doctrine that Marx, through Ludwig Feuerbach, wrested from the Church in the nineteenth century. Feuerbach, in his influential work *The Essence of Christianity*,[3] said theology must be replaced by anthropology, and religion by humanism. Following him, Marx claimed that the critique of religion was over, and that religion, the opium of the people, the sigh of the oppressed masses, would wither away when their ills were remedied. Feuerbach secularized Christianity; Marx was his heir.

Critics have commented on the originality of the encyclicals. They are original because they are the first attempt by a Pope to get back what Marx took from Christianity. Instead of attacking Marxism directly, as did his predecessors, John Paul II usurps Marx's ground, just as Marx usurped Christianity's. That is the battle raging in the encyclical, a battle all but lost to the bulk of American readers who neither know, nor really care much about, Marx or Marxism. In the United States, Marxism and socialism are no threat and have little popular appeal. In Western Europe and Latin America they are alive. In Eastern Europe they are in power.

In writing *On Human Work* the Pope left the theological development for the end. In the earlier chapters he relies on just a few biblical quotations, mostly from *Genesis*. This structure underlies the claim that John Paul is taking on Marx on Marx's own ground. The moral tone throughout is Christian, yet the audience the Pope wants to reach, and the minds for which he is fighting, are not likely to be moved by theology. They will be moved by moral ideals, and it is the Pope's aim to win the battle for those minds. The last chapter, which seems almost an afterthought with citations piled one on another, bows to the fact that *On Human Work* is not only a work inspired by theology, but that there are actually theological references one could make all along the line, if one were so inclined. For those who want them, they are there. But those who want them really do not need them, and any who really need them would not be convinced by them anyway. The Pope knows what he is doing.

The last chapter cites the spirituality of work and gives a Christian interpretation to work based on the *New Testament.* The rest of the encyclical relies on *Genesis,* especially on the command to subdue the earth, a text which the Pope makes bear more weight than it can withstand, and which becomes a device for making the points he wishes to make. He takes a great deal of Marx's analysis of work and *a posteriori* derives it from *Genesis.* Nonetheless, he persuasively and skillfully weaves it into a Christian perspective, relying heavily as well on his own predilection toward personalism.

In arguing for my claims I shall draw first a comparison between the language of the encyclicals and that of Marx. I have no quarrel with the Pope's principles. I applaud and agree with them. I shall ask whether the description the Pope gives of the current state of affairs is accurate, or whether it is slanted through its language. The way one describes the world is vital to how one evaluates it; and how one evaluates it is vital to how one might act to remedy its perceived defects. My aim primarily is to explain why the encyclicals have fallen mainly on deaf ears in the United States and why the ears that have heard it have been led to the idea of a counterculture.

THE PRIORITY OF LABOR OVER CAPITAL

Let us look a little more closely at the text, rather than just at the spirit of the encyclicals, which is what most Americans who have reacted to it have tended to do.

From the very start, in the first paragraph of *On Human Work,*[4] Pope John Paul II says, "Work is one of the characteristics that distinguish man from the rest of creatures" (p. 1). The claim is remarkable in an encyclical. Traditionally, the notion of humankind as rational animals with divinely created souls has been the Christian distinguishing characteristic of parenthood. The opening shot invites comparison with Marx's statement in *The German Ideology* that "Men...begin to distinguish themselves from animals as soon as they begin to *produce* their means of subsistence, a step which is conditioned by their physical organization."[5] Work as a distinguishing characteristic of human beings is Marx's insight, and one that is traditionally linked to him. In the Christian tradition the interpretation of *Genesis* has not focused on work as a distinguishing characteristic of people, but as a punishment for sin. Pope John Paul II knows all of this. He clearly and at the outset adopts Marx's characterization of humankind and incorporates it into the Christian position. He refuses to yield to Marx the moral high ground on labor, and the only way to seize that ground is to claim it as one's own and to incorporate it into an overall view where it fits more or less comfortably.

Talk about humankind as rational beings, with emphasis on the immortal soul, will not fill the bill when it comes to labor—at least that is the clear signal we get in the opening paragraph of the encyclical. Of course, the Pope does not mention Marx. He assumes the statement is clear enough and shocking enough in the opening paragraph of an encyclical to alert the reader to what he is doing. Those who miss the allusion to Marx will read the rest of the text without the central connection the Pope makes here. Since most Americans will miss it, the encyclical on this level is not written with them in mind.

The opening salvo is just the first of many appropriations of famous passages in Marx. Two paragraphs later, in the encyclical's "Introduction," the Pope writes: "Man's life is built up every day from work, from work it derives its specific dignity" (p. 3). Once again, the Christian tradition has been that people derive their dignity from their immortal souls, made in the image of God. That people derive their dignity from work is not part of the Christian tradition. It is part of Marx's claim, and it forms the basis of his celebrated 1844 Paris manuscript on alienated labor. Marx claims there that people are made by work; that in work they fulfil and realize their capacities; and, that to the extent they are not able to do this, they are alienated from and by their work. The Pope quietly slips from the claim that people's lives derive their dignity from work to the more traditional Christian claim of the dignity and rights of those who work (p. 4). But in the Christian tradition the dignity of the worker does not rest on the claim that a person's life *derives* its dignity from work. The Pope has assimilated a piece of Marx, and linked it to a traditional doctrine.

The Pope concludes the Introduction by highlighting the point that "human work is a key, probably the essential key, to the whole social question" and that the solution "must be sought in the direction of 'making life more human'" (p. 7). That human work is the key to the social problem is once again the basic claim of Marx in his analysis of politics, law, and all other social problems. Pope John Paul II takes the phrase "making life more human" from *Gaudium et Spes;* but the phrase "more human" fits Marx's notion of humankind and human conditions better than it does the view in which an individual's essence, and so humanity, comes from God. From the latter perspective, how human life can be "more human" is puzzling. The conditions of life can be better and more appropriate to the dignity of a person, but human life cannot be more human.

The development of humankind in relation to nature, another new ecological theme in an encyclical (p. 13), parallels Marx's statement that "The universality of man appears in practice in the universality which makes all nature his *inorganic* body."[6] The biblical injunction to "subdue the earth" has been given as a justification for what some have called the rape of nature. Marx's view of nature as an extension of humankind, on the other hand, has been used in defense of the protection of nature. Here, the Pope attempts to seize the moral initiative on ecology from Marx.

On page 14 the Pope says "in the first place work is 'for man' and not man 'for work.'" Compare Marx: "the worker…in his work…does not affirm himself but denies himself….His labor is…not the satisfaction of a need; it is merely a *means* to satisfy needs external to it"[7] and "My work would be a *free manifestation of life,* hence an *enjoyment of life*….[Because] I work *in order to live*….[m]y work *is not* my life."[8] The theme that work is for people and not people for work is at the heart of Marx's critique of alienated labor. On page 16 the Pope says: "Man is treated as an instrument of production, whereas he—he alone, independent of the work he does—ought to be treated as the effective subject of work and its true maker and creator." Once again, Marx's theme of alienation is borrowed and placed in *Genesis.* Listen to Marx: "The *alienation* of the worker in his product means not only that his labor becomes an object, …but that it exists *outside him,* …as something alien to him, and that it becomes a power on its own confronting him."[9]

Marx critiques three aspects of alienated labor under capitalism: first, the alienation of the worker from the product of his or her labor; second, the alienation of the worker from the labor process; and third, the alienation of the worker from other people. The Pope addresses the first aspect in section 6 of Chapter II of the encyclical, "Work in a Subjective Sense"; the second in section 7, "A Threat to the Right Order of Values"; and, not surprisingly, the third in section 8. Marx finds the solution to this third aspect of alienation, that of the worker from other people, in species-being, a Feuerbachian notion in which people are related to other people. The Pope proposes a similar theme "Worker Solidarity." The parallel development is not a coincidence. This is Pope John Paul II's answer to Marx's critique of labor under capitalism. He appropriates the critique, and places it in a personalist context. The citations from *Genesis* cannot support the doctrine he builds and, wisely, he does not place undue emphasis on those quotations.

In further defense of the claim that the encyclical does not have Americans as its primary audience, note the Pope's choice of words for section 8: "Worker Solidarity." "Solidarity" to the American ear calls up—if one is of the older generation—the labor union movement, and the song "Solidarity Forever." It has the ring of the 1930s to it; it is a little passé and archaic. The only other connotation it has for an American is the Solidarity movement in Poland. The Pope's choice of the word resonates with Poland and with the labor union movement there. Americans do not use the term in the same way, and would tend to speak of communion or community instead.

As the Pope develops the theme of solidarity, he refers to "the proletariat question" (p. 17). There is no proletariat question in the United States. Americans do not describe workers or union members as the proletariat. "Proletariat" is a Marxist term used to describe workers, and "the proletariat question" is framed in Marxist terms. This becomes even clearer a few lines later in the encyclical when the Pope links that issue with "exploitation." The Pope openly borrows the terminology of Marx to describe work and working conditions. He is appropriating the Marxist terms and using them for his own purposes, his own solution. But he clearly speaks the language of Marx. He does so knowingly to assimilate and Christianize Marx's critique in the struggle for people's hearts, minds and souls. But the language and the analysis leave most Americans cold. Americans do not think in rigid class terms, in terms of bourgeoisie and proletariat, and in terms of the exploitation of all workers by capitalists; Europeans and Latin Americans do.

The Pope's discussion of the proletariat question recapitulates Marx's analysis of alienated labor and, again, we can match the one to the other. The Pope's statements that "through work man not only transforms nature, adapting it to his own needs, but he also achieves fulfillment as a human being" (pp. 20–21); that "in work, whereby matter gains in nobility, man himself should not experience a lowering of his own dignity"; that "work can be made into a means for oppressing man, and that in various ways it is possible to exploit human labor, that is to say, workers" (p. 21); and so on, all have direct correlations to Marx's writings.

The parallels continue in Chapter III, "Conflict between Labor and Capital in the Present Phase of History." The very title of the chapter is Marxist. Americans speak of the conflict between labor and management. In appropriating Marx's use of the term "capital," the Pope not only appropriates Marx's term but assimilates his analysis, and his critique of capitalism. This is tactically and rhetorically an effective device if one's audience is those for whom Marxism has an appeal. It is not effective tactically or rhetorically for most Americans who will either not catch the references or who will not recognize the descriptions as a reflection of their experience.

The Pope points to the conflict between "capital" and "labor," "that is to say between the small but highly influential group of entrepreneurs, owners or holders of the means of production, and the broader multitude of people who lacked these means and who shared in the process of production solely by their labor" (p. 24). The terms and their definitions are direct paraphrases of Engels' definitions in a footnote to the 1888 English edition of *The Communist Manifesto*. Engels there defines the bourgeoisie as "the class of modern Capitalists, owners of the means of social production and employers of wage-labour" and the proletariat as "the class of modern wage-labourers who, having no means of production of their own, are reduced to selling their labour-power in order to live."[10]

In describing the conflict between capital and labor the Pope says, "This conflict...found expression in the ideological conflict between liberalism, understood as the ideology of capitalism, and Marxism, understood as the ideology of scientific socialism and communism....The real conflict between labor and capital was transformed into a systematic class struggle" (p. 24). To see the relation of management and labor in this way is to see it precisely as Marx describes it in *The Communist Manifesto*. That the conflict between management and labor in the United States is a conflict between liberalism and Marxism would come as news to both management and labor. The Pope then equates Marxism with its Soviet version—thereby robbing it of its original legitimacy—saying that the Marxist program "presupposes the collectivization of the means of production" (p. 24), whereas for Marx it involves the socialization of the means of production.

The Pope then notes "...we cannot go into the details [of Marxism], nor is this necessary, for they are known both from the vast literature on the subject and by experience" (p. 25). Clearly, he assumes his audience is familiar with Marxism and the debates surrounding it, an assumption that is false with respect to most Americans. The Pope's confrontation with Marxism is clear, and the alternative that the Pope proposes is based on "the principle of the priority of labor over capital" which "has always been taught by the church" (p. 25). But that principle is one that we find also in Marx. The Pope says "capital cannot be separated from labor" (p.27). Marx said "Capital is *stored-up labor*"[11]—a claim that follows more obviously from his labor theory of value than the Pope's statement follows from Christian doctrine.

The Pope's aim is not only to seize the moral initiative on labor and economic issues from Marx, but also to replace the Marxist perspective with a Christian one. Thus far in the encyclical he has adapted only Marx. Finally, after describing the relation between labor and capital in Marxist terms, the Pope suddenly and abruptly attacks economism. An American reader may well be lost here. The Pope's attack on what he calls "economism" is his attack on the economic determinism attributed to the later Marx. Here the Pope makes the crucial equation of Marxism and philosophical materialism. He says that the error of economism is the error of materialism which includes "the primacy and superiority of the material, and directly or indirectly places the spiritual and personal (man's individual activity, moral values and such matters) in a position of subordination to material reality" (p. 29). He continues, stating that "In dialectical materialism too man is not first and foremost the subject of work...but continues to be understood and treated, in dependence on what is material, as a kind of 'resultant' of the economic or production relations prevailing at a given period" (p. 30). This is true of Soviet dialectical materialism—the Pope's real target—even if not of the early Marx.

What initially is puzzling is that after this diversion, the Pope continues discussing work and ownership in Marxist terms: "On the one side are those who do the work without being the owners of the means of production, and on the other side those who act as entrepreneurs and who own these means or represent the owners" (p. 31). The description was accurate in Marx's time, and still may be accurate of some places. It does not capture accurately the fact that in the United States, through pension funds, workers are in fact owners of a significant portion of the means of production.

We have here the crux of the Pope's strategy. The target is materialistic Soviet Marxism-Leninism and its offshoots. All the allusions to Marxism and the continued use of Marx's analysis of work and of capitalism are a concerted effort to assimilate them into the Christian view and message, to seize the initiative with respect to workers and the poor, and to separate them from metaphysical materialism. The condemnation of materialism and of dialectical materialism—a term coined by Plekhanov and never used by Marx—comes abruptly, and forces us to see that simply assimilating Marx is not enough. One must see that, despite the use of similar language, only a Christian, personalist base, and not a materialist base, can do justice to the message the Pope has been developing.

The Pope attacks "rigid" capitalism and argues for "joint ownership of the means of work, sharing by the workers in the management and/or profits of business, so-called shareholding by labor" (p. 32.). He says "merely taking these means of production (capital) out of the hands of their private owners is not enough to ensure their satisfactory socialization" (p. 33). Having attacked both capitalism and Soviet collectivism, he suggests a number of intermediary bodies that resemble most of all the structures of Yugoslav self-management socialism.

Chapter IV also is strongly reminiscent of Marxism. It starts with the duty to work—a duty not recognized as such in the United States, but one enforced by law in the Soviet Union which outlaws parasitism. The discussion of direct and indirect employers brings in the exploitation of the less developed by the more developed countries, and the dependency thesis—two doctrines developed by Lenin and taken over whole in the Pope's analysis of international relations of rich and poor countries.

Pope John Paul II says the state "must make provision for overall planning with regard to the different kinds of work by which not only the economic life, but also the cultural life of a given society is shaped; ...they must also give attention to organizing that work in a correct and rational way" (p. 41). That these are proper tasks of the state are views compatible with Marxism but not with the notion of a free economy. The "rational planning" (p. 42) he refers to is a Marxist ideal (as I have noted already) in which the anarchy of the marketplace is rationalized. The U.S. view is that such planning does not work; and if it does not work, it cannot be a moral imperative to be followed.

In speaking of wages, the Pope departs from the Marxist position to some extent. Wages, for Marx, necessarily involve exploitation, whereas the Pope calls for a just wage in the tradition of the social encyclicals of his predecessors.

The Pope defends unions and the right to strike, the rights of the disabled, the right of emigration. The final chapter on "Element for a Spirituality of Work" presents the theological basis for the Christian assessment of work.

The Pope's opponent throughout is Marx whom, as I have claimed, he fights on his own ground. Unless one sees this, one misses a major point of the encyclical. The Pope appropriates what he sees as correct in Marx's position, without attributing it to Marx. Implicitly, the Pope suggests that Christianity held those positions before Marx, even if it were Marx who brought them to the fore. The Church, it can be noted, did not institute the workers' movement or attack alienation or economic exploitation until after Marx had done so. The social encyclicals were responses to Marxist initiatives as well as to existing conditions, and the two social encyclicals from the hands of Pope John Paul II continue to be so.

Capitalism is the name the Pope uses for free enterprise of whatever kind. There is no nuanced examination of the present-day structures of free enterprise. All existing forms of free enterprise are indiscriminately attacked in the same language that Marx, and later Lenin, used in attacking capitalism. This is an important reason why the encyclical fell on predominantly deaf ears in the United States. The Pope was not speaking directly to Americans but to those for whom Marxism has an appeal, and he was presenting an alternative to them that built on the strength of Marx's critique, while adding a spiritual and religious dimension lacking in Marx. To say this is not to criticize the encyclical but to understand it. Those who read the encyclical as countercultural should consider carefully the extent to which they may be misreading it.

A Tendency toward Imperialism

The encyclical *On Social Concern* also is not addressed, except indirectly, to Americans, even though they may seem to be the villains and those called upon to do the most. Marxism is present in three ways. The first is in the Pope's analysis of what he refers to as the "capitalist" countries and the doctrine of "liberal capitalism." The second is in his adoption of the Leninist claims of imperialism and of the dependency of the less developed countries on the more developed ones. The third is in the use of dialectics and dialectical language. All three are once again acceptable to the European and Latin American audiences who are familiar with Marxism, but these references are alien to Americans.

I shall comment briefly on these three Marxist ingredients by turning to a more extended analysis of the Pope's so-called "East-West Battlefield Thesis."

In Chapter III, "Survey of the Contemporary World," the Pope notes the poverty in the world and "the widening of the gap between the areas of the so-called developed North and the developing South" (p. 21). The gap is, in fact, between the rich nations of the North—the United States and Canada, most of Western Europe, and Japan—on the one hand, and most of the rest of the world on the other. South America and Africa are in the Southern hemisphere. India, Pakistan, Bangladesh and other poor countries are in the North, but are also less developed. The Soviet Union, Eastern Europe, and perhaps China are the Second World, even though China ranks among the less developed countries. The Pope's critique in any case is primarily of the rich countries. He notes as well the housing crisis, unemployment, illiteracy, and the international debt.

If my thesis about *On Human Work* is correct, we should not be surprised to find that the Pope, in the encyclical *On Social Concern,* again assimilates the Marxist critique of capitalism. The Pope seizes the moral appeal of the Marxists and addresses an audience to which Marxism is a live option. Marxism remains the major threat to Christianity, even if it is not the major target of this encyclical. The point continues to be to seize the initiative from those Marxists who appeal to the poor, the down-trodden, the oppressed, the exploited, and to develop the message that Christianity is their original and true champion. Not only are Americans not the target audience, but the United States can be read as the dominant unnamed object of attack.

The Pope states that the central reason for the ills he identifies is the *"existence of two opposing blocs,* commonly known as the East and the West" (p. 33). His analysis is strongly reminiscent of Mao Tsetung's. Mao, in his work *On Contradictions,* claimed that in any analysis one should look for the principal contradiction. Within the principal contradiction, one should look for the principal aspect of the contradiction; and within the framework of the principal contradiction, or opposition, one can look for secondary and other contradictions.[12]

Somewhat disconcertingly for the American reader, Pope John Paul II follows this methodology in his analysis of world conditions. In the spirit of dialectics he searches for, and finds, polar oppositions—political opposition, ideological opposition, and military opposition. He distinguishes contradictions in social life—not in the sense of logical inconsistencies—but in the Hegelian-Marxist dialectical sense of opposing forces. There is nothing wrong with using the dialectical method, either for description or for analysis. Yet it is not used frequently in U.S. analyses and the terminology is foreign to American ears, which helps explain why the analysis is somewhat strange to Americans.

The Pope claims "Each of the two blocs tends to assimilate or gather around it other countries or groups of countries, to different degrees of adherence or participation" (p. 33). This may seem like a neutral statement, but it is far from such. It implicitly equates the relation of Poland to the Soviet Union and of England to the United States. It is certainly the case that each smaller country is allied with one of the blocs. But Poland in a very real sense is an occupied country. The Soviet Union did not simply "gather around it other countries." It did "assimilate" the Baltic states. To equate the situation of Czechoslovakia vis-à-vis the Soviet Union to the situation of France vis-à-vis the United States is scarcely accurate. Hence, to equate the blocs as similar—for example, from a moral point of view—will seem to Americans simply not to be the case. It is difficult to believe that it seems to be the case for the Poles, and for the Polish Pope. Or is it? It is not difficult to imagine the description as appealing to many people in Europe and Latin America, despite its inaccuracies.

The Pope describes the ideological level of oppositions as one between liberal capitalism and Marxist collectivism. Liberal capitalism, we are told, "developed with industrialization during the last century" (p. 33). What that doctrine or ideology is at the present time is far from clear. Whatever it is, it is surely not what it was in the nineteenth century. The welfare state has made an important difference, a difference which the pat opposition of liberal capitalism to Marxist collectivism ignores. Once again, it is not surprising that most Americans have not resonated to the description of their country in terms they do not accept and scarcely recognize.

The third tension, the military one, characterized by cold war, wars of proxy, and the threat of an open and total war (p. 34) is all too well known.

The Pope continues in the same apparently evenhanded manner to say that the "two *concepts* of the development of individuals and peoples" are both "imperfect and in need of radical correction" (p. 35). Is it really evenhanded to say both concepts are in need of radical correction? From an American perspective, the United States does not occupy any country, while the Soviet Union does. The United States has given and continues to give a great deal of aid to less developed nations, while the Soviet Union gives very little. Americans have championed freedom and human rights while the Soviet Union has restricted freedom and ignored human rights.

The Pope goes on in this supposedly evenhanded manner saying, "Each of the two *blocs* harbors in its own way a tendency toward *imperialism,* as it is usually called, or toward forms of neo-colonialism" (p. 37). Here the Marxist bias and analysis are again clear. Lenin, in his widely known book *Imperialism: The Highest Stage of Capitalism,*[13] defended the thesis that through colonialism the European nations were able to transfer the worst exploitation to their colonies. The European nations thus were able to exploit their own workers less, allow them higher standards of living and, by doing so, fend off a proletarian revolution. The analysis does not fit the United States well. The United States itself was once a British colony. It has no colonies and has never had any. It has not conquered and subjugated any foreign peoples. To accuse it of imperialism or of colonialism or of neo-colonialism, as if those charges were self-evidently true, is not something most Americans are willing to accept. In some senses of imperialism a case might be made. But the case has to be made. With respect to the Eastern bloc, since the Soviet Union brought communism into the countries of Eastern Europe with its troops, which have remained, the claim of imperialism makes more sense.

The Pope's claim that "the West gives the impression of abandoning itself to forms of growing and selfish isolation" (pg. 39) is puzzling in the light of the earlier claims about imperialism and neo-colonialism, which seem antithetical to isolationism. Americans may well wonder, especially since no countries are named, to what countries the Pope is referring.

In Chapter V the Pope returns once again to the two blocs analysis, and says, "...a world which is divided into blocs, sustained by rigid ideologies, and in which instead of interdependence and solidarity different forms of imperialism hold sway, can only be a world subject to structures of sin" (p. 68). Two typical ones are "on the one hand, the *all-consuming desire for profit,* and on the other, *the thirst for power,* with the intention of imposing one's will upon others" (p. 71). Will Americans see themselves in the description of having an all-consuming desire for profit "at any price" (p. 71)? Some people may have such a desire. But it is not accurate to characterize all Americans in this way, nor is it accurate to characterize the government in this way. The characterization is typically Marxist, and perhaps widely believed of America in many parts of the world. It can be rightly rejected by Americans as an overgeneralization.

Nor will Americans understand the "principle that the goods of creation *are meant for all.* That which human industry produces through the processing of raw materials, with the contribution of work, must serve equally for the good of all" (p. 76). What does that principle mean? It seems to be addressed to the West and to the rich. Does it truly mean that all manufactured goods must be distributed to all who want or need them, regardless of who makes the product or of anyone's ability to pay? The principle deals with distribution and ignores production and, in this way, follows the Marxist critique of capitalism. The Pope once again seizes the initiative from the Marxists and assimilates and Christianizes their critique. This may play well in Europe and Latin America. It has not played well in the United States.

The Pope tells us in Chapter VI that "The Church's social doctrine is *not* a 'third way' between *liberal capitalism* and *Marxist collectivism,* nor even a possible alternative to other solutions less radically opposed to one another: rather, it constitutes a *category of its own,"* which aims "to *guide* human behavior" (p. 83). The guidance it provides is clearer for those to whom the encyclical is primarily addressed, namely, to Europeans and Latin Americans, than it is for those in the United States.

A SUPREME IRONY

I have claimed that Americans have not responded to the Pope's social encyclicals because they are written in a style and diction foreign to Americans and because, in a real sense, they seem not to be written for Americans. Yet, surely, it will be argued, the Pope clearly wants the rich countries—especially the United States—to help the poor countries. He also wants the United States to change its liberal capitalist ideology and the system built on it, as well as to stop the production and sale of arms, and to help the less developed countries develop. This is true; and it is on this aspect of the encyclicals that those who argue for a counterculture may seize. But this is compatible with my thesis that the Pope, primarily or directly, does not address America because that is not where his major concern lies. His major concern lies with Eastern and Western Europe and with Latin America.

The Catholic Church in the United States, despite its vocal dissent on some issues, is the strongest in the world. The Catholic churches in the United States are filled. Americans do not suffer the anticlericalism of Europe; nor do we find in the United States the liberation theology movement which causes the Pope so much concern, in part because of the Marxist doctrines with which it is mixed. For the Pope the major threat is Marxism, and the major opponent is the Soviet Union. The United States is not really a problem for him; rather it is a possible solution. It is the possible solution to poverty, among other things.

I do not wish to claim that the Pope's social encyclicals have nothing to say to Americans or that Americans have nothing to learn from them. I do not think that either claim is true. There is much worthy of note and study in the two encyclicals. Whether or not the Pope understands the United States or speaks directly to Americans in his social encyclicals is of little importance in the last analysis. If the Pope has something to say from which Americans can learn—and he surely does—then our aim should be to learn from him what we can. Because of the reasons I have given, for the larger U.S. audience this will mean that intermediaries will have to translate the positions the Pope espouses into the American idiom and develop independent arguments for them. They must develop the moral principles and make relevant what often seems extremely abstract, unclear, and sometimes contradictory to U.S. readers. The American bishops have given us an example of how to do that.

The American bishops address many of the same themes and come to many of the same conclusions as does the Pope. They do so in the American idiom. They do not take as their target Marx or Marxism, nor do they try to assimilate the moral ground to which Marxism laid claim. They do not do so because Marxism is in no way a threat or challenge to the Church in the United States.

It is difficult to imagine Pope John Paul II offering a first draft of his encyclical for criticism and reaction—even to the bishops, much less to the general public, as the American bishops did—before issuing the final version. Therein may lie part of the Pope's failure to understand the American mind. Democracy, participation, and freedom are at least as essential to it as is profit. The Pope's failure to appreciate this, and his description of America in Marxist terms might lead one to believe that the rigid ideology of which he speaks is not America's but the Pope's view of America.

If my analysis has been persuasive, Americans should not be surprised that the Pope had a special interest in addressing the problems he did in the way he did. It would be naive to think the Pope wrote his social encyclicals with no agenda in mind or to consider them a-temporal or a-historical. It is naive to think that they are universal in the sense of being addressed to all equally. To the extent that they are universal in the moral principles they articulate, they are necessarily vague, general, invite interpretation, and require concrete development. We should not be disappointed to find little in the way of clear policy guidelines. Providing these was not its aim. Following the bishops' lead, a U.S. response can take the development of appropriate, morally based, policy guidelines as its aim, developing them from the encyclicals but with an appreciation of the strengths of the U.S. system which the Pope, for strategic, tactical, or for other reasons, ignores.

In his two encyclicals Pope John Paul II has sought to take the moral initiative away from the Marxists in Europe and the liberation theologians in Latin America. To the extent that the Pope has succeeded in Christianizing the Marxist approach to labor and social issues, he has accomplished no mean feat. In the process he has adopted too uncritically the Marxist critique of capitalism and used it as a device for analyzing the world situation. The appeal to those who accept that point of view is understandable. Although Americans, among others, are justified in not accepting his analysis uncritically, we can well be tolerant of the Pope's description of capitalism and of the West in Marxist terms if we keep in mind his aim.

In the long run, the success of John Paul's social encyclicals will depend on whether they are successful in allowing the Church to seize the moral initiative from Marxism on oppression, alienation, exploitation, and the poor. To those who find in the encyclicals a call to create an American counterculture, they should be careful of the Marxist presuppositions and critiques of free enterprise they may unconsciously and uncritically assimilate from the encyclicals. It would be a supreme irony if Pope John Paul II's encyclicals led critics in America unwittingly and uncritically to adopt the very Marxist positions he wishes to replace.

Notes

1. John Paul II, *On Human Work*, Washington, D.C.: Office of Publishing and Promotion Services, United States Catholic Conference, 1981; *On Social Concern*, Washington, D.C.: Office of Publishing and Promotion Services, United States Catholic Conference, 1988. All page references in the text are to these editions.

2. John Locke, *The Second Treatise of Government*, Indianapolis: The Bobbs-Merrill Company, Inc., 1975, Chapter V, "Of Property."

3. Ludwig Feuerbach, *The Essence of Christianity*, trans. by George Eliot, New York: Harper Torchbooks, 1957.

4. *On Human Work*, p. 1.

5. *The German Ideology*, in *Karl Marx and Frederick Engels: Collected Works*, New York: International Publishers, Vol. 5, p. 31.

6. *Economic and Philosophic Manuscripts of 1844*, in *Collected Works*, Vol. 3, p. 275.

7. *Ibid.* p. 274

8. *Comments on James Mill, Elemens d'economie politique*, in *Collected Works*, Vol. 3, p. 228.

9. *Economic and Philosophic Manuscripts, Collected Works*, Vol. 3, p. 272.

10. *Manifesto of the Communist Party, Collected Works*, Vol. 6, p. 482.

11. *Economic and Philosophic Manuscripts, Collected Works,* Vol. 3, p. 247.

12. *On Contradiction, Selected Works of Mao Tse-tung,* Peking: Foreign Language Press, 1975, Vol. 1, pp. 331–337.

13. *Imperialism: The Highest Stage of Capitalism, V. I. Lenin Selected Works,* London: Lawrence & Wishart Ltd., 1936, Vol. 5.

19. Feminist Analysis: A Missing Perspective

Maria Riley

This chapter first appeared in *Logic of Solidarity: Commentaries on Pope John Paul II's Encyclical on Social Concern,* eds. Gregory Baum and Robert Ellsberg, in 1989.

> The decision to feed the world
> is the real decision. No revolution
> has chosen it. For that choice requires
> that women shall be free.
> *Adrienne Rich*[1]

Sollicitudo Rei Socialis speaks so clearly and forcefully of the failure of development and the consequent sufferings of so many persons, it is difficult to be critical of it without appearing to nitpick. John Paul II's powerful moral message declares that the right to a dignified human life supercedes all the justifications our political and financial activities put forward to cloak our unbridled desire for profit and drive for power (no. 37). It is a bracing corrective to the evolution of human society as we have lived it during the past three decades. However, the very importance of this encyclical demands that its blind spots be illuminated so that it is not dismissed out of hand for some of its obvious failures.

In the opening section of the encyclical, John Paul II states that his objective is twofold: (1) to affirm the continuity of the social doctrine with special reference to *Populorum Progressio;* and (2) to renew that social teaching as "suggested by the changes in historical conditions" (no. 3). It is in his selective reading of the changes in historical conditions that I take issue with the encyclical. John Paul II does not recognize the subtle but profound shifting in human consciousness and in social structures that is occurring globally as a result of the women's

276

movement. Most major critiques of the process of development over the last twenty years now recognize the essential role of women in society. They also recognize, at least in their rhetoric, that a significant cause of the failure of development has been the ignoring of women's role. For example, the UNICEF report, *Within Human Reach: A Future of Africa's Children,* states:

> Women remain the providers of 60 to 80 percent of the household food needs in many parts of sub-Saharan Africa. Women are the key actors in ensuring the survival and well-being of children, and their educational level is the single most important factor related positively to high infant survival rates. Expanding women's social and economic opportunities and increasing their control over household finances and their participation in community affairs, therefore, are the most significant measures that can be taken to enhance children's health and the welfare of families.[2]

The conclusions of such studies continue to illustrate that the promotion of women is not only a matter of justice to women, it is also essential to the survival and well-being of societies.

In *Pacem in Terris,* 1963, John XXIII identified the then incipient women's movement as one of the "signs of our times." He wrote:

> It is obvious to everyone that women are now taking a part in public life. This is happening more rapidly perhaps in nations with a Christian tradition, and more slowly, but broadly, among peoples who have inherited other traditions or cultures. Since women are becoming ever more conscious of their human dignity, they will not tolerate being treated as inanimate objects or mere instruments, but claim, both in domestic and in public life, the rights and duties that befit a human person [no. 41].

Since 1963 the global women's movement has continued to grow and mature in its appreciation of the necessity to make its voice and agenda known, particularly in relation to development.

The United Nations declared 1975 the International Women's Year (IWY) in response to the early indicators from women in Africa,

Asia, and South America that something was awry in the development process that many nations were pursuing under the direction of Western-dominated agencies, such as the World Bank and the International Monetary Fund. Women, who throughout the world are responsible for the daily sustenance of the family, were the first to feel the lack of resources, particularly in food and in availability of land for subsistence farming, that followed upon the changes initiated by development processes. One of the primary purposes of the International Women's Year, subsequently extended to the International Women's Decade, was to examine the development process and its effects upon women and those dependent upon women, the young and the old.

The history of thinking about women's role in development illustrates the growing maturity of analysis over the last twenty years. In the early 1970s, development planners talked about "integrating women into the development process." Women from the so-called developing countries were quick to point out they did not need to be integrated into development, they already were the primary subsistence food producers and petty traders of most economies. By the late 1970s, the language had changed to "supporting women in development." But as the quality of life continued to deteriorate in so many countries during the 1980s, it became more and more evident how integral women are to the sustaining of life in all societies. This reality is especially apparent in less industrialized countries. The failure to include women in all phases of the development process insures the failure of that process, as history and experience have proven.

Feminist critiques of current development models and of current planning, programming, and evaluation of development projects are among the most creative and promising of all development work today.[3] The literature is expanding rapidly. Not all the literature is written by feminists; much of it is written by other groups concerned with addressing the needs of the poor.[4]

Sollicitudo Rei Socialis shows no awareness of this body of material. This is a serious and debilitating lacuna in the encyclical. There are a number of ways in which this lacuna is evident. In developing my feminist critique of the encyclical, I will concentrate on three problem areas: its methodology, analysis, and strategies. In so doing, I am not arguing so much with what the encyclical says, as with what it does not say.

METHODOLOGY

Feminists are not the only group of persons to raise questions about the methodology used to write papal encyclicals. But given the absence of any awareness of women's experience and critique of development in this document, the question of methodology must be addressed from a feminist perspective.

John Paul II speaks of the church's threefold approach to developing social teaching: (1) its "principles of reflection," (2) its "criteria of judgment," and (3) its basic "directive for action." The methodology is fundamentally deductive. Women ask, who defines these principles, criteria, and directives? From where do they come? Historically, women's voices and experience have not been formative of Catholic social thought. This, of course, is not a new insight. Women's voices and experience have been absent from all authoritative teaching and deliberation in the church.

The absence of women is symbolic of a fundamental flaw in the methodology for developing this encyclical. The process of feminist analysis continues to emphasize two key principles of analysis: (1) how a person arrives at a particular perspective powerfully influences that perspective; and (2) who is included and who is excluded in the process shape the content of the analysis. In a way, the process used for developing this encyclical contradicts its content. To contribute to building a society that is just, equitable, and life-affirming for all, the methods in constructing it must be correspondingly open and respectful of differences. They must attempt to break down existing stereotypes and oppressive hierarchies of power and control. The process is integral to the justness of the product. Such an insight demands models that are participatory and inclusive—inclusive not only of women but also of representatives of all groups outside the dominant culture, which in this case is predominately white, male, clerical, and European.

This insight is not restricted to feminist thinking; liberation theologians would raise similar critiques. However, it is important to include it in this analysis because women are often not consciously included in the call for inclusiveness among male liberation theologians. Unfortunately, this works out in practice to be the equivalent of unconscious exclusion of women. At this moment in history, women need to assume a "hermeneutic of suspicion" in the face of the pandemic patriarchy that shapes our cultures, especially the culture of the church. It plagues even liberation theologies.

ANALYSIS

There is much in *Sollicitudo Rei Socialis* with which feminist analysis finds common cause, in particular in its effort to extend the meaning of the word "development" beyond economic categories. John Paul II continues and enlarges upon Paul VI's reflection on the meaning of development in *Populorum Progressio*. Paul VI defined development in human terms, including not only economic but also social, political, personal, and spiritual dimensions of life.

The International Women's Decade 1975–1985 declared equality, development, and peace as its three goals. The early documentation clearly analyzed the linkages among these goals, particularly from the experience of women:

> Equality is here interpreted as meaning not only legal equality, the elimination of *de jure* discrimination, but also equality of rights, responsibilities, and opportunities for the participation of women in development, both as beneficiaries and as agents. The issue of inequality as it affects the vast majority of women of the world is closely related to the problem of underdevelopment, which exists mainly as a result of unjust international economic relations....
>
> Development is here interpreted to mean total development, including development in the political, economic, social, cultural, and other dimensions of human life, as also the development of economic and other material resources and also the physical, moral, intellectual, and cultural growth of the human person....It [development] also requires a change in the attitudes and roles of both men and women. Women's development should not only be viewed as an issue in social development but should be seen as an essential component in every dimension of development....
>
> Without peace and stability there can be no development. Peace is thus a prerequisite to development. Moreover,

peace will not be lasting without development and the elimination of inequalities and discrimination at all levels.[5]

This vision of development resonates with John Paul II's reflection on "Authentic Human Development" (nos. 27–34).

Feminist analysis also resonates with the pope's condemnation of militarization and its consequent squandering of resources that could be directed toward fulfilling human needs. DAWN, the Third World women's network on women and development issues, identifies militarization and violence as major causes of the current crisis.[6] The pope recognizes the living victims of war—refugees. However, feminists would add the concrete observation that 80 percent of all refugees are women and their dependent children.[7]

Women also find common cause with John Paul II's identification of the preferential option for the poor. Once again, however, they would move beyond generalities and abstractions to put a human face on the poor. That human face is disproportionately female. Women and their dependent children make up more than 66 percent of the world's poor and the number is growing. Women's poverty consists not only in the lack of resources, but also in the lack of opportunity and in the growing incidence of women worldwide who are the sole responsible parent to children. This trend has been identified as the "feminization of poverty."[8] It is more correctly understood as the pauperization of women and children.

Women join others in applauding the growing concern for the environment in recent social teaching. In addition to the encyclical's stated reasons for that concern—the protection of the ordered system of the cosmos, the limitation of our natural resources, and the deterioration of the quality of life—more and more ecologists and feminists speak of a growing awareness of the "community of creation." In identifying with the "community of creation" they are pointing out the mutual dependence of all life—human, animal, plant. This shift toward understanding that we are all mutually linked enables the human community to realize that its ecologically destructive habits are slowly destroying the very foundation of all life, including human life.

A feminist analysis of the failure of development over the last several decades would agree with many of the generalizations in *Sollicitudo Rei Socialis,* but differences begin to emerge in the identification of some of the causes of that failure. Feminist analysis would point not so much to what the encyclical says, but to what it does not say, because it lacks a gender analysis. I will develop several examples: some root causes of the failure of development, reflections on the demographic "problem" as developed in the encyclical, and an analysis of the culture of militarism. In so doing I hope to illustrate how Catholic social teaching would be enriched and enlarged by including feminist analysis and reflection.

Sollicitudo Rei Socialis identifies the failure of development primarily in global terms: East-West conflict, militarization, international debt, homelessness, and unemployment. It affirms the profound insight of Paul VI in *Populorum Progressio* that the social question has become worldwide in dimension. It briefly alludes to the national and local social questions but chooses to analyze the current situation from a global perspective (no. 9).

Feminist analysis, on the other hand, asserts that local or micro questions are integrally linked with global or macro questions. It insists that we will never move to a more successful theory and practice of development until we recognize and attend to those linkages.

Moreover, feminist analysis consciously seeks to illustrate that all issues have a political, economic, social, and cultural dimension in contrast to some analytical thinking that tends to define issues as political, or economic, or social, or cultural, or to ignore the intrinsic links among these dimensions. Using women's experience as a lens, feminist analysis rejects dualistic approaches that "dichotomize relationships between private and public sphere, production and reproduction, the household and the economy, the personal and the political, the realms of feeling and intuition and those of reason."[9] Recognizing that all is connected, it seeks a more holistic approach to the analytical process.

In analyzing the failure of development, feminists focus on three areas usually overlooked in development theory: the household, women's work, and women's multiple roles. They focus on poor households—and on women within those households—insisting that they are a good starting point for an understanding of the situation of women in development because it "enables us not only to evaluate the extent to which development strategies benefit or harm the poorest and most oppressed section of the people, but also to judge their impact on a range of sectors and activities critical to socio-economic development and human welfare."[10]

For example, assessing the International Monetary Fund's structural adjustment requirements for new or refinanced loans to debtor nations by its impact on the household economy, gives an immediate indicator of the human failure of that policy. It is not adequate to evaluate development on abstractions such as the gross national product. It must be evaluated on its impact on ordinary people, especially the poor.

This particular policy demands cuts in public expenditures on social programs such as health, housing, and education, as well as such needs as water, utilities, roads. These cuts are accompanied by a devaluation of the currency. Such policies particularly affect women by reducing their sources of income and services while simultaneously increasing the demands upon their time and creativity to fill the gaps left by the diminishment of social services. That there is survival at all in this situation is in great measure due to the resourcefulness of women in developing income-generating and income-saving projects, and in developing cooperative ventures with friendship and extended family networks.[11] But that women-resource is under terrific stress in many societies today and cannot sustain the burden of survival much longer.

Another example of failure of development strategy because it ignored the work of women has been in the economic policies aimed at developing an agricultural economy for export. If those plans are critiqued from the point of view of women, we discover one of the causes of widespread hunger. Africa presents a clear case in point. African women are the subsistence farmers of the societies. Communal farmland commandeered into export cropping often leaves women with no access to land. Consequently they are unable to fulfill their traditional obligation of feeding the family.

These examples illustrate that by failing to take into account women's roles in socio-economic development, the policies adopted often exacerbate the very problems they seek to resolve.[12] In a very real sense we can say that women and children are the early indicators of the failure of a development policy.

This failure to recognize women's essential and multiple economic roles in a society reflects a "deeply gendered ideology, which simultaneously minimizes the value of the tasks necessary for social reproduction, while promoting a pattern of economic growth based on the exploitation of the socio-economic vulnerabilities of a female population."[13] It is also one of the causes of the failure of development and the continuing deterioration of the quality of life for growing numbers of persons worldwide. *Sollicitudo Rei Socialis* fails to recognize this dynamic in the development process. I would argue that it fails to do so because it too is shaped by a "deeply gendered ideology."

This ideology reveals itself in the rather cursory treatment the encyclical gives to the "demographic problem" (no. 25). This question is at the heart of all feminist analysis, because it is primarily women who carry both the glory and the burden of children worldwide. No other reality has such impact on women's lives. The encyclical reflects absolutely no understanding of women's experience in reproduction.

While briefly alluding to the difficulties for development due to population growth in the countries of the Southern hemisphere, it offers no analysis of that growth. Yet population studies over the years have identified clear linkages between poverty and the number of children in a family in developing countries. There is a ratio between the number of children a couple have and their search for economic security in old age in societies that have no social security programs. There is also a ratio between the number of children who survive early childhood and the number of children a family has. If infant and youth mortality is high, couples will continue to have children to ensure that some survive into adulthood.

But the most important statistic that demographers have identified is the connection between increasing women's educational and life opportunities and the lowering of the birth rate per woman. In *Women...A World Survey,* Ruth Leger Sivard writes:

> Since education influences women's economic participation and earning power, and also the number of children they have and the health their children will have, progress here can be the harbinger of expanding opportunities in the future. Education develops the human potential. In the modern world it is seen as vital for a fully productive role in life for women as well as men.[14]

The population question must be analyzed within the social, economic, political, and cultural structures that shape women's lives. This statement is valid in the so-called developed countries of the Northern hemisphere as well. As long as the church continues to ignore the context of women's lives when it raises the issues of childbirth, its voice in this profound human concern will not be heard.

The question of militarization is critical in feminist analysis. *Sollicitudo Rei Socialis* condemns the growth of militarism in the world on political, economic, and social grounds. It decries the East-West conflict with its surrogate wars in developing countries (nos. 20–23). It names arms production and arms trade as a "serious disorder" (no. 24). It identifies the stockpiling of atomic weapons as a symbol of the death-dealing direction of the contemporary world. It speaks to the victims of conflicts, refugees, and it condemns terrorism.

Sollicitudo Rei Socialis is in continuity with the church's long history of teaching that seeks to promote peace and justice in our world. It is a history, however, that for the most part concentrates on the problems of war between nation states, the possibility of a just war, the morality of deterrence, the immorality of the destruction of innocent noncombatants.

Feminism enters the question of militarism through its analysis of the culture of patriarchy.[15] Its analysis of war is shaped by the critical feminist insight that the "personal is political." The simplest definition for this insight is to assert that men's power and women's subordination is a social, economic, political, and cultural reality—that what happens in personal relationships between women and men reflects social structures. Those structures are patriarchal.

According to feminist analysis, the root cause of war is the will to dominate. John Paul II speaks of the dual sin shaping our world, "the all-consuming desire for profit" and the "thirst for power, with the intention of imposing one's will upon others" (no. 37). Radical feminist analysis identifies the root of the will to dominate in men's will to dominate and control women. It is the "original sin." From this root come all other forms of domination. The will to dominate appears subtly in patriarchal social structures and in the cultural ideology that supports those structures.[16] It appears overtly in all acts of violence: rape, torture, sexual abuse, incest, pornography, domestic violence, terrorism, the destruction of the earth. It finds its ultimate expression in war, as one nation, usually governed by men, seeks to dominate other nations.

Feminism in particular criticizes militarism, pointing out how the military mind-set is shaped with an emphasis on domination of the "other," the weak ones, of which women are primary symbols. It points to the history of women and land being considered the booty of the victorious army.

Today it points to the prostitution of women that so commonly accompanies a military presence in a country. Feminists' anger toward militarism and war is deep and abiding.

Feminist analysis brings a cultural analysis to the problems of militarism and war that would enrich and enlarge the reflections of *Sollicitudo Rei Socialis*. It also points to some of the directions that would promote it—namely, the transformation of dominant structures to structures of mutuality. However, until women and their insights are included in the framing of Catholic social teaching, it is difficult to project that it will ever include a critique of the culture of patriarchy.

The insights of feminist analysis on the failure of development are slowly moving from the margins into the mainstream of development thinking. This movement illustrates the growing realization of women's essential role in society. Future evolution, we hope, will know how to use the new insights gained from gender analysis to become the basis for framing policy. The clear message of the results of the International Decade for Women 1975–1985 is that the movement of women beyond poverty, dependence, and violence is contingent upon the evolution of societies, both national and international, beyond the current imbalances of economic and political power that shape our world. But concomitantly, a society's ability to move toward justice for all is contingent upon the liberation of women. Because *Sollicitudo Rei Socialis* reflects none of this thinking, it must be judged a dated document.

STRATEGIES

John Paul II calls for a response of solidarity to overcome the structures of sin that currently shape the interdependence of our world. He recognizes that interdependence in an unequal world begets structured inequality. He recommends the "virtue" of solidarity—that is, a "firm and persevering determination to commit oneself to the common good, that is to say, to the good of all and to each individual because we are all really responsible for all" (no. 38).

In seeking to define solidarity he uses several key words and phrases: "moral responsibility," "to see the 'other' as neighbor," "the path to peace and to development," "a Christian virtue," "goes beyond itself, to take on the specifically Christian dimension of total gratuity, forgiveness, and reconciliation," "new model for the human race, the communion of the Trinity," and "on the individual, national, and international level."

He further delineates the appropriate responses of different persons in seeking solidarity:

> The exercise of solidarity within each society is valid when its members recognize one another as persons. Those who are more influential because they have a greater share of goods and common services should feel responsible for the weaker and be ready to share with them all they possess. Those who are weaker, for their part, in the same spirit of solidarity should not adopt a purely passive attitude or one that is destructive of the social fabric, but while claiming their legitimate rights, should do what they can for the good of all. The intermediate groups, in their turn, should not selfishly insist on their particular interests, but respect the interests of others [no. 39].

The exercise of solidarity is the pope's strategic moral response to the problems of injustice he has identified throughout the encyclical.

A feminist reflection on the meaning of solidarity moves beyond the concept of interdependence and even the common good to recognize an essential unity within the community of creation. This understanding of solidarity is rooted in several key feminist moral insights: the centrality of relationship in life, mutuality, and the underlying integral unity of experience.

A key foundation of a feminist moral ethic is to recognize the centrality of relationship in human experience. This insight arises from women's experience as primary nurturers of the family. Reflection on this experience opens new understandings of the presence of God in history. For Christian feminists, this reflection focuses on Jesus' radical acts of relationship, especially with the outcasts of society—the lepers, the woman at the well, the Syro-Phoenician woman, tax collectors, and prostitutes. He joined them in solidarity, and for that reason he too became an outcast in his society. Jesus' journey toward Calvary was not a journey toward self-sacrifice so much as it was a journey of radical acts of love that deepened relationships, embodied and extended community, and passed on the gift of life.

In concluding her reflection of a Christian feminist ethic, Beverly Harrison writes: "We are called to express, embody, share, celebrate the gift of life and to pass it on. We are called to reach out, to deepen relationships or to right wrong relations—i.e., those which deny, distort, or prevent human dignity from arising—as we re-call each other into the power of personhood."[17] In a feminist understanding, solidarity is first of all an experience of relationship, rather than an abstract virtue.

But if relationships are to express true solidarity, they must be built on mutuality. *Sollicitudo Rei Socialis* condemns the relationships of domination that presently rule our world, particularly in the "desire for profit...and the thirst for power" (no. 37). As I stated before, feminism identifies this will to dominate as part of the culture of patriarchy. Mutuality in relationship is the feminist alternative to domination. Mutuality moves beyond equality to recognize the reciprocity of giving and receiving, caring and being cared for. In its negative expression, it recognizes the reciprocity of evil, of harming and being harmed, of hating and being hateful. Solidarity, without mutuality, easily slips into paternalism or maternalism.

Finally, a feminist ethic would argue for a renewed understanding of the integral unity that underlies all experience. This unity transcends all the rational categories of dualism, which systems of philosophy have developed to explain experience, such as body/soul, intuition/knowledge, thinking/feeling, public/private, church/world, sacred/secular.

Applying these key insights of a feminist ethic to our understanding of solidarity extends and deepens its meaning as developed in *Sollicitudo Rei Socialis*. A feminist perspective on solidarity would insist that our very salvation as persons is linked. For example, a feminist ethic understands that racism is not only unjust to persons of differing racial and ethnic backgrounds; it destroys the soul of the racist. Likewise, sexism is unjust not only to women; it destroys the soul of the sexist. In the context of this essay, economic and political domination of so-called developed nations is not only unjust to weaker, poorer nations; it is destroying the soul of the powerful nations. Solidarity in the liberation struggles of peoples is a mutually salvific act. For us of the developed world, it is at the heart of our redemption.

Sollicitudo Rei Socialis is an important but dated document. Its failure resides in its blindness to the essential contribution that feminists, both women and men, are making to the development debate. I suggest that the framers and consultants of this document are trapped by the myopic position that "women's issues" are marginal to the so-called great issues of our day. This particular myopia results from a patriarchal mind-set. Mainline development theory and practice has also been shaped by patriarchal thinking. Ironically, it has been the very failure of that development over the last several decades that has opened the way among some groups to reassess the development process from women's perspectives. It is becoming clearer that "women's issues" are not marginal; they are central to the search for the kind of development in which people matter. *Sollicitudo Rei Socialis* would have been enriched by the voices and insights of women.

Notes

1. Adrienne Rich, "Hunger," *The Dream of a Common Language* (New York: Norton, 1978), p. 13.

2. *Within Human Reach: A Future for Africa's Children,* a UNICEF Report (New York: United Nations Publication, 1985), p. 52.

3. The word "feminist" carries a variety of meanings for readers. Because in its root form it refers to the female, it can be considered exclusionary of men. However, current, but not universal, usage includes both women and men. In the context of this essay, I am using feminist to mean a person, woman or man, who believes in the essential equality between women and men, and seeks to create social attitudes, policies, and structures that reveal and sustain that equality.

4. See, for example, Gita Sen and Caren Grown, *Development, Crisis, and Alternative Visions: Third World Women's Perspectives* (New York: Monthly Review Press, 1987); and *The State of the World's Children, 1988* (Oxford: Oxford University Press, 1988).

5. *Report of the World Conference of the United Nations Decade for Women: Equality, Development, and Peace* (New York: United Nations Publication, 1980), pp. 3–4.

6. Sen and Grown, *Development,* pp. 67ff.

7. Joni Seager and Ann Olson, *Women in the World Atlas* (New York: Simon and Schuster, 1986), p. 27.

8. This term was first used by Diana Pearce in "The Feminization of Poverty: Women, Work and Welfare," *Urban and Social Change Review* (Feb.

1978) and later popularized by the *Final Report of the National Advisory Council on Economic Opportunity* (Washington, D.C.: Government Printing Office, 1981). Although it was first used in reference to the growing poverty of women in the United States, it has also been applied to the growing poverty of women worldwide.

9. Peggy Antrobus, "Gender Analysis," unpublished manuscript.

10. Sen and Grown, *Development,* p. 24.

11. Peggy Antrobus, "The Empowerment of Women," unpublished manuscript.

12. Ibid.

13. Ibid.

14. Ruth Leger Sivard, *Women...A World Survey* (Washington, D.C.: World Priorities, 1985), p. 18.

15. I am using the term "patriarchy" in its current understanding as the system of male control over all the structures of a society—political, economic, social, and cultural.

16. Feminism also points out that religion has served to legitimate patriarchal culture.

17. Beverly Harrison, "The Power of Anger in the Act of Love: An Ethic for Women and Other Strangers," *Union Seminary Quarterly Review*, 36, Supplementary Issue (1981), p. 53.

20. Concern and Consolidation

Donal Dorr

This chapter first appeared in the author's book *Option for the Poor: A Hundred Years of Vatican Social Teaching* in 1992.

The two terms "concern" and "consolidation" in the title of this chapter sum up the main thrust of John Paul's papacy in the period 1981–92. It has been a time when the Vatican has appeared anxious about many aspects of Church life and has made strong efforts to reinforce and consolidate traditional teaching. It is more than a coincidence that "concern" is also the first word in John Paul's second social encyclical (*Sollicitudo Rei Socialis,* translated into English as "On Social Concern"), written in late 1987 half-way through this period. And the word "consolidation" may serve as a one-word summary of his third social encyclical *Centesimus Annus,* issued in 1991 to commemorate the hundredth anniversary of *Rerum Novarum.*

Many Concerns

In the area of social justice John Paul's concern ranged widely. He continued his custom of making a number of pastoral visits each year to various parts of the world. On many of these occasions he took the opportunity to speak out strongly against injustices of various kinds. But there seems to be a certain change of tone and emphasis between what he was saying up to 1983 and what he said in later years. In the first period he spoke out very strongly on issues of political oppression, challenging governments quite directly. In the later period his statements on political matters seem rather more muted. This may be related to the ongoing concern in Rome about what are seen as the excesses of liberation theologians and to the Vatican's sustained effort to counteract their influence.

Early in 1983 Pope John Paul undertook what was probably the most controversial of his missionary journeys: he traveled to Central America and Haiti and gave major addresses in El Salvador, Nicaragua, Guatamala, and Port au Prince. In these there are clear indications of both aspects of the pope's concern: his outrage in the face of regimes that were blatantly oppressive; and his fears that the Church's role might be reduced to that of working for political and economic liberation—above all if this liberation were seen in Marxist terms.

What the pope said in El Salvador and Nicaragua brought out more clearly than ever before his reservations about the Marxist answer to problems of social injustice; he objected to what he saw as an "instrumentalization" of the Gospel and to its subjection to an "ideology" (e.g., in Managua AAS 75, 720–22). Linked to this is his warning to priests and members of religious communities not to confuse their role with that of political organizers. For instance, he said to priests in San Salvador (*L'Oss. Rom.* 7–8 Oct. 1983, 4), "Remember that…you are not social directors, political leaders, or officials of a temporal power...."[1]

During this same trip, however, the pope made a very outspoken demand in Haiti that things must change; he insisted on the crying need for justice, and for equitable distribution of goods, as well as for participation by the people in decision-making and for freedom in the expression of opinion (Port au Prince AAS 75, 768–69).

At this time also he spoke to a group of people who were among the most oppressed in the whole world—the American Indians of Guatemala. To them he made what is perhaps the strongest and most specific statement he has ever made on a burning issue of justice. He assured them that "…the Church at this moment knows the marginalization which you suffer, the injustices you endure, the serious difficulties you encounter in defending your lands and your rights." He encouraged them to resist these injustices: "Your brotherly love should express itself in increasing solidarity. Help one another. Organize associations for the defense of your rights and the realization of your own goals" (AAS 75, 742–43).

The pope told these oppressed people of the attitude of the Church in the face of the injustices they suffer:

> …in fulfilling her task of evangelization, she seeks to be near
> you and to raise her voice in condemnation when your dig-
> nity as human beings and children of God is violated....For

>this reason, here and now, and in solemn form, in the name
>of the Church I call on the government to provide an ever
>more adequate legislation which will protect you effectively
>against abuses…(AAS 75, 742–43—my translation).

In the same paragraph the pope very significantly demanded that the process of authentic evangelization should not be branded as subversion. In other words, he was vindicating the right of the Church to speak and act in the interests of justice even when this is interpreted by authorities such as those in Guatemala as a political activity, or as subversive of the State authority.

Both aspects of the pope's concern found expression in his address to the Council of Latin American Bishops (CELAM) at Port au Prince on 9 March 1983. In the first section of his talk he expressed his concern about poverty and injustice: "A sincere analysis of the situation shows that at its root one finds painful injustices, exploitation of some by others, and a serious lack of equity in the distribution of wealth and the benefits of culture." In the third section of the address he warned against distortions of the Gospel and one-sided or partial interpretations of Puebla: "…it is necessary to spread and…to recover the *wholeness* of the message of Puebla, without deformed interpretations or deformed reductions, and without unwarranted applications of some parts and the eclipse of others" (AAS 75, 775–76—my translation).

In more recent years the pope has continued to stress the importance of social justice. But his talks have not been perceived as a clarion call in the same way as in his earlier years as pope. When he visited Southern Africa in 1989 there was considerable disappointment about the reticence and caution of his remarks about the struggle for liberation in South Africa (e.g., AAS 81, 331–34). And the addresses of his second visit to Brazil seemed more reserved on issues of justice than those of his earlier visit, e.g., his address in the shantytown of Vitória (*L'Oss. Rom.* 4 Nov. 1991, 4) and to Amazonian Indians at Cuiabá (*L'Oss. Rom.* 28 Oct. 1991, 10).

There is, however, one issue of justice on which the pope has focused particular attention—that of the rights of cultural and ethnic minorities. On this question he spoke out strongly on numerous occasions, e.g., to the Indians and Inuit of Canada in 1984 (AAS 77, 417–22), also in 1984 to Koreans (AAS 76, 985 and 947), in 1985 to

Africans in the Cameroons (AAS 78, 52–61), to Amerindian people in Ecuador again in 1985 (AAS 77, 859–69), to the Aborigines of Australia in 1986 (AAS 79, 973–79), in 1991 to Amazonian Indians in Brazil (*L'Oss. Rom.* 28 Oct. 1991, 10), and in 1992 in West Africa (*L'Oss. Rom.* 26 Feb. 1992, 8).

Liberation Theology

From the early 1980s onwards the Vatican began appointing many conservative bishops in Latin America (and in other sensitive areas). This was a clear indication of the concern felt in Rome about what were perceived to be the dangers of liberation theology. In 1984 this concern took a more obvious form when the Vatican Congregation for the Doctrine of the Faith issued its *Instruction on Certain Aspects of the "Theology of Liberation."* The document was widely understood to be the work of Cardinal Ratzinger, though there was some insistence on the fact that its contents were approved by the pope. It mounted a strong attack on liberation theology (or at least some versions of it) from several points of view. Among the notable points are:

—its insistence on the priority of personal sin over social sin (IV, 12—5);

—its emphasis on the incompatibility of Marxist theory with Christian faith (VII, 9) and its assumption that the theologies of liberation have adopted Marxist positions which are incompatible with the Christian vision (VIII, 1);

—its accusation that theologies of liberation have radically politicized the faith (IX, 6), have perverted the Christian meaning of "the poor" by confusing "the poor" of Scripture with the Marxist proletariat and have then transformed the fight for the rights of the poor into a class struggle (IX, 10), and have rejected with disdain the social doctrine of the Church (X, 4).

There was a very strong reaction to this document, including a comprehensive and sustained attack on it by one of the leading liberation theologians, Juan Luis Segundo. Like other liberation theologians he claimed that what the document put forward was a gross distortion of the main thrust of liberation theology. But he went much further: he argued that the theology with which it was imbued was one which located transcendence outside human history (e.g., Segundo 48, 72, 154); and for him this represented a regression to a pre-Vatican II theology.

The 1984 *Instruction* had included a promise of a further document on the theme of liberation. As a result of the poor reception given to the *Instruction* a consensus soon emerged that it needed to be supplemented if not superseded by another Vatican document. The new *Instruction on Christian Freedom and Liberation* was duly issued by the Congregation for the Doctrine of the Faith in 1986. Its teaching was widely seen as representing the view of the pope himself (cf. Hebblethwaite [1987] 85). While stressing the continuity between the two documents, it presented a balanced account of liberation theology without the harsh judgments and warnings of the earlier document.

This second document reaffirmed many of the themes of liberation theology such as the special place of the poor (21), the link between earthly liberation and eschatological hope (60), the Church's "special option for the poor" (68) and the need for changes in the structures of society (75). It recognized that armed struggle against oppression could be justified in extreme cases as a last resort; but it suggested that in today's world passive resistance would be more effective and morally acceptable (79). It warned against "the myth of revolution" (78); it stressed the importance of solidarity, subsidiarity (73, 89) and participation (86) and the need for a cultural transformation of society (81).

This second *Instruction* could be seen as an acknowledgment by Rome that the main teachings of liberation theology were thoroughly Christian. However, neither it nor its predecessor gave any indication of sympathy for liberation theology as a *project*—or indeed any real understanding of it. They showed no enthusiasm for the notion that theology emerges from reflection on the ongoing struggle for justice and liberation, or for the idea that theology should be worked out with and for ordinary "grassroots" people (cf. Boff 416). And the Vatican continued its policy of appointing Church leaders who were quite unsympathetic to such an approach.

International Debt

Throughout the 1980s the problem of international debt was becoming ever more serious and urgent, and had been moving ever higher on the social justice agenda (cf. Potter; Dorr [1991] 11–14). In response to this situation the Pontifical Council for Justice and Peace issued in 1986 a document entitled "At the Service of the Human Community: An Ethical Approach to the International Debt Question." It explored the problem of debt in some detail, pointing out the burdens imposed on poor nations and especially on the poorer people.

The document was by no means radical in its analysis or its proposals. For instance, it did not condone the idea that debtor nations should repudiate their debts unilaterally or that payment defaults should be allowed to happen (13, 25); it suggested, however, that in the cases of the poorest nations the loans should be converted by the creditors into grants (26). And it did not put forward any serious and sustained criticism of the policies of the International Monetary Fund (IMF), on the grounds that "it is not up to the Church to judge the economic and financial theories behind their analyses and the remedies proposed" (28).

Proposals put forward in the document were that the international creditors should take immediate action to meet emergency situations (13) and that, as part of a more long-term solution, they should reduce interest rates (19), reschedule debts (25), and eliminate protectionist measures which hinder exports from poorer countries (18). The document went on to suggest that international financial agencies (World Bank, IMF, etc.) should have more representatives from developing countries and should allow these countries a greater share in determining their policies (29). The guiding principle of the authors was that people and their needs should be given priority over financial rectitude (e.g., 22, 31).

Pope John Paul has spoken occasionally on the issue of debt, following much the same lines as those of the Council for Justice and Peace; for instance, in an address to diplomats in 1991 (*L'Oss. Rom.* 14 Jan. 1991, 3).

A New Social Encyclical

The twentieth anniversary of *Populorum Progressio* was in 1987. To commemorate it John Paul issued his second social encyclical *Sollicitudo Rei Socialis,* known in English as "On Social Concern." It was dated 30 December 1987 but was not actually issued until February 1988. It gave rise to a certain amount of controversy in the United States where it was criticized by neo-conservatives such as Michael Novak for appearing to be as critical of the capitalism of the West as it was of the Marxism of Eastern bloc countries (cf. Walsh, p. xx). The main contribution of the document lay in its teaching on solidarity; and this was largely ignored not only in the mass media but even in theological and religious reviews.

After some initial observations on the significance of *Populorum Progressio,* the pope goes on to make an extended "Survey of the Contemporary World" (SRS Chapter 3). It is quite significant that he chooses this approach. It means that his teaching is not abstract and deductive in style but is rooted in a penetrating socio-political and historical analysis of the situation.[2]

In this survey John Paul does not simply give a value-free account of the situation. He does not hesitate to make moral judgments. For instance he complains that the gap between "the North" and "the South" has persisted and is often widening. He criticizes in a strong and even-handed manner the systems of both "the West" (liberal capitalism) and "the East"(Marxism), maintaining that each of them has a tendency towards imperialism and neo-colonialism (SRS 22). And he cries out in protest against the arms trade, the plight of refugees, the horror of terrorism (SRS 24) and the damaging effects of international debt (SRS 19).

Invoking various indicators of genuine human development, the pope has no hesitation in claiming that there has been a failure or delay in fulfilling the hopes of development which were so high when *Populorum Progressio* was written (SRS 12, 20). One reason for this, according to the encyclical, is the political, geo-political and ideological opposition between the East and the West. The pope strongly condemns the way in which the ideological conflict between East and West has widened the gap between "the North" and "the South." He blames both sides for fostering the formation of ideological blocs, for the arms race, for failing to promote genuine interdependence and solidarity, and for imposing on other countries two opposed concepts of development, both seriously flawed (SRS 20–25; cf. Coleman 92).

When he uses the terms "the North" and "the South" the pope immediately points out that this terminology is "only indicative, since one cannot ignore the fact that the frontiers of wealth and poverty intersect within the societies themselves" (SRS 14). He shows a preference for a different set of terms, namely, the First World, the Second World, the Third World and the Fourth World. The advantage of this usage is that it brings out the fact that these different worlds are all part of our *one world* (SRS 14). (In a footnote he clarifies that "the Fourth World" refers especially to "the bands of great or extreme poverty in countries of medium and high income.")

Development

The main purpose of this encyclical was to meet the need for "a fuller and more nuanced concept of development" in continuity with that of *Populorum Progressio* (SRS 4). Like his predecessor, John Paul II understands development to cover all aspects of human life. His emphasis, like that of *Populorum Progressio* (and of Lebret from whom Paul VI borrowed the phrase) is on "being more" rather than "having more" (SRS 28; cf. Goulet 134). In the light of this he speaks out not only against the underdevelopment of the poor countries but also against what he calls "superdevelopment" existing "side-by-side with the miseries of underdevelopment"; this he explains as "an *excessive* availability of every kind of material goods for the benefit of certain social groups" linked to a civilization of "consumerism" and waste (SRS 28).

Development includes an economic and social component. The encyclical refers to a number of ways in which this can be measured, such as the availability of goods and services, of food and drinking water, good working conditions and life expectancy (SRS 14), as well as proper housing (SRS 17), the extent of unemployment and underemployment (SRS 18) and the burden of international debt (SRS 19).

But the pope insists that development cannot be assessed simply in terms of such economic and social indicators. To limit development to its economic aspect, he says, leads to the subordination of the human person to "the demands of economic planning and selfish profit" (SRS 33; cf. 28). One must also take account of cultural aspects such as literacy and education, and of political aspects such as respect for human rights and human initiative, the extent of discrimination, exploitation and oppression, and also the degree to which people are allowed to be involved in building their own nation or, on the other hand, deprived of initiative and left dependent on a bureaucracy (SRS 15; cf. 33).

One difficulty about using these indicators of development is that it gives the impression that there is just one pattern of human development which all nations must follow. It is as though there were one "ladder of progress" on which various countries have reached different heights. But the pope does not make this assumption. In fact he is careful to insist that different groups of people have *"differences of culture and value systems* which do not always match the degree of *economic development"* (SRS 14).

The pope sets out to present a theological basis for his teaching on development. He works this out by reflecting first on Old Testament texts such as the Genesis accounts of the relationship of Adam to the earth, to the animals and to God (SRS 29–30); then he goes on to reflect on the role of Christ in human history and human progress—and the role of the Church in promoting this vision of the meaning of life (SRS 31).

Towards the end of the encyclical the pope takes up briefly the topic of liberation. He says

> Recently…a new way of confronting the problems of poverty and underdevelopment has spread in some areas of the world, especially in Latin America. This approach makes *liberation* the fundamental category…(SRS 46).

He refers to the two Vatican documents on the topic of liberation. He also speaks of the intimate connection between development and liberation and goes on to say that "the process of *development* and *liberation* takes concrete shape in the exercise of *solidarity"* (SRS 46). In this way he attempts to integrate the theology of development elaborated by Paul VI and himself with what might be called a moderate theology of liberation. This does not really work very well; for the approach and pattern of thought in the encyclical as a whole has little in common with the "from the ground up" approach of the liberation theologians.

Solidarity

John Paul maintains that genuine development must be understood in terms of solidarity (SRS 33). In fact his notion of solidarity is the very heart of his understanding of development. His treatment of this topic in the encyclical is a notable contribution to moral theology. But, rather than discussing it in abstract philosophical terms, he situates what he has to say in the context of the distinctive contribution of *Populorum Progressio* to our understanding of human development. He sees his treatment of solidarity as an expansion of the brief reference made by Paul VI in *Populorum Progressio* to "the duty of solidarity" (PP 44, 48).

As I noted above, Paul VI's account of development began with self-fulfillment. He then extended it outward by including among the criteria of genuine development an increased concern for others and a desire to cooperate with others for the common good (PP 21). John Paul develops this further, offering his teaching on solidarity as a strong bridge to span the gap that might arise between personal fulfillment and concern for others. What he has to say about it can be summarized schematically as follows:

—Firstly, he spells out the fact of *interdependence*. By this he means that we live within a system which determines how we relate to each other in the economic, cultural, political, and religious spheres (SRS 38). (For instance, the livelihood of coffee-farmers in Brazil or Kenya depends on the markets of North America and Europe; and the television "soap operas" of the USA and Australia now influence the values of people in remote parts of Africa and Asia.)

—Secondly, solidarity is a *moral response* to the fact of interdependence. People are now convinced "of the need for a solidarity which will take up interdependence and transfer it to the moral plane" (SRS 26). This is a moral call to overcome distrust of others and to collaborate with them instead (SRS 39).

—Thirdly, such *acts* of collaboration spring from the *virtue* of solidarity (SRS 39). As a virtue, solidarity is not just a feeling but "a firm and persevering determination to commit oneself to the common good" (SRS 38). It is an attitude of commitment to the good of one's neighbor, coupled with a readiness to sacrifice oneself in the service of the other (SRS 38). (I shall return in the next section to the pope's account of solidarity as a virtue.)

—Fourthly, the virtue of solidarity transforms the *interpersonal* relationships of individuals with the people around them. It causes the more powerful people to feel responsible for those who are weak and makes them ready to share what they have with them. It leads those who are weak or poor to reject destructive or passive attitudes. It enables those in an in-between position to respect the interests of others (SRS 39).

—Fifthly, the virtue of solidarity is exercised also by whole *nations* in their relationships with other nations. Nations, like people, are linked in a system which makes them dependent on each other. Within this international system, the powerful and wealthy nations are morally bound to resist the temptation to "imperialism" and "hegemony"; they must not dominate, oppress or exploit the others (SRS 39). What the pope proposes here is a community of *peoples,* each with its own unique culture. "Solidarity" means taking seriously the different value-systems of the various cultures (cf. SRS 14), rather than the imposition of a Western model of development on other peoples.

—Sixthly, by transforming the relationships both between individuals and between nations, the virtue of solidarity brings about a radical change in society as a whole. (I shall develop this point below.)

—Seventhly, there is a sense in which one might speak not merely of "human solidarity" but even of "ecological solidarity." The pope does not quite use this phrase, but it seems to sum up what he has in mind. For he speaks of "a greater realization of the limits of available resources and of the need to respect the integrity and the cycles of nature" (SRS 26). He insists that we are morally obliged to respect "the cosmos," i.e., "the beings which constitute the natural world" (SRS 34). He goes on to expound at some length on the moral obligations imposed on us by our ecological situation (SRS 34). Later, he speaks of "the urgent need to change the spiritual attitudes which define each individual's relationship with self, with neighbor, with even the remotest human communities, and with nature itself" (SRS 38). This indicates that the moral dimension of genuine human development involves a sense of responsibility for the whole cosmos; such moral responsibility is either a part of the virtue of solidarity itself or else it is a sister virtue that has very much in common with it.

—Finally, there is the matter of what happens if people refuse the challenge to be in solidarity with others—if they respond with disinterest instead of concern, if their attitude is one of "using" others rather than respecting them. If individuals or groups or nations act in this way they may grow more wealthy but they cannot be said to be truly "developed," for they are ignoring the crucial *moral* dimension of human development (SRS 9). The pope notes that the lack of solidarity between the nations has "disastrous consequences" for the weaker ones; but it also has serious "negative effects even in the rich countries" (SRS 17).

These include negative economic effects such as inadequate housing and growing unemployment (SRS 17, 18). Even more serious are the moral and political effects. For instance, failure of the nations to overcome their distrust of each other leads to continued imperialism and a turning away from the path to peace (SRS 39, 22); and the so-called "developed" nations of East and West become locked into ideological and military opposition (SRS 20), wasting on an arms race the resources needed for development (SRS 22).

Solidarity as a Virtue

As I pointed out when examining the encyclical *Laborem Exercens,* the pope there employed the term "solidarity" as it is commonly used, to denote the mutual support by which members of an oppressed group strengthen each other to resist injustice. In an earlier work written before he became pope he gave a more philosophical account of solidarity as a virtue. He saw it as an *attitude,* a commitment on the part of those who form a community, to participate in the life of that community in a way that promotes the common good.

In the present encyclical the pope puts forward a more theological analysis of the virtue of solidarity. Firstly, it is an enabling power which gives us the capacity to respect others:

> Solidarity helps us to see the "other"—whether a person, people or nation—not just as some kind of instrument with a work capacity and physical strength to be exploited at low cost and then discarded when no longer useful, but as our "neighbor," a "helper" (cf. Gen. 2:18–20), to be made a sharer, on a par with ourselves, in the banquet of life to which all are equally invited by God (SRS 39).

In this way the virtue of solidarity enables us to overcome distrust and to collaborate with others (SRS 39). Consequently, the exercise of this virtue is the path to true peace (SRS 39). The pope points out that the achievement of peace requires not only justice but also "the practice of the virtues which favor togetherness, and which teach us to live in unity, so as to build in unity, by giving and receiving, a new society and a better world" (SRS 39). So solidarity presupposes justice but goes beyond it by including generosity and care for others.

The aspect of generous self-sacrifice is developed more fully by the pope when he goes on to focus attention on the *Christian* character of the virtue of solidarity. He suggests that "solidarity seeks to go beyond itself, to take on the specifically Christian dimensions of total gratuity, forgiveness, and reconciliation." John Paul finds the basis for this selfless love in the fact that each person is the living image of God (SRS 40). He goes on to say that, for the Christian, the ultimate inspiration for solidarity comes from a unity that is even deeper than any unity based on natural and human bonds; this is a *communion* which is a reflection of the unity of the three Persons in one God (SRS 40).

Structures of Sin

The pope's account of solidarity is part of his sustained effort in this encyclical to overcome the individualistic viewpoint which marred moral theology in the past; by emphasizing solidarity he is saying that virtue is not just a private affair. But just as virtue is not a private matter, neither is sin. So the pope takes up the notion of the social dimension of sin under the title "structures of sin" (SRS 36).

He tries to strike a balance between two extremes. On the one hand he wants to correct the idea that sin is a purely personal action. So he insists that sin becomes embodied in attitudes, traditions and institutions which endure long after "the actions and the brief lifespan of an individual" (SRS 36). On the other hand he resists the idea that structural evil is the primary reality—a notion that is linked to the Marxist emphasis on the need for a revolution to overthrow the structures. John Paul insists that structures of sin are "rooted in personal sin, and thus always linked to the *concrete acts* of individuals who introduce these structures, consolidate them and make them difficult to remove" (SRS 36). In giving primacy to personal, deliberate sin the pope no doubt saw himself as correcting a dangerous tendency of liberation theology.

John Paul also insisted that structures of sin are to be understood not merely in terms of social analysis (SRS 36) but in theological terms:

...hidden behind certain decisions, apparently inspired only
by economics or politics, are real forms of *idolatry:* of
money, ideology, class, technology (SRS 37).

The essence of this idolatry is an absolutizing of certain human attitudes—for instance an all-consuming desire for profit and thirst for
power at any price (SRS 37). In making this point the pope was repeating one of the favorite themes of the liberation theologians (e.g., Gutiér-
rez, Segundo 55–65, Galilea 230). However, as Baum notes, his heavy
stress on the personal roots of social sin means that he pays less attention than Medellín to its unconscious aspects such as the blindness
caused by ideology and the dominant culture (Baum [1989] 113–16).

If the structures of sin are so pervasive and powerful how can we
hope to bring about genuine development? At the personal level there
must be a conversion in the biblical sense, that is " a change of behavior
or mentality or mode of existence" (SRS 38). The social dimension of
this conversion is the virtue of solidarity. Solidarity brings about a radical change in society because it gives people the ability to oppose dia-
metrically the all-consuming desire for profit and the thirst for power,
and the structures of sin which spring from them (SRS 37–38). In this
way it provides the foundation of a whole new set of structures, which
can be called *"the civilization of love"* (SRS 33). So the crucial importance of solidarity in the pope's theology of development is that for him
it is the only effective response to the mis-development and corruption
of our world.

Inadequacies

Pope John Paul's account of the virtue of solidarity is a valuable
one. He has made a praiseworthy attempt to give solid theological content to a word that is widely used in the world today, a word that
describes a feature of modern moral consciousness at its best. There can
be no doubt that he has met a real need, since a moral account of human
development that is confined to such traditional words as "charity" and
"justice" can seem at times to lack the flavor of real life.

However, there are some points at which his account of solidarity
seems to be insufficiently developed. There is the fact that the treatment of
solidarity in this encyclical fails to put any particular emphasis on the spe-

cial role that God has given to those who are weak and poor in bringing liberation to all. Linked to this is the very cursory treatment in the encyclical of the whole notion of a preferential option by the Church for the poor (SRS 42, 46).[3] These are issues of theology, but they can have very practical implications. For, if the poor are called to be key agents of change, it is unlikely that they can play this role without some confrontation (cf. Baum [1989] 120–21); and if the Church is committed to an option for the poor then it too must face up to the challenge of serious confrontation.

This points to another inadequacy in the encyclical's treatment of solidarity: the model of social change which the pope envisages here seems to be very much a consensus model. As noted previously, when John Paul spoke to the shanty-dwellers of Brazil and the Philippines and to the American Indians of Guatemala, he encouraged them to take responsibility for their lives, to struggle against injustice and to stand up for their rights; he reaffirmed this approach in *Laborem Exercens;* and it could be linked to the views he expressed in Poland before he became pope.

In the first edition of *Option for the Poor,* completed in early 1983, I made much of these facts. I saw them as indications that John Paul was willing to break with the tradition established by his predecessors; that he had come to acknowledge that, at least in some circumstances, progress can come only through confrontation. But I must admit that the position adopted in *Sollicitudo Rei Socialis* is a backward step in this regard. In this encyclical the pope does not encourage the poor and powerless to see themselves as key agents of change. Nor does he repeat here what he had said before he became pope about the role of opposition as one aspect of solidarity. Quite the contrary; his treatment here is distinctly more reserved in this regard.[4] Perhaps this reserve may be attributed to the pope's determination to distance himself from the stance of the liberation theologians—not so much in terms of their teaching but in respect of their encouragement to the poor to see themselves, and organize themselves, as the key agents in the struggle for liberation.

Closely related to this is a certain blandness and unreality in the encyclical's treatment of the relationship between different groups or classes in society (SRS 39). What is lacking is a social analysis which would take more seriously the causes of the class structure in society and which could then go on to examine ways in which tensions between the different classes can be overcome or lessened.

Another significant point about the treatment of solidarity in *Sollicitudo Rei Socialis* is that it appears to lack an *affective* dimension. This is surprising since the pope's account of solidarity obviously owes a great deal to the strong affective bonds which have linked him so closely to his own people in their history and their struggles. His treatment of solidarity could be enriched significantly by a fuller account of the *experience* of solidarity and the strong *feelings* that are part of it.

By the "experience" of solidarity I mean the actual sharing of life with a group of people. When one shares the living conditions of a community one can begin to share their sufferings and joys, their fears and their hopes. Out of this lived solidarity grow the bonds of affection that make one feel part of this people and enable them to accept one as truly part of themselves. These bonds of shared life and feelings evoke and nourish a strong sense of responsibility for the whole community and especially for its weaker members. So the virtue of solidarity should not be defined as purely an attitude of the *will* in contrast to "mere feelings." The gap between the fact of interdependence and the undertaking of an appropriate moral response is not adequately bridged by academic knowledge or even by prayer. Study and prayer must be situated within the context of some degree of shared life with people and the bonds of affectivity to which such sharing gives rise.

It is interesting to note that with the collapse of communism in the Soviet bloc the issue on which the encyclical became controversial—its equal criticism of East and West—has already been overtaken by history. Much more significant is its treatment of solidarity. Despite the incompleteness or weaknesses in what it has to say on this topic, its teaching adds a significant component to the corpus of Catholic social teaching (cf. SRS 1, 3, 41), one that should endure and be fully integrated into moral theology.

A Document on Ecology

As I pointed out in the previous section, Pope John Paul took some account of the ecological issue in his second social encyclical. But Vatican teaching on this topic lagged a long way behind that of the World Council of Churches and even behind the teaching of various groups of Catholic bishops (e.g., the bishops of the Philippines and the bishops of the Appalachian region of the USA). This gap was further widened in 1989 when the Council of the European Catholic Bishops cosponsored with the Conference of European Churches a major conference in Basel, out of which came a strongly worded and inspiring statement entitled "Peace with Justice for the Whole of Creation." This adopted a very radical stance. It called for a "complete reversal of the concept of sustained economic growth" (87a) and for a reduction of 50 per cent in the *per capita* energy consumption in industrialized countries (87d). At this time, too, the Vatican was under pressure to join with the World Council of Churches in sponsoring a world convocation on Justice, Peace and the Integrity of Creation, or JPIC as it had come to be called (cf. Dorr [1991] 77–81). No wonder then that the pope felt it was time to give a more comprehensive treatment to the topic of ecology.

This came in his message for the World Day of Peace on January 1st, 1990. In this document the pope insists strongly on the close links between peace, justice and ecology, noting that one of the threats to peace is "lack of *due respect for nature,* ...[and] the plundering of natural resources" (1). These in turn are often caused by unjust land distribution and exacerbated by the need of heavily indebted countries to increase their exports in order to service their debts (11).

The document seeks to provide a biblical and theological basis for ecological concern. In God's plan there was "a fixed relationship" between humankind and the rest of creation.[5] When the first humans deliberately went against this divine plan the result was that the earth was in "rebellion" against humanity and all of creation became "subject to futility" (cf. Rom 8:20–21). So human sin has repercussions on the rest of creation (3–5).

Perhaps the most significant aspect of the document is its insistence that there is "an integrity to creation" (7); the universe is "a 'cosmos' endowed with its own integrity, its own internal, dynamic balance" which must be respected (8). Environmental pollution and the reckless exploitation of natural resources show lack of respect for life and are ultimately to the disadvantage of humankind (7).

The document seems to envisage two reasons why we should respect the integrity of creation:

—Firstly, those who fail to do so are rejecting God's plan for creation.

—Secondly, to fail to respect creation is to damage human life.

However, neither of these points provides us with a criterion for deciding what degree of "interference" with nature would amount to lack of respect for its integrity.

There is an urgent need for some criteria to govern our relationship with the rest of creation. Christians now find themselves pulled in two opposite directions. On the one hand, most governments are committed to an ever greater economic growth, linked to an ever-expanding degree of "exploitation" of the resources of nature. On the other hand, a growing number of concerned people are calling for a halt to this model of economic growth and even a reversal of it.

Justice for Women

In 1988 the pope issued an important document on the dignity of women. The most significant part of the document is that in which he sets out to show that there is a true equality between women and men. He offers an elaborate analysis of the text in the Bible where the first woman is said to be a helpmate for the first man. He concludes that the wife is "subject to" the husband only in the same sense as the husband is "subject to" her; each is called to be at the service of the other (7, 10, 24–25).

This teaching could go a long way to overcome the older Catholic tradition in which wives were expected to obey their husbands without any suggestion that this was to be reciprocated. However, this radical change of direction has gone almost unnoticed. Much more newsworthy is the strong stance taken by the pope against the ordination of women. Feminists and others claim that this amounts to a denial of the equality of women. But the Vatican maintains that what is at issue is not the fundamental equality of women but an unchangeable tradition based on Christ's choice of men as his apostles.

Notes

1. These have been constant themes of the pope (e.g., his Letter to the Religious of Latin America (*L'Oss. Rom.*, 30 July 1990, 4) repeated above all during his visits to Latin America—for instance, during his second visit to Mexico

(*L'Oss. Rom.,* 14 May 1990, 3) and his second visit to Brazil (*L'Oss. Rom.,* 28 October 1991, 12).

2. Cf. Land and Henriot, 65–74; however, their attempt to show that the pope uses "the pastoral cycle" seems a little contrived.

3. The pope does, however, point out that the Church feels called by the Gospel to take a stand alongside the poor in their public but nonviolent demands for justice (SRS 39).

4. I accept the view of Coleman ([1991] 39 and 42) on this issue. He says: "I agree with Dorr that some movement (at least in verbal acknowledgment) has taken place in Catholic social thought to give room to conflict models of society. I do not think, however, that Catholic social thought has really budged all that much from its historic bias toward harmony models" (42).

5. Some months later, the pope took up again the issue of human stewardship of the earth. In an address to participants in a study week on the environment he said, "It is precisely the special value of human life that counsels, in fact compels us, to examine carefully the way we use other created species" (*L'Oss. Rom.,* 28 May 1990, 5). In Comacchio in Northern Italy he said that the transformation of the environment enables people to become more human (*L'Oss. Rom.,* 8 October 1990, 4–5).

21. The New "New Things"

George Weigel

This chapter first appeared in *A New Worldly Order: John Paul II and Human Freedom,* ed. George Weigel, in 1992.

The social encyclical issued by Pope John Paul II in May 1991 is a landmark event in contemporary religious thought about human freedom and its embodiment in culture, economics, and politics. Written to honor the centenary of *Rerum Novarum,* the 1891 letter of Pope Leo XIII that began the papal tradition of modern Catholic social teaching, *Centesimus Annus* ("The Hundredth Year") is both a look back at the *res novae,* the "new things" that seized the attention of Leo XIII, and a look ahead at what we might call the "new 'new things,'" the new facts of public life at the end of the twentieth century and the turn of the third Christian millennium. Like other papal documents, *Centesimus Annus* reaffirms the classic themes of Catholic social thought. But it is John Paul II's creative extension of the tradition that makes this encyclical a singularly bold document, one that is likely to redraw the boundaries of the Catholic debate over the right-ordering of culture, economics, and politics for the foreseeable future.

Centesimus Annus is not, however, a matter of Catholic inside baseball. The encyclical addresses itself to "all men and women of good will." Moreover, scholars and religious leaders outside the formal boundaries of Roman Catholicism have shown an increasing interest in modern Catholic social teaching as perhaps the most well-developed and coherent set of Christian reference points for conducting the public argument about how we should order our lives, loves, and loyalties in society today. (Curiously enough, John Paul II is sometimes more appreciated as a witness to Christian orthodoxy outside his church than within it: as a prominent Southern Baptist put it to a group of Catholic colleagues in early 1991, "Down where I come from, people are saying, 'You folks finally got yourself a pope who knows how to pope.'")

Centesimus Annus should be of special interest to Americans. For better or for worse—and usually for both—the United States is the test-bed for modernity, and for whatever-it-is that's going to come after modernity. We are the world's only superpower, and we are a superpower whose moral *raison d'être* is freedom. As a nation "conceived in liberty," and as the leader of the party of freedom in world politics, the United States ought to pay careful attention to what the most influential moral leader in the contemporary world has to say about the many dimensions of freedom, and about the intimate relation between freedom and truth: particularly the "truth about man," which has been such a prominent theme in the teaching of John Paul II since his election in 1978.

Speaking in Miami in September 1987, the pope described the United States in these terms:

> Among the many admirable values of this nation there is one that stands out in particular. It is freedom. The concept of freedom is part of the very fabric of this nation as a polit-ical community of free people. Freedom is a great gift, a great blessing of God.
>
> From the beginning of America, freedom was directed to forming a well-ordered society and to promoting its peace-ful life. Freedom was channeled to the fullness of human life, to the preservation of human dignity, and to the safe-guarding of all human rights. An experience of ordered free-dom is truly a part of the cherished history of this land.
>
> This is the freedom that America is called to live and guard and to transmit. She is called to exercise it in such a way that it will also benefit the cause of freedom in other nations and among other peoples. The only true freedom, the only freedom that can truly satisfy, is the freedom to do what we ought as human beings created by God according to his plan. It is the freedom to live the truth of what we are and who we are before God, the truth of our identity as chil-dren of God, as brothers and sisters in a common humanity. That is why Jesus Christ linked truth and freedom together, stating solemnly, "You will know the truth and the truth will

set you free" (John 8:32). All people are called to recognize
the liberating truth of the sovereignty of God over them as
individuals and as nations.

So much for the image of John-Paul-the-Polish-authoritarian, so
assiduously propounded by the prestige press (and by the party of dissent in American Catholicism). The truth of the matter is precisely the
opposite: were one to hang a moniker on this remarkable bishop of
Rome, one might well call him the "pope of freedom."

What John Paul II means by "freedom," of course, is not precisely
what America's cultural elites have had in mind since the fevered "liber-
ations" of the 1960s. And so an argument is engaged: What is this freedom that is a "great gift, a great blessing of God"? How is it to be lived
by free men and women, in free societies that must protect individual
liberty while concurrently advancing the common good?

Enter *Centesimus Annus.*

The Truth About Man

Viewed most comprehensively, *Centesimus Annus* is a profound
meditation on human nature, on man's quest for a freedom that will
truly satisfy the deepest yearnings of the human heart. John Paul II
regards that human search for true freedom as something "built in" to
the very nature of man's way of being in the world, and "built in" precisely by a God whom we are to find, and worship, in freedom.

The "Problem" of Freedom

Centesimus Annus begins with a review of the teaching of Leo
XIII in *Rerum Novarum.* For there, in 1891, the Church began to grapple
with the new problem of freedom that had been created by the upheavals
of the Industrial Revolution (in economics) and the French Revolution
(in politics). "Traditional society was passing away and another was
beginning to be formed—one which brought the hope of new freedoms
but also the threat of new forms of injustice and servitude." That threat
was particularly grave when modernity ignored "the essential bond
between human freedom and truth." Leo XIII understood, his successor

argues, that a "freedom which refused to be bound to the truth would fall into arbitrariness and end up submitting itself to the vilest of passions, to the point of self-destruction." In the last decade of this bloodiest of centuries, it is difficult to suggest that Leo XIII was prematurely pessimistic about certain aspects of the modern quest for freedom.

From Leo XIII on, Catholic social teaching's "answer" to the "problem" of freedom has begun with a moral reflection on man himself, and an insistence on the dignity and worth of each individual human being as a creature endowed with intelligence and will, and thus made "in the image and likeness of God." Therefore the beginning of the answer to the rapaciousness of Manchesterian liberalism in economics was "the dignity of the worker...[and] the dignity of work." And the beginning of the answer to the massive repression and injustice of twentieth-century tyrannies was Leo XIII's insistence on the "necessary limits to the state's intervention in human affairs." Why are those limits "necessary"? Because "the individual, the family, and society are prior to the State, and...the State exists in order to protect their rights and not stifle them."

The Catholic human rights revolution of the late twentieth century thus owes a debt of gratitude to the last pope of the nineteenth century, Leo XIII, for it was Leo who first posed Christian *personalism* as the alternative to socialist collectivism (which subsumed human personality into the mass) and to radical individualism (which locked human personality into a self-made prison of solipsism). John Paul II, from the moment he took office in October 1978, has been a vigorous proponent of basic human rights, particularly the fundamental right of religious freedom. This pattern continues in *Centesimus Annus,* in which the pope decries the situation in those countries "which covertly, or even openly, deny to citizens of faiths other than that of the majority the full exercise of their civil and religious rights, preventing them from taking part in the cultural process, and restricting both the Church's right to preach the gospel and the right of those who hear this preaching to accept it."

"Rights": Deepening the Debate

For that reason, it is all the more striking that the human rights language is a bit more muted in *Centesimus Annus* than in John Paul's earlier encyclicals—and far more muted than it was in Pope John

XXIII's *Pacem in Terris*. The pope has not lost any interest in the problems of human rights. Rather, he now seems determined to deepen (and, in some respects, to discipline) the debate over "rights" by linking rights to *obligations* and to *truth*.

On this latter point, conscience is not a kind of moral free agent, in which an "autonomous self" declares something to be right because it is right "for me." No, conscience is "bound to the truth." And the truth about man is not to be confused with "an appeal to the appetites and inclinations toward immediate gratification," an appeal that is "utilitarian" in character and does not reflect "the hierarchy of the true values of human existence."

Nor are "rights" simply a matter of our immunities from the coercive power of others, important as such immunities are: rights exist so that we can fulfill our obligations. Thus a man should be free economically so that he can enter into more cooperative relationships with others, and meet his obligations to work in order to "provide for the needs of his family, his community, his nation, and ultimately all humanity." Ownership, too, has its obligations: "Just as the person fully realizes himself in the free gift of self, so too ownership morally satisfies itself in the creation, at the proper time and in the proper way, of opportunities for work and human growth for all."

By hearkening back to the Christian personalism of Leo XIII, while at the same time "thickening" the concept of "rights" in the Catholic tradition, John Paul II has, in *Centesimus Annus,* provided a powerful example of Christian anthropology at its finest. But this is no abstract philosophical exercise. For having set the proper framework for thinking about public life, the pope immediately brings his analysis of the "truth about man" to bear on the revolution of 1989 in Central and Eastern Europe.

REVOLUTION OF THE SPIRIT

The fundamental error of socialism is anthropological in nature. Socialism considers the individual person simply as an element, a molecule within the social organism, so that the good of the individual is completely subordinated to the functioning of the socio-economic mechanism. Socialism likewise maintains that the good of the individual can be realized without reference to his free choice, to the unique and exclusive responsibility he exercises in the face of good or evil. Man is thus reduced to a series of social relationships, and the concept of the person as the…subject of moral decision disappears, the very subject whose decisions build the social order.

From this mistaken conception of the person there arise both a distortion of law…and an opposition to private property. A person who is deprived of something he can call "his own," and of the possibility of earning a living through his own initiative, comes to depend on the social machine and on those who control it. This makes it much more difficult for him to recognize his dignity as a person, and hinders progress toward the building up of an authentic human community.—*Centesimus Annus, 13*

Western political scientists and international-relations specialists have had a hard time figuring out just what happened in Central and Eastern Europe in 1989. "Delayed modernization" seems to be the preferred answer from the ivory tower: the economic systems of the communist world couldn't compete, and the only way to change them was to get rid of the political regimes that had imposed collectivism in the first place. It is, in truth, a deliciously Marxist "answer" to the utter collapse of Marxism—and a worrisome indication of how deeply quasi-Marxist themes have sunk into the collective unconscious of the new knowledge class.

Pope John Paul II, for one, isn't buying any of this.

Centesimus Annus is well worth careful study for its marvelous third chapter alone. For in "The Year 1989," the pope offers a succinct, pointed, and persuasive analysis of the roots of the Revolution of 1989. The fundamental problem with communism, or "real socialism," was not its economic decrepitude. Rather, communism failed because it denied "the truth about man." Communism's failures were first and foremost moral failures. "The God That Failed" was a false god whose acolytes led societies and economies into terminal crisis.

Yalta Revisited

Pope John Paul begins his historical analysis of 1989 in 1945, with the Yalta Agreements. "Yalta," in fact, looms very large indeed in the vision of the Polish pontiff. The Second World War, "which should have re-established freedom and restored the right of nations, ended without having attained these goals"—indeed, it ended with "the spread of Communist totalitarianism over more than half of Europe and over other parts of the world." Yalta, in other words, was more than a political decision; it was a moral catastrophe and a betrayal of the sacrifices of the war, a betrayal rooted in incomprehension of the nature of Marxist-Leninist totalitarianism.

A failure of moral intuition led to a failure of politics. And thus the first truth about Central and Eastern Europe was that the "Yalta arrangement" could not be regarded as merely a historical datum with which one had to deal. Dealing had to be done (not for nothing did Pope John Paul grow up under the tutelage of Cardinal Stefan Wyszynski of Warsaw, a tenacious primate who gained the Church crucial breathing room in the 1950s). But there should be no illusions. The only "dealing" that would contribute to a genuine peace was a dealing based on the conviction that no peace worthy of the name could be built on the foundations of Yalta.

As it began, so would it end. The origins of this bizarre and, in the pope's terms, "suffocating" empire found their parallels, forty-four years later, in the ways in which the empire fell.

The moral catastrophe of Yalta was attacked at its roots by "the Church's commitment to defend and promote human rights," by a confrontation with Stalin's empire at the level of ethics, history, and culture. Communism, and particularly communist atheism, the pope said time and again, was "an act against man." And the antidote to the false humanism of Marxism-Leninism would come from a truly Christian humanism in which men and women once again learned the human dignity that was theirs by birthright.

1979: A Return to Poland

That understanding had never been completely snuffed out in Central and Eastern Europe. But there was fear. And it seems in retrospect that the people of the region—first in Poland, and then elsewhere—began to face down their fear during John Paul II's first, dramatic return to Poland in June 1979. His message during that extraordinary pilgrimage was decidedly "pre-political." It was a message about ethics, culture, and history devoted to explicating "the truth about man" that Poles knew in their bones—the truth that their regime had denied for two generations. It was not a message about "politics" in the narrow sense of the struggle for power. But it was high-octane Politics in the more venerable sense of the term: as the ongoing argument about the good person, the good society, and the structure of freedom. And that upper-case Politics led, over time, to the distinctive lower-case politics of the revolution of 1989, the revolution that reversed Yalta.

John Paul II believes that, among the "many factors involved in the fall of [these] oppressive regimes, some deserve special mention." The first point at which "the truth about man" intersected with lower-case "politics" was on the question of the rights of workers. The pope is quite willing to drive home the full irony of the situation:

> It cannot be forgotten that the fundamental crisis of systems claiming to express the rule and indeed the dictatorship of the working class began with the great upheavals which took place in Poland in the name of solidarity. It was the throngs of working people which foreswore the ideology which presumed to speak in their name. On the basis of a hard, lived experience of work and of oppression, it was they who recovered and, in a sense, rediscovered the content and principles of the Church's social doctrine.

That reappropriation of "the truth about man" led to another of the distinctive elements of the revolution of 1989: its non-violence. Tactical considerations surely played a role in the choice of non-violence by what we used to call "dissidents": the bad guys had all the guns, and the good guys knew it. But it is hard to explain why the mass of the people remained non-violent—particularly given the glorification of armed revolt in Polish history and culture—unless one understands that a moral revolution preceded the political revolution of 1989.

Other Factors in the Fall

The pope is aware that the economic systems of Central and Eastern Europe were in a shambles by the mid-1980s, and that this played a role in the collapse of Stalin's empire. But he also urges us to consider the economic disaster of command economies, not as a "technical problem" alone, but rather as "a consequence of the violation of the human rights to private initiative, to ownership of property, and to freedom in the economic sector." Marxist economics, just like Leninist politics, refused to acknowledge "the truth about man."

State atheism in the Eastern bloc also carried the seeds of its own destruction, according to John Paul. The "spiritual void" the state created by building a world without windows or doors "deprived the younger generation of direction and in many cases led them, in the irrepressible search for personal identity and for the meaning of life, to rediscover the religious roots of their national cultures, and to rediscover the person of Christ himself as the existentially adequate response to the desire in every human heart for goodness, truth, and life." The communists had thought they could "uproot the need for God from the human heart." They learned that "it is not possible to succeed in this without throwing the heart into turmoil."

And communism onto the ash heap of history.

John Paul II's carefully crafted discussion of the revolution of 1989 makes no claims for the Church's role as agent of the revolution that will strike a fair-minded reader as implausible or excessive. Nor is the Holy See unaware of the many other factors that conspired to produce the peaceful demolition of Stalin's empire: the Helsinki process, which publicly indicted communist regimes for their human rights violations and created a powerful network of rights activists on both sides of the Iron Curtain; the fact of Mikhail Gorbachev; and SDI, which any number of Vatican officials consider, privately, to have been decisive in forcing a change in Soviet policy.

But John Paul II is determined to teach a more comprehensive truth about the revolution of 1989: that a revolution of the spirit, built on the sure foundation of "the truth about man," preceded the transfer of power from communist to democratic hands. The revolution of 1989, viewed through this wide-angle lens, began in 1979. It was a revolution in which people learned first to throw off fear, and only then to throw off their chains—non-violently. It was a revolution of conservation, in which people reclaimed their moral, cultural, and historical identities. It was, in short, a revolution from "the bottom up"—the bottom, in this case, being the taproots of the historic ethical and cultural self-understandings of individuals and nations.

The Free Economy

Not only is it wrong from the ethical point of view to disregard human nature, which is made for freedom, but in practice it is impossible to do so. Where society is so organized as to reduce arbitrarily or even suppress the sphere in which freedom is legitimately exercised, the result is that the life of society becomes progressively disorganized and goes into decline.

Moreover, man, who was created for freedom, bears within himself the wound of original sin, which constantly draws him toward evil and puts him in need of redemption. Not only is this doctrine an integral part of Christian revelation; it also has great hermeneutical value insofar as it helps one to understand human reality. Man tends towards good, but he is also capable of evil. He can transcend his immediate interest and still remain bound to it.

The social order will be all the more stable, the more it takes this fact into account and does not place in opposition personal interest and the interests of society as a whole, but rather seeks to bring them into a fruitful harmony. In fact, when self-interest is violently suppressed, it is replaced by a burdensome system of bureaucratic control which dries up the wellsprings of initiative and creativity. When people think they possess the secret of a perfect social organization which makes evil impossible, they also think that they can use any means, including violence and deceit, in order to bring that organization into being. Politics then becomes a "secular religion" which operates under the illusion of creating paradise in this world. But no political society...can ever be confused with the Kingdom of God.—*Centesimus Annus, 25*

Pope John Paul II does not hesitate to draw out the implications of his Christian anthropology of human freedom, and his analysis of the dynamics of the revolution of 1989, in the field of economics: *Centesimus Annus* contains the most striking papal endorsement of the "free economy" in a century. The endorsement comes in the form of the answer to a pressing question:

> Can it be said that, after the failure of communism, capital-ism is the victorious social system, and that capitalism should be the goal of the countries now making efforts to rebuild their economy and society? Is this the model which ought to be proposed to the countries of the Third World which are searching for the path to true economic and civil progress?
>
> The answer is obviously complex. If by "capitalism" is meant an economic system which recognizes the funda-mental and positive role of business, the market, private property, and the resulting responsibility for the means of production, as well as free human creativity in the eco-nomic sector, then the answer is certainly in the affirma-tive, even though it would perhaps be more appropriate to speak of a "business economy," "market economy," or simply "free economy." But if by "capitalism" is meant a system in which freedom in the economic sector is not cir-cumscribed within a strong juridical framework which places it at the service of human freedom in its totality, and which sees it as a particular aspect of that freedom, the core of which is ethical and religious, then the reply is cer-tainly negative.

In other words, if by "capitalism" is meant what the West at its best means by capitalism—a tripartite system in which democratic poli-tics and a vibrant culture discipline and temper the free market—then that is the system the pope urges the new democracies and the Third World to adopt, because that is the system most likely to sustain a human freedom that is truly liberating.

Some Striking Points

The defenders of the liberal status quo have insisted that this endorsement carries a lot of conditions with it. Well, of course it does. No thoughtful defender of the market will deny the need for its careful regulation by law, culture, and public morality. What is striking about *Centesimus Annus* comes in passages like these:

- The modern business economy has positive aspects. Its basis is human freedom exercised in the economic field, just as it is exercised in many other fields.

- It is precisely the ability to foresee both the needs of others and the combinations of productive factors most adapted to satisfying those needs that constitutes another important source of wealth in modern society. Besides, many goods cannot be adequately produced through the work of an isolated individual; they require the cooperation of many people in working towards a common goal. Organizing such a productive effort, planning its duration in time, making sure that it corresponds in a positive way to the demands which it must satisfy, and taking the necessary risks—all this too is a source of wealth in today's society. In this way, the role of disciplined and creative human work and, as an essential part of that work, initiative and entrepreneurial ability becomes increasingly evident and decisive.

- Another task of the State is that of overseeing and directing the exercise of human rights in the economic sector. However, primary responsibility in this area belongs not to the State but to individuals and to the various groups and associations which make up society. The State could not directly ensure the right to work for all its citizens unless it controlled every aspect of economic life and restricted the free initiative of individuals.

- Indeed, besides the earth, man's principal resource is man himself.

Centesimus Annus thus marks a decisive break with the curious materialism that has characterized aspects of modern Catholic social teaching since Leo XIII. Wealth-creation today, John Paul II readily acknowledges, has more to do with human creativity and imagination, and with political and economic systems capable of unleashing that creativity and imagination, than with "resources" *per se*. And that, John Paul II seems to suggest, is one of the "signs of the times" to which Catholic social thought must be attentive.

An Empirical View of the "Option"

In fact, one of the distinctive characteristics of *Centesimus Annus* is its empirical sensitivity. John Paul II has thought carefully about what does and what doesn't work in exercising a "preferential option for the poor" in the new democracies, in the Third World, and in impoverished parts of the developed world. The "preferential option," the pope seems to suggest, is a formal principle: its content should be determined, not on the basis of ideological orthodoxy (that's what was rejected in the revolution of 1989), but by empirical facts. And as far as this pope seems concerned, the evidence is in. What works best for the poor is democratic polities and properly regulated market economies. Why? Because democracy and the market are the systems that best cohere with human nature, with human freedom, with "the truth about man."

It will take some time for this new departure in Catholic social thought to be digested by those committed to what the pope calls the "impossible compromise between Marxism and Christianity," as well as by those who continue to search for a chimerical Catholic "third way" between capitalism and socialism. (At a meeting in Rome shortly after the encyclical was published, for example, the dean of the social-science faculty at the Pontifical Gregorian University told me that "Capitalism A [i.e., the properly disciplined capitalism the pope endorses] exists only in textbooks." I privately told the dean, a Latin American Jesuit, that if he really believed that, he had no business running a faculty of social science.) But the text of *Centesimus Annus* itself is plain: the authoritative teaching of the Catholic Church is that a properly regulated market, disciplined by politics, law, and culture, is best for poor people. It works. And it gives the poor an "option" to exercise their freedom as economic actors that is available in no other system.

CULTURE WARS

It is not possible to understand man on the basis of economics alone, nor to define him simply on the basis of class membership. Man is understood in a more complete way when he is situated within the sphere of culture through his language, history, and the position he takes toward the fundamental events of life, such as birth, love, work, and death.

> At the heart of every culture lies the attitude man takes to
> the greatest mystery: the mystery of God. Different cultures
> are basically different ways of facing the question of the
> meaning of personal existence. When this question is elimi-
> nated, the cultural and moral life of nations is corrupted.—
> *Centesimus Annus, 24*

John Paul II is rather more concerned about the "culture" leg of
the politics-economics-culture triad than about the argument between
market economists and those still defending state-centered schemes of
development. The latter debate has been settled. The real issue is the
ability of a culture to provide the market with the moral framework it
needs to serve the cause of integral human development.

Once again, "1989" is on the pope's mind. Can the new democracies develop societies that provide for the free exercise of human creativity in the workplace, in politics, and in the many fields of culture
without becoming libertine in their public moral life? Will "consumerism"—that is, consumption as an ideology, not as a natural part of
what dissidents used to call a "normal society"—replace Marxism-
Leninism as the new form of bondage east of the Elbe River?

The pope is not persuaded by libertarian arguments. "Of itself," he
writes, "the economic system does not possess criteria for correctly distinguishing new and higher forms of satisfying human needs from artificial new needs which hinder the formation of a mature personality." And
so the market cannot be left on its own. "A great deal of educational and
cultural work is urgently needed," so that the market's remarkable
capacity to generate wealth is bent toward ends congruent with "the
truth about man"—which is not, John Paul continually urges, an economic truth only (or even primarily).

The pope seems convinced that consumerism-the-ideology is to
be blamed, not on the market system, but on the moral-cultural system's
failures to discipline the market:

> These criticisms [of consumerism in its hedonistic form] are
> directed not so much against an economic system as against
> an ethical and cultural system....If economic life is absolu-
> tized, if the production and consumption of goods become
> the center of social life and society's only value...the reason

is to be found not so much in the economic system itself as in the fact that the entire socio-cultural system, by ignoring the ethical and religious dimension, has been weakened, and ends by limiting itself to the production of goods and services alone.

Centesimus Annus is by no means a dreary exercise in papal scolding. John Paul II knows that the things of this world are important, and that material goods can enhance man's capacity for living a freedom worthy of one made in the image and likeness of God. "It is not wrong to want to live better," according to the pope. "What is wrong is a style of life which is presumed to be better when it is directed toward 'having' rather than 'being,' and which wants to have more, not in order to be more but in order to spend life in enjoyment as an end in itself."

So what is to be done? John Paul II is highly critical of the excesses of the welfare state, which he styles the "social assistance state." Here, the pope argues, is another abuse of human freedom: "By intervening directly and depriving society of its responsibility, the Social Assistance State leads to a loss of human energies and an inordinate increase of public agencies, which are dominated more by bureaucratic ways of thinking than by concern for serving their clients, and which are accompanied by an enormous increase in spending."

Reconstructing Civil Society

John Paul's preference, which is an expression of the classic Catholic social-ethical principle of "subsidiarity," is for what, in the American context, would be called "mediating structures": "Needs are best understood and satisfied by people who are closest to [the poor, the weak, the stricken] and who act as neighbors to those in need." Such mediating structures—religious institutions, voluntary organizations, unions, business associations, neighborhood groups, service organizations, and the like—are the backbone of what Václav Havel and others in Central and Eastern Europe have called "civil society." And the reconstruction of civil society is the first order of business in establishing the foundations of democracy. This is a message that could well be taken to heart in the West, too.

In sum, what is needed is a public moral culture that encourages "lifestyles in which the quest for truth, beauty, goodness, and communion with others for the sake of common growth are the factors which determine consumer choices, savings, and investments." We do not live in hermetically sealed containers labeled "economic life," "politics," and "lifestyle." John Paul insists that it is all of a piece. There is only one human universe, and it is an inescapably moral universe in which questions of "ought" emerge at every juncture. As the pope puts it, "Even the decision to invest in one place rather than another, in one productive sector rather than another, is always a moral and cultural choice."

And as with economics, so with politics. I have stressed here the importance of "1989" in the pope's historical vision. But by "1989" the pope means a set of events fraught with meaning for the West as well as for the East. John Paul II has vigorously positioned the Church on the side of the democratic revolution throughout the world, not because he is a geopolitician, but because he is a moral teacher and a pastor. The Church, he insists, "has no models to present." But, as an expression of its fundamental concern for "the truth about man," the Church "values the democratic system inasmuch as it ensures the participation of citizens in making political choices, guarantees to the governed the possibility of both electing and holding accountable those who govern them, and of replacing them through peaceful means when appropriate."

Democracy and the Ultimate Truth

John Paul II is almost Lincolnian in wondering whether nations "so conceived and so dedicated can long endure," particularly given the attitude toward the relation between rights and obligations, and between rights and the truth, that is common among Western cultural elites today. It is not as Cassandra but as a friend of democracy that John Paul II lays down this challenge:

> Nowadays there is a tendency to claim that agnosticism and skeptical relativism are the philosophy and the basic attitude which correspond to democratic forms of political life. Those who are convinced that they know the truth and firmly adhere to it are considered unreliable from a democratic point of view, since they do not accept that truth is determined by the majority, or that it is subject to variation

according to different political trends. It must be observed in this regard that if there is no ultimate truth to guide and direct political activity, then ideas and convictions can easily be manipulated for reasons of power. As history demonstrates, a democracy without values easily turns into open or thinly disguised totalitarianism.

And yet, the pope continues, "the Church respects the legitimate autonomy of the democratic order," and the Church "is not entitled to express preferences for this or that institutional or constitutional solution." Rather, the Church is the Church, and thus "her contribution to the political order is precisely her vision of the dignity of the person revealed in all its fullness in the mystery of the Incarnate Word."

Centesimus Annus is an extraordinary statement of faith: faith in freedom; faith in man's capacity to order his public life properly; above all, faith in God, who created man with intelligence and free will. It may well be the greatest of the social encyclicals, given the breadth of the issues it addresses, the depth at which questions are probed, and the empirical sensitivity John Paul II shows to the "signs of the times" as they illuminate freedom's cause today. (It is also, despite the occasional heavy patch, the most reader-friendly of John Paul's major letters.) With *Centesimus Annus,* the "pope of freedom" has not only marked the centenary of a great tradition. He has brilliantly scouted the terrain for the next hundred years of humanity's struggle to embody in public life the truth that makes us free.

22. Reordering the World

J. Bryan Hehir

This chapter first appeared in *Commonweal* in 1991.

In 1891 Leo XIII shaped his encyclical *Rerum Novarum* on the theme of "new things"; a hundred years later John Paul II has given us *Centesimus Annus* as we debate the need for a "new world order." One way to read this new encyclical is as the pope's contribution to the "new order" debate. Such a reading is defensible if *Centesimus Annus* is read in the context of John Paul's other major social teachings, *Laborem Exercens* (1981) and *Sollicitudo Rei Socialis* (1987), as well as his 1979 address to the United Nations. Long before the change that has occurred in world politics, the pope had argued that the old order was morally unacceptable and had been developing his conception of reform for the international order. He had articulated his view of a world less controlled by the superpowers, his conception of a united Europe—separated from the "logic of the blocs"—and his conviction that the peoples and the nations of the developing world deserve a different status from the one accorded them by the Cold War.

Now that those fundamental changes have taken place, *Centesimus Annus* celebrates the change and moves on to an analysis of what the moral order requires within and among states.

When Leo XIII wrote *Rerum Novarum,* his primary concern was to respond to the suffering of workers in the industrializing world, but he also designed the encyclical to complement his larger effort to restore the Church's voice and role to a central place in the public life of the world. The effects of nineteenth-century political, intellectual, and economic life and the stances of his two predecessors (Gregory XVI and Pius IX) had effectively pushed the Church to the margins of public life. A major accomplishment of Leo's papacy was the way in which he began the process—intellectually, socially, and politically—of a creative dialogue between church and world.

The setting for *Centesimus Annus* could hardly be more different. Throughout the world today, the role of faith and religious life is intricately tied to major political, economic, and social developments. The driving currents of change in Eastern Europe, the Middle East, and Latin America cannot be explained without an understanding of the personal and social role of faith. More specifically, the place of the Catholic Church on this wider horizon of religion and politics is dramatically different from the situation that Leo confronted. *Centesimus* is guaranteed a hearing in the academies, the embassies, the factories, and the *favelas* of the world because John Paul is seen as one of the catalysts of the transformed world scene. The chapter of the encyclical called "The Year 1989" constitutes a rare insight by a participant in the ending of the Cold War.

That participant is, however, primarily a pastor and teacher. Hence, the long-term value of the encyclical is the contribution it makes to the social teaching inaugurated by Leo. A significant portion of *Centesimus* is devoted to a rereading of the teachings of Leo, Pius XI, and Pius XII. The developing edge of the teaching in *Centesimus* is exemplified, but not exhausted, by three themes: the role of the market, the teaching on the state, and the evaluation of the use of force.

THE MARKET ECONOMY

In the century of social teaching, no other document has come close to the specificity of analysis offered in *Centesimus* about the role of the "free market" in the economy. At one level the qualified endorsement of the market mechanism is analogous to Pius XII's statements about democracy in the 1940s. There is in *Centesimus* a carefully contained but authentic statement of support in principle for the market economy.

The analysis of the role of the market is two-dimensional. At one level the pope offers a clinical commentary on the empirical assets of the market mechanism ("the most efficient instrument for utilizing resources and effectively responding to needs") and of the capitalist style of economic organization ("which recognizes the fundamental and positive role of business, the market, private property, and the resulting responsibility for the means of production, as well as for human creativity in the economic sector"). The clinical assessment takes the market reality seriously and acknowledges values in it that John Paul's predecessors may have assumed but did not assert.

The second level of the analysis places the empirical fact of the market within a moral framework, and describes three moral limits: (1) many human needs are not met by the workings of the market; (2) there are whole groups of people without the resources to enter the market; and (3) there are goods that "cannot and must not be bought and sold."

The market economy poses a double challenge: how to take advantage of what it does well, and how to supplement its acknowledged limits. John Paul's answer is that the market must be placed in the broader context of state and society. He sees the need for a "juridical framework" within which the market will function, a setting of law and policy that will contain the market and address the human needs it leaves unattended.

But what will be the juridical framework at the international level of the economy? The market mechanism is not only a choice that countries can make; it is almost certainly the framework within which the international economy will function. The decentralized nature of international politics has always made the establishment of such a framework very difficult.

THE STATE

A theory of the role of the state in society runs through *Centesimus;* an entire chapter is devoted to the role of state and culture. The tension in John Paul's treatment of the state is that it both expresses his conviction that the state should be involved "directly and indirectly" in fostering economic activity and in defending "the weakest" participants in the economic sectors, and also reflects his determination to keep the power of the state limited by law and free of totalitarian pretensions. This dialectic is found in previous social encyclicals that espoused an activist state, but one constrained by the principle of subsidiarity.

Centesimus is more detailed on both dimensions. Its brief critique of "the welfare state" is new in papal teaching, and it is useful. It stresses the way in which the state—even in pursuit of desirable social objectives—can become an oppressive bureaucracy, and it emphasizes the role of voluntary associations in delivering social services. This critique is puzzling, however, because the range of activities that Catholic teaching—including this encyclical—requires the state to perform, particularly in defense of the poor, is usually identical with the role "the welfare state" has fulfilled in many industrial democracies. It would not be surprising if critics of these functions try to use this language to limit the state's role in the future.

THE USE OF FORCE

A basic theme of this papacy has been to foster non-violent methods of social change and to raise the moral barriers against the use of force between states. The Gulf War made the pope even more determined to pursue this course. He refers to the critique he consistently made during the war, and he uses his commentary on "1989" to argue for the possibility of achieving major social objectives—even in the face of state power—without resort to force.

A detailed assessment of how *Centesimus Annus* fits into the wider philosophy of John Paul II on war would be an article in itself; but one surely comes away from the Gulf debate and this encyclical with a sense that the moral barriers against the use of force are now drawn more tightly by this pope. Where he is moving on this question is not yet clear but bears careful watching.

23. Tested by Our Own Ideals

Michael Novak

This chapter first appeared in *National Review* in 1991.

The encyclical *Centesimus Annus* does what many of us had long hoped some church authority would do: it captures the spirit and essence of the American experiment in political economy. The pope showed an extraordinary grasp of American ideas, achievements, and points of view. His vision of a free economy, within a culture moral and religious to its core, guided and energized by a democratic polity, is American in spirit and definition. Thus Pope John Paul II has brought economic liberty (plus democracy) into Catholic social teaching, just as Vatican II brought in religious liberty. In both cases, these are predominantly American contributions to the church universal.

The big points in this encyclical will surely be covered elsewhere. I'd like to concentrate on a few small points, since it is in its details that this papal letter shows its true brilliance. Just one example: The pope describes the desperate need poor families have of jobs. But instead of declaring a Humphrey-Hawkins "right to work" that the state would have to enforce, he writes: "Primary responsibility [for human rights in the economic sector] belongs not to the state but to individuals and to the various groups and associations which make up society." Then comes a sentence I love: "The state could not directly ensure the right to work for all its citizens unless it controlled every aspect of economic life and restricted the free initiative of individuals." Having experienced the prison fashioned by the Marxist version of "economic rights," the pope pops that notion of rights on its glass chin, and the fragments fall to the floor.

Another detail shines out in the section on drugs, which the pope points to as a sign of "consumerism" at its worst: "These criticisms are directed not so much against an economic system as against an ethical and cultural system." What a neat—and accurate—way of putting it.

Three Systems in Society

Throughout, this philosophically trained pope distinguishes the three separate but related systems of advanced free societies: the political system, the economic system, and the moral-cultural system. To each he gives its due, as he also gives its due to their necessary unity, as checks and balances to one another. (It does not seem hard for a person trained to discuss the Trinity to grasp a concept of three-in-one.)

Further neat distinctions are made, for the first time in a papal document, between human capital and capital based on land, and between nations in the "South" that are poor and those that use human capital to create much wealth despite their lack of natural resources. The pope identifies the chief causes of the wealth of nations—not a Marxist "labor theory of value," but enterprise, innovation, organizing skill, and creativity: "Today the decisive factor increasingly is *man himself,* that is, his knowledge, especially his scientific knowledge, his capacity for interrelated and compact organization, as well as his ability to perceive the needs of others and to satisfy them." The pope's further elaboration of new modern virtues such as enterprise, initiative, creativity, and civic responsibility is also superb.

The Moral/Cultural Agenda

Most important of all, perhaps, is the extended attention given throughout *Centesimus Annus* to the moral and cultural sector of life—how it impinges on the political economy, often inspiring, correcting, and guiding it while imparting to it dynamism and character. A pope who has experienced both communist and free societies understands instantly the economic differences that moral/cultural factors give rise to. For free societies in the twenty-first century, questions of culture and morals are likely to be near the top of the agenda. Amid rising tides of intellectual relativism and moral sickness, free societies face real problems in developing their human capital and in maintaining against human weakness the intense pressure of judgment by the Almighty, whence springs so much social dynamism (cf. Abraham Lincoln).

Finally, the pope describes the views of those (like Richard Rorty, Arthur Schlesinger, and many others in this country) who argue that only agnosticism, relativism, and unbelief keep democracy safe: "Those who are convinced that they know the truth and firmly adhere to it are considered unreliable from a democratic point of view." Then, recalling recent experiences under Marxism, the pope turns the tables on them.

> It must be observed in this regard that if there is no ultimate truth to guide and direct political activity, then ideas and convictions can easily be manipulated for reasons of power. As history demonstrates, a democracy without values easily turns into open or thinly disguised totalitarianism.

Centesimus Annus is a great encyclical, the greatest in a hundred years. It is the single best statement in our lifetime by the Catholic Church, or any other religious body, of the moral vision of a political economy such as that of the United States. That is why even Pope John Paul's diagnosis of serious faults in such systems is not offensive; his criticism hoists us on our own ideals. It is, so to speak, criticism "from within." It is as if the pope had written: "We hold these truths in faith: that all men are created equal and endowed by their Creator with certain unalienable rights, among which are the right to life..." and so on. Quite recognizable, that.

If in Vatican II Rome accepted ideas of religious liberty, in *Centesimus Annus* Rome has assimilated American ideas of economic liberty. Moreover, the pope has brought Rome to understand liberty as Americans do:

> Confirm thy soul in self-control,
> Thy liberty in law.

Look again at the Statue of Liberty: holding aloft the lamp of reason, in her other hand the Book of the Law, and bearing a visage as stern and purposive as that of any third-grade teacher in the history of our land.

24. An Argument About Human Nature

Richard John Neuhaus

This chapter first appeared in *The Wall Street Journal* in 1991.

"Can it perhaps be said that, after the failure of communism, capitalism is the victorious social system, and that capitalism should be the goal of the countries now making efforts to rebuild their economy and society?" John Paul asks the question in *Centesimus Annus.* The answer: If by capitalism is meant the "primitive" and often "ruthless" system criticized by Leo XIII in *Rerum Novarum* a century ago, "the reply is certainly negative." But then this: "If by capitalism is meant an economic system which recognizes the fundamental and positive role of business, the market, private property, and the resulting responsibility for the means of production, as well as free human creativity in the economic sector, then the answer is certainly in the affirmative."

John Paul affirms a new capitalism. But the term he prefers is simply "free economy." Of course socialism is economically disastrous, but what he calls the "evil" of the system imposed by the communist "empire" is its denial of freedom. Readers will miss the gravamen of this encyclical if they do not recognize that it is, first and most importantly, an argument about human nature. Capitalism is the economic corollary of the Christian understanding of man's nature and destiny.

The pope says that we can now see how prescient Leo XIII was in his scathing critique of the socialist idea 100 years ago. John Paul underscores, too, *Rerum Novarum*'s vigorous defense of private property as essential to human freedom, dignity, and prosperity. According to the pope's argument, interpretations of Catholic social teaching along socialist or semi-socialist lines, together with the idea that the Church proposes a "third way" between capitalism and socialism, are in serious error.

A Challenge to Conventional Wisdom

Centesimus Annus must surely prompt a careful, and perhaps painful, rethinking of conventional wisdom about Catholic social teaching. It may be, for instance, that the controlling assumptions of the American bishops' 1986 pastoral letter, *Economic Justice for All,* must now be recognized as unrepresentative of the Church's authoritative teaching.

John Paul repeatedly insists that economic growth and the production of wealth are essential to economic justice. Private property must be put to its proper purpose: "Ownership of the means of production...is just and legitimate if it serves useful work. It becomes illegitimate, however, when it is not utilized or when it serves to impede the work of others, in an effort to gain a profit which is not the result of the overall expansion of work and the wealth of society."

The free economy in advanced societies is still not free enough, says the pope. It must develop more fully to include labor and management in a free "community of work" and "circle of exchange" in which business is viewed as a "society of persons." At several points he emphasizes the importance of trade unions, insisting, however, that they must be genuinely free associations that are clear about "the impossible compromise between Christianity and Marxism."

The pope writes that Catholic social teaching, from *Rerum Novarum* to the present, "criticizes two social and economic systems: socialism and liberalism." In the European manner, he means by liberalism what in this country is commonly called libertarianism. *Centesimus* is as hard on the libertarians as it is on the socialists. While economics is important indeed, man must never be reduced to the merely economic. To think that the entirety of social life is to be determined by market exchanges is to run "the risk of an 'idolatry' of the market, an idolatry which ignores the existence of goods which by their nature are not and cannot be mere commodities."

Putting Economics in Its Place

While the bulk of the 114 pages of the encyclical is devoted to economics, its import is to deflate the importance of the economic. Economics, politics, culture—these three define the social order, and the greatest of these is culture. At the heart of culture is the spiritual and moral.

Capitalism, if it is to work, cannot be amoral. "Important virtues are involved in this process," the pope writes, "such as diligence, industriousness, prudence in undertaking reasonable risks, reliability and fidelity in interpersonal relationships, as well as courage in carrying out decisions which are difficult and painful but necessary, both for the overall working of a business and in meeting possible setbacks."

The economics of freedom does not assume the practice of unqualified altruism. The pope has no illusions about human nature. "Man, who was created for freedom, bears within himself the wound of original sin which constantly draws him towards evil and puts him in need of redemption." Self-interest is often wrongly perceived, but it cannot be eliminated. An economy that is fit for human nature must take legitimate self-interest into account. "The social order will be all the more stable, the more...it does not place in opposition personal interest and the interest of society as a whole, but rather seeks ways to bring them into fruitful harmony. In fact, where self-interest is violently suppressed, it is replaced by a burdensome system of bureaucratic control which dries up the wellsprings of initiative and creativity."

Similarly, profit is not to be despised. "The Church acknowledges the legitimate role of profit as an indication that a business is functioning well." At the same time, "profitability is not the only indicator of a firm's condition." The "most valuable asset" of a company is its people. When they are "humiliated and their dignity offended," this both is "morally impermissible" and "will eventually have negative repercussions on the firm's economic efficiency."

The pope points out that the production of wealth has increasingly less to do with the exploitation of natural resources and more to do with the employment of human resources—with the intelligence, skills, and creativity of people who recognize that individual good and common good are inseparably joined in the expanding solidarity of "the community of work."

THE ABUSE OF FREEDOM

Despite his respect for the market mechanism, the pope is severely, even harshly critical of much in those advanced societies that do practice economic freedom. No proponent of capitalism should want to deny the justice of his critique, for the problem, John Paul makes abundantly clear, is not with economic freedom but with the abuse of that freedom. The remedies are essentially cultural, political, and, finally, spiritual. He bitingly condemns the "consumerism" that results when "freedom refuses to be bound to the truth and falls into arbitrariness and ends up submitting itself to the vilest of passions, to the point of self-destruction." The practice of abortion, he observes several times, is an alarming indicator of the degradation of human dignity.

Catholics with a stake in protecting anti-capitalist prejudices have claimed that John Paul is faulting capitalism for the social sins that he deplores. That claim flies in the face of the pope's own words: "These criticisms are directed not so much against an economic system as against an ethical and cultural system.... If economic life is absolutist, if the production and consumption of goods become the center of social life and society's only values, the reason is not to be found so much in the economic system itself as in the fact that the entire socio-cultural system, by ignoring the ethical and religious dimension, has been weakened, and ends up by limiting itself to the production of goods and services alone."

In other words, there is only so much that economics can do. The free market cannot produce the virtuous society that the economy itself requires. That is the task of culture and, most particularly, of morality and religion.

As economics is limited, so also is the role of politics. "The State," the pope writes, "has the task of determining the juridical framework within which economic affairs are to be conducted, and thus of safeguarding the prerequisites of a free economy." Thus, for example, monopolies must not be permitted to exclude competition in the market. The free economy cannot be conducted in an "institutional, juridical, or political vacuum." "On the contrary, it presupposes sure guarantees of individual freedom and private property, as well as a stable currency and efficient public services." In a free society, the state is a servant with carefully circumscribed duties.

John Paul is highly critical of the expansive ambitions of government in what he calls the "Welfare State" or the "Social Assistance State." He reluctantly allows that in "exceptional circumstances," mainly in economically undeveloped societies, the state may make "supplementary interventions." But such interventions "must be as brief as possible, so as to avoid removing permanently from society and business systems the functions which are properly theirs, and so as to avoid enlarging excessively the sphere of State intervention to the detriment of both economic and civil freedom."

This insight is based on two principles that run through the encyclical. The first is the principle of priority. The individual, his free associations, and society itself are all prior to the state in both dignity and rights. The second is the principle of subsidiarity: "A community of a higher order should not interfere in the internal life of a community of a lower order, depriving the latter of its functions, but rather should support it in case of need and help to coordinate its activity with the activities of the rest of society, always with a view to the common good."

CHALLENGES TO THE "NEW CAPITALISM"

While *Centesimus* is a ringing affirmation of the free economy, there is nothing in it to justify complacency among the friends of capitalism. Socialism is dead, but "the new capitalism" has hardly met the challenges raised by the pope. He presses three of these with particular urgency.

First, the principle of subsidiarity requires that advanced societies redesign their social policies to return power to "the intermediate groups" of family and voluntary associations. Social policies should be designed and implemented at the levels nearest to those most immediately affected by them.

Second, the pope offers a number of proposals for the more effective inclusion of poor nations in the world economy's "community of work" and "circle of exchange." As the spiritual leader of nearly a billion Christians, most of them poor, the pope necessarily has much to say about poverty. The chief problem of the poor, he contends, is not capitalism but their "marginalization" from capitalism. While acknowledging the ways in which poor nations are responsible for their own plight, John Paul insists that the more developed economies must do much more to address their marginalization.

Third, business leaders are called upon to disenthrall themselves from the illusion that their decisions are morally neutral. What business does either advances or impedes the prospect, nationally and globally, of "a society of free work, of enterprise, and of participation." Each of us is accountable to that common good and, finally, to the judgment of God.

Far from being an uncritical blessing of the market economy, then, the message of *Centesimus Annus* is that the work of "the new capitalism" has hardly begun.

25. Neoconservative Economics and the Church's "Authentic Theology of Integral Human Liberation"

David L. Schindler

This chapter first appeared in the author's *Heart of the World, Center of the Church* in 1996.

Having critically examined some of the basic principles of neo-conservative theology, we now move our discussion to the terrain of John Paul II's *Centesimus Annus* (= CA), investigating how the neoconservatives respond in their post-*Centesimus Annus* writings to the encyclical's call for an "authentic theology of integral human liberation." Specifically, we shall have to ask whether their conception of the order of freedom, which converges with that of Anglo-American liberalism, truly liberates.

The pope himself makes clear the precise state of the question. The Marxist solution has failed, he says (*CA*, n. 42). At the same time, "the realities of marginalization and exploitation remain in the world, especially the Third World, as does the reality of human alienation, especially in the more advanced countries" (*CA*, n. 42). Summing up the Church's undiminished desire for an authentic liberation theology, *Centesimus Annus* states:

> The crisis of Marxism does not rid the world of the situations of injustice and oppression which Marxism itself exploited and on which it fed. To those who are searching today for a new and authentic theory and praxis of liberation, the church offers not only her social doctrine and, in general, her teaching about the human person redeemed in Christ, but also her

concrete commitment and material assistance in the struggle against marginalization and suffering.

In the recent past, the sincere desire to be on the side of the oppressed and not to be cut off from the course of history has led many believers to seek in various ways an impossible compromise between Marxism and Christianity. Moving beyond all that was short-lived in these attempts, present cultural circumstances are leading to a reaffirmation of the positive value of an authentic theology of integral human liberation. (*CA,* n. 26)[1]

In facing these realities, John Paul takes care to insist that the Church has no economic models to offer; models that are effective can "only arise within the framework of different historical situations through the efforts of all those who responsibly confront concrete problems in all their social, economic, political and cultural aspects as these interact with one another" (*CA,* n. 43). The pope nonetheless does not take back his judgment that Marxism has been a failure: in saying that the Church offers no economic models, he does not thereby affirm a symmetry between communist and Western/free market proposals. On the contrary, he endorses the economic freedom and human creativity characteristic of a market economy. He nonetheless does so in the context of a carefully qualified criticism of capitalism.

Western liberalism of course takes on different forms. As we have seen, there is the distinction often made between the liberalism of Continental Europe, or again of Latin America, and the liberalism of Anglo- or North America; and there is a corresponding distinction made between the "monopoly" or "patrimonial" capitalism characteristic of the former and the "open" or "rational" capitalism characteristic of the latter. My assumption is that the pope's criticism of a "radical capitalistic ideology" in fact applies to Continental liberalism ("monopoly" capitalism). But this leaves the further question: does it apply to Anglo-American liberalism ("rational" capitalism) as well? It is the latter that is now being proposed most often and significantly as the way forward, as a liberalism whose freedom liberates in a sense compatible with, if indeed not inspirational for, the social teaching of Pope John Paul II. In short, it is the distinctly Anglo-American liberal capitalism that is now being widely proposed as the model for the countries of

Eastern Europe to adopt, in their transition from a "command economy" to a market economy.

Hence my question: does Anglo-American liberalism liberate? How does Anglo-American liberalism stand vis-à-vis the "authentic theology of integral human liberation" reaffirmed by *Centesimus Annus?*

I

At the heart of any discussion of economics lies the question of human creativity, in its character as image of God. Thus, for example, John Paul II, in his encyclical *Laborem Exercens* (= *LE*), stresses the creativity of man, which he characterizes as a "'transitive' activity... beginning in the human subject and directed toward an external object," and consequently as involving "dominion...over 'the earth'" (*LE,* n. 14; cf. 13–15). The pope emphasizes the importance of this creativity, and this consequent mastery of the earth and dominion over the visible world, as the expression of man's imaging of God (*LE,* nn. 13-15).

The principle asserted here is axiomatic for those in North America today who would defend the compatibility between the pope's proposals and their own proposals on behalf of a distinctly Anglo-American version of liberal capitalism. Thus Michael Novak states:

> Jews, Catholics, and indeed other men and women who have rejected the old order in the name of initiative and creativity have done as well as the Calvinists Weber singled out.
>
> In any case, Pope John Paul II has supplied just such a new rationale for the building of a new order, through his own concepts of the acting person; the inalienable right to personal economic initiative; the virtues associated with the act of enterprise; and human creativity grounded in the *Imago Dei* endowed in every woman and man by the Creator himself.[2]

Again, in the final section of *CESC,* which he entitles "The Heart of the Matter: Creativity," Novak states: "In fact, the true moral strength of capitalism lies in its promotion of human creativity" (235).

My contention is that Novak is right in seeing the notion of creativity as foundational for both the pope's and his own conception of social-economic order; but that he nonetheless cannot claim agreement with the pope regarding the primitive *meaning* of creativity. And, given the nature of the issue of creativity—namely, that it concerns, by the express claim of both parties, the foundations of economic order—it follows that a difference on this issue will function as a kind of "fault line" which shifts and rearranges every significant element or building block of that order.[3]

Thus the pope says that human creativity, and the "dominion" over the earth that is tied thereto (and thus by further implication the primitive meaning of "*acting* person," "economic *initiative*," and "the virtues associated with the act of *enterprise*"), are all basic to the human being, in the sense that they reveal the human being in its character as image of God. He then goes on to say that this creativity and "dominion" remain "in every case and at every phase within the Creator's original ordering" (*LE*, n. 15).[4]

The hermeneutical key to the pope's meaning here lies in the phrase "within the Creator's original ordering." The proper interpretation of this phrase is in fact given by the pope himself in the texts cited in the previous chapter: namely, "that Christ the Lord, Christ the New Adam, in the very revelation of the mystery of the Father and of his love, fully reveals man to himself"; and that, after Christ and dependent upon him, Mary "is the most perfect image of freedom."

In the light of these texts, we must say that man images the *creativity* of God the Father and Creator only in and through the *receptivity* of Jesus Christ and his mother Mary. The divine creativity of which human creativity is the image, in other words, is first that of Sonship and not that of Fatherhood. We are "sons in the Son": we represent the creativity of the Father only through the Son (cf. Col. 1:15–16), and indeed through the archetypal creature, Mary—the freedom or love of both of whom consists first in receptive obedience.[5]

Thus my first and basic point: human freedom is *receptive* freedom before it is *creative* freedom—or, better, is a freedom that becomes authentically creative only by being anteriorly receptive.

The implication of the *fiat*, in short, is not that we should be less creative, but that, in and through being receptive, we might rather become creative in the proper sense, by generously extending to others what has first been given and what we have therefore always-already first received. All that is, is gift. All that we are and do and make and produce must therefore emerge from a sense of gift: I gratefully receive from God ("immanent" activity: *fiat*), and this provides both the warrant for and the deepest meaning of my giving to others ("transitive" activity: *magnificat*—my soul's magnification of the Lord and of the riches of his creation). It is only by means of the *fiat* and *magnificat,* in short, that human creativity can be liberated toward its true purpose, which, again, is to bring about a civilization of love, or indeed to assist all created entities in all aspects of their being to give glory to God.

Recall again the distinction often made between the liberalism of Continental Europe and that of Anglo-Saxon countries: in the former there is "monopoly" capitalism, where freedom of enterprise is restricted to a privileged social group; in the latter there is "open" capitalism, where the majority have access to the market. If what I have written thus far is accurate, this distinction does not suffice to resolve all the problems, or indeed even the most fundamental problem. For the question remains whether a capitalism that grants the majority (politically) free access to the market may not still be weighted with a false sense of freedom. A freedom whose nature is wrongly understood does not become good simply because it is widely distributed rather than restricted to a few.

I am proposing that liberalism of *any* stripe—including the liberalism of "open" capitalism—remains unacceptable insofar as its freedom remains conceived as primarily creative—or rather, insofar as its creativity is not conceived as anteriorly receptive.[6] Indeed, here we discover the basic definition of a liberalism which, at its deepest level, threatens the integrity of Christianity, because it poisons at its source the meaning of autonomy. In overlooking receptivity in favor of creativity as primary in the basic human act, such a liberalism overlooks the implications of the relation that is constitutive of the human being as *creature.*[7] At stake is the nature of the solidarity characteristic of a "civilization of love"—and thus the nature of the "new order" which we are to propose to the world.

II

But we need to make clearer the sense in which Novak, Weigel, and Neuhaus themselves link their proposals on behalf of "capitalism"—

that is, the "new capitalism"—to a definite theology of creation and a corresponding spirituality. As we have seen, in his earlier work which has played a central role for neoconservatism, Novak implies by the very title that his proposals are tied to a spirituality: *The Spirit of Democratic Capitalism* (= *SDC*).[8] Novak's "democratic capitalism is not just a system but a way of life" (*SDC,* 29). The book is about "the life of the spirit which makes democratic capitalism possible. It is about its theological presuppositions, values, and systemic intentions" (*SDC,* 14). The order of democratic capitalism "calls forth not only a new theology but a new type of religion" (*SDC,* 69).[9] The substance of what is stated here by Novak is repeated in the 1990 essays by all three authors.

The concerns of Novak and Neuhaus expressed here are repeated in their post–*Centesimus Annus* books.[10] But with an important difference: they now propose the theology and spirituality outlined above in terms of the "new sense of order" (*CESC,* 229), or again "the breakthrough to the development of a spirituality of economic enterprise" (*DWDG,* 69), which they contend is found in *Centesimus.* The matter is summed up well by Novak:

> To complement Max Weber's thesis about the new sense of order needed to transform a traditional society into a capitalist society, and the role of certain Calvinist traditions in supplying that sense, I have followed Pope John Paul II in stressing the Catholic (and catholic) ethic of the human person as an active and creative person, in realizing her or his vocation to create, to show initiative, and to accept responsibility. (*CESC,* 229; cf. also 232)

Thus the American Catholic neoconservative proposals regarding capitalism are suffused with a definite theology and spirituality. This point, again, is important because it highlights the fact that, in accepting the economic dimensions of their proposals, we are already being invited to accept as well a particular ethos or way of life. Their economic proposals are already shaped by, and in turn call for, a definite moral-cultural order.

Of course this fact, stated as such, is not yet problematic: for the central claim of the three thinkers is that the new social-economic-moral order they are proposing is in fact consistent with that of John Paul II, at least as now articulated in *Centesimus Annus*.[11]

What is most decisive here is the matter of creativity. The American thinkers under discussion understand creativity to image God in a sense which they take—expressly and emphatically—to be compatible with that of the Scottish-Enlightened and Puritan thinkers of eighteenth-century Anglo-America. The burden of the neoconservatives' argument is that the latter's sense of a "vocation to create, to show initiative, and to accept responsibility" is fundamentally in harmony with that affirmed by the pope—at least in *Centesimus Annus*. In what follows we will examine the issue of self-interest and profit. We will see how, with regard to self-interest and profit, the ordering of freedom in terms of primacy of creativity leads to a significant disharmony with *Centesimus Annus*'s call for an authentic theology of liberation.

In terms of the ideas of *self-interest* and *profit*, Adam Smith's classical statement focuses the issue sharply: "It is not from the benevolence of the butcher, the brewer, the baker, that we expect our dinner, but from their regard to their own interest. We address ourselves, not to their humanity but to their self-love, and never talk to them of their own necessities but of their advantages."[12] Thus the baker bakes a good loaf of bread because that is the way to ensure profit, and thereby to do good business. The baker intends his own good and in the process creates a good also for the other: namely, a good loaf of bread. The good both of the product and of the other (the potential consumer) is thus instrumentalized to the baker's own self-interest; but Smith's point is that both the baker and his customer are better off for that self-interest.[13] In short, it is to the baker's self-love and not to his humanity that we should address ourselves, if we wish the good that the baker has to offer us.

CA's teaching on self-interest and profit is carefully qualified. Humanity bears within itself the wound of original sin, and therefore its inclination to evil can never be eradicated. Man can never wholly overcome his disposition toward selfishness. This fact must be recognized, says the pope; and, as a consequence, we should beware of any attempts at a violent removal of self-interest from society (*CA*, n. 25). Such attempts lead in fact to a burdensome system "of bureaucratic control which dries up the wellsprings of initiative and creativity" (*CA*, n. 25). Those who would seek to eliminate self-interest through some sort of perfect social-political organization in fact turn politics into a "'secular religion' which operates under the illusion of creating paradise in this world" (*CA*, n. 25) and thereby violates "the patience of God" (*CA*, n. 25).

Regarding profit, the pope states: "The church acknowledges the legitimate role of profit as an indication that a business is functioning well" (*CA*, n. 35). In acknowledging the legitimate role of profit as a regulator of the life of a business, the pope insists at the same time that profit is not the only regulator (*CA*, n. 34). Profit must be integrated in the light of human and moral factors (*CA*, n. 34). It is unacceptable for a business to order its accounts well financially while continuing to offend people's dignity. "[T]he purpose of a business firm is not simply to make a profit, but is to be found in its very existence as a community of persons who in various ways are endeavoring to satisfy their basic needs and who form a particular group at the service of the whole of society" (*CA*, n. 34).

The pope's recognition of the legitimate place of profit in the functioning of business, in sum, is accompanied by the insistence that profit is never to be abstracted from—but on the contrary is always to be integrated within—the whole good of the human being and of human society.

A baker trying to live out his Christianity in his life as a businessperson, to imbue the reality of his economic life with the Gospel—in a word, to live in the spirit of the "new" liberation theory and praxis indicated in *Centesimus Annus*—would thus attempt to order profit differently from the way suggested by Smith. He would seek first to make a loaf of bread that was intrinsically good—in terms of its taste and health-producing qualities and the like—and he would seek to do this from the beginning for the sake of being of service to others in society, of enhancing their health and well-being. To be sure, he would recognize profit as a necessary condition of his continuing ability to provide this service to others. He would recognize that he was realizing his own good in this service to others. But that is just the point: his legitimate concern for profit, and his own "self-interest," would be integrated from the beginning and all along the way into the intention of service.

In contrast, say, to a Buddhist understanding, an authentic Gospel spirituality does not entail an elimination of the self and its interests, in the self's mutual relation with others.[14] The intention of the Gospel finally is that there be mutual enhancement in each such relation. But the Gospel requires nonetheless that a normative distinction be made with respect to primacy within that relation: a self that first (ontologically, not temporally) serves the other, and thereby finds itself, is not identical with a self that first seeks itself, and thereby serves the other. A selfishness become mutual is not yet mutual generosity.

What I have said should thus suffice to show that an appeal to *creativity* as such as basic to the human act is not yet enough, because that creativity will in fact always carry a definite sense of order in the self's relation to the other. As indicated, creativity is a transitive act: it goes out to the other. But, when pressed in the face of the issue of self-interest as just raised, we can see that the sense of "going out to the other" is precisely what now requires further differentiation. My suggestion has been that the receptivity that images the *fiat* and *magnificat* is what first and most deeply disposes the self to open to the other as gift—and hence to the other as other—and that immanent activity of this sort is thus the necessary condition for the transitive activity called creativity if it is to be conceived as (structurally) generous rather than selfish.[15]

The emphasis of the neoconservatives with respect to self-interest and profit is indicated in Neuhaus's statement that, in recognizing that the incentives to work certainly include the desire for material gain, the pope "does not despise that desire, but generously affirms self-interest as natural and good" (*DWDG*, 189). In that connection, Neuhaus goes on, the pope "affirms the role of profit in business" (*DWDG*, 190). To be sure, Neuhaus points out that John Paul thereby affirms profit as "an indicator" that business is functioning well, and not as a good in itself, and that the pope's concern is "to underscore the intimate connection between profits and people" (*DWDG*, 190). But he then says that this is "not simply an idealistic or rhetorical flourish. The pope is not asking people to run their businesses on the basis of disinterested altruism" (*DWDG*, 190). On the contrary, human and moral factors are themselves important for the life of a business—in the sense expressed in Neuhaus's conclusion: "So it is also for the sake of business itself—it is in the self-interest of business—that the 'human and moral factors' must be taken very seriously. Once again John Paul highlights the sometimes curious ways in which 'how the world works' can work to the benefit of all" (*DWDG*, 190).

The qualifiers and the emphasis in Neuhaus's statements here are crucial. The pope's recognition of the ineliminability of self-interest (due to sin) is not synonymous with the judgment that self-interest is thereby natural and good. A harmony between personal interests and the interests of society as a whole which is sought on the basis of business's self-interest is not synonymous with a harmony sought on the basis of other-centered service (*CA, n.* 34). Again, in this connection, altruism is not the only alternative to a primacy of self-interest: altruism and Gospel love are not identical.[16] Finally, to say that taking the human and moral factors seriously is coincident with business's self-interest is exactly to beg the question of which—the human and moral factors or the self-interest—is primary, that is, granting their coincidence.

On the matter of self-interest, then, both *Centesimus* and Neuhaus recognize the ineliminability of self-interest, due to sin. Both recognize that any attempt to remove self-interest through force—premature eschatology—will lead only to equal or greater evils. Both insist that we must not place personal interest and the interests of society as a whole in opposition but rather try to bring them into harmony. But what seems clear in John Paul, as it is not in Neuhaus, is that, while the self and its "interests" are never to be eliminated, the dynamic purpose of human existence, "in every case and at every phase," remains that of *transforming* each of our actions into, and *ordering* them in terms of, other-centered love.

That I have not unfairly and rigidly interpreted what might be judged at most a harmless ambiguity in Neuhaus's thought can be seen more clearly now by surveying further some of the basic features of the spirituality and order offered by him (and Novak).

Notes

1. In the last sentence quoted here, Pope John Paul II makes reference to the Congregation for the Doctrine of the Faith's *Instruction on Christian Freedom and Liberation* ([= *ICFL*], 1986), which states that "a theology of freedom and liberation which faithfully echoes Mary's Magnificat preserved in the church's memory is something needed by the times in which we are living" (*ICFL*, n. 98). The Instruction goes on:

Liberation in its primary meaning, which is salvific, thus extends into a liberating task, as an ethical requirement. Here is to be found the social doctrine of the church, which illustrates Christian practice on the level of society.

The Christian is called to act according to the truth and thus to work for the establishment of that "civilization of love" of which Pope Paul VI spoke....The love which guides commitment must henceforth bring into being new forms of solidarity. To the accomplishment of these tasks urgently facing the Christian conscience, all people of good will are called.

It is the truth of the mystery of salvation at work today in order to lead redeemed humanity toward the perfection of the kingdom which gives true meaning to the necessary efforts for liberation in the economic, social and political orders and which keeps them from falling into new forms of slavery. (*ICFL*, n. 99)

2. *The Catholic Ethic and the Spirit of Capitalism* (= *CESC*) (New York: The Free Press, 1993), 232.

3. Cf. *CESC*, the preceding chapter.

4. Cf. also *LE*, n. 54: "At the beginning of man's work is the mystery of creation. This affirmation, already indicated as my starting point, is the guiding thread of this document...."

5. Cf. Balthasar, *A Theology of History* (New York: Sheed and Ward, 1963), 25–33 ("Existence as Receptivity"); and *Unless You Become Like This Child* (San Francisco: Ignatius Press, 1991). Cf. also the striking words of Karol Wojtyla: "Being the father of many, many people, I must be a child: the more I am a father, the more I become a child" (368); "One must choose to give birth even more than to create. In this consists the radiation of fatherhood" (341); "And you too, like me, must be liberated from freedom through love" (355). (Citations are from "The Radiation of Fatherhood," in Wojtyla's *Collected Plays and Writings on the Theater* [Berkeley: University of California Press, 1987], 323–368.) Of course, one must see the intrinsic link among these statements: the creative act (e.g., the act of self-possession of the adult) must become anteriorly receptive (hence childlike and indeed feminine), in order to be truly liberated (and liberating: authentically creative). On the primacy of receptivity, see my "Christology and the *Imago Dei*: Interpreting *Gaudium et Spes*," *Communio* 23 (Spring 1996): 156–184.

6. In connection with how I have framed the question here, see Richard Neuhaus's *Doing Well and Doing Good: The Challenge to the Christian Capitalist* (= *DWDG*) (New York: Doubleday, 1992), 168, where he argues that what the pope means by "radical capitalism," or again "liberalism" (in its unacceptable sense), is what Americans distinguish rather as "libertarianism." The burden of Neuhaus's book is then to show that a(n) (Anglo-American) liberalism so distinguished from libertarianism can be coupled with the pope's social teaching. It is just this claim that it is my purpose to examine.

7. See the discussion in Chapters Nine and Ten, *DWDG*.

8. New York: American Enterprise Institute/Simon and Schuster; 1982.

9. Of course, as we have seen, it is a hallmark of neoconservative social thought also to insist that democratic capitalism, in contrast to traditionalist or socialist societies, is marked by a pluralist spirit (*SDC*, 49). I will return to this

neoconservative claim that their proposals are "pluralistic," in contrast to what they call the "monism" of more traditional societies.

10. Novak, *CESC;* Neuhaus, *DWDG.*

11. Cf., for example, Neuhaus: "While the breakthrough to the development of a spirituality of economic enterprise did not come directly out of the American context, *Centesimus* demonstrates an unprecedented sensitivity to the dynamics of the American social order" (*DWDG*, 70–71).

12. Adam Smith, *An Inquiry into the Nature and Causes of the Wealth of Nations* (New York: Modern Library, 1937), 14.

13. Thus the argument is made that, according to Smith, self-interest can be harnessed to serve the common good and virtuous behavior by being channeled properly through social institutions. Cf. *(inter alia)* Michael Novak, *Free Persons and the Common Good* (Lanham, MD: Madison Books, 1989), esp. 55–69. Cf. also Jerry Z. Muller, *Adam Smith in His Time and Ours* (New York: The Free Press, 1993). Of course, it is just the crucial ambiguity in this argument that I mean to address now in the context of *Centesimus Annus.*

14. Nor does it entail a simple opposition between the self and the other, after the manner of Nygren's opposition between *eros* and *agape:* see the preceding chapter, 108–109, n. 22.

15. Thus an appeal to creativity which remains undifferentiated in the face of a distinction between self-centered and other-centered transitive activity becomes guilty of a *petitio principii.* When it then claims a harmony between a Gospel creativity (cf. the pope's authentic liberation theology) and an eighteenth-century "Enlightened" creativity, that is, without clarifying the difference between generous transitive activity and selfish transitive activity, it falls into an equivocation. It is an equivocation of this sort which seems to characterize the main elements of the neoconservative—Anglo-American liberal—"new order."

16. Altruism typically understands the primacy of the other in such a way that it excludes the self; charity does not. That is, although charity (Christian generosity) demands that primacy be given to the other, it does so all the while recognizing that, *in* losing oneself (and only in losing oneself), one will find oneself. A primacy of the other which is *exclusive of self-realization* (altruism, with its "disinterested" self) is not synonymous with a primacy of the other which is *inclusive of self-realization* (charity). In a word, there are three and not two possibilities here: self-centeredness, altruistic other-centeredness, and charitable other-centeredness.

26. Christian Social Ethics
   After the Cold War

David Hollenbach

This chapter first appeared in *Theological Studies* in 1992.

The dramatic revolutions in Central Europe in 1989 and the continuing disintegration of the Soviet Union since the failed putsch of August 1991 are having profound effects on Christian social-ethical reflection. This section of these "Notes on Moral Theology: 1991" will review a representative sample of the literature that has begun clarifying the impact of these revolutionary events on the ethical agenda. The end of the repressive totalitarianism in these regimes is certainly cause for rejoicing. It raises the issue of what *kind* of non-Communist vision of economic life should be pursued in the future. This question is important not only in the Eastern European context, but in the North Atlantic region and the Southern Hemisphere as well.

It has been addressed at considerable length in Pope John Paul II's encyclical *Centesimus Annus,* issued on May 1, 1991 to commemorate the one-hundredth anniversary of Leo XIII's *Rerum Novarum.* This is a lengthy and complex document. Though it is impossible here to discuss all of the topics treated in the encyclical, it will be useful to highlight some of its main points and selected responses to them.

THE COLLAPSE OF COMMUNISM

A central theme of the document is the failure of "real socialism," a term the pope uses to describe the social systems of Eastern Europe and the U.S.S.R. He presents two sorts of analysis of the reasons for this failure, one more theoretical and the other more practical and historical. On the theoretical level, "the fundamental error of socialism is anthropological in nature." It subordinates the good of the individual person to the functioning of the socio-economic mechanism. "The concept of the person as the autonomous subject of moral decision disappears." This leads to the destruction of the "subjectivity" of society, by which the pope means a civil society that respects the freedom, initiative, and legitimate autonomy of many diverse communities such as families and the other intermediate groups classically referred to in Catholic social thought under the heading of the principle of subsidiarity. Most fundamentally, "real socialism" has failed because it was atheistic. In denying God, it denied the transcendent dignity of the person. "It is by responding to the call of God contained in the being of things that man becomes aware of his transcendent dignity. Every individual must give this response, which constitutes the apex of his humanity, and no social mechanism or collective subject can substitute for it."[1] State absolutism, in other words, is really a form of idolatry that sacralizes the political sphere and attacks the transcendent freedom and dignity of persons in the process. From there it is but a short step, the pope argues, to a view of class conflict that is "not restrained by ethical and juridical considerations, or by respect for the dignity of others (and consequently of oneself)."[2] The nub of the theoretical critique of "real socialism," therefore, is that its denial of transcendence leads to a denial of authentic humanity.

From a more practical point of view, the encyclical enumerates three factors that especially contributed to the collapse of Communist regimes. The first was the violation of the rights of workers. First in Poland and then elsewhere working people stood up nonviolently against regimes and ideologies that presumed to speak in their name.[3] Second, the inefficiency of the Communist economic systems became evident. This inefficiency was not simply a technical problem, but "rather a consequence of the violation of human rights to private initiative, to ownership of property, and to freedom in the economic sector."[4] Third, the official atheism of these regimes created a "spiritual void" that deprived youth of a sense of human purpose. This ultimately led many of them, "in the irrepressible search for personal identity and for the meaning of life, to rediscover the religious roots of their national cultures, and to rediscover the person of Christ as the existentially adequate response to the desire in every human heart for goodness, truth, and life."[5] Not only as a theoretical matter, therefore, but very practically as well, the reaffirmation of the transcendent showed the inadequacy of "real socialism."

Before turning to a discussion of the encyclical's vision of the alternative, it will be useful to note some other analyses of the failure of the Communist system in the recent ethical literature. In February 1990 (thus more than a year before *Centesimus Annus* was issued), Brazilian theologian Leonardo Boff attended a series of meetings in what was then East Germany to discuss the significance of the events of 1989 for the future of liberation theology. In his reflections on these discussions, he maintains that what failed in Eastern Europe was "command social-ism," "patriarchal socialism," or "authoritarian socialism." Following the dictatorial model developed by Lenin, after the Second World War so-called scientific socialism was imposed on Eastern Europe from "outside" and "above" by Soviet troops.[6] The breakdown of this kind of socialism is beneficial for everyone. But this does not mean the end of all socialist models. For Boff, "it is evident that socialism will have a future if it has the capacity to enter into the path of a democracy that is worthy of the name: a popular democracy, structured from below, with the greatest possible participation, and open to the inevitable differences among people." This commitment to popular participation is more basic than efforts to create a society in which all are equal. It must, however, be accompanied by solidarity, i.e. "collaboration with others and the joint construction of history." Such participation and solidarity will, in turn, lead to social equality, to respect for differences among people, and finally to "communion" among persons.[7] These commitments rep-resent "the true nucleus of utopian socialism."[8] Boff does not present a detailed description of capitalism, though he presupposes that an eco-nomic system based on private property and the market is inherently exploitative and "creates so many victims on a world-wide scale."[9] Because of this presupposition, he views capitalism as itself an obstacle to popular democracy. Its "internal logic" leads to inequalities, to an asymmetrical relationship between capital and labor, and to the forma-tion of monopolies and oligopolies. So even though the collapse of "really existing socialism" in Eastern Europe means that the socialist vision is "sadly and in purification passing through its 'Good Friday,'" it will yet know its "Easter Sunday."[10]

Max Stackhouse and Dennis McCann proclaim a very different conclusion in the "Postcommunist Manifesto" they jointly issued in

January 1991. Marx and Engels' Manifesto began with the words "A specter is haunting Europe—the specter of communism."[11] Stackhouse and McCann turn this sentence upside down: "The specter that haunted the modern world has vanished. That specter is Communism."[12] This fact has important implications for Christian social ethics. For, in their view, much of the modern Christian tradition had identified itself with the failed socialist project:

> The Protestant Social Gospel, early Christian realism, much neo-orthodoxy, many forms of Catholic modernism, the modern ecumenical drive for racial and social inclusive-ness, and contemporary liberation theories all held that democracy, human rights, and socialism were the marks of the coming kingdom. For all their prophetic witness in many areas, they were wrong about socialism.[13]

They were wrong in believing that capitalism is "greedy, individu-alistic, exploitative and failing" while socialism is "generous, commu-nity-affirming and coming." In fact the truth is quite the opposite: capitalism is the more cooperative system and socialism the more exploitative. And "no one who has experienced 'really existing social-ism' now believes that it was God's design. What we now face is more than a delay in the socialist *parousia*. It is the recognition that this pre-sumptive dogma is wrong." The collapse of Communism calls for more than a readjustment in ecumenical social thought. It "demands repen-tance." This does not mean, however, that Stackhouse and McCann think the churches should embrace the status quo in capitalist societies. Rather they advocate "a reformed capitalism—one that uses law, poli-tics, education, and especially theology and ethics to constrain the temp-tations to exploitation and greed everywhere."[14]

A recent issue of the World Council of Church's *Ecumenical Review* is devoted to the theme of "Ecumenical Social Thought in the Post-Cold-War Period." Several of the articles move in the same direc-tion as do Stackhouse and McCann. Paul Abrecht, who was director of the Church and Society Sub-unit of the WCC from 1948 to 1983, argues that for the past twenty years that body has emphasized the importance of the creation of a "new world economic order." The model of that order was taken to be some form of socialism. Consequently, "the collapse of socialism in Central and Eastern Europe and its disarray throughout the world has shocked those who pinned their hopes on the socialist model."[15] The fact that the WCC was not intellectually prepared to deal with the events of the past few years, Abrecht says, was particularly evident at the world convocation on "Justice, Peace, and the Integrity of Creation" held in Seoul in March 1990. The report of this conference does not even mention the end of the cold war.

> Most important of all, the inability of the convocation to agree on an "exposition" or interpretation of the present social situation and the causes of injustice and violence in our times resulted in a series of concluding affirmations and covenants so abstract and so generally phrased as to be of little use in guiding Christian social thought and action in the world.[16]

Abrecht traces the historical roots of this vacuum to the fact that WCC proponents of revolutionary and liberation models of social change "were more explicit about what they opposed in the present system than about the character of the new one which they envisaged."[17] Abrecht's conclusion on the situation in WCC circles is somber:

> After twenty years of "revolutionary" thought and action on economic and social justice issues, ecumenical thought in these areas is at a dead end. There is no longer a theological-ethical consensus which commands any measure of agreement. Cut off from its historic theological-ethical roots and obliged to recognize that the concept of a revolutionary transformation of the world economic and social order is an illusion, ecumenical social thought faces a crisis of historic proportions.[18]

A major reconstruction is called for, which Abrecht does not think will be easily achieved. But the collapse of Communism in Eastern Europe reinforces two key insights of an earlier generation of Protestant ecumenical thinkers: "the interdependence of democracy and social justice," and the ecumenical critique of "Marxism's spiritual and ethical illusions."[19] On these bases an effort of renewal and self-criticism can begin.

Is Capitalism Victorious?

Some years ago Peter Berger argued in *The Capitalist Revolution* that the future will—or at least ought to—belong to capitalism. In a second edition of that book published in 1991, he admits that recent events have led to "a certain euphoria among those who have been in favor of capitalism all along" and that "it is nice for a change to be able to indulge in a bit of *Schadenfreude*" over the difficulties being experienced by ideological adversaries.[20] Nevertheless, Berger does not think that the appeal of the socialist idea will entirely vanish, for it has greater mythopoetic power to generate loyalty than does capitalism, especially among the intelligentsia. Some will find a way to sustain a "socialist faith" despite the evidence all around them. They will try to do this by refusing to call a spade a spade:

> Since *capitalism* continues to be a negatively charged word in many places, especially among intellectuals, it is often avoided in favor of the less upsetting synonym *market economy*. Conversely, where *socialism* is still a word that uplifts some hearts, it will also be avoided as the term to describe a *non*market economy; instead reference may be made to *command, Communist,* or even *Stalinist* economies.

In Berger's view, such distinctions "are semantic games. What is being described is, very clearly, a broad shift from socialist to capitalist models of economic organization."[21] Those who hold out against this conclusion "now appear as people who argue that the earth is flat."[22]

If drawing distinctions between capitalism and market economies is playing semantic games, *Centesimus Annus* may be fairly accused of playing them. The passage that has received most attention by commentators addresses the question of the significance of the collapse of Communism. John Paul asks whether this means that capitalism has been victorious and should consequently become the goal of the countries of Eastern Europe and the Third World. His response is carefully constructed and deserves quotation at some length:

> The answer is obviously complex. If by "capitalism" is meant an economic system which recognizes the fundamental and positive role of business, the market, private

property and the resulting responsibility for the means of production, as well as free human creativity in the economic sector, then the answer is certainly in the affirmative, even though it would perhaps be more appropriate to speak of a "business economy," "market economy," or simply "free economy." But if by "capitalism" is meant a system in which freedom in the economic sector is not circumscribed within a strong juridical framework which places it at the service of human freedom in its totality, and which sees it as a particular aspect of that freedom, the core of which is ethical and religious, the answer is certainly negative.[23]

Further, the pope warns several times that the collapse of Eastern European models of society should not be confused with the victory of what we might call "really existing capitalism." For example, he says that "it is unacceptable to say that the defeat of so-called 'Real Socialism' leaves capitalism as the only model of economic organization."[24] Or again, after discussing the continuing reality of marginalization and exploitation, especially in the Third World, and the reality of human alienation, especially in advanced societies, the pope adds a strong note of warning:

The collapse of the Communist system in so many countries certainly removes an obstacle to facing these problems in an appropriate and realistic way, but it is not enough to bring about their solution. Indeed there is a risk that a radical capitalist ideology could spread which refuses even to consider these problems, in the *a priori* belief that any attempt to solve them is doomed to failure, and that blindly entrusts their solution to the free development of market forces.[25]

What then is the encyclical saying? Rocco Buttiglione has proposed an interpretation of its "complex" answer to the question of whether capitalism has been victorious. It has been reported that Buttiglione participated in the drafting of the encyclical, so his views should be carefully noted.[26] He observes that the word "capitalism" has different meanings charged with different emotions on different sides of the Atlantic and in the Northern and Southern Hemispheres. In the United States it "implies free enterprise, free initiative, the right to work out one's own destiny through one's own efforts." It is "a thoroughly positive and respectable word" because of its link with a form of widespread entrepreneurship which grew organically in American soil. In Europe, on the other hand, the development of the industrial revolution was often under the control of small groups led by banks with decisive support from the state. In that context "capitalism" came to connote "the exploitation of large masses through an elite of tycoons who dispose of the natural and historical resources of the land and expropriate and reduce to poverty large masses of peasants and artisans." In Latin America, because of its distinctive history, "capitalism is simply synonymous with social injustice," at least among the intellectuals and a large section of the masses.

Buttiglione suggests, therefore, that there are different kinds of capitalism or at least different meanings to the word. The formal rules of market exchange may be the same in Europe, the United States, and Latin America. But where control of the market is concentrated in the hands of a privileged group, these rules will produce very different effects.[27] In some countries, only a small percentage of the population has the prerequisite skills and resources necessary to gain access to the market. Thus "they have no choice but to accept whatever conditions are offered them by those who have a monopoly of access to the market." In such a context, Buttiglione suggests, radical change will be needed. "Something just short of a social revolution is needed to create a market: a peaceful revolution of freedom."[28]

This line of argument is surely central in the encyclical. John Paul strongly affirms the efficiency and productivity of market economies. And he endorses entrepreneurship and economic initiative in terms that remind Max Stackhouse of Max Weber's discussion of the "Protestant ethic."[29] At the same time, the pope repeatedly stresses that many persons are unable to participate in the marketplace because they lack the resources needed to do so. The following passage is illustrative: "The fact is that many people, perhaps the majority today, do not have the means which would enable them to take their place in an effective and humanly dignified way within a productive system in which work is truly central....Thus, if not actually exploited, they are to a great extent marginalized; economic development takes place over their heads."[30] The pope's argument is here in full agreement with the United States Catholic bishops' statement that "Basic justice demands the establishment of minimum levels of participation in the life of the human community for all persons."[31] The lack of such participation (which the pope calls marginalization) continues to be present in advanced societies "in conditions of 'ruthlessness' in no way inferior to the darkest moments of the first phase of industrialization." It is the condition in which "the great majority of people in the Third World still live." And on the global level, "the chief problem [for poor countries] is that of gaining fair access to the international market."[32] The pope calls the conditions that lead to such marginalization "structures of sin which impede the full realization of those who are in any way oppressed by them."[33] And he says the Church can contribute to an "authentic theory and praxis of liberation" through its social teaching and its "concrete commitment and material assistance in the struggle against marginalization and suffering."[34] It was statements such as these that likely led *The Economist* of London to comment that, though the encyclical supports free markets, "thoroughgoing capitalists cannot take off their sackcloth yet."[35]

RETHINKING PRIVATE PROPERTY

One of the keys to the encyclical's discussion of the need to overcome marginalization is its innovative treatment of ownership in the long chapter on "Private Property and the Universal Destination of Material Goods." Earlier Catholic social thought, both in Aquinas and in the modern period, defended the legitimacy of private property. But this teaching (again in Aquinas and especially since Pius XI) did not regard the right to private property as an unlimited one. The use of privately owned goods was subject to strict limits because the material world was created by God for the benefit of all human beings, not just a few. This is the so-called "universal destination of material goods." As John Paul puts it, "The original source of all that is good is the very act of God, who created both the earth and man so that he might have dominion over it by his work and enjoy its fruits (Gen 1:28). God gave the earth to the whole human race for the sustenance of all its members without excluding anyone." It is only through their intelligence and work, however, that human beings make the earth fruitful. John Paul, echoing Locke and Leo XIII, affirms that persons make part of the earth their own through work. "This is the origin of individual property." But its accumulation is limited by "the responsibility not to hinder others from having their own part of God's gift."[36] This again echoes Locke, who maintained that the natural law limited the acquisition of property by the requirement that there be "as much and as good left in common for others."[37]

It is clear that in Aquinas, Locke, and earlier modern Catholic social thought this line of reasoning envisions private property as initially the ownership of land and natural resources based on individual labor. John Paul's innovation arises from his awareness that this paradigm does not describe the reality of an advanced technological and industrial world. In such context, the "givenness" of the world of land and natural resources is easily overshadowed by the creativity of human intelligence. Thus the temptation arises to say that the product of human work comes solely from the activity and initiative of the individuals who do the working. This can lead to belief that the fruits of industry belong solely to those who actively produced them. This would undercut the limits on the right to private property asserted by the earlier tradition. So John Paul maintains that "a deeper analysis" of the scope and limits of the right to property is called for than that based on a paradigm of agriculture and mining.[38]

This deeper analysis begins with the assertion that "it is becoming clear how a person's work is naturally interrelated with the work of others. More than ever, work is *work with others* and *work for others:* it is a matter of doing something for someone else."[39] Entrepreneurship based on the knowledge of the needs of others and the development of creative ways of meeting those needs is an important source of wealth in modern society. Such activity "requires the cooperation of many people working toward a common goal." Moreover, the ability to engage in it depends on "the possession of know-how, technology, and skill."[40] The possession of these resources today plays a more important role in generating wealth than ownership of land or natural resources. But the pope applies the same moral criteria to the human capital of knowledge and skill that the tradition formerly applied to land: its moral purpose is to serve the needs and well-being of the human community. It will do so when it is organized in ways that lead to "ever more extensive working communities" bound together "by a progressively expanding chain of solidarity."[41] Paralleling the earlier argument that the earth and its natural resources were created by God for the benefit of the whole human community, John Paul argues that human beings as such—with their capacity for creative intelligence—have been created by God for solidarity with others in the economic sphere. The resources of "know-how and technology" are not the purely private possession of anyone. They are meant to be at the service of others. They should be used to open up ways for the vast numbers of people who are marginalized from the market to become active participants in it. Thus Archbishop Jorge Maria Mejía, who as secretary of the Vatican's Council for Justice and Peace was doubtless close to the drafting of the encyclical, has commented that it presents the principle of the universal destination of material goods in a new way. "Today, therefore, 'the know-how,' 'technology,' and 'skill' (§32) are part of these 'goods' destined for all, but that do not reach everyone and are not enjoyed by all."[42]

This line of argument was anticipated in *Laborem Exercens,* where John Paul wrote that through work a person "enters into two inheritances: the inheritance of what is given to the whole of humanity in the resources of nature and the inheritance of what others have already developed on the basis of those resources." In productive activity persons never act independently. There is always an element of dependence: "dependence on the Giver of all the resources of creation and also on other human beings, those to whose work and initiative we owe the perfected and increased possibilities of our own work."[43]

For example, the small group of high-tech entrepreneurs who founded the Apple computer corporation were dependent on a historical heritage of technological and scientific knowledge given them by others through education. They did not create that corporation simply out of their own resources, even though they began it in the apparent isolation of the garage behind the home of one of the founders. Even highly creative and innovative activity is linked by moral bonds of interdependence with a vast community of other human beings. So *Centesimus Annus* concludes that if ownership of physical capital or control of "know-how" and "skill" impedes the participation of others in this network of solidarity, it "has no justification, and represents an abuse in the sight of God and man."[44] Put positively, this means that the alternative to the failed Communist system is what the pope calls "a society of free work, of enterprise and of participation." This will be a society with a mixed economy, in which the market is "appropriately controlled by the forces of society and the State, so as to guarantee that the basic needs of the whole society are satisfied."[45]

REFORMING CAPITALISM

Thomas S. Johnson spells out the challenge this involves very pointedly in an essay written for a conference held at the University of San Francisco to commemorate the *Rerum Novarum* centenary. Johnson is a Catholic layman who was President of Manufacturers Hanover Trust Corporation at the time the essay was written. He believes that the collapse of Communism changes the framework for debate about the shape of social and economic life in two interrelated ways. First, the argument over the relative advantages of economic "decision-making by bureaucrats versus an open marketplace has been settled."[46] Second, we have an opportunity to shed the ideological baggage and conceptual rigidities that often encumbered debate during the cold-war period. This will enable us "to focus our energy and attention on eliminating the significant faults and inadequacies of capitalism that we know to exist, while at the same time preserving those special properties that imbue the markets with their special genius."[47] Johnson illustrates both the genius and the faults of the market from the example of the city where he works. In New York City the fruits of the free and competitive spirit abound. "The atmosphere is dynamic, resulting in the best there is to offer, not only in the areas of business and commerce but also in the arts, entertainment, education, and scholarship." At the same time, the city is beset with serious problems: devastating homelessness, drug abuse, crime, decaying infrastructure. Most deeply troubling are those who lack the skills to enter the city's economy, "large groups of people whose spirits have been crushed and who live literally without hope. They are the people who have been left out of the process—the very poor in a city of enormous wealth."[48] The end of Communism thus calls for much more than victory celebrations. It will require the best available thinking by business, political, educational, and religious leaders to identify ways of addressing these devastating problems. The challenge is succinctly put in Johnson's title: "Capitalism after Communism: Now Comes the Hard Part."

Perhaps the most useful contribution of Johnson's essay to this thinking is its stress on the fact that different societies in the capitalist world organize markets in notably different ways. Just a few of the differences he cites can be noted here. In Japan, ownership patterns differ from those in the United States, for in Japan much ownership is is in the form of cross holdings by one company in another. There are also significant differences among market systems in the degree to which productive property is state-owned. For example, until recently, more than fifty percent of West German gross national product was produced by state enterprises. In Japan and many European societies there is much more coordination among companies and the other institutions of society and their governments than in the United States. The role of government in redressing inequalities is also notably different from country to country. It is extensive in Sweden, minimal in Hong Kong. In Western Europe, the provision of health care and housing "is measurably greater, and arguably fairer, than what is provided in the United States." And this has been accomplished while aggregate growth has on average been greater than in the United States.[49]

Johnson's point is that there is more than one way to organize a market economy. The serious debates of the post-cold-war world concern the human costs and human benefits of the various systems of ownership, market structure, and governmental redistribution that are possible. He thinks Christian ethics can make an important contribution to these debates on the basis of several key principles. As a minimum, all human beings should have the "freedom to live a life in which they can choose to follow God's will. At the least, this measure must assure that human beings are removed from bondage—either the literal bondage imposed by a political system or the de facto bondage that results from such a low level of sharing in the wealth that does exist that all hope for progress is extinguished and individual work is always seen as inadequately rewarded."[50] Second, all persons have a responsibility to contribute to the future of their community and to preserve resources for future generations. This has important implications for the tax system and for savings and investment. It is "the responsibility of those who have relatively greater wealth to save and invest more, so that others will be given the opportunity...to raise their participation in the economic system in the future."[51] Finally, since in market economies work is increasingly done in large corporate organizations, the structures and activities of these corporations must be evaluated in light of their impact on those who work in them. This means giving careful thought to "ways to include workers as full members of an enterprise, including empowering them to participate genuinely in decision-making."[52]

Johnson's essay was written in the context of the United States for an American audience. Though published just as *Centesimus Annus* was being issued, it provides a helpful framework for interpreting the encyclical's implications in this country. *Centesimus Annus* states that the Church "has no models to present" for the precise way social-economic affairs should be organized. Such models must be developed in light of the historical situations in different societies. Rather the pope's intent is to provide an "ideal orientation" based on recognition of the values of the market and enterprise, of the need for these to be oriented to the common good, and of the importance of broadening the possibilities of participation.[53] Nevertheless the encyclical goes beyond the restatement of general moral principles and indicates that not all models of a market economy are compatible with its orientation. Johnson's discussion of the diverse forms of market economy is a stimulus to careful consideration of what the encyclical says in this regard.

In the pope's reading of post-World War II history, the spread of Communist totalitarianism evoked three different responses in Europe and other parts of the world. The first sought to counter Communism by rebuilding democratic societies, in which free markets and economic growth were encouraged, but which avoided "making market mechanisms the only point of reference for social life" by subjecting markets "to social control." Some of the restrictions on the market are "a solid system of social security and professional training, the freedom to join trade unions and the effective action of unions, the assistance provided in cases of unemployment, the opportunities for democratic participation in the life of society." This calls for action by both society and state to protect workers "from the nightmare of unemployment" by seeking "balanced growth and full employment" and "through unemployment insurance and retraining programs." Wages must be adequate for living in dignity, "including a certain amount for savings." And legislation is needed to block exploitation "of those on the margins of society," including immigrants.[54] These limits are some of the elements of the "strong juridical framework" that the encyclical says is necessary if a free economy is to serve freedom in its totality.[55]

The second kind of post-war response to the spread of Communism is described as a system of "national security" that aimed at making Marxist subversion impossible by "controlling the whole of society in a systematic way" and by increasing the power of the state. This gravely threatens freedom, and it is clearly rejected by the encyclical.

Though no specific regimes are named, the pope clearly has in mind those like Chile under Pinochet.[56]

The third post-war response is called that of "the affluent society or the consumer society." It sought to defeat Marxism by showing that it could satisfy material human needs more effectively than Communism. According to the pope, this consumer society shared a reductively materialist view of the person with Communism.[57] I think the pope is here referring to significant currents in the societies of Western Europe and North America. But I doubt this description gives a full account of what is going on in those countries, nor does he claim this.

It is nevertheless clear that the first of these post-war models is approved by the encyclical while the second and third are rejected. I have written elsewhere that the functioning economic system that most closely resembles what the pope is describing is the social-market economy *(Sozialmarktwirtschaft)* of Germany.[58] An editorial in *La Civiltà Cattolica* commented that German and Scandinavian social democratic movements have been notably successful in implementing the objectives outlined by the pope.[59] And in Britain, Frank Turner has written that *Centesimus Annus* "sometimes reads like an unusually well written Labour manifesto," and is certainly closer to the program of the Labour Party than it is to laissez faire or libertarian objectives. Turner observes, however, that the democratic socialist parties of Western Europe themselves are often ironically prone to accepting "the primacy of economic criteria and the values of corporate pragmatism."[60] To the extent that they do, they are challenged by *Centesimus Annus* from the Left. Thus there is considerable room for debate about the specifics of social-economic systems that would be compatible with the ethical teaching of the document. In my judgment, the principles it lays out call for major changes both in the domestic arrangements presently in place in the United States as well as in the global marketplace.

THE ROLE OF GOVERNMENT

As noted above, *Centesimus Annus* says that the responsibility for bringing about these changes falls on both "society and the state." This reemphasizes the traditional principle of subsidiarity of Catholic social thought, which rests on the distinction between civil society and the state. This distinction emphasizes the fact that a free society is composed of many freely formed and freely active communities.[61] The idea of civil society has been a central theme in the revolutions of Eastern Europe. Adam Michnik, a Polish intellectual who was a leader of the Solidarity movement, put it this way: "[In totalitarian regimes] the State is teacher and civil society is the pupil in the classroom, which is sometimes converted into a prison or a military camp. In civil society, by contrast, people do not want to be pupils, soldiers, or slaves; they act as citizens."[62] Michnik, who is Jewish, says that one of the principal influences on his thinking about the role played by a strong civil society in sustaining democracy was "a priest from Kraków, Fr. Karol Wojtyla."[63] As John Paul II, Fr. Wojtyla has strongly reaffirmed this role.

At the same time, John Paul repeatedly links the principle of subsidiarity to the ideas of solidarity and the common good. For this reason, as Kenneth Himes has pointed out, the pope's understanding of subsidiarity is clearly different from the laissez-faire view that the market will solve all problems and that the role of government should be as small as possible.[64] In discussing the role of government in promoting the goals of economic justice, the encyclical makes a distinction that should be considered carefully, especially in the context of the United States:

> The State must contribute to the achievement of these goals both directly and indirectly. Indirectly and according to the *principle of subsidiarity,* by creating favorable conditions for the free exercise of economic activity, which will lead to abundant opportunities for employment and sources of wealth. Directly and according to the *principle of solidarity,* by defending the weakest, by placing certain limits on the autonomy of the parties who determine working conditions, and by ensuring in every case the necessary minimum support for the unemployed worker.[65]

I would interpret this passage in the following way. The indirect role of government in addressing issues such as poverty and unemployment is through macroeconomic policies that stimulate growth and create jobs. These policies create the conditions in which the individuals and the many communities of civil society can freely exercise their initiative and creativity. In Michnik's words, this will enable people to act like citizens, not pupils or slaves. It will enable them to work together and for each other in families, in entrepreneurial activity, and in personalized forms of service and self-help. But if and when this leaves serious problems in place, government should undertake more. For example, legislation regarding working conditions, fair labor practices, and minimum wages are called for. In addition, more direct stimulation of job opportunities, unemployment insurance and other forms of social support will be called for.

In my judgment, this provides a key to understanding what *Centesimus Annus* says about the welfare state or what it calls "the social assistance state." The pope notes that the range of state intervention to remedy "forms of poverty and deprivation unworthy of the human person" has expanded in recent years. "In some countries," he suggests, this has led to "malfunctions and defects in the Social Assistance State," which are the result of an inadequate understanding of the principle of subsidiarity. These defects are the sapping of human initiative and energy through excessive bureaucratization. State interventions to alleviate poverty, the pope says, are "justified by urgent reasons touching the common good" (this is the principle of solidarity). But subsidiarity implies that such interventions are "supplementary" to the primary source of economic welfare, which is active participation in economic life through work. They are also supplementary to the direct assistance that, if possible, should be provided by families, neighbors, and others who are closest to those in need.[66]

These specifications of when governmental involvement is called for should be kept clearly in view in discussions of the encyclical's relevance to the debate about welfare reform in the United States. It is clear that the encyclical will be embraced by those who argue that recent increases in poverty in this country, especially among children in single-parent families, is due to a welfare dependency in large part *caused* by misguided governmental programs. This is the view of Daniel Patrick Moynihan, who argues that the remedy for poverty is parental self-sufficiency and parental responsibility to contribute to the well-being of their children. Moynihan also argues, however, quoting Judith Gueron, that "the responsibilities of government are to provide the means for parents to become self-sufficient—such as employment services and supports—and to provide income when their best efforts fall short."[67] This is not the place to review the complexity of the welfare debate in this country. But two additions to what Moynihan has said are crucial. First, poverty is not due simply to welfare dependency. In fact, a substantial majority of those receiving social assistance do so either because employment is simply unavailable or because they lack the skills needed for available jobs. Second, many of the poor in the United States work full time. They are poor simply because their wages are too low. For both of these reasons, the poverty problem has more complex causes than those who blame dependency acknowledge. Efforts to alleviate it will have to be correspondingly complex.[68] The encyclical recognizes this in its call for a blend of individual initiative, voluntary assistance, and both indirect and direct government intervention. It does not offer a blueprint for how these should be combined, but it is a strong call to place discussion of these matters on the public agenda.

CONSENSUS ON THE COMMON GOOD?

The need for a serious discussion of how to deal with poverty in America will highlight one final theme of the encyclical's vision of Christian ethics after the Cold War. In the name of subsidiarity, the pope opposes all forms of totalitarianism. But he also warns the West of the opposite danger: the loss of a vision of and commitment to the common good. He writes of "a crisis within democracies themselves, which seem at times to have lost the ability to make decisions aimed at the common good."[69] In advanced societies "the individual is often suffocated between two poles represented by the State and the marketplace. At times it seems as though he exists only as a producer and consumer of goods, or as an object of State administration."[70] This experience leads to distrust and apathy in the face of political and financial power, with consequent decline in political participation and civic spirit. This, I think, is a key element in the pope's critique of "consumerism."

On the most obvious level, a consumer society for the pope is one in which persons organize their lives around the pursuit of material gratification and maximal profit independent of concern for the effects on others.[71] More deeply, it is a society that regards all political, cultural, and religious values as matters of personal preference to be selected cafeteria-style. On this level, a consumer society is one in which the spirit of marketplace has reached into the sphere of politics, culture, and religion. When this happens, there develops "a tendency to claim that agnosticism and skeptical relativism are the philosophy and the basic attitude which correspond to democratic forms of political life." This further leads to a politics in which the preference of the majority determines all. And this, the pope concludes, is "open or thinly disguised totalitarianism."[72] If, therefore, a marketplace of exchange based on personal preference becomes the overarching framework in society, the market itself becomes totalitarian. *Centesimus Annus* raises a strong voice against this tendency. "There are goods which by their very nature cannot and must not be bought and sold."[73] Some of these goods are directly at stake in the marketplace, such as the dignity of working people, the survival of the poor, and the greater participation of developing countries in the global economy. But the pope also implies that the image of the marketplace of ideas is inadequate to portray what is at stake in discussions of how a democratic society should govern itself.

Centesimus Annus repeatedly asserts that democracy and freedom are rooted, not in agnosticism and skepticism, but in commitment to the truth: *"Obedience to the truth about God and man* is the first condition of freedom."[74] This is sure to set many Americans' teeth on edge. Truth claims in politics, we tend to believe, are the prelude to oppression, not freedom. But we have something very important to learn from the recent experience of Central and Eastern Europe. The Czech philosopher Erazim Kohák has written that the "the entire tenor of Czech dissent, whose most prominent figures are playwright-philosopher Václav Havel and priest-theologian Václav Maly, has been on *life in the truth....* In word and deed, Czech dissidents have demonstrated their conviction that there is truth, that there is good and evil—and that the difference is not reducible to cultural preference."[75] Kohák acknowledges that these dissidents are marching to a very different drummer than the one heard by the French philosophers Foucault and Derrida and the American Richard Rorty.[76] So is the pope. And like the pope, Kohák asks whether the newly liberated Central European countries should abandon their commitment to living in truth, the importance of which they learned when faced with the lies imposed by apparatchiks, for the "mindless consumerism of the Atlantic basin."[77]

I am uneasy with simplistic uses of the term "consumerism." But a careful reading of *Centesimus Annus* will show that what the term means there is not simplistic at all. It is used to criticize those strands of the culture of North Atlantic nations that have abandoned the effort to achieve a greater solidarity than the market can produce. This solidarity is rooted in the human capacity for self-transcendence and for justice. The pope's insistence that freedom comes from obedience to the truth about one's fellow human beings is similar to John Courtney Murray's insistence that the opening words of the American Declaration of Independence were an affirmation that "there are truths, and we hold them." The encyclical has learned enough from the democratic experience to affirm that the discovery of these truths will come not from theology alone but from a truly interdisciplinary inquiry, that it demands attention to the practical experience of diverse peoples, and that "many people who profess no religion" will contribute to it.[78] But to this democratic experience, it makes an indispensable contribution: the need for solidarity and a commitment to the fact that human beings are not for sale, whether they be the poor in the advanced societies of the North Atlantic or those who live in the developing countries of the Southern hemisphere. Those who have been led to believe that *Centesimus Annus* endorses "really existing capitalism" should take a hard look at the text. I hope that this modest "note" will encourage both such careful reading and subsequent talking in the spirit of solidarity and commitment to the common good that permeates the encyclical.

Notes

1. Pope John Paul II, *Centesimus Annus*, English translation (Vatican City: Libreria Editrice Vaticana, 1991) no. 13; the English text is available in *Origins* 21 (1991) 1–24. Throughout the English translation of the encyclical, the male gender is used to refer to all human beings. It would be possible to retranslate the Latin into English in a way that uses sexually inclusive language. I have refrained from doing so because the encyclical as a whole reveals an astonishing lack of concern for the economic and social problems faced by women in both advanced and developing countries. After describing the serious economic problems in both kinds of society, the document makes its sole reference to the problems faced by women in a single sentence: "The situation of women is far from easy in these conditions" (no. 33). In my judgment, this is worse than inadequate.

2. Ibid. no. 14.

3. Ibid. no. 23.

4. Ibid. no. 24.

5. Ibid.

6. Leonardo Boff, "La 'implosión' del socialismo autoritario y la teología de la liberación," *Sal Terrae* 79 (1991) 321–41, at 322.

7. Ibid. 331–32.

8. Ibid. 327.

9. Ibid. 339.

10. Ibid. 334.

11. Karl Marx and Friedrich Engels, "Manifesto of the Communist Party," in Louis S. Feuer, ed., *Basic Writings on Politics and Philosophy: Karl Marx and Friedrich Engels* (Garden City, N.Y.: Doubleday, 1959) 6.

12. Max L. Stackhouse and Dennis P. McCann, "A Postcommunist Manifesto: Public Theology after the Collapse of Socialism," *Christian Century* 108 (Jan. 16, 1991) cover and 44–47. This citation if from the cover.

13. Ibid. cover and 44.

14. Ibid. 44.

15. Paul Abrecht, "The Predicament of Christian Social Thought after the Cold War," *Ecumenical Review* 43 (1991) 318–28, at 319.

16. Ibid. 324.

17. Ibid. 323.

18. Ibid. 325.

19. Ibid. 326.

20. Peter L. Berger, "Capitalism: The Continuing Revolution," *First Things* 15 (1991) 22–27, at 23. This is an excerpt from *The Capitalist Revolution: Fifty Propositions about Prosperity, Equality, and Liberty*, with new Introduction (New York: Basic Books, 1991).

21. Ibid. 23.

22. Ibid. 24.

23. *Centesimus Annus*, no. 42.

24. Ibid. no. 35.

25. Ibid. no. 42.

26. Giancarlo Zizola writes that a group headed by Buttiglione (whom he calls a "theoretician of the Communion and Liberation movement") was involved in revising an earlier draft produced by the Vatican Council on Justice and Peace, and that the pope himself made subsequent revisions ("Les revirements d'une encyclique," *L'Actualité religieuse dans le monde* 90 [June 15, 1991] 10–11).

27. Rocco Buttiglione, "Behind *Centesimus Annus*," *Crisis* 9 (July/Aug., 1991) 8–9, at 8.

28. Ibid. 9.

29. *Centesimus Annus* nos. 32 and 34. See Stackhouse, "John Paul on Ethics and the 'New Capitalism,'" *Christian Century* 108 (May 29–June 5, 1991) 581.

30. *Centesimus Annus* no. 33.

31. National Conference of Catholic Bishops, *Economic Justice for All* (Washington, D.C.: United States Catholic Conference, 1986) no. 77; available in *Origins* 16 (1986) 408–56.

32. *Centesimus Annus* no. 33.

33. Ibid. no. 38.

34. Ibid. no. 26.

35. "God's Visible Hand," *Economist* 319 (May 4, 1991) 42.

36. *Centesimus Annus* no. 31.

37. John Locke, *Second Treatise on Civil Government*, in *Social Contract*, ed. Sir Ernest Barker (New York: Oxford Univ. 1967) 18. The degree to which Locke took this requirement seriously is disputed. Those who, like C. B. MacPherson, see Locke as a paradigmatic "possessive individualist" think he did not. A recent interpretation that argues Locke believed in strict limits on property and that his views are closer to Thomas Aquinas than to modern individualism is that of Andrew Lustig, "Natural Law, Property, and Justice: The General Justification of Property in Aquinas and Locke," *Journal of Religious Ethics* 19 (1991) 119–49. To the extent that John Paul echoes Locke, it is Lustig's rather than MacPherson's Locke that is at issue.

38. *Centesimus Annus* no. 6.

39. Ibid. no. 31.

40. Ibid. no. 32.

41. Ibid. nos. 32 and 43.

42. Jorge Maria Mejía, "Centesimus Annus: An Answer to the Unknowns and Questions of Our Times," *Ecumenical Review* 43 (1991) 401–10, at 406. This issue of *Ecumenical Review* is devoted to articles commemorating the *Rerum Novarum* centenary.

43. John Paul II, *Laborem Exercens*, English translation (Washington, D.C.: United States Catholic Conference, 1981) no. 13; available in *Origins* 11 (1981) 225–44.

44. *Centesimus Annus* no. 43.

45. Ibid. no. 35; emphasis in the original.

46. Thomas S. Johnson, "Capitalism after Communism: Now Comes the Hard Part," in John A. Coleman, S.J., ed., *One Hundred Years of Catholic Social Thought: Celebration and Challenge* (Maryknoll, N.Y.: Orbis, 1991) 240–55, at 247.

47. Ibid. 240–41.

48. Ibid. 241.

49. Johnson, 248 and passim.

50. Ibid. 248.

51. Ibid. 249.

52. Ibid. 253.

53. *Centesimus Annus* no. 43.

54. Ibid. nos. 15 and 19.

55. Ibid. no. 42.

56. Ibid. no. 19.

57. Ibid.

58. David Hollenbach, "The Pope and Capitalism," *America* 164 (June 1, 1991) 591.

59. "Capitalismo nell'Encyclica 'Centesimus Annus,'" *La Civiltà Cattolica* 142/3383 (1991) 417–30, at 426.

60. Frank Turner, S.J., "John Paul's Social Analysis," *The Month* (August, 1991) 344–49, at 347–48.

61. See Michael Walzer, "The Idea of Civil Society: A Path to Social Reconstruction," *Dissent* (Spring, 1991) 293–304.

62. Interview with Adam Michnik, "Towards a Civil Society: Hopes for Polish Democracy," *Times Literary Supplement* (February 19–25, 1988) 188 ff., at 198.

63. Ibid.

64. Kenneth Himes, O.F.M., "The New Social Encyclical's Communitarian Vision," *Origins* 21 (1991) 166–68, at 167.

65. *Centesimus Annus* no. 15.

66. Ibid. no. 48.

67. Daniel Patrick Moynihan, "Social Justice in the *Next* Century," *America* 165 (Sept. 14, 1991) 132–37, at 137.

68. For a careful and balanced discussion of this complexity, see David Ellwood, *Poor Support: Poverty in the American Family* (New York: Basic Books, 1988); William Julius Wilson, *The Truly Disadvantaged: The Inner City, the Underclass, and Public Policy* (Chicago: Univ. of Chicago, 1987); and Alan Wolfe, "The Right to Welfare and the Obligation to Society: A Communitarian Balance," in *Responsive Community* 1/2 (1991) 12–22.

69. *Centesimus Annus* no. 47.

70. Ibid. no. 49.

71. Ibid. no. 41.

72. Ibid. no. 46.

73. Ibid. no. 40.

74. Ibid. no. 41.

75. Erazim Kohák, "Can There Be a Central Europe?" *Dissent* (Spring, 1990) 194–97, at 195–96.

76. For Rorty's rejoinder to Kohák, Havel, and Jan Patočka (the philosopher who was the symbolic and spiritual leader of the Charter '77 movement

that brought down the Communist regime in Czechoslovakia) on the question of truth, see his "The Seer of Prague," a review of three books by Patočka, one of them edited by Kohák, *New Republic* 205 (July 1, 1991) 35–39.

77. Kohák 195.

78. *Centesimus Annus* no. 60.

List of Contributors

Gregory Baum is Emeritus Professor on the Religious Studies Faculty of McGill University in Montreal, Canada.

Pamela Brubaker is Assistant Professor of Christian Ethics at California Lutheran University.

Lisa Sowle Cahill is Professor of Christian Ethics at Boston College.

Léonie Caldecott is a freelance writer living in Oxford, England who specializes in the arts, religion and women's issues.

Charles E. Curran is the Elizabeth Scurlock University Professor of Human Values at Southern Methodist University.

Richard T. DeGeorge is Distinguished University Professor of Philosophy at the University of Kansas.

Donal Dorr is an Irish missionary priest and author who has taught philosophy and theology in Ireland.

Joseph Fuchs is Professor Emeritus of Moral Theology at the Gregorian University in Rome.

James Gaffney is Professor of Moral Theology at Loyola University, New Orleans.

Richard Grecco is Auxiliary Bishop of the Diocese of London, Ontario, Canada.

Leslie C. Griffin is an attorney with the United States Department of Justice who previously taught moral theology at Notre Dame.

Germain Grisez holds the Flynn Chair in Christian Ethics at Mount St. Mary's College, Emmitsburg, Maryland.

Bernard Häring is Professor Emeritus of Moral Theology at the Accademia Alfonsiana in Rome.

J. Bryan Hehir is Professor of the Practice in Religion and Society at Harvard Divinity School and Counselor at Catholic Relief Services.

Richard M. Hogan is a priest of the Archdiocese of St. Paul and Minneapolis who has coauthored *Covenant of Love: Pope John Paul II on Sexuality, Marriage, and Family in the Modern World.*

David Hollenbach is the Margaret O'Brien Flatley Professor of Catholic Theology at Boston College.

John M. LeVoir is a priest of the Archdiocese of St. Paul and Minneapolis who has coauthored *Covenant of Love: Pope John Paul II on Sexuality, Marriage, and Family in the Modern World.*

Richard A. McCormick is the John A. O'Brien Professor of Christian Ethics at the University of Notre Dame.

Ronald Modras is Professor of Theology at St. Louis University.

Richard John Neuhaus is the President of the Institute on Religion and Public Life and editor of *First Things.*

Michael Novak holds the George Frederick Jewett Chair in Religion and Public Policy at the American Enterprise Institute in Washington, D.C.

Marc Ouellet is Professor of Dogmatic Theology at the John Paul II

Institute on Marriage and the Family at the Pontifical Lateran University in Rome.

Michael D. Place is President and CEO of The Catholic Health Association of the United States.

Maria Riley is the Director of the Global Women's Project at the Center of Concern in Washington, D.C.

David L. Schindler is the Gagnon Professor of Fundamental Theology at the John Paul II Institute for Studies on Marriage and Family in Washington, D.C.

Janet E. Smith is Associate Professor of Philosophy at the University of Dallas.

George Weigel is the President of the Ethics and Public Policy Center in Washington, D.C.